The Essential Writings of Sudhir Kakar

With an introduction by
T.G. VAIDYANATHAN

UNIVERSITY PRESS

OXFORD
UNIVERSITY PRESS

YMCA Library Building, Jai Singh Road, New Delhi 110 001

Oxford University Press is a department of the University of Oxford. It furthers the
University's objective of excellence in research, scholarship, and education
by publishing worldwide in

Oxford New York

Athens Auckland Bangkok Bogota Buenos Aires Calcutta
Cape Town Chennai Dar es Salaam Delhi Florence Hong Kong Istanbul
Karachi Kuala Lumpur Madrid Melbourne Mexico City Mumbai
Nairobi Paris São Paolo Shanghai Singapore Taipei Tokyo Toronto Warsaw

with associated companies in Berlin Ibadan

Published in India
By Oxford University Press, New Delhi

ISBN 019 565149 9

Typeset in Times (10/12)
By Urvashi Press, Meerut 250 001
Printed in India by Rashtriya Printers, New Delhi 110 020
Published by Manzar Khan, Oxford University Press
YMCA Library Building, Jai Singh Road, New Delhi 110 001

For my *masi* Kamla Chowdhry,
who made the journey possible

Acknowledgement

I would like to thank David Davidar of Penguin Books India Pvt. Ltd. for giving permission to reprint essays from *Intimate Relations*, *The Analyst and the Mystic*, and *Colours of Violence*, for this edition.

Contents

Introduction

By common consent, Sudhir Kakar is our foremost psychoanalyst and has done more than anyone to keep the discipline alive and relevant in contemporary India by, among other things, extending the range of its applications from popular cinema to Hindu-Muslim relations in the subcontinent. My own introduction to his work was quite fortuitous. I had just rediscovered Naipaul—both the lyrical and, oftentimes, mystical Naipaul of *An Area of Darkness* (1964), which I had read inattentively when it had first come out, and his more abrasive *avatar* in *A Wounded Civilization* (1977). The latter was still appearing in periodic installments in the *New York Review of Books* in 1976 and it was the 'Defect of Vision' essay that intrigued me. Naipaul is discussing Gandhi—the section begins with him and has gone on for more than five pages, with Naipaul fanning through Gandhi's English and South African sojourns picking out the 'visual' failures from the famous autobiography—when, suddenly, looking for intellectual back-up, he invokes the name of 'Dr. Sudhir Kakar, a psychotherapist at Jawaharlal Nehru University in New Delhi, who is himself Indian and has practised both in Europe and in India . . . .' Kakar was then on a fellowship from the Indian Council of Social Science Research while still at the Centre for the Study of Social Systems in JNU and almost the first sentences that Naipaul quotes (from a letter of Kakar's) are uncannily prophetic of the shape of the work that is to follow in the next twenty years: 'Generally among Indians there seems to be a different relationship to outside reality, compared to the one met with in the West. In India it is closer to a certain stage of childhood when outer objects did not have a separate, independent existence but were intimately related to the self and its affective states.' This is much more memorably (and cautiously, too!) formulated in the now famous passage in *The Inner World* where Kakar resorts, for once, to military metaphors to explain why 'Indians tend to maintain more troops at the narcissistic position' than westerners. Needless to say, Naipaul goes to town on the 'underdeveloped ego' of Gandhi and some less notable Indians—both real and fictional—for arraigning an entire civilization. He goes on to illustrate the advantages enjoyed by western man (because, apparently, of his 'developed ego') which helps him 'to withdraw and analyse' the sexual act 'even at the moment of orgasm' while the Indian can only weakly mutter 'It happened.' Perhaps the difficulties of the Indian are only compounded by the reserve enjoined by the English language. As Kakar has pointed out in his 1995 essay, 'Culture in Psychoanalysis', Hindi is more concrete and much more direct and unfettered. And, *pace* Naipaul, it is not as if all westerners—including some distinguished Nobel laureates—invariably enjoy the distinction he so generously bestows on them. For instance, even the 'cultured' Robert Jordan in Hemingway's *For Whom the Bell Tolls* (1941), after enjoying sexual felicity with the cuddly Maria—played to perfection by Ingrid Bergman in the 1943 Paramount movie—can only ask her 'Did thee feel the earth move?' which certainly does not display the objectivity that Naipaul finds in western man.

When we look back at the impressive body of Kakar's work (his earliest 'psychological' foray was a study, at Harvard, of that innovative American genius, Frederick Taylor, who revolutionized factory management, nearly thirty years ago), we can only marvel at its astonishing continuity and unity of intention. Early surmises snake their way to the present and find fuller and more complete expression in later writings so that we have a solid body of work where there are few internal fissures. His more recent writing seems merely to carry forward early leads and formulations. Of the latter, none is more prophetic than the truly seminal *The Inner World* which appeared in 1978. In a short 'Introduction', of some 13–14 pages, there are some scattered remarks on anthropological research of childrearing practices in India where he observes that 'they are not to be viewed as 'causative.' Anthropological studies balance 'observations gleaned from clinical psychotherapy' which 'reflect but a small, elite sample of a large, heterogeneous population.' A scrupulous, if not always successful, attempt to keep a fine balance between the conflicting claims of psychoanalysis and anthropology, between—in a recent Kakar formulation—'psychological imperialism in one case and psychological naivete on the other' has been the hallmark of his early work.

Twenty years on, we find him wrestling with the same issues and defending his territory from the inroads made, in the meantime, by the 'psychological anthropologist' who, in Kakar's view, 'often idealizes the culture he or she is involved with,' often oblivious of the internal 'inconsistency and conflict.' This is so especially with the notion of 'multiple-mothering' in India. This leads the 'psychological anthropologist' to posit a saint-like Indian child—seemingly afflicted by a premature *vairagya*—who voluntarily renounces or puts by a host of childish things (including surprisingly, his strong ties to his mother) and submits himself joyfully, it would seem, to a manly sacrifice of infantile and incestuous wishes. Attributing further an ability for inductive generalization which would appear well beyond his tender years, the 'psychological anthropologist' sees the child gaining an 'insight' (after a long struggle for enlightenment) that 'all the mothers' are, after all, one and the same. This near-mythical man-child, needless to say, does not figure in the pages of *The Inner World*.

What we find instead in *The Inner World* is a portrait of a prolonged infancy—where 'the second and third development stages seem not to take place sequentially but are compressed into one'—during which the Indian child is '*intensely* and *intimately* attached to his mother' (italics mine) 'in spite of the customary presence in the extended family of many other potential caretakers and "substitute mothers".' Mind you, Kakar is careful to point out that the Indian child 'exclusively directs his demands and affections towards his mother'; that 'this attachment is manifested in (and symbolized by) the physical closeness of the infant and his mother.' Not only do Indian children 'sleep by their mother's side at night,' during the day 'she carries the youngest, or the one most needing attention, astride her hip, the others within arm's reach' all through the day whatever task she is engaged in. His summing up leaves little room for any ambiguity: 'Constantly held, and cuddled, crooned and talked to, the Indian infant's experience of his mother is a heady one, his contact with her is of an intensity and duration that differentiate it markedly from the experience of infancy in western worlds.' In the light of all this, it is hard to see just how the 'psychological anthropologist' can maintain that 'intense emotional involvement' is absent in Hindu mother–child relationships. We can only conclude that, as Kakar has drily observed, when Indian mothers do 'unreservedly convey their love to their babies' ('especially at night when the infant is lying by her side'), the western anthropologist is unfortunately, if necessarily, absent.

The mistake that most western critics of Kakar make is in attempting to impale his very culture-specific psychology onto the drive psychology model of classical psychoanalysis: Freud, Melanie Klein, and the Klein-inspired Carstairs. But Kakar's sources are mythological and psychoanalytical at the same time. Kakar's good–bad mother typology has more to do with the dual nature of India's Mother Goddess (Durga-Kali) than with the early formulations of Melanie Klein or her 'Indian' exponent, G.M. Carstairs. The resemblances are purely adventitious! The 'psychological anthropologist', aided and abetted by the hostility to religion, inbuilt into psychoanalysis, sees 'secular' caretaker mothers where Kakar sees the goddess in her beauteous and terrifying forms.

Kakar's next selection in the opening section of 'Childhood and Identity' from *The Inner World* is a little surprising for it is not even part of the main text but the sole appendix to the book! But 'The Child in Indian Tradition' is intended to throw light on current child-rearing practices and Kakar in his lightning survey of the past—and he takes in the two great epics, the 'patriarchal' 'Laws of Manu,' the *bhakti* poets—finally settles on 'the traditional Ayurvedic system of medicine' for a closer look. He is too honest a chronicler not to shift the rather dubious chaff from the shining grain—of truth—in Ayurveda. While admitting that 'credulity is strained' when we read about 'the predictable behaviour of the unborn child—'predictions based on the longings of the mother during pregnancy, he is quick to point out that 'the voices of ancient doctors . . . sound positively Spockian as they expound on the relationship between child-rearing practices and personality development.' What is perhaps not so obviously Spockian is the 'consistently humane attitude towards the child' as it moves through the various stages of childhood in Ayurveda. Kakar remarks with some justice that from 'the timing and content of the various childhood *samskaras*', it would appear that 'one of the major thrusts of these rituals is the gradual integration of the child into society, with the *samskaras*, as it were, beating time to a measured movement that takes the child away from the original mother–infant symbiosis into full-fledged membership in his community' (without the benefit, we might add retrospectively, of a phalanx of caretaker-mothers!).

Kakar's tantalizingly brief sketch of Ayurveda's portrait of Indian childhood needs to be placed alongside his long section on the cultural and theoretical aspects of Ayurveda in *Shamans, Mystics and Doctors* (1982). For truly, as Gananath Obeysekere has remarked, 'Without some awareness of the theory of Ayurvedic medicine it is not possible for us to understand much of what goes on in the minds of men in the South Asian world.'

Kakar's next selection, 'The Revolutionary Yogi: Childhood of Swami Vivekananda,' is clear about its terms of reference. For, even this early, Kakar rejects not only the pathographic approach which would treat Vivekananda as 'a "classic" manic-depressive' but also the hagiographic approach of his western disciples and admirers, like Nivedita, Nikhilananda and Romain Rolland. Kakar's chief purpose is to illustrate the dilemmas attendant on the forging of 'a modern Indian identity,' a phrase repeated several times in the closing pages of the book. Caught between a westernized father and a traditional Hindu mother, Vivekananda grew up torn between fantasies of grandeur and the reality of dependence on an overwhelming maternal presence. We have here an embryonic version of what is soon to become a Kakar trademark: the theory of 'oedipal alliance' as opposed to the more classical Oedipus complex. The struggle to free himself from his mother and forge a strong 'masculine' self—both at the personal level and at the collective plane of a religio-nationalist politics—was never-ending and Vivekananda's Himalayan 'crisis', at 35 (in 1897), is treated by Kakar expertly and sensitively. One of Kakar's key psychoanalytic notions in the book—that of a 'second birth' when 'Indians tend to maintain more troops at the narcissistic position, with the advance platoons poised to rejoin them whenever threatened or provoked' where westerners have fewer 'troops of occupation at the home base of archaic narcissism'—is well deployed here to show that, in Vivekananda's case, the developmental transition was complicated by his fantasy of being 'his father's father,' a fantasy that was seriously dented when he fainted before the ice-phallus of Shiva in the cave at Amarnath during the aforementioned 'crisis'. In the final analysis, Kakar sees Vivekananda's lifelong attempts to forge 'a modern Indian identity' as foundering before the inner psychic pull of the Mother Goddess. Heroically, but vainly, would 'Narendra' repeatedly implore Kali to make him a man: 'O thou Mother of the Universe, vouchsafe manliness unto me! . . . take away my unmanliness, and—*Make me a Man*!' Perhaps, Kakar's own self-confessed 'counter-transference' towards his subject makes this mini-biography in many ways—at the least for this writer—a very special essay!

'Lord of the Spirit World' which forms part of 'Part 1: Local and Folk Traditions' of Kakar's 1982 publication, *Shamans, Mystics and Doctors*, takes us to an Indian healing centre—the Balaji temple at

Mehndipur in Rajasthan—where patients from all over northern India gather seeking relief from many afflictions, both mental and physical. The most common ailment, of course, is 'spirit possession' (or 'hysteria') and Kakar takes the reader through three such cases (two young Hindu married girls and a 19-year old Muslim girl)—'fifteen out of twenty eight, eleven of whom were women—which 'evidenced such a core hysteric personality,' although he is careful to point out that although 'possession is more than hysteria, the hysterical personality seems to make the best use of possession states'. For this is where the influence of 'culture' comes in: unlike the visually diffuse world of the western hysteric, 'the rich mythological world' of the Indian hysterical personality 'takes on the coloring of a specific historical and cultural setting.' And so for the Indian psychoanalyst, Freud's libido theory—relegated in the West to 'the realm of an aesthetic metaphor'—is still central because, for him, psychoanalysis itself is still 'the child of the hysterical woman.' But while 'psychoanalysis and western psychotherapies' concentrate on the text of the mental illness—'on its understanding, translation and genesis'—the healing rituals of the Balaji shrine are more concerned with the context of the illness by 'changing the person's feelings about himself or herself.' The very pilgrimage to the Balaji shrine—'a sacred journey'—shifts the illness from being just 'a medical metaphor' to one where it has become 'a religious–spiritual metaphor' of 'the pilgrim's progress towards wholeness.' Also the 'temple's healing culture' involves the 'integration and involvement of the patient's relatives' as well. The 'healing at Balaji' lays emphasis 'on ending the patient's alienation from his social and cosmic order.' The unconscious content of the psyche here in India is 'neither fixed and immutable nor malignant and threatening' like the 'psychoanalytic id' but is 'fundamentally capable of a benign transformation.' And so 'the *duta* . . . god's messenger' takes the place of the troublesome *bhuta* (which is frequently 'Muslim' and hence 'farthest away from his "good" Hindu self'). In noting all this, Kakar refrains from any value judgement whatsoever, especially of a cultural kind. To each culture, Kakar would seem to say, its own preferred ideals: western psychotherapy valorises 'modern individualism,' while traditional healing stresses 'faith and surrender to a power beyond the individual.'

'The Body Image' is a small, 6-page fragment from a much larger chapter on 'the cultural and theoretical perspectives' of Ayurveda. The 'Indian body image' (used interchangeably with the 'Hindu body image' throughout the essay) emphasizes 'its intimate connection with the cosmos' unlike the western image 'of a clearly etched body, sharply different from the rest of the objects in the universe.' The 'Hindu body' gives rise to a whole class of diseases which Gananath Obeyesekere has called 'cultural diseases,' and Kakar sees even the culture's nagging ontological anxiety (with questions like 'Who am I?') as a defense against 'the fundamental anxiety aroused by an image of the body in unflagging transformation.' Again, where the West conceives of the environment in 'nutritional and human terms,' in 'what is going on *within* the fortress of the individual body,' the Indian belief system considers the effects of the 'natural world'—which would take in the planetary constellations, the earth, magnetic fields, seasonal and daily rhythms, precious stones and metals—on 'the human body and psyche.' Most importantly, in the Indian body image, there is a 'very high emotional investment in the body' leading to one of Kakar's rare (if cleverly disguised) judgements: 'Somehow, it seems quite appropriate that India's national bird is the peacock!'—the exclamation mark at the end being a dead giveaway— unlike the western rejection of the 'insides of the body' as a 'cistern,' with the implication that 'with the *possible* exception of tears' (italic mine), observes Kakar drily, it is 'for that reason alone dirty.' Yet another 'disguised' value judgement, perhaps, balancing the earlier one almost aesthetically.

In 'Clinical Work and Cultural Imagination,' Kakar explains 'the cultural rootedness of psychoanalysis' by drawing on his own clinical experience with two markedly different patients, Ramnath and Pran, drawn from entirely different social strata. 51-year Ramnath is a Delhi grocer with an 'unspecified "fearfulness"' and it is his case (albeit a 'failure': 'More than Ramnath's expectations, it was the disappointment of mine, I now realize, on which the analysis floundered . . . perhaps I had given up on him before he gave up on me' Kakar ruefully confesses) that leads to the postulation of the notion of 'psychological modernity' as the *sine qua non* of psychoanalytic treatment. But this 'psychological modernity,' Kakar is careful to point out, 'is not coterminous with historical modernity, nor are its origins in a special geographical location, even if it received a sharp impetus from the European Enlightenment.' So both 'traditional and modern individuals . . . share . . . the essence of psychological modernity' the 'core' of which is 'internalization rather than externalization.' But after dowering the traditional individual with 'psychological modernity,' Kakar does an unexpected U-turn and proceeds to invest the 'urban Indian analysand' with the 'cultural particularities of the self,' especially the particularity of the 'male Indians' experience of the powerful mother.' Such an 'urban Indian analysand' is Pran—a 35-year old journalist—whose '320 sessions have been pervaded by his mother to a degree unsurpassed in my clinical work.' And yet Kakar finds Pran non-pathological in the Indian context since his 'level of functioning,' including the sexual, 'is quite impressive.' By showing that Pran is, after all, as Indian as the next man, Kakar resumes his battle with the old adversary—the 'many anthropologists of Indian society'—to make the point that 'the traditional Hindu villager is not the only Indian there is with the rest being some sort of imposters or cultural deviants.'

We can now turn to that *locus classicus* in the entire Kakar *oeuvre*, 'The Maternal Feminine in Indian Psychoanalysis,' which carries the much-discussed Mohan case study which has appeared in four separate publications so far (1989, 1990 (twice) and 1997). It can be read alongside the Pran case-study and the Deven and Kiran studies clubbed together as 'Maternal Enthrallment' in Kakar's recent *Culture and Psyche* (1997). It is in the Mohan case study that Kakar first makes explicit the link between culture and psyche that has become his trademark by showing how in the Indian context 'the construction and experience of the self are influenced by culture from the very beginning of life' unlike 'Freud's "timetable" of culture entering the psychic structure relatively late in life as "ideology" of the superego . . . which has continued to be followed by other almanac-makers of the psyche,' including 'self-object' theorists like Heinz Kohut. To get inside 'Mohan's inner life,' Kakar explores the myths of Ganesa and Skanda, from the *Shiva Purana*, which are still 'vibrantly alive' in India and 'constitute a cultural idiom which aids the individual in the construction and integration of his inner world.' 'Here Ganesa and Skanda are personifications,' Kakar observes, 'of the two opposing wishes of the older child at the eve of the Oedipus stage. He is torn between a powerful wish for independent and autonomous functioning and an equally strong pull towards surrender and re-immersion in the enveloping maternal fusion from which he has just emerged.' For Mohan, 'the Ganesa position is often longed for' although 'it does not . . . represent an enduring solution to the problem of maintaining phallic desire in the face . . . of the Great Mother.' The Skanda position, too, runs into trouble when his lust turns rampant. The Goddess intercedes and Skanda began to see his mother in each of the wives of the gods he sought to seduce. So for Skanda, as for Mohan, all the women he desired turned into his mother and he be-different agenda—analyses one of Mohan's reported fantasies where he imagines himself having intercourse with the naked corpse of a beautiful woman hanging from a tree while other members of the same jungle tribe are eating parts of the hanging corpses which they themselves have hung on the trees. Kurtz interprets this by using an episode in the *Padma Purana* which involves Shiva's sexual sacrifice to argue that 'without Shiva's sacrifice, without his voluntary turn away from incest, the group of goddesses threatened to consume and destroy even Devi (the natural mother) herself. In fact, M is wishing for such a group action against his mother . . .' But you can't use 'counterfactual conditionals' (to borrow Harvard philosopher, the late Nelson Goodman's well-known concept), especially in a myth, to argue what could have happened in the myth if Shiva had not made his sexual sacrifice. In effect, Kurtz is writing his own *purana*!).

Kakar's 'The Cloistered Passion of Radha and Krishna'—taken from his 1986 publication *Tales of Love, Sex and Danger*, written jointly with the New York psychoanalyst and university don, John Ross—uses the legendary Radha–Krishna love story most ingeniously to illustrate his thesis on the Indian male—first sounded by Girindrasekhar Bose in the 20s, as Kakar himself acknowledges in his landmark 'Maternal-Feminine' essay—namely, his susceptibility to the 'primitive idea of being a woman.' After deftly referring to a couple of 'western' case histories—including that of Aaron Green, that maverick psychoanalyst in Janet Malcolm's *The Impossible Profession* (1980)—Kakar summarizes an Indian vignette where the patient 'in initiating an illicit love affair with the wife of a businessman had crossed daunting social barriers of caste and class.' This patient's 'visions' 'of Hindu gods and goddesses in amorous embrace' and his experience of their 'sensations and feelings in his own person' leads Kakar seamlessly to examine the history of the Radha–Krishna legend as paradigmatic of Indian sexuality.

Kakar does a rapid survey of the history of 'love' in India to find that 'love' moved from being 'a matter of straightforward desire and its gratification' (in the two great epics) to its first flowering in the 'first six to seven centuries of the present era' after suffering an eclipse in 'the Buddhist domination of society' which followed the epic era. However the 'transformative moment' of love—from desire's sensations to love's adoration—occurred in the twelfth century in Jayadeva's celebration of the Radha–Krishna legend in his *Gitagovinda* which takes its place beside Beroul's celebrated work on the romance of Tristan and Isolde in Europe and Nizami's on Layla and Majnun in the Islamic

Isolde in Europe and Nizami's on Layla and Majnun in the Islamic world as predating and possibly prefiguring 'important cultural–historical changes in Europe, India and the Middle East.'

Jayadeva merely hints at the illicit nature of the Radha–Krishna love. It was the later poets, 'notably Vidyapati, who tend to focus more on Radha and her love than on Krishna.' 'As with most things Indian,' Kakar remarks astutely, the reemergence of passionate love 'originated in the religious sphere' after its ossification in Sanskrit and Tamil love poetry. It is with the rise of devotional religion and the arrival of the great *bhakti* poets that the rigidities and petrifactions of conventional love poetry were at last broken. No longer was woman described in standard, prescribed ways—with 'thighs round and plump, like the trunk of an elephant or a banana tree'—but because she is herself, 'a whole object or person.' This, for Kakar is 'a developmental milestone that brings to a close the early dyadic struggles of infancy.' And with '*bhakti* . . . pre-eminently feminine in its orientation,' we are in familiar Kakar territory because erotic love here is described 'from the woman's viewpoint or at least from her position as imagined by the man.' This crossing of gender boundaries in India is what gives the Radha–Krishna poems their 'erotic excitement.' Kakar quotes with relish Sur Das and Chandi Das, where 'the inversion of sexual roles is all the more striking in the depiction of sexual intercourse,' to make his case against western phallocentricity. In the *bhakti* cults, Kakar reminds us, 'the worshipper must create an erotic relationship with Krishna, the transcendence of boundaries of gender become imperative for the male devotee, 'who endeavours to become as a woman in relation to the Lord.' This is why Indian saints feminize themselves and countless poet-saints bear testimony to this. But Kakar is careful to distinguish this 'from pathological cases where similar fantasies and feminine behaviour might well be a manifestation of "homosexual libido".'

Kakar's case is now complete. The Indian male's wish to be a woman is 'not a later distortion of phallic strivings but rather another legacy from our 'prehistoric' experience with our mothers. This Indian ambisexuality represents 'the climax of pre-oedipal development before castration anxiety and guilt enter to limit and dull the sexual quest.' And thus does Kakar return us to that seemingly odd adulterous Indian patient with which he began his reflections on love in India. Not for nothing, we now realize, has the book been dedicated—in all seriousness, no doubt!—'To Lovers.'

Kakar's Gandhi essay is likely to stay in the popular imagination for its fascinating vignettes on two Gandhi acolytes: the little known Prema Kantak (most analysts would say 'classically hysterical' is how Kakar introduces her but his actual treatment of her goes well beyond the strictly psychoanalytical and is positively hilarious!) and the 'tall, strapping . . . handsome rather than pretty' Madeline Slade ('renamed Mira by Gandhi') who, after 35 years in India, 'refused to talk about Gandhi' with Kakar when he met her in 1964 in the forests above Baden near Vienna. Both, incidentally, answer to the description of psychoanalyst Ralph Greenson—incidentally, he was Marilyn Monroe's personal therapist in her last days—of women 'who come to analysis not to seek insight but to enjoy the physical proximity of the analyst.' But Kakar's 'Gandhi and Women' has a more lasting value. It does a 'psychoanalytic deconstruction' of the famous autobiography by 'bringing out its latent meanings' arising chiefly 'from the narrator's unconscious purposes rather than . . . any deliberate efforts at omission or concealment.' Kakar's 'deconstruction' takes us through the well-known episodes in Gandhi's life—the much-discussed incident revolving round the night of his father's death, the English interludes during Gandhi's stay there, the South African period and the 1906 vow of celibacy—without causing any major surprises, till he comes to Gandhi's 'experiments with food' in South Africa as reported by an adoring, yet detached, disciple, Millie Polak. Kakar quotes from Gandhi a passage—not from the autobiography—on 'control of palate' and finds it 'reminiscent of St. Augustine' except that 'Augustine treats imbibition as he does all sensory output' whereas 'Gandhi . . . makes of food a primary regulator of the genital impulses.' This is not the only appearance the Christian saint makes in the Gandhi section of *Intimate Relations* (although, somewhat surprisingly, he merits only a single entry in the index). Gandhi's autobiography, itself, is found to have 'much in common' with St. Augustine's *Confessions* and this is the occasion of some very incisive remarks on Mahadev Desai's English translation (with the aid of a passage dealing with 'the Master's sexual conflicts') which he finds 'full of Augustinisms': 'den of vice,' 'jaws of sin' etc. Offering his own translation of the same passage, Kakar points out that the Mahadev Desai translation 'seems to be judging them in a Christian theological sense that is missing in Gandhi's own account.' Kakar retrieves for reconsideration two native concepts that Gandhi employs in the Gujarati original: *vishaya* and *vikara*. So, rather than 'sinful,' Gandhi finds sexuality 'poisonous' (*vishaya*) and as something that 'distorts' (*vikara*). Lust, for Gandhi, was not sinful but poisonous, 'contaminating the elixir of immortality.' 'To be passionate,' for Gandhi, 'is not to fall from a state of grace, but to suffer a distortion of truth.' We are dealing with a Hindu, not a Christian *Weltanschauung*.

So now we have Gandhi, 'a passionate man who suffered his passions as poisonous of his inner self and a sensualist who felt his sensuality distorted his inner purpose.' But there were also long periods when 'his sensuality was integrated with the rest of his being.' And so Kakar sets out in a short passage to describe Gandhi's 'acceptable sensuality' based on 'old movie clips and reminiscences of those who knew him in person' and remarks—invoking the great Christian saint again!—'The Christian St. Augustine would have been altogether shocked.' Some 22 pages later, St. Augustine makes yet another appearance, this time in an extended quote from the *Confessions* which describes 'celibacy garbed in soothing maternal imagery.' This leads Kakar to his master thesis on Gandhi (read: Indian male): 'the unconscious fantasy of maintaining an idealized relationship with the maternal body.' Still, the 'cherished oneness with the maternal-feminine could not always be maintained,' Kakar points out, since it was 'often threatened by the intrusion of phallic desire.' And hence Gandhi's 'obsession with food at these times, evident in the letters and writings . . .' Gandhi's 'experiments with various kinds of food'—the autobiography might more appropriately be called *My Experiments with Food!*—appear, as Kakar observes, 'as part of an involuted and intuitive effort to recover and maintain his merger with his mother.'

Popular cinema in India—the new home of the non-rational in India—received scant attention in the past, although, of late, it would seem a compulsive object of study for sundry intellectuals in search of a subject. But Kakar is the first serious thinker to throw psychoanalytic light on Hindi cinema as Wolfenstein and Leites (and, more ornately, Parker Tyler) had done on American cinema nearly fifty years back. The essay begins on a disarming personal note—his movie-going days began, we learn, in Lahore in the 40s where a grand-uncle owned a cinema theatre ('Prabhat Talkies') and Kakar seems to have virtually gorged himself on Hindi movies which he now clinically classifies on the basis of a *threefold* caste hierarchy!—but quickly moves on to consider weightier issues. Acknowledging their role in keeping 'the road to childhood open,' Kakar goes on to consider popular cinema 'as a collective fantasy, a group dream.' Fantasy—'the bridge between desire and reality'—is further extolled in psychoanalyst Robert Stoller's lyrical tribute, as 'the vehicle of hope, healer of trauma . . . cleanser of the soul.' Noting in passing that not even the German cinema—during the economic crisis of the 1920s—or the Japanese cinema—in the aftermath of the Second World War—'elevated fantasy to such an overwhelming principle,' Kakar locates the reasons for the ubiquity of fantasy in—the Hindi cinema in the realm of 'cultural psychology' rather than in the domain of the socio-economic. In India, since 'the child's world of magic is not as far removed from adult consciousness as it may be in some other cultures'—remember Kakar's thesis of Indians maintaining 'more troops at the narcissistic position?'—Hindi films 'seem to provide this regressive haven for a vast number of our people.'

'Dogmatic rationalists' err in dismissing Hindi films as 'unrealistic.' This is to needlessly reduce the scope of the real to 'exclude the domain of the psychologically real.' Adapting Bruno Bettelheim's classic dictum on fairy tales to movies, Kakar declares that 'Hindi films may be unreal in a rational sense but they are certainly not untrue,' for they exhibit 'a sure-footed grasp of the topography of desire.' There follows a masterly summary of Raj Kapoor's *Ram Teri Ganga Maili*—using the Freudian 'third eye' which 'merely cracks reality's stony surface to release its inner shape of fantasy'—in the course of which Kakar offers an absolutely novel theory of rape in Hindi films (which caused consternation when I attempted to introduce it at a feminist seminar in Bangalore in the early 90s). 'The wished-for father-daughter intimacy became a major fantasy in India,' observes Kakar, 'because of the fact that in the Indian family the father's withdrawal from the daughter is quite precipitate once she attains puberty.' At this period of 'inner turmoil' for the girl, 'the rape by the father is then the forbidden sexual aspect of her encompassing longing for intimacy.' For the Indian male, the locus of the rape fantasy is in the trauma of the 'second birth' (see Kakar's *The Inner World*, pp. 126–33). 'In the cavernous darkness of the cinema hall, the fantasy may at last surface gingerly and the associated masochistic pleasure be enjoyed vicariously in the pain and subjugation of the woman with whom one secretly identifies.'

Kakar breaks up the chronology of the early Hindi film broadly into the Majnun–lover phase—the Majnun–lover ('coiner of poetic phrases,' his natural habitat the *kotha*, 'a home for vile *bodies*' (italics mine), the phrase an inadvertent echo, perhaps, of the title of Evelyn Waugh's wickedly satirical novel, *Vile Bodies*!) here seeks to retain the paradise that was lost 'before the separation from the mother's anima took place' (Kakar observes in passing that 'it is only the phallic illusion of modern

western man which has tended to deny their legitimacy and reality')—
and the Krishna–lover phase (none other than the eveteasing hero of oh,
so many, many Indian films). Kakar's observations are refreshingly
original and wholly free of the realistic hang-ups that so often plague
criticism of Bombay films. Honed to perfection by Shammi Kapoor (of
Junglee fame), the Krishna–lover is, for Kakar, the 'phallus humbling
the pride of the unapproachable woman.'

However, it is in treating Amitabh Bachchan—recently voted the top
actor of the millennium by the users of the BBC's Online services—
"who has personified a new kind of hero and lover' : the 'good–bad
hero'—that Kakar breaks new ground. Rather like Karna in the *Mahabharata*, the Bachchan hero 'reflects the psychological changes in a vast
number of people who are located in a halfway house—the transitional
sector. . . .' The good–bad hero is 'neither overtly emotional like Majnun nor boyishly phallic like the Krishna lover'; he is very much like
the hero described by Faiz in his well-known poem, 'Do Not Ask of
Me, My Love.' Kakar's short essay—less than 16 pages, really—
bristles with so many startling insights into the Indian psyche that one
wishes he could have devoted a full-length study to the subject. He
could do it yet!

So much has been written on the 19th century Bengali saint, Sri
Ramakrishna, but, in Indian hands, it has largely been hagiography. And
so it is fascinating to see Kakar taking up the gauntlet. Early on, he is
careful to point out that Ramakrishna's *bhakti* mysticism, which bears
'a strong family resemblance'—a coinage made famous by Ludwig
Wittgenstein in his *Philosophical Investigations* (1953)—'to the mysticism of monotheistic faiths' needs to be distinguished from both
Upanishadic and Yogic mysticism where love or yearning for communion with god do not play any role. Psychoanalysis, notoriously
hostile to the mystical state, is 'ripe for radical revision' here given that
the mystic's capacity for 'love and work' (Freud's twin criteria of mental health) are absolutely unimpaired. Already in the work of Winnicott,
Lacan and Bion—the latter two described as 'the mystics of
psychoanalysis'—there is an attempt 'to develop a phenomenology of
creative experiencing.' Kakar's choice of Ramakrishna's 'ecstatic
mysticism' as the occasion for his 'radical revision' is clearly a response
to Freud's notorious unease at Ramakrishna's 'florid ecstasies.' Drawing freely from Mahendranath Gupta's well-known work on
Ramakrishna, Kakar takes the reader through much hallowed territory—the saint's first 'personal darshan of the Mother' ('a very Hindu.

story of a man forcing the Goddess to appear by threatening to decapitate himself'), followed by an eight-year period when 'he systematically followed the prescribed practices laid down by the different schools of Hindu mysticism.' The esoteric meditations of Tantra (under the tutelage of a female guru, Brahmani Bhairavi) were followed by 'the non dualistic way of Vedanta and Shakta mysticism 'to which he felt personally most attuned.' Now 'devotional mysticism,' Kakar points out, does not 'demand an elimination of a sense of individual identity.' It just required the 'recovery of a childlike innocence and a quiet renunciation of the major adult categories.' Of the various developmental stages of devotional mysticism, it is *bhava* ('feeling,' 'mood') that Kakar chooses to gloss for the reader. Characterising *bhava*s as 'psychic looseners' that 'jar the soul of the narcissistic sheath of self-limiting routine' into 'creative experiencing,' Kakar moves on to discuss '*darshan*' or 'vision' rather than 'its psychiatric counterpart hallucination' to be clear of the 'connotations of psychopathology associated with psychiatric categories.' In addition to several 'unconscious visions' (or 'visions of the unconscious'? Kakar speculates)—'the hallucinations, unbidden and unwelcome' that belong to the period of his insanity (*unmada*),—Ramakrishna had numerous conscious visions, some of which he saw in 'the traditional Yogic imagery of Kundalini.' Luckily, for the student of Hindu mysticism, 'Ramakrishna does not seem to have been overly enamoured of these states.' As a result he 'consciously tried to keep a trace of the observing ego. . . .' As he himself maintained, 'I want to taste sugar, not become sugar.' Sometimes, however, in spite of himself, he did dissolve into sugar—or, 'salt doll' (to use Ramakrishna's favourite metaphor) 'which went to measure the depth of the ocean' and dissolved! It is this 'yearning' that Freud and some orthodox Freudians, like Melanie Klein, see as the desire to return to the 'good' mother and a defensive denial of her terrifying aspects. With uncommon psychoanalytic honesty, Kakar admits that while the evidence for Ramakrishna's hostility towards his father is nil, the 'evidence for the denial of the dreaded mother is slightly greater'—as witness his first mystical vision in the Kali temple. However the 'radical revisionist' cogently and plausibly argues that 'the ambiguous evidence of one particular vision is not enough to compel an acceptance of the Kleinian notions on mystical motivation.'

There is much to be said, Kakar observes, 'for the hypothesis that experiences of separation and loss'—viz, his father's terminal illness, the death of his brother during Ramakrishna's adolescence 'when the developing ego is particularly vulnerable to stress'—'spurred Ramak-rishna into mystical states.' But these experiences are not 'sufficient to explain the totality of his mysticism.' Rather, as Kakar points out, Ramakrishna's acute sensitivity to the theme of separation was itself due to his 'mystical gift (or curse) of a specific kind of creative experiencing.' Again, the sole and primary object of 'creative experiencing' of the mystic is none of the psychoanalyst's stock in trade—mother, father, sex, aggression, etc.—but 'the unknowable ground of creativeness as such.' When Kakar observes that it is 'the throes of romantic love that gives inklings of our original freshness of vision' we nod in wistful agreement. But when Kakar extends the scope of 'creative experiencing' to include the achievements not only of a Buddha and a Ramakrishna but of a Freud and an Einstein as well, we are not so sure!

Kakar concludes his reflections on 'Ramakrishna and the Mystical Experience' by turning his attention to male sexuality which, for Ramakrishna, 'constituted the biggest obstacle to mystical experiencing.' Not surprisingly, Ramakrishna baulked at Tantric Yoga where, 'at its culmination,' God as a female is sought to be 'pleasured' by the devotee. Ramakrishna repeatedly warned his disciples against the allurements of *kamini–kanchani* ('literally, women and gold') and advised them 'to avoid the female sex altogether.' Still, to regard even sitting with a woman or talking to her (albeit for a long time!) as 'a kind of sexual intercourse' looks needlessly harsh to bewildered man bound in all too earthly chains and Ramakrishna's relaxation of this restriction for the evolved soul would seem far too paltry a concession. To vary his own aphorism, you may not want to dance once you reach the roof. Ramakrishna, himself, never quite overcame his uneasiness in the presence of female devotees and his attempted renunciation of male sexual desire is the subject of a truly terrifying vision which Kakar analyses with his customary acumen. The masculine aspects of identity were 'never completely submerged' in Ramakrishna in spite of 'the persistent impulse towards being feminine' which had to do 'with the greater tolerance of his community and its culture towards such identifications.' This is the reason why the example of Ramakrishna (and Gandhi, too, we might add, with his Chaitanya-like terror of the seductive powers of women) will be permanently relevant for us.

The companion piece from *The Analyst and the Mystic*—'The Guru as Healer'—is understandably more general since it addresses the important question of the role of the guru as 'healer' in the modern medical sense. Kakar does a quick survey of the nature and function of the guru since Vedic times when he was not yet the figure of awe and authority he is today but merely an instructor in the performance of religious duties. In the following Upanishadic era, the guru begins 'to replace Vedic rituals as the path to spiritual liberation.' The great Sankara (AD 7) is the best exemplar of the ancient Upanishadic tradition of the guru. Relying as much on reason as on scriptural authority, the student was here exhorted by the guru 'to test and verify the teachings through his own experiences.' The guru acted as a facilitator by constructing 'experience-near situations' to illustrate his teaching. The master-disciple relationship was governed by 'perfect equality in self realization, with radical insight as its goal.' Intimacy, not merger, prevailed between guru and disciple. But with the rise and spread of both *bhakti* and Tantric cults, devotional surrender of the disciple became *de rigueur*. Love, not understanding, now governs the guru--disciple relationship as the labyrinthine mazes of Upanishadic thought and logic give way to a complete and willful surrender as the guru is increasingly deified. As the guru moves away from man to god, there is a parallel shift of the disciple from man to child ('progressive', if you think in religious terms, 'regressive', if you think psychoanalytically). The ideal disciple is 'a natural renouncer of all adult categories, especially of rational 'inquiry and of the sexual gift.' The guru is now Brahma, Vishnu and Maheshwara—a formulation familiar to all modern Hindus. In the last hundred years, since the rise of the Brahmo and Arya Samaj movements, there have been attempts at the revival of Vedic rituals and Upanishadic religions but, more recently, we have seen the rise of 'reluctant gurus' like Jiddu Krishnamurti. But, on the whole, the guru today remains a 'mystical, charismatic' figure, although Kakar is careful to point out that this is not simply due to the 'victory of irrationality over reason, servility over autonomy, or of a contemporary dark age over an earlier golden era.' Today, 'the major, if not the most significant, role of the guru is that of a healer of emotional suffering.' In fact, it is the 'psychotherapeutic function' of the guru, his 'healing capabilities' that is most visible, not his 'great spiritual attainments.' This would be true of even such an 'intellectual guru' like J.K.! For the most frequent malaise today is a prolonged depletion of self esteem and most guru-seekers need restoration of a 'lost sense of self worth.' The need for a healing guru is acute during the 'second birth' phase in the identity development of the Hindu male. In 'extreme states of narcissistic starvation' when 'the terrors of self-dissolution' deluge the fragmented self, the personal guru alone is 'the primary cultural self-object experience for adults in Hindu tradition and society.'

Taking issue with western psychiatric pathologizing of the guru–disciple relationship, Kakar finds 'a full-blown guru fantasy' (a phrase he is to use again here and in his '94 essay, 'Clinical Work and Cultural Imagination') present universally however much 'one may prefer the Enlightenment virtues of reason and ideological egalitarianism.' Indeed, the guru–disciple relationship offers 'a developmental second chance for obtaining the required nutrients for the cohesion, integration and vigour of the self.' The 'surrender of the self' demanded by the guru of the disciple is 'ubiquitous' in diverse mystical traditions. 'Surrender', in self psychology, 'is the full flowering of the idealizing transference.' The only alternative to surrender to the guru is 'constant conflict.' (Muktananda). But, then, gurus are neither just human beings nor, for that matter, just 'objects'—'in the inelegant language of psychoanalysis'—but 'functions.' The guru, in India at any rate, is 'the culturally sanctioned addressee of a collective request for the transforming experience,' the 'transformational object' (Christopher Bollas). 'The idealizing transference leading to the merging experience' is, in Kakar's formulation, 'the core of the healing process in the guru–disciple relationship.' In addition to 'surrender,' an equally important feature of the guru–disciple relationship is 'intimacy,' although 'the sought-for intimacy' could be 'archaic in nature, before the birth of language.' This is the reason why 'the guru–disciple interaction touches deeper, more regressed layers of the psyche which are generally not reached by psychoanalysis.' And thus it is that 'the guru as benign self-object opens the devotee's closed world of archaic destructive relationships to new possibilities' through the uniquely Hindu phenomenon of '*darshanat.*' Accompanying the guru's look is the symbolic power of his words, 'enhanced by the group setting,' 'through the *sound* which conveys the experience of the guru's presence within the psyche' (italic mine), although their sense is not understood! And, finally, there is 'the taking of *prasada*, food offerings touched or tasted by the guru' and other related behaviour which helps in 'a loosening up of individual bodily and psychic boundaries' and brings about 'a co-mingling with a self-object.'

In spite of all the good things Kakar has to say of the guru-disciple relationship, Kakar is analyst enough to quietly ponder 'how a guru deals with the massive idealizing transference of so many disciples.' He concludes (with the quiet astonishment of a fellow sufferer, no doubt!)

that the guru's counter-transference is actually a source of two-fold relief, that the guru's calm, cheerful, loving mien is perhaps 'a consequence rather than a cause of his role as a healer.' There is a witty, yet warm, detachment in such a remark.

Kakar's portrait of Sadhvi Ritambhara in The *Colours of Violence* (1996), 'The Virtuous Virago,' is his first serious foray into a realm he had studiously avoided in his earlier writings ('perhaps the most difficult to write,' he has since confessed): the political psychology of mass movements. A spokesperson of the *sangh parivar*, Ritambhara was 'well on her way to become the leading firebrand in the Hindu cause.' Kakar chooses to dissect a 'standard' speech to lay bare the face of Hindu fundamentalism. Drawing her imagery and allusions from the epics, the speech, 'replete with symbolic resonances, evocations and associations,' appeals to 'a group identity while creating it.' The speech is 'delivered in rhyming verses' as 'people tend to believe verse more than prose especially in Hindu India where the transmission of sacred knowledge has been traditionally oral.' Ritambhara invokes the gods and heroes of Hinduism offered as 'ego ideals' as well as 'the overarching Hindu community.' She also 'devoutly hails' Mahavira, Buddha, Guru Govind Singh and nineteenth century reformers like Dayanand Saraswati. Valmiki, legendary author of the *Ramayana*, finds a place in Ritambhara's peroration as he has been recently elevated 'as the patron saint of the Harijans.' From the gods and heroes of the past, a link is established to the *karsevak*s who lost their lives in their bid to build the temple at Ayodhya. The rebuilding, itself, is seen as an act of mourning 'for lost honour, lost self-esteem, lost civilization, lost Hinduness.' Ritambhara's speech, in the original Hindi, is in 'its brilliant, loud colours . . . impossible to reproduce in the muted palette of English' and yet, apparently, the impossibility has been surmounted in Kakar's own translation, albeit with unexpectedly witty results!

In Ritambhara's construction of a post-Babri Masjid Hindu identity, Kakar sees 'the necessary splitting that enhances group cohesion.' The process involves idealizing 'Hindu tolerance, compassion' etc, on the one hand, and scapegoating 'the bad, the dirty, and the impure' Muslim on the other. Longish passages detailing 'persecutory fantasies in the collective Hindu imagination' are given (in Kakar's own English translation, the adequacy and accuracy of which I take for granted) and, in doing so, Kakar permits himself one of his rare authorial intrusions when he observes 'There is a considerable denial of reality in maintaining that the Hindus are relatively deprived or in danger of oppression

by the Muslim. Such a denial of reality is only possible through the activation of the group's persecutory fantasy in which the Muslim changes
from a stereotype to an archetype,' even 'arch tyrant.'

The India that Ritambhara conjures for her audience is that of 'a
mutilated body.' However, this 'feeling of helplessness which persecution anxiety engenders reverses the process of idealization' and 'reveals
the fragility of the group's grandiose self,' because what 'a group most
idealizes about itself is intimately related to its greatest fear.' Still,
Kakar is too honest not to confess his own feelings on the subject—
'since I am a Hindu myself'—could have coloured 'some of my
interpretations.' His own 'brand of Hinduism, liberal–rationalist (with a
streak of agnostic mysticism)' finds the Hindu to be 'no different from
any other ethnic community or even nation which feels special or superior to other collectivities, especially their neighbours and rivals.' Kakar
finds the Hindu fundamentalist guilty of narcissism—especially with its
twin corollaries of a 'smug superiority' and 'an arrogant self
righteousness'—which provokes 'distaste among even the most
tolerant.' However, Kakar refuses to judge such behaviour as
'pathological' because there is in it 'the human aspiration towards self
transcendence' through immersion in a group.

Hindutva, finally, does offer 'another alternative vision of India's
future', an alternative to both modernists and traditionalists. Still, Ayodhya is 'not an end but only a beginning since the forces buffeting Hindu
(or, for that matter, Muslim) grandiosity do not lie within the country
but are global in their scope.' This observation should receive wide acceptance.

The second selection from *The Colours of Violence*—'Meeting the
Mullahs'—can only be described as a *tour de force*, a sustained, single-
breath (as in the very Indian game of *kabbadi*!) foray into Muslim
terrain by an 'agnostic–mystic' Hindu psychoanalyst as we have just
learnt. I say 'Hindu,' advisedly, for Kakar openly confesses to 'the persistence of my Hindu childhood image of the mullah as the wild-eyed
man with a flowing beard who spewed fire and brimstone every Friday
afternoon in the mosque.' Kakar, we need to remember, grew up in
small, district towns in west Punjab (which are all now in Pakistan) in
undivided India before 1947. Consequently, his 'first reaction to the
mullah' was recoil 'at the hectoring tone, the imperative voice' which
led to his labelling him a 'fanatic.' 'Emotionally,' he was influenced 'by
fantasies from a Hindu past,' 'cognitively' by 'the concepts of a West-
inspired liberalism.' The 'temptation' was 'to pathologize the mullah as

an obsessional, if not psychopathic or even paranoid.' But he settles for listening 'if I wished to understand Muslim fundamentalism without resort to reductionist psychological cliches.'

The 'Muslim fundamentalist,' then, in Kakar's sympathetic hands, is briefly turned into a 'physician' who moves from 'diagnosis' to 'pathogenesis.' The 'sorry plight of Muslims,' now, is compared to their early 'exalted status' when, during the Crusades, Sultan Salah-ul-din (Saladin), 'commanding a force of 13,000 . . . killed 300,000 Christians on a single day.' 'Today, with all the oil, dollars, and weapons in the world, Muslims are slaves to the dictates of Western powers' and have trouble 'keeping their own faith alive.' Television is declared a 'sickness' which has 'entered Muslim homes where families fritter away whole evenings in ungodly entertainment rather than in reading from or discussing the Qur'an.' The 'remedy' is a 'return to the fundamentals of faith as contained in the Qur'an.'

Fundamentalism (here, Muslim), for Kakar, is 'psychologically speaking' 'a theory of suffering,' just as modern individualism, too, is 'another theory of suffering and its cure.' Interestingly here, when he explicates the notion of 'psychological individuality' which depends upon 'internalization rather than externalization' (unlike fundamentalism which locates the source of suffering not in the individual mind but outside, in 'a historical process'), Kakar uses the very words he had used in 'Clinical Work and Cultural Imagination' to describe the Delhi grocer, Ramnath's suffering! Kakar does refer to 'a narcissistic injury to the group self' and, twice, refers to 'sadomasochistic injury' in the mullah's imagery. Still, as with Sadhvi Ritambhara, 'the violent virago,' Kakar refuses to reduce the mullah's discourse to 'psychopathology.' For while it may appear as 'illness to the outsider, fundamentalism is a cure for the insider.' Kakar would appear, then, to have steered cautiously between the Scylla of Hindu fundamentalism and the Charybdis of its Muslim counterpart without losing his psychoanalytic way or bearings.

In 'Religious Conflict in the Modern World,' Kakar's wrap-up of the main arguments of *The Colours of Violence*, he sees the current worldwide religious revival as 'a complex attempt at the resacralisation of cultures beset with the many ills of modernity.' But, for him, 'the much-touted revival' is 'less of religiosity than of cultural identities based on religious affiliation.' But the several threats to individual identity do not create 'a group identity' but merely 'bring it to the fore,' although traditionally psychoanalysts have tended to see 'group aspects of personal identity' as 'a late creation in individual development.' Such 'stereotypes' demand, in Kakar's view, a 'careful revision.' Arguing, in his now familiar trademark vein, that 'the self . . . is a system of reverberating representational worlds,' Kakar questions the wisdom of the almanac-makers of the psyche who see 'these constituent inner worlds' as 'primary' or 'deeper' and argues, instead, for 'an archeological layering of the various inner worlds.'

The group aspect of identity, for Kakar, is 'powerfully formed by the processes of introjection, identification and projection during childhood.' In this process, 'the child tries to disown the bad representations through projection.' These 'disowned bad representations' need 'reservoirs' (in Vamik Volkan's apt description)—for Hindus these are Muslims and vice versa—and these act as 'convenient repositories for subsequent rages and hateful feelings for which no clear-cut addressee is available.' Kakar illustrates this with a telling and wellknown example: 16th century France with its bitter Catholic–Protestant feud.

Arguing that, along with religious selfhood (with its 'I-ness'), we have 'a second track of We-ness' (which is 'the experience of being part of a community of believers'), Kakar points out that 'religious community is the interactive aspect of religious identity' and it is the threat 'to the community aspect of religious identity' that gives birth 'to communalism, intolerance, and the potential for social violence.' It is 'the change from community to communalism' that makes 'the community aspect of religious identity hyperconscious.' In 'communalism as a state of mind,' 'the individual's *assertion* of being part of a religious community' is 'preceded by a full *awareness* of belonging to such a community,' as the 'We-ness' of the community is replaced by the 'We-*are*' of communalism. In an elegant variation of a famous declaration in the U.N. Charter, Kakar observes 'Riots *do* start in the minds of men, minds conditioned by our earliest inner experience of self-affirmation and assertion.'

More than 'language, region, or other markers of ethnic identity,' religions bring to conflict between groups 'a greater emotional intensity and a deeper motivational thrust.' And, although we like to believe that religions are about love, compassion etc., we are confronted with the reality that 'violence is present in all religions'—including Hinduism (which talks of the Kali Yuga) and Buddhism (with its Seven Days of the Sword)—'as a positive and even necessary force for the realization of religious goals.'

Kakar's closing remarks—with echoes and pastiches of classical

English literature (Shakespeare's *Hamlet*), popular American literature (Mario Puzo's The *Godfather*, and even a famous aphorism of the 19th century Liberal politician, the Rt. Hon. Augustine Birrell—offer a cautious, if optimistic, political prognosis. Casting himself in the role of an 'optimistic realist,' Kakar sees 'multiculturalism' as the *mantra* of the future. Quoting, with approval, the American poet, Theodore Roethe, 'In a dark time, the eye begins to see,' Kakar ends with a matching quote from the *Mahabharata*, 'Hope is the sheet anchor of every man . . .' After Pokhran (I & II), what else is there, anyway?

Looking back at Kakar's work, spanning some three decades, we see an amalgam and fusion of widely disparate world-views, the forging and consolidation of 'a modern Hindu identity', something Swami Vivekananda and, somewhat more recently, Gandhi struggled with all their lives with varying degrees of success. In both, the feminine side seemed to win out after a long, bitter struggle with the western-rationalist male side. In the case of Kakar—going largely by the evidence of his written work—the familiar pattern seems to be gaining ascendancy as the near-oxymoronic formulation in *The Colours of Violence*—'liberal–rationalist (with a streak of agnostic mysticism)' on a broadly Hindu base—looks pretty much like reversing itself with the 'liberal–rationalist' pole now the minor key and the 'agnostic–mystic' Hindu pole the major chord in the swelling diapason (or 'grand narrative,' if you like, a concept for which Kakar has a sneaking fondness despite the rising tide of post-modernism) of his work.

Kakar's work on childhood and adult-male formation—with the maternal–feminine principle the thematic fulcrum of both—will undoubtedly stand the test of time and will serve as a milestone or benchmark for any future research on the subject. His brief foray into mysticism—with the mystic tantalizingly poised between childhood and adulthood—certainly breached the Maginot line separating psychoanalysis and religious experience without altogether creating a unified field of human endeavour. Which particular direction his future work will take is difficult to predict, though he has already given us a few hints. Aging—on which, like his master, the late Erik Erikson, he has written already—could occupy his attention now and, certainly, female (Indian) sexuality—a proverbial thorn for psychoanalysis—is eagerly awaiting further exploration.

Kakar will remain indispensable to our understanding the condition of Indian men and women in contemporary India. His recent interests going by *Indian Love Stories* (1999), which he edited, *The Ascetic of*

Desire (1998) and a translation of the *Kamasutra*, with Wendy Doniger, is in the pipeline—would seem to have veered in the general direction of fiction, fictionalized biography (?) and translation. I expect this trend to intensify and continue as we enter the new millennium.

T.G. VAIDYANATHAN

I

Childhood and Identity

1

Mothers and Infants

The first months of human life are a period of wordless oblivion which is of root significance for individual development. At once timeless and fleeting, infancy is the foundation for all later psychological experience. Moreover, the nature of an individual's first relationship—with his mother—profoundly influences the quality and 'dynamics' of social relations throughout his life.

Recognition of the crucial role of this original relationship, the mother-infant 'dyad' as the genetic psychologist Edward Simmel has called it,[1] for the development of all subsequent social relations has been relatively late in coming in the social sciences. Thus, although Freud mentioned its importance in 1895 in one of his earliest papers and often elaborated on the psychological reciprocity between mothers and infants, he came to appreciate its full significance in emotional development only towards the end of his life. By 1938, he described the mother's importance to the infant as 'unique, without parallel, established unalterably for a whole lifetime as the first and strongest love-object and as the prototype of all later love-relations—for both sexes'.[2] It is within this dyad that a person first learns to relate to the 'Other' and begins to develop his capacity to love (in its widest sense); it is here that an individual originates as a social being. As adults, all of our affiliations and intimacies bear the stamp of our particular kind of infancy. Indeed, as anthropologists such as Kardiner, Benedict and Mead have shown, the specific emotional colouring of many of a society's cultural institutions can be directly attributed to the dominant quality or mode of the first relationship, not in the sense of simple causal connection, but in the complementarity and reciprocal influence between the mother–infant dyad and other institutionalized forms of social relations.

In spite of the general consensus on its significance, the mother–infant dyad remains intellectually elusive and relatively unexplored. In part, because of its archaic, wordless nature, it is but dimly reflected in the free associations of psycho-analytic patients and hence in clinical reconstructions. Hypotheses and speculations on the emotional development of the infant and on what actually transpires between him and his mother in the course of their repeated early encounters are thus derived from a variety of sources: direct observation of infants, experimental data in neo-natal cognition, treatment of psychotic patients, and deductions from the conceptual framework of psycho-analysis. The following short summary of existing knowledge of the emotional state of infancy is highly condensed.[3] Such a description, however minimal, is a necessary background for the elaboration of the dominant mode of the mother–infant relationship in Hindu society and for an interpretation of its consequences for adult personality, its influence on the organization of social relations and its relevance to the elaboration of cultural ideals.

During the first few months of life, the infant lives in a psychological state which has variously been termed 'undifferentiated', 'non-differentiated', or 'unintegrated'. These terms are basically similar; all imply that at the beginning of life there is no clear and absolute distinction between conscious and unconscious, ego and id, psyche and *soma*, inside and outside, 'I' and what is 'not-I', nor even between the different parts of the body. Only gradually, through constant exchanges with the mothering person, does the infant begin to discriminate and differentiate these opposites which are initially merged, and thus to take his first steps on the road to selfhood. The emotional or affective quality of this process of differentiation and inner integration is determined by the vicissitudes of the infant's tie to his mother. Whether all that is 'not-I' will forever remain vaguely threatening, replete with forebodings of an undefined nature, a danger to be avoided, or whether the infant will emerge from this phase feeling that the outside world is benevolently disposed and basically trustworthy; whether a reassuring sense of inner continuity and wholeness will predominate over a sense of falling to pieces and life forever lived in disparate segments: these are some of the developmental questions which originate in infancy. Furthermore, there is no comparable period of life in so far as the adaptive learning that takes place, learning which is mediated almost solely through the mother's instrumentality, when the mother is the principal caretaker of infants as she is in most cultures.

It is the mother's face—which the baby's eyes begin to 'grasp' and follow from about the age of four weeks, even when nursing—which becomes crystallized as the first visual precept from a jumble of light blurs, the first meaningful image out of a chaos of 'things' without meaning. It is on the mother's body, on her breast and through her hands that tactile perception and orientation are learned and practised. It is her rhythms of movement and quiet, her body warmth and smell, which differentiate the baby's other sensitivities, his sense of equilibrium and movement and his sensuality, while her voice is the sound stimulus which is the prerequisite for his own development of speech. Thus, the mother's *sensory presence* is of vital importance for the infant's earliest developmental experiences and awakenings.[4]

This emphasis on the mother's significance and power does not mean that the infant is completely helpless or passive in his relationship with her. From the beginning, he too is actively involved—looking, listening and, with the development of manual co-ordination, touching, handling, grasping—in maintaining connection and communication with his mother. Ethologists have designated this innate predisposition to activity—the five basic instinctive responses of sucking, clinging, following, crying and smiling—as a 'species-specific behaviour pattern' designed to further the human infant's survival by keeping him near the mother. Whether the ethological hypothesis is appropriate remains a controversial issue;[5] and even given the infant's predisposition to this kind of activity and the innate equipment which makes it possible, 'the vital spark has to be conferred on the equipment through exchanges with another human being, with a partner, with the mother'.[6] She is the 'facilitating environment' for these earliest processes of development. Without her contact and facilitation, the infant's first experiences take place in a psycho-social void, and his development is likely to be severely disturbed.

The infant's development and the relationship with the mother which nurtures it are optimal only when that relationship becomes a kind of psychological counterpart to the biological connection of pregnancy. Psychologists have variously described this optimal condition as 'mutuality', 'dual unit', 'reciprocity' or 'dialogue'. All these terms seek to convey that what is good and right for one partner in the relationship is also good and right for the other. The reciprocity between the mother and infant is a circular process of action–reaction–action in which, ideally, the mother welcomes her infant's unfolding activities and expressions of love with her own delighted and loving responses, which in turn stimulate the baby to increase his efforts and to offer his mother further expressions of gratification and attachment. This mutuality is by far the most important factor in enabling an infant to create a coherent inner image of a basically reassuring world and to lay the foundation for a 'true self'; without it, he is likely to become a bundle of reactions which resignedly complies with, or is in constant struggle against, the outer world's infringements. It is the mother who helps her infant learn to deal with anxiety without feeling devastated, and to temper and manage the inevitable feelings of frustration and anger.

For many years, psycho-analytic psychologists were preoccupied with the infant's need for succour in its most literal form: the need to be fed. The manifest nature of this need, together perhaps with the symbolic nostalgia and charm evoked by the image of a nursing baby and his mother, led to an almost exclusive focus on the variability of feeding practices in the mother–infant relationship as the central dynamic factor in personality formation. Anthropological observations of feeding and weaning activities were relied upon in an almost ritualized manner, as a primary source for the explanation of dominant personality characteristics within a given culture. Without underestimating the effect of the nursing situation and the feeding moment on personality—the vicissitudes of orality, as psycho-analysts would call it—it is fair to note that the nutritional need and its satisfaction is only one element, albeit an important one, in the total configuration of the mother–infant dyad. For the crucial social interaction, through which an individual begins to separate himself out and become a person, the infant needs his mother as a whole human being, not merely as a satisfier of hunger and thirst; or, to state it plainly, what the infant requires is not a breast but a mother. Feeding must be viewed as a part of a total communication process in which not only the mother's breast but also the quality of her movement, voice and touch affects the quality of the infant's sensory and emotional lease on life. The breast can be viewed, then, as a symbol for the mother, while feeding and weaning are but symbols for the inevitable processes of attachment and separation in human development. That is, whether or not they are representative of the quality of mothering in any culture, they are the most tangible (and symbolically loaded) aspects of nurturing. What psychologists and anthropologists alike must observe more carefully is not the false controversy between breast and bottle feeding, or how conscientiously the mother carries out her nursing duties, or how and when she weans her child, but the total emotional climate, the gestalt, of mothering.

PSYCHO-SOCIAL MATRIX OF INFANCY: FEMININE IDENTITY IN INDIA

Whether her family is poor or wealthy, whatever her caste, class or region, whether she is a fresh young bride or exhausted by many pregnancies and infancies already, an Indian woman knows that motherhood confers upon her a purpose and identity that nothing else in her culture can. Each infant borne and nurtured by her safely into childhood, especially if the child is a son, is both a certification and a redemption.

At the same time, each individual woman approaches motherhood at her particular crossroads of *desa, kala, srama and gunas*, and with her unique constellation of values, expectations, fears and beliefs about the role and the experience of mothering. She meets her newborn infant with the emotional resources and limitations of her particular personality; these are the 'matrix' of her child's infancy.[7] Her identity as a Hindu woman has evolved out of the *particulars* of her life cycle and childhood, out of the dailiness of her relationships as daughter in her parents' family and as wife and daughter-in-law in her husband's family, and out of the universals of the traditional ideals of womanhood absorbed by her from childhood onwards. Whether a particular mother is reserved or responsive to a particular infant, and in what circumstances, depends on a wide range of variables, not the least of which is her ordinal position in her original family (whether she was a firstborn female or the fourth daughter in a row, or the first little girl after a line of sons . . .) as well as the sex and ordinal position of the infant who now needs and claims her love and care. It is not the purpose of this study to explore the range of individual maternal receptivity. Rather, we will focus on the vivid ideals of womanhood and motherhood in India, the common themes which in a traditional society such as India pervade and circumscribe the identities of individual women.

First of all, where and when tradition governs, an Indian woman does not stand alone; her identity is wholly defined by her relationships to others. For although in most societies, a woman (more than a man) defines herself in relation and connection to other intimate people, this is singularly true of Indian women. The dominant psycho-social realities of her life can be condensed into three stages:

First, she is a daughter to her parents.

Second, she is a wife to her husband (and daughter-in-law to his parents).

Third, she is a mother to her sons (and daughters).

How, then, do daughters fare in 'mother India'? The frank answer is that it is difficult to know, at least as exhaustively and 'in depth' as I would like to. The reason for this lies in the fact that data, of all kinds, are uneven or unavailable. Anthropological accounts refer, implicitly or explicitly, to the development of boys, and skim the subject of female childhood or skip it altogether. Myths, too, are sparing of their bounty towards daughters, for in a patriarchal culture myths are inevitably man-made and man-oriented. Addressing as they do the unconscious wishes and fears of men, it is the parent–son rather than the parent–daughter relationship which becomes charged with symbolic significance.[8]

These limitations are real enough, but they need not be forbidding. On the contrary, they challenge the psycho-analytic researcher to mine the existing material thoroughly and to construct an interpretive bridge for future work. There are, for example, in anthropological accounts, both a consistent indication of the marked preference for sons all over India, and at the same time, somewhat paradoxically, abundant allusion to the warmth, intimacy and relaxed affection of the mother–daughter bond.[9] Statistics document the higher rate of female infant mortality, and call attention to the fact that whatever health care and schooling are available in India, daughters are the last to receive it.[10] In the realm of literature, although the mainstream mythology and classical texts of Hinduism have been the preserves of men, there are parts of the oral tradition—ballads, folk-songs and couplets sung by women in different parts of the country, a few folk-tales—which give us clues to the psychological constellation of daughterhood in India. Leavened with clinical impressions, these various sources can be judiciously drawn together to sketch a portrait of Indian girlhood.

The preference for a son when a child is born is as old as Indian society itself. Vedic verses pray that sons will be followed by still more male offspring, never by females. A prayer in the *Atharvaveda* adds a touch of malice: 'The birth of a girl, grant it elsewhere, here grant a son.'[11] As MacDonell observes, 'Indeed daughters are conspicuous in the *Rigveda* by their absence. We meet in hymns with prayers for sons and grandsons, male offspring, male descendants and male issue and occasionally for wives but never daughters. Even forgiveness is asked for ourselves and grandsons, but no blessing is ever prayed for a daughter. When *Agni* is born it is as if it were a male infant. They clap their hands and make sounds of rejoicing like the parents of a new-born son. There is no such rejoicing over the birth of a daughter.'[12] The ancient *Pumsavana* rite, still performed over pregnant women in tradi-tional Hindu households, is designed to elicit the birth of a male infant and to magically change the sex of the unborn child if it be a female.

Contemporary anthropological studies from different parts of India and the available clinical evidence assure us that the traditional preference for sons is very much intact.[13] At the birth of a son drums are beaten in some parts of the country, conch-shells blown in others and the midwife paid lavishly, while no such spontaneous rejoicing accompanies the birth of a daughter. Women's folk-songs reveal the painful awareness of inferiority—of this discrepancy, at birth, between the celebration of sons and the mere tolerance of daughters. Thus, in a north Indian song the women complain:

Vidya said,   'Listen, O Sukhma, what a tradition has started!
Drums are played upon the birth of a boy,
But at my birth only a brass plate was beaten.'[14]

And in Maharashtra the girl, comparing herself to a white sweet-scented jasmine (*jai*) and the boy to a big, strong-smelling thorny leaf (*kevada*), plaintively asks: 'Did anyone notice the sweet fragrance of a *jai*? The hefty *kevada* however has filled the whole street with its strong scent.'[15]

Of course there are 'valid' ritual and economic reasons—we will come to the psychological ones later—for 'sexism' in Indian society. The presence of a son is absolutely necessary for the proper perfor-mance of many sacraments, especially those carried out upon the death of parents and imperative to the well-being of their souls. In addition to her negligible ritual significance, a daughter normally is an un-mitigated expense, someone who will never contribute to the family income and who, upon marriage, will take away a considerable part of her family's fortune as her dowry. In the case of a poor family, the parents may even have to go deep in debt in order to provide for a daughter's marriage. The *Aitareya Brahmana* (like other older texts) probably refers as much as anything else to the economic facts of life when it states flatly that a daughter is a source of misery while a son is the saviour of the family.[16]

As in other patriarchal societies, one would expect the preference for sons, the cultural devaluation of girls, to be somehow reflected in the psychology of Indian women. Theoretically, one possible consequence of this kind of inequity would be a heightened female hostility and envy towards males, together with a generally pronounced antagonism between the sexes. I do not have sufficient evidence to be categorical; yet my impression is that these phenomena do not, in general, characterize the inner world of Indian women. The dominant myths, for example—unlike, say, *A Thousand and One Nights*—show little evidence of strain in relationships between the sexes. And, as I have shown elsewhere, aggression occurring between members of the same sex is significantly greater than between members of opposite sexes in India.[17]

It can be argued that male dominance and strong taboos against feminine aggression may inhibit the expression of female resentment against men and serve to redirect this hostility against male children. For if a woman perceives that the fundamental premise of the absolute status hierarchy between the sexes is merely gender, and if she is prevented from expressing her rage and resentment at this state of affairs, either because of cultural taboos, social inferiority or her dependence upon men, then her unconscious destructive impulses towards male children are liable to be particularly strong, this being her only possible revenge against a pervasive oppressive masculinity. Again, excepting certain communities, this does not appear to be characteristic of Indian women, given the evidence of songs, tales and other kinds of folklore.[18]

The third possibility is that girls and women in a dramatically patriarchal society will turn the aggression against themselves and transform the cultural devaluation into feelings of worthlessness and inferiority. There is scattered evidence that such a propensity indeed exists among many communities of Indian women, that hostility towards men and potential aggression against male infants are often turned inward, subsumed in a diffuse hostility against oneself, in a conversion of outrage into self-depreciation. At least among the upper middle class women who today seek psychotherapy, the buried feeling, 'I am a girl and thus worthless and "bad"', is often encountered below the surface of an active, emancipated femininity. One patient, for example, staunchly maintained that her parents' separation took place because of her father's disappointment that she was born a girl and not a boy, although in fact, as she herself was aware, the parents had separated shortly before her birth. Some of the traits connected with low self-esteem—depressive moodiness, extreme touchiness and morbid sensitivity in interpersonal relations—come through in the testimony of modern, educated Indian girls in the non-clinical interviews reported by Margaret Cormack in *The Hindu Woman*.[19] And their less educated, rural sisters give vent to similar feelings through the medium of folk-songs: 'God Rama, I fall at your feet and fold my hands and pray to you, never again give me the birth of a woman.'[20]

I have deliberately used the words 'possibility' and 'propensity' in the above discussion rather than ascribe to Indian women a widespread depressive pattern. In the first place, for the cultural devaluation of women to be translated into a pervasive psychological sense of worthlessness in individual women, parents' and other adults' behaviour and attitudes towards the infant girls in their midst—the actualities of family life—must be fully consistent with this female depreciation. Secondly, the internalization of low self-esteem also presupposes that girls and women have no sphere of their own, no independent livelihood and activity, no area of family and community responsibility and dominance, no living space apart from that of the men, within which to create and manifest those aspects of feminine identity that derive from intimacy and collaboration with other women. And, in fact, these two circumstances exist in India, to mitigate the discriminations and inequities of patriarchal institutions.

From anthropological accounts and other sources, we know of the lenient affection and often compassionate attention bestowed by mothers on their daughters throughout their lives.[21] 'I turn the stone flour mill with the swiftness of a running deer; that is because my arms are strong with the mother's milk I drank.'[22] This, and other couplets like it, sung by women all over India, bear witness to the daughter's memory of her mother's affection for her and to the self-esteem and strength of will this has generated in turn. Thus, in the earliest period of emotional development, Indian girls are assured of their worth by whom it really matters: by their mothers.

The special maternal affection reserved for daughters, contrary to expectations derived from social and cultural prescriptions, is partly to be explained by the fact that a mother's unconscious identification with her daughter is normally stronger than with her son.[23] In her daughter, the mother can re-experience herself as a cared-for girl. And, in Indian society, as we shall see later, a daughter is considered a 'guest' in her natal family, treated with the solicitous concern often accorded to a welcome outsider, who, all too soon, will marry and leave her mother for good. Mindful of her daughter's developmental fate, the mother re-experiences the emotional conflicts her own separation once aroused, and this in turn tends to increase her indulgence and solicitude towards her daughter.

In addition to her mother's empathic connection with her, as an

Indian girl grows up her relationships with others within the extended family further tend to dilute any resentment she may harbour for her brothers. Among the many adults who comprise a Hindu family there is almost always someone in particular who gives a little girl the kind of admiration and sense of being singled out as special that a male child more often receives from many. In such a family system, every child, irrespective of sex, stands a good chance of being some adult's favourite, a circumstance which softens the curse of rivalry, envy and possessiveness which often afflicts 'modern' nuclear families. And of course when a girl is the only daughter, such chances are increased immeasurably. Thus in folk-tales, however many sons a couple may have, there is often one daughter in their midst who is the parents' favourite.

Finally, in traditional India, every female is born into a well-defined community of women within her particular family. Although by no means does it always resound with solidarity and goodwill, the existence of this exclusive sphere of femininity and domesticity gives women a tangible opportunity to be productive and lively, to experience autonomy and to exercise power. It also allows a special kind of inviolate feminine privacy and familiar intimacy. Getting along with other women in this sphere, learning the mandatory skills of householding, cooking and childcare, establishing her place in this primary world: these relationships and these tasks constitute the dailiness of girlhood in India. Moreover, this experience of 'apprenticeship' and the activities that transpire in this feminine sphere are independent of the patriarchal values of the outside world. And when necessary, other women in the family—her mother, grandmother, aunts, sisters and sisters-in-law—are not only an Indian girl's teachers and models but her allies against the discriminations and inequities of that world and its values. Often enough, in the 'underground' of female culture, as reflected in ballads, wedding songs and jokes, women do indeed react against the discriminations of their culture by portraying men as vain, faithless and infantile.[24] All these factors help to mitigate (if not to prevent) the damage to a girl's self-esteem when she discovers that in the eyes of the culture she is considered inferior to a boy, a discovery which usually coincides with the awareness of gender identity in late childhood.

Late childhood marks the beginning of an Indian girl's deliberate training in how to be a *good woman*, and hence the conscious inculcation of culturally designated feminine roles. She learns that the 'virtues' of womanhood which will take her through life are submission and docility as well as skill and grace in the various household tasks. M.N. Srinivas, for example, reports on the training of young girls in Mysore:

It is the mother's duty to train her daughter up to be an absolute docile daughter-in-law. The *summum bonum* of a girl's life is to please her parents-in-law and her husband. If she does not 'get on' with her mother-in-law, she will be a disgrace to her family, and cast a blot on the fair name of her mother. The Kannada mother dins into her daughter's ears certain ideals which make for harmony (at the expense of her sacrificing her will) in her later life.[25]

In the *bratas*, the periodical days of fasting and prayer which unmarried girls keep all over India, the girl's wishes for herself are almost always in relation to others; she asks the boons of being a good daughter, good wife, good daughter-in-law, good mother, and so forth.[26] Thus, in addition to the 'virtues' of self-effacement and self-sacrifice, the feminine role in India also crystallizes a woman's connections to others, her embeddedness in a multitude of familial relationships.

If the self-esteem of Indian girls falters during the years of early puberty, this is intimately related to the fact that at precisely this developmental moment, a time of instinctual turbulence and emotional volatility, her training in service and self-denial in preparation for her imminent roles of daughter-in-law and wife is stepped up. In order to maintain her family's love and approval—the 'narcissistic supplies' necessary for firm self-esteem—the girl tends to conform, and even over-conform, to the prescriptions and expectations of those around her.

The adult personality of Indian women is not only moulded through this (unconscious) manipulation of her precarious feelings of worthiness as an adolescent, it is also distinctly influenced by the culturally sanctioned maternal indulgence of daughters. As we have noted above, daughterhood in India is not without its rewards, precisely because the conditions of womanhood are normally so forbidding. In contrast to the son's, a daughter's training at her mother's hands is normally leavened with a good deal of compassion, for which, as ever, there are traditional as well as psychological explanations. Manu expressly enjoins that kindness be shown to the daughter as she is 'physically more tender and her emotions are more delicate', and other ancient commentators forbid any harshness towards her, even in words.[27] The learned Medhatithi puts the whole matter into its 'proper', that is, its ritual, perspective:

'By reason of the marriage having taken the place of *Upanayana** it follows that just as in the case of men all the ordinances of the *Srutis*, *Smritis* and custom become binding upon them after the *Upanayana*, before which they are free to do what they like and are unfit for any religious duties, so for women also there is freedom of action before marriage, after which they also become subject to the ordinances of the *Srutis* and *Smritis*.'[28] Little wonder that for an Indian girl rebellion against the constraints of impinging womanhood, with its circumscription of identity, becomes impossible. She internalizes the specific ideals of womanhood and monitors her behaviour carefully in order to guarantee her mother's love and approval, upon which she is more than ever dependent as she makes ready to leave home. For all the reasons described above, the irony of an Indian girl's coming-of-age is that to be a good woman and a felicitous bride she must be more than ever the perfect daughter.

Sita: the ego ideal

For both men and women in Hindu society, the ideal woman is personified by Sita, the quintessence of wifely devotion, the heroine of the epic *Ramayana*. Her unique standing in the minds of most Hindus, regardless of region, caste, social class, age, sex, education or modernization, testifies to the power and pervasiveness of the traditional ideal of womanhood. Sita, of course, is not just another legendary figure, and the *Ramayana* is not just another epic poem. It is through the recitation, reading, listening to, or attending a dramatic performance of this revered text (above all others) that a Hindu reasserts his or her cultural identity as a Hindu, and obtains religious merit. The popular epic contains ideal models of familial bonds and social relations to which even a modernized Hindu pays lip service, however much he may privately question or reject them as irrelevant to the tasks of modern life.

Sita, like the other principal figures in the epic—Rama, Lakshman, Hanuman—is an incomparably more intimate and familiar heroine in the Hindu imagination than similar figures from Greek or Christian mythology are in the fantasies and deliberations of an average westerner. This intimate familiarity does not mean historical knowledge, but rather a sense of the mythical figure as a benevolent

---

*The sacrament for boys, usually occurring between the ages of five and eight, which initiates them as full-fledged members of the society.

presence, located in the individual's highly personal and always actual space-time. From earliest childhood, a Hindu has heard Sita's legend recounted on any number of sacral and secular occasions; seen the central episodes enacted in folk plays like the *Ram Lila*; heard her qualities extolled in devotional songs; and absorbed the ideal feminine identity she incorporates through the many everyday metaphors and similes that are associated with her name. Thus, 'She is as pure as Sita' denotes chastity in a woman, and 'She is a second Sita', the appreciation of a woman's uncomplaining self-sacrifice. If, as Jerome Bruner remarks, 'In the mythologically instructed community there is a corpus of images and models that provide the pattern to which the individual may aspire, a range of metaphoric identity',[29] then this range, in the case of a Hindu woman, is condensed in one model. And she is Sita.

For western readers unacquainted with the myth, the legend of Sita, in bare outline, goes like this: One day as King Janaka was ploughing, an infant sprang up from the ground whom he named Sita.* The child grows up to be a beautiful girl whom the king promises to give in marriage to any man who can bend the wonderful bow in his possession. Many suitors—gods, princes, kings, demons—vie for Sita's hand but none is even able to lift the bow, until Rama, the reincarnation of Vishnu and the hero of the epic, comes to Janaka's country and gracefully snaps the bow in two. After their wedding, Sita and Rama return to Ayodhya, which is ruled by Rama's father, Dasharatha.

After some time Dasharatha wants to abdicate in favour of Rama who is his eldest son. But because of a promise given to the mother of one of his younger sons, he is forced to banish Rama to the forest for fourteen years. Rama tries to persuade Sita to let him proceed in his exile alone, pointing out the dangers, discomforts and deprivations of a homeless life in the forest. In a long, moving passage Sita emphasizes her determination to share her husband's fate, declaring that death would be preferable to separation. Her speech is an eloquent statement of the *dharma* of a Hindu wife:

For a woman, it is not her father, her son, nor her mother, friends nor her own self, but the husband, who in this world and the next is ever her sole means of salvation. If thou dost enter the impenetrable forest today, O Descendant of Raghu, I shall precede thee on foot, treading down the spiky *Kusha* grass. In truth, whether it be in palaces, in chariots or in heaven, wherever the shadow of the feet of her consort falls, it must be followed.[30]

---

*The name Sita means a furrow, a universal symbol for the feminine genitalia.

Both Rama and Sita, mourned by the citizens of Ayodhya who adore their prince and future king, proceed to the forest in the company of Rama's brother Lakshman. The *Ramayana* then recounts their adventures in the forest, most prominent and terrible among them being Sita's kidnapping by the powerful king of the demons, Ravana, and her abduction to Lanka. In Lanka, Ravana's kingdom, Sita is kept imprisoned in one of the demon-king's palaces where he tries to win her love. Neither his seductive kindnesses nor his grisly threats are of any avail as Sita remains steadfast in her love and devotion to Rama.

Meanwhile, Rama raises an army from the *Vanar* (monkey) tribes in order to attack Lanka and bring back Sita. After a long and furious battle, he is victorious and Ravana is killed. Doubting Sita's fidelity through the long term of her captivity, Rama refuses, however, to accept her again as his wife until she proves her innocence and purity by the fire ordeal in which the fire-god Agni himself appears to testify to her virtue. The couple then return to Ayodhya where amidst the citizens' happy celebrations Rama is crowned king.

But Sita's ordeal is not yet over. Hearing of rumours in the city which cast suspicion on the purity of his queen, Rama banishes her to the forest where she gives birth to twins, Lava and Kusha. She and her children live an ascetic life in a rustic hermitage, Sita's love for Rama unfaltering. When the twins grow up, she sends them back to their father. On seeing his sons, Rama repents and Sita is brought back to Ayodhya to be reinstated as queen. On her arrival, however, Rama again commands her to assert her purity before the assembled court. His abiding mistrust, and this further demand prove too much for the gentle queen who calls on her mother, the earth, to open up and receive her back. The earth obliges and Sita disappears where she was born.

How are we to interpret the legend of Sita? Philip Slater has pointed out that a myth is an elaborately condensed product, that there is no one 'correct' version or interpretation, for no matter how many layers one peels off, there will remain much to be explained.[31] In the interpretation that follows, I will set aside such elements as social history, religious ritual and artistic embellishment, although I am well aware of their importance to myth-making. Rather, my aim is to attend to the themes in the Sita legend from a psychoanalytic and psycho-social perspective. In this kind of interpretation we must ask questions such as: How does the myth influence the crystallization of a Hindu woman's identity and character? What role does it play in helping to ward off or assuage feelings of guilt and anxiety? How does it influence her attitude towards and images of men? How does it contribute to the individual woman's task of 'adapting to reality' and to the society's task of maintaining community solidarity? And finally do the different mythological versions of a single underlying theme correspond to different 'defensive editions' of unconscious fantasy at different life stages of those to whom the myths speak?[32]

The ideal of womanhood incorporated by Sita is one of chastity, purity, gentle tenderness and a singular faithfulness which cannot be destroyed or even disturbed by her husband's rejections, slights or thoughtlessness. We should note in passing that the Sita legend also gives us a glimpse into the Hindu imagery of manliness. Rama may have all the traits of a godlike hero, yet he is also fragile, mistrustful and jealous, and very much of a conformist, both to his parents' wishes and to social opinion. These expectations, too, an Indian girl incorporates gradually into her inner word.

The legend of Nala and Damayanti provides a variation on the ideal of the good wife; Damayanti cheerfully accompanies Nala, her husband, into the forest after he has gambled away everything they own, including his clothes. And when he leaves her sleeping in the forest at night, taking away half of the only garment she possesses to clothe his own nakedness, Damayanti does not utter a single word of reproach as she wanders through the forest, looking for her husband. The 'moral' is the familiar one: 'Whether treated well or ill a wife should never indulge in ire.'

In another popular myth, Savitri, in spite of the knowledge that her chosen husband is fated to die within a year, insists on marrying him and renouncing the luxuries of her palace to join him in his poverty. When at the end of the year, Yama, the god of death, takes away her husband, Savitri follows them both. Although Yama assures her that she has loved her husband faithfully, that she need not sacrifice her own life but should return, Savitri replies that wherever her husband goes she must follow for that is the eternal custom: 'Deprived of my husband, I am as one dead!'[33]

In the Savitri myth, the ideal of fidelity to one man takes on an added dimension and categorical refinement: Exclusive devotion to one's husband becomes the prerequisite for the all-important motherhood of sons. Thus, as Savitri follows Yama to his country, the land in which all wishes come true, she refuses to accept his assurance that with her husband's death all her wifely obligations have expired. Only through her demonstration of wifely devotion, even after her husband's death, can she finally persuade Yama to revive him and grant her the boon of offspring: 'Of Satyavan's loins and mine, begotten by both of us, let there be a century of sons possessed of strength and prowess and capable of perpetuating our race.'[34]

To be a good wife is, by definition, to be a good woman. Thus Markandeya discourses to Yudhishthira of 'wives restraining all their senses and keeping their hearts under complete control. [They] regard their husbands as veritable gods. For women, neither sacrifice, nor *sraddhas* (penances), nor fasts are of any efficiency. By serving their husbands only can they win heaven.'[35] This is the ideal, purveyed over and over again, in numberless myths and legends, through which the Hindu community has tried to mould the character and personality of its female members. Moreover, a woman is enjoined that her devotion to her husband should extend also to his family members, especially to his parents. A married woman's duties have been nowhere more fully described than in Draupadi's advice to Satyabhama, Lord Krishna's wife:

Keeping aside vanity, and controlling desire and wrath, I always serve with devotion the sons of Pandu with their wives. Restraining jealousy, with deep devotion of heart, without a sense of degradation at the services I perform, I wait upon my husbands . . . Celestial, or man, or Gandharva, young or decked with ornaments, wealthy or comely of person, none else my heart liketh. I never bathe or eat or sleep till he that is my husband hath bathed or eaten or slept. . . . When my husband leaveth home for the sake of any relative, then renouncing flowers and fragrant paste of every kind, I begin to undergo penances. Whatever my husband enjoyeth not, I even renounce . . . Those duties that my mother-in-law had told me in respect of relatives, as also the duties of alms-giving, of offering worship to the gods . . . and service to those that deserve our regards, and all else that is known to me, I always discharge day and night, without idleness of any kind.[36]

I have quoted from the ancient texts in detail in order to emphasize the formidable consensus on the ideal of womanhood which, in spite of many changes in individual circumstances in the course of modernization, urbanization and education, still governs the inner imagery of individual men and women as well as the social relations between them in both the traditional and modern sectors of the Indian community.

Together with this function as a more or less conscious ideal which leaves indelible traces in the identity formation of every Hindu woman, the Sita myth also plays an unconscious role as a defence against the anxiety aroused by a young girl's sexual impulses, whose expression would almost seem to be invited by the nature of family life in traditional India. Freud has clarified for us the universal themes of infantile psycho-sexual development in terms of the vicissitudes of the libido. He left it primarily to others to differentiate among the social influences and cultural variations. Thus, sexual development in Hindu daughters is *socially* influenced by the communal living pattern, the close quarters of the extended family and the indulgent adult attitudes towards infant sexuality. In this intimate daily setting where constant close contact with many members of the family of both sexes and several generations is part of a little girl's early bodily experience; where the infant girl is frequently caressed and fondled by the many adults around her; and where playful exploratory activities of an explicitly sexual nature among the many cousins living in the same house or nearby in the neighbourhood are a common early developmental experience, often indulgently tolerated by the more or less 'permissive' adults—a promiscuous sexual excitation, as well as the fear of being overwhelmed by it, looms large in the unconscious fantasies of an Indian girl. Later, as she leaves childhood behind, the identification with Sita helps in the necessary renunciation of these childhood fantasies, in the concentration of erotic feeling exclusively on one man, and in the avoidance of all occasions for sexual temptation and transgression. Sita sets the compelling example: Although Rama's emissary, the monkey-god Hanuman, offers to rescue Sita from her ordeal of imprisonment in Lanka by carrying her on his shoulders and transporting her through the air to her waiting husband, she must refuse the offer since it means touching Hanuman's body, and of her own free will she may, on no account, permit herself to touch any man except her husband. This enigmatic tension between the memory of intense and pleasurable childhood sexuality and the later womanly ideal which demands restraint and renunciation, between an earlier indiscriminate 'availability' and the later unapproachability, may account for that special erotic presence in Indian women which has fascinated the imagination of many writers and artists.

Perhaps the most striking mythological elaboration of the connection between the young girl's sexuality, in particular, her fantasied erotic wishes towards her father, and her later repudiation of these wishes by transforming them into their opposite, aloofness and chastity, is the myth of Arundhati, who, next to Sita, is the most famous chaste wife in Hindu mythology. I have reproduced the myth in detail not only to illustrate this aspect of feminine identity in India but also because of its special relevance for psycho-analytic theory, for it explicitly acknowledges the existence of infantile sexuality:

Brahma (the Creator) had displayed desire for his daughter, Sandhya (Twilight), as soon as she was born, and she had desired him. As a result of this, Brahma cursed Kama (Eros), who had caused the trouble, to be burnt by Siva. When everyone had departed, Sandhya resolved to purify herself and to establish for all time a moral law: that new-born creatures would be free of desire. To do this, she prepared to offer herself as an oblation in the fire. Knowing of her intention, Brahma sent the sage Vasistha to instruct her in the proper manner of performing *tapas*. Vasistha disguised himself as a *brahmacarin* with matted locks and taught her how to meditate upon Siva. Siva then appeared to her and offered her a boon. She said, 'Let all new-born creatures be free of desire, and let me be reborn as the wife of a man to whom I can just be a close friend. And if anyone but my husband gazes upon me with desire, let his virility be destroyed and let him become an impotent eunuch.' Siva said, 'Your sin has been burnt to ashes, purified by your *tapas*. I grant what you ask; henceforth, creatures will only become subject to desire when they reach youth, and any man but your husband who looks upon you with desire will become impotent.' Then Sandhya, meditating upon the chaste Brahmin for her husband, entered the sacrificial fire. Her body became the oblation, and she arose from the fire as an infant girl, named Arundhati. She grew up in a sage's hermitage and married Vasistha.[37]

Another version of the myth offers a diametrically opposite resolution of the conflict. Here the 'plot' works to lift the repression of childhood memories and to remove defences against erotic impulses and guilt feelings, and, according to the principle of the identity of opposites, the daughter of Brahma is reborn not as the most chaste of women, but as Rati, the incarnation of sexuality and the goddess of sexual pleasure. The unconscious fantasy elaborated in this version belongs of course to adolescence rather than to the oedipal years of childhood.

On still another level, the identification with Sita contributes to the Hindu woman's adaptation to married life in her husband's extended family and to the maintenance of this family as a functioning unit. Such a family, composed as it is of other men besides her husband, affords the Hindu wife temptations and opportunities for sexual transgression, the indulgence of which would destroy the necessary interdependence and co-operation of the Indian family. At some level of consciousness, every Hindu couple is aware, for instance, of Sita's exemplary behaviour towards Rama's brother Lakshman during the fourteen years of their exile together. There exist, of course, elaborate codes and rituals of social behaviour and discretion between the male and female members of an extended family, such as the injunction that the elder brother never directly address his younger brother's wife (nor enter her room when she is alone). Like most taboos, these are broken in fantasy. In a

Bengali folk-song; for example, a woman expresses her desire for amorous relations with the elder brother of her husband, regretting that he is not the younger brother so that her desire might be gratified.[38] These taboos are designed to preclude intolerable jealous passions and disruptive rivalries; the reigning presence of Sita in the Indian inner world, in all her serene forbearance, is an important psychological reinforcement of these special codes.

The short description of daughterhood and the elaboration of the Sita ideal of womanhood cannot fully account for an Indian woman's emotional preparation for motherhood. Her chronological and developmental stage of life at marriage, her experiences and relationships within her husband's family, and the meaning of childbirth in her particular personal and social setting: these factors too are paramount; taken together, they are the 'psycho-social matrix of infancy' in India.

Life stage at marriage

An Indian girl is usually married during early adolescence, between the ages of twelve and eighteen; the average age of a Hindu bride is fifteen to sixteen.[39] In urban areas, or among higher castes, where daughters are more likely to receive some kind of formal education, the age may be somewhat higher. The traditional ideal holds that a girl should be married soon after her first menstrual period, for it is feared that 'if she remains long a maiden, she gives herself to whom she will'. The custom of early marriage, it seems, recognizes and is designed to guard against the promiscuous resurgence in adolescence of a girl's playful childhood sexuality and the threat this would pose to Hindu social organization. To marry one's daughters off propitiously is considered one of the primary religious duties of Hindu parents. Indeed, 'Reprehensible is the father who gives not his daughter at the proper time.' If married at eleven or twelve, the girl may remain in her parents' home for another three to four years before moving away to live with her husband. In any case, when she joins her husband's family, she is still a young adolescent and vulnerable to the universal psychological problems of this age.

First of all, before her departure for her husband's family and household, a very special relationship tends to develop between an Indian girl and her mother,[40] who becomes at this time her daughter's confidante and counsellor in the bewildering turmoil of adolescence and the newness of the prospect of marriage. Although the relationship between daughter and mother is surely characterized by the tension between the conflicting modalities of 'getting away' and 'coming nearer', the daughter none the less seeks to recreate the emotional closeness to the protective mother of her childhood. She has also formed intimate attachments to girl friends of her age in the village or neighbourhood among whom the secret fears and delights concerning the physical changes of puberty are shared, and fantasies about men and marriage are collectively evoked as each girl tries to envision and secure a clear sense of herself as a woman. These processes—the renunciation of dependency on the 'pre-oedipal' mother, the integration of what she was as a girl with the woman she is now suddenly becoming, and the acceptance of her inevitable marriage to a stranger—all these require time, her mother's support and love, the reassuring exchange of confidences with peers, and the 'trying out' of new, as yet unexperienced identities in fantasy. This whole process of feminine adolescent development is normally incomplete at the time an Indian girl gets married and is transplanted from her home into the unfamiliar, initially forbidding environment of her in-laws.

The alien, often threatening, and sometimes humiliating nature of the setting in which an Indian girl's struggle for identity and adult status takes place cannot be stressed enough. In much of northern India, for example, the exogamous rule, that the bride comes from a village which does not border on the groom's village, strictly applies. In some other parts of the country, marriage customs are governed by a further rule which stipulates that a man who lives in a *gotra* village—that is, a village which is predominantly composed of a related caste group—is unacceptable as a potential bridegroom for any daughter of the village. In his study of social life in a village in Delhi, Oscar Lewis found that the 266 married women of the village came from 200 different villages, a pattern repeated by those who married outside this, their native village.[41] Consequently, this small village of 150 households was linked with over 400 other villages in its region; at the same time, no woman in the village could call for company, or in a moment of crisis or loneliness, on a friend or neighbour or relative known to her from childhood.

Whatever the contribution of these marriage rules to the integration of Indian society, and it is considerable, this integration is ultimately based on the insistence that women not only renounce their erotic impulses and primary loyalties to their parents—a universal developmental requirement—but also sever their attachments, in fact and in fantasy, to all the other boys and men they have known during their early lives who inevitably belong to one of the forbidden extended kinship or village groups. Instead, upon marriage, an Indian woman must direct her erotic tenderness exclusively towards a man who is a complete stranger to her until their wedding night, and she must resolve the critical issues of feminine identity in unfamiliar surroundings without the love and support of precisely those persons whom she needs most. Little wonder that the themes of the young girl pining for her parental home, her grief at separation from her mother, constantly recur in popular folk-songs and ballads.[42] The staunch presence of ideal feminine figures like Sita and Savitri is crucial to making the traumatic transition which an Indian girl undergoes at precisely the most sensitive and vulnerable period of her development.

Status within her husband's family: not wife but daughter-in-law

An Indian girl's entry into the married state and the new world of social relations within her husband's family thus does not take place under auspicious psychological conditions. In spite of her inner ideals and conscious resolutions to be a good wife and an exemplary daughter-in-law, a bride comes into her husband's family with a tremendous burden of anxiety and nostalgia, with a sense of antagonism towards her mother-in-law who has, after all, usurped the place of her own sorely missed and needed mother, with a mixture of shy anticipation and resentment towards her husband's sisters and other young female relatives who have presumed to replace the sisters and cousins and friends at home, and with ambivalent feelings of tenderness and hostility towards the unknown person who is now her husband and claims her intimacy.[43] And if her husband turns out to be unworthy, she knows that there is no recourse for her. Manu enjoins: 'Though destitute of virtue or seeking pleasure elsewhere, or devoid of good qualities, yet a husband must be constantly worshipped as a god by a faithful wife.'[44] And: 'By violating her duty towards her husband, a wife is disgraced in this world, [after death] she enters the womb of a jackal and is tormented by the punishment of her sin.'[45] These precepts, in spirit if not in these precise words, have been instilled into Hindu girls from the age of earliest understanding. For, as mentioned above, although treated with indulgence and demonstrative affection in the years immediately before her marriage, an Indian girl is so indulged partly because of her status as a guest in her own house. Her 'real' family is her husband's family.

Whatever her future fortunes, when she marries, an Indian girl knows that, in a psychological sense, she can never go home again.*

In the social hierarchy of her new family, the bride usually occupies one of the lowest rungs. Obedience and compliance with the wishes of the elder women of the family, especially those of her mother-in-law, are expected as a matter of course. Communication with the older men is minimal (if it exists at all) since they, as mentioned earlier, are traditionally expected to maintain a posture of formal restraint in the presence of the newcomer. Unflinchingly and without complaint, the new daughter-in-law is required to perform some of the heaviest household chores, which may mean getting up well before dawn and working till late at night. Any mistakes or omissions on her part are liable to incur sarcastic references to her abilities, her looks or her upbringing in her mother's home. For it must be noted once again that the new bride constitutes a very real threat to the unity of the extended family. She represents a potentially pernicious influence which, given family priorities, calls for drastic measures of exorcism. The nature of the 'danger' she personifies can perhaps best be suggested by such questions as: Will the young wife cause her husband to neglect his duties as a son? As a brother? A nephew? An uncle? Will social tradition and family pressure be sufficient to keep the husband–wife bond from developing to a point where it threatens the interests of other family members? Will 'sexual passion' inspire such a close relationship in the bridal couple that the new girl becomes primarily a wife rather than a daughter-in-law and her husband transfers his loyalty and affection to her rather than remaining truly a son of the house?

These are, of course, not either/or choices; however, custom, tradition and the interests of the extended family demand that in the realignment of roles and relationships initiated by marriage, the roles of the husband and wife, at least in the beginning, be relegated to relative inconsequence and inconspicuousness. Any signs of a developing attachment and tenderness within the couple are discouraged by the elder family members by either belittling or forbidding the open expression of these feelings. Every effort is made to hinder the development of an intimacy within the couple which might exclude other members of the family, especially the parents. Oblique hints about 'youthful

---

*Literally, of course, she may return to visit her family and village of origin; this is particularly likely in the case of a new, young wife at the time of confinement and childbirth.

infatuations', or outright shaming virtually guarantee that the young husband and wife do not publicly express any interest in (let alone affection for) each other; and they are effectively alone together only for very brief periods during the night. If women's folk-songs are any indication, even these brief meetings are furtive affairs; there is hardly a song which does not complain of the ever-wakeful *sas* (mother-in-law) and *nanad* (sister-in-law) preventing the bride from going to her husband at night. Madhav Gore's study of a sample of Indian men of the Agarwal community further confirms that these constraints, masterminded by the older women, usually succeed in their aims: 56 per cent of the men described themselves as being closer to their mothers than to their wives, while only 20 per cent felt they were closer to their wives.[46]

I do not intend to imply that marriage in India lacks intimacy—that mutual enhancement of experience within culturally determined patterns of love and care which is the commonly held criterion of a 'good marriage' in the West. Rather, in India, this intimacy develops later in married life, as both partners slowly mature into adult 'householders'. Ideally, parenthood and the shared responsibility for offspring provide the basis for intimacy, rather than the other way around as in the West. This postponement of intimacy is encouraged by the family, for in the years of middle age the husband–wife bond no longer seems to threaten the exclusion of other family members, but incorporates or rather evolves out of the responsibility to take care of the next generation. Thus it is not antithetical to communal and family solidarity but, in its proper time, a guarantor of it.

Has the newly-married girl's situation in her husband's family no redeeming, or even relieving, features? I have neglected to point out that an Indian girl prepares for the harsh transition of marriage for some time before her actual departure for her husband's household. Stories, proverbs, songs, information gleaned from conversations with newly-married friends who come back home on visits, all more or less 'prepare' her for her role as an obedient daughter-in-law. Moreover, as in many other parts of the world, puberty rites such as seclusion during her menstrual period, or fasting on certain days, are designed to separate the young girl, both physically and symbolically, from her parents and to enable her to tolerate 'oral deprivation', for in her husband's household, at any meal, she will be the last one to eat.

These and other procedures bring the Indian girl to the end of childhood and introduce her, in a measured, ritual way, to the realities of womanhood. If married *very* young, the bride's initiation into her new life and family is gradual, interspersed with long visits to her parents' home where much of the accumulated loneliness and resentment can be relieved by the indulgent love showered on her by everyone, and particularly by her own mother's constant presence as a sympathetic listener and a gentle mentor. The young wife's isolation in her husband's home, moreover, is not necessarily as extreme as I have implied. She often develops relationships of informal familiarity and friendly consolation with certain younger members of her husband's family; and it usually happens that one or another of the many children in the family forms a strong attachment to her. But above all, it should be emphasized that the suspicion and hostility towards her rarely degenerate into deliberate oppression. This reflects a cultural tradition of restraint and prudence, which manifests itself in the Hindu conscience. Respect for and protection of the female members of society are a prime moral duty, the neglect of which arouses anxiety and a sense of being judged and punished. Manu the law-giver, a misogynist by modern standards, leaves no doubt about the virtuous treatment of the female members of the family: 'Where women are honoured, there gods are pleased; but where they are not honoured, no sacred rite yields rewards . . . Where the female relations live in grief, the family soon wholly perishes; but that family where they are not unhappy ever prospers . . . . The houses on which female relations, not being duly honoured, pronounce a curse, perish completely, as if destroyed by magic.'[47] Thus, the head of the family, or other elder males who feel themselves entrusted with the family's welfare, gently but firmly seek to mitigate the excesses of the mother-in-law and the elder women. On balance, however, the conclusion is unavoidable that the identity struggle of the adolescent Indian girl is confounded by the coincidence of marriage, the abrupt and total severance of the attachments of childhood, and her removal from all that is familiar to a state of lonely dependency upon a household of strangers.

Pregnancy and the anticipation of motherhood

The young Indian wife's situation, in terms of family acceptance and emotional well-being, changes dramatically once she becomes pregnant. The prospect of motherhood holds out a composite solution for many of her difficulties. The psychological implications of her low social status as a bride and a newcomer; the tense, often humiliating relationships with others in her husband's family; her homesickness and sense of isolation; her identity confusion; the awkwardness of marital intimacy, and thus, often, the unfulfilled yearnings of her sexual self— these are tangled up in a developmental knot, as it were. With the anticipation of motherhood, this knot begins to be unravelled.

The improvement in an Indian wife's *social* status once she is pregnant has been universally noted by cultural anthropologists.[48] Elder family members, particularly the women, become solicitous of her welfare, seeing to it that she eats well and rests often. Many irksome tasks, erstwhile obligations and restrictions are removed, and gestures of pride and affection towards her as a daughter-in-law of the house increase markedly.

The growing feeling of personal well-being throughout the course of pregnancy is also reinforced by social customs. Thus, in many parts of India, the expectant mother goes back to stay at her own mother's house a few months before the delivery. This stay helps her to strengthen her identification with her mother, a prerequisite for her own capacity for motherhood. The anticipation of the birth itself, in spite of the primitive medical facilities available, does not seem to provoke strong anxiety or fears of dying since she knows her own parents, the all-powerful protectors, will be constantly at her side during labour. Once having given birth, the new mother can bask in her delight in her child and also in her satisfaction with herself, all of this taking place in a circle of greatly pleased and highly approving close kin.

This unambiguous reversal in an Indian woman's status is not lost on her; moreover, the belief that pregnancy is a woman's ultimate good fortune, a belief that amounts to a cultural reverence for the pregnant woman, is abundantly broadcast in the favourite folk-tales and familiar myths of Hindu tradition. Thus, this passage from a Bengali tale: 'Suddenly it seemed that God had taken notice of the prayer. The youngest queen, Sulata, was expecting. The king was overjoyed at the happy news. His affection for Sulata grew even more. He was always looking after her comforts and attending to her wishes.'[49]

The roots of this solicitous respect for the pregnant woman lie deep in a religious and historical tradition which equates 'woman' with 'mother', and views the birth of a male child as an essential step in the parents' and the family's salvation. 'To be mothers women were created, and to be fathers men,' Manu states categorically.[50] Further on in the *Laws*, appraising the status of motherhood, he adds, 'The teacher is ten times more venerable than the sub-teacher, the father a hundred times more than the teacher, but the mother is a thousand times more than the father.'[51] 'She is a true wife who hath borne a son,' Shakuntala tells Dushyanta as she reminds him of his forgotten marriage vows, for wives who produce children are 'the root of religion and of salvation. They are fathers on occasions of religious acts, mothers in sickness and woe.'[52] And the goddess Parvati, with divine disdain for convention, remarks: 'Among all the pleasures of women, the greatest pleasure is to unite with a good man in private, and the misery that arises from its interruption is not equalled by any other. The second greatest misery is the falling of the seed in vain, and the third is my childlessness, the greatest sorrow of all.'[53]

Numerous passages in legends and epics vividly describe the sufferings of the souls of departed ancestors if a couple remain childless and thus unable to guarantee the performance of the rituals prescribed for salvation. 'Because a son delivers his father from the hell called *put*,' Manu says, 'he was therefore called *put-tra* [a deliverer from *put*] by the self-existent himself.'[54] Hindu society is of course not unique in revering motherhood as a moral, religious, or even artistic ideal,[55] but the absolute and all-encompassing social importance of motherhood, the ubiquitous variety of motherhood myths, and the function of off-spring in ritual and religious (not to mention economic) life all give to motherhood in Indian culture a particularly incontrovertible legitimacy.

Subjectively, in the world of feminine psychological experience, pregnancy is a deliverance from the insecurity, doubt and shame of infertility: 'Better be mud than a barren woman', goes one proverb. Moreover, until very recently, in Hindu society, as among the Jews, Muslims and certain West African tribes, a childless wife could be repudiated (even if not divorced) by her husband who was permitted then to take another wife. On the positive side, pregnancy marks the beginning of the psychological process which firmly establishes a Hindu woman's adult identity. The predominant element in this identity, the ideal core around which it is organized, is what Helene Deutsch has called 'motherliness'.[56] Its central emotional expressions are those of *tenderness, nurturing* and *protectiveness*, directed towards the unborn child. Many of the other psychic tendencies generally associated with the young woman's life-stage now become subordinate. The need for emotional closeness with her 'pre-oedipal' mother and the wish to be loved can be transformed into the wish to love; hostility, especially towards her new surroundings, can be directed towards the protection of her child from the environment; the longing of her reawakened sensuality can be temporarily sublimated, given over to physical ministrations to her child.

To be sure, the development of motherliness as the dominant mode in a Hindu woman's identity and its harmony with other personality traits vary among individual women. Nonetheless, a Hindu woman's 'motherliness' (including manifestations of maternal excess) is a relatively more inclusive element of her identity formation than it is among western women. Given her early training and the ideals of femininity held up to her, motherhood does not have connotations of cultural imposition or of confinement in an isolating role.

For an Indian woman, imminent motherhood is not only the personal fulfilment of an old wish and the biological consummation of a lifelong promise, but an event in which the culture confirms her status as a renewer of the race, and extends to her a respect and consideration which were not accorded to her as a mere wife. It is not surprising that this dramatic improvement in her social relations and status within the family, the resolution of her emotional conflicts and the discovery of a way of organizing her future life around the core of motherliness tend to be experienced unconsciously as a gift from the child growing within her. The unborn child is perceived as her saviour, instrumental in winning for its mother the love and acceptance of those around her, a theme which recurs in many legends and tales. Thus Rama repents and is ready to take Sita back from her exile in the forest after he sees his sons for the first time; Dushyanta remembers and accepts Shakuntala as his legitimate wife after he comes face to face with his infant son; while in the two Bengali folk-tales of Sulata and Kiranmala, it is through their children's instrumentality that the injustice done to the mothers is redressed and they assume their rightful places as queens. In the case of a Hindu woman, at least in the imagery of the culture, maternal feelings of tenderness and nurturance occur in combination with a profound gratitude and the readiness for a poignantly high emotional investment in the child.

THE 'GOOD MOTHER'

Although in the usage of pediatrics and medicine 'infant' refers to a child who cannot yet walk, the actualities of childhood and identity development in India suggest that the psycho-social *quality* of infancy extends through the first four or five years of life, the entire span of time in which feeding, toileting and rudimentary self care, as well as walking, talking and the initial capacity for reasoning, become matters of course. This extension of the definition is not arbitrary. As we shall see, in India, the first developmental stage of childhood, characterized by a decisive, deep attachment to the nurturing mother, by dependence upon her for the necessities and the pleasures of succour and comfort, and by the 'crisis' of trust in the benign intentions of others towards oneself, is prolonged in such a way that the second and third developmental stages seem not to take place sequentially but are compressed into one. Thus, it is not until between the ages of three and five that an Indian child moves away (in a psychological sense) from the first all-important 'Other' in his life, his mother. And it is at this time that he[57] confronts simultaneously the developmental tasks of separation and individuation, of autonomy and initiative, of wilful self definition and oedipal rivalry, and moves as it were from 'infancy' to 'childhood' all at once.

During this period of prolonged infancy, the Indian child is intensely and intimately attached to his mother. This attachment is an exclusive one, not in the sense of being without older and younger siblings close in age who claim, and compete for, the mother's love and care, but in that the Indian child up to the age of four or five exclusively directs his demands and affections towards his mother, in spite of the customary presence in the extended family of many other potential caretakers and 'substitute mothers'.[58] Nor does the father play a significant caretaking role at this time.

This attachment is manifested in (and symbolized by) the *physical closeness* of the infant and his mother. Well up to the fifth year, if not longer, it is customary for Indian children to sleep by their mother's side at night. During the day she carries the youngest, or the one most needing attention, astride her hip, the others within arm's reach, as she goes about on visits to neighbours, to the market, to the fields and on other errands. At home, if not suckling or nestling in his mother's lap, the infant is playing on the floor or resting in a cot nearby. Constantly held, cuddled, crooned and talked to, the Indian infant's experience of his mother is a heady one, his contact with her is of an intensity and duration that differentiate it markedly from the experience of infancy in western worlds. At the slightest whimper or sign of distress the infant is picked up and rocked, or given the breast and comforted. Usually it is the infant's own mother who swiftly moves to pacify him, although in her occasional absence on household matters it may be a sister or an aunt or a grandmother who takes him up to feed or clean or just to soothe with familiar physical contact. It is by no means uncommon to see an old grandmother pick up a crying child and give him her dried-up breast to suck as she sits there, rocking on her heels and crooning over him. The intensity of the infantile anxiety aroused by inevitable brief separations from the mother is greatly reduced by the ready availability of the other female members of the extended family. Hindu cultural tradition enjoins women not to let their infants cry, and maternal practice in India anticipates the findings of contemporary empirical research on infancy which attributes infant distress, when a baby is not hungry, cold or in pain, to separation from the mother (or her substitute).

From the moment of birth, then, the Indian infant is greeted and surrounded by direct, sensual body contact, by relentless physical ministrations. The emotional quality of nurturing in traditional Indian families serves to amplify the effects of physical gratification. An Indian mother is inclined towards a total indulgence of her infant's wishes and demands, whether these be related to feeding, cleaning, sleeping or being kept company. Moreover, she tends to extend this kind of mothering well beyond the time when the 'infant' is ready for independent functioning in many areas. Thus, for example, feeding is frequent, at all times of the day and night, and 'on demand'. And although breast feeding is supplemented with other kinds of food after the first year, the mother continues to give her breast to her child for as long as possible, often up to two or three years: in fact, suckling comes to a gradual end only when there is a strong reason to stop nursing, such as a second pregnancy. Even then, weaning is not a once-and-for-all affair, for an older child may also occasionally suckle at his mother's breast. It is not uncommon to see a five- or six-year-old peremptorily lift up his mother's blouse for a drink as she sits gossiping with her friends, an event which is accepted as a matter of course by all concerned.

Similarly, without any push from his mother or other members of the family, the Indian toddler takes his own time learning to control his bowels, and proceeds at his own pace to master other skills such as walking, talking and dressing himself. As far as the mother's and the family's means permit, a young child's wishes are fully gratified and his unfolding capacities and activities accepted, if not always with manifest delight, at least with affectionate tolerance.

The predisposition of an Indian mother to follow rather than lead in dealing with her child's inclinations and with his tempo of development does not spring from some universal component of maternal pride. In part, it reflects the cultural conception of and respect for the specific 'inborn' individuality of every child. In part it has been influenced by the facts of life in traditional India; given the infant mortality rate which used to range above twenty per cent, a surviving child was accorded by his mother the most deferential care, for he would become the parents' source of economic support in later life, and through his participation in the rituals of death and mourning, their guarantee of *religious* merit and of righteous passage into the next life. But above all, this quality of deference and indulgence in Indian motherhood has *psychological* origins in the identity development of Indian women. As I have described above, in daughterhood an Indian girl is a sojourner in her own family, and with marriage she becomes less a wife than a daughter-in-law. It is only with motherhood that she comes into her own as a woman, and can make a place for herself in the family, in the community and in the life cycle. This accounts for her unique sense of maternal obligation and her readiness for practically unlimited emotional investment in her children. These are the cultural, social, religious and developmental threads which are woven together in the formation of conscious attitudes and unconscious images in the mother which, in turn, give Indian infancy its special aura and developmental impact.

Given the experience of his mother's immediacy and utter responsiveness, an Indian generally emerges from infancy into childhood believing that the world is benign and that others can be counted on to act in his behalf. The young child has come to experience his core self as lovable: 'I am lovable, for I am loved.' Infancy has provided him with a secure base from which to explore his environment with confidence. This confidence in the support and protection of others, together with the memory traces of maternal ministrations, provide the basic modality for his social relations throughout the life cycle. In other words, Indians are apt to approach others with an unconscious sense of their own lovability and the expectation and demand that trustworthy benefactors will always turn up in times of difficulty. Suspicion and reserve are rare. Many character traits ascribed to Indians are a part of the legacy of this particular pattern of infancy: trusting friendliness with a quick readiness to form attachments, and intense, if short-lived, disappointment if friendly overtures are not reciprocated; willingness to reveal the most intimate confidences about one's life at the slightest acquaintance and the expectation of a reciprocal familiarity in others; and the assumption that it is 'natural both to take care of others . . . *and* to expect to be cared for'.[59] Considering the oppressive economic environment in which most Indians live, I find no other explanation than the emotional capital built up during infancy for the warmth that is abundantly and unreservedly given and received in the most casual encounters, for the bouts of spontaneous laughter (and crying), and for the glow of intimacy and vitality that characterizes social relations.

Setting aside our consideration of the unconscious for a moment, we can observe that an Indian child tends to experience his mother almost totally as a 'good mother'. The proportion of Indian men who express or experience an active dislike, fear or contempt for their mothers at a conscious level is infinitesimally small. This is strikingly apparent in clinical work; in initial interviews and in the early stages of psychotherapy, patient after patient invariably portrays his mother as highly supportive and extremely loving. In studies of family relations, sociologists and anthropologists confirm the existence of a very close mother–son relationship of the 'good mother' variety in different regions and social classes throughout India.[60]

Literary evidence further corroborates her sentimental prevalence Thus, short stories and novels by Indian writers such as Sarat Chandra and Premchand tend to portray the mother in her benign and nurturing aspect, with a nostalgia uncomplicated by the slightest trace of hostility or guilt. Nor do autobiographical accounts deviate from this psychological stance of conscious devotion to the 'good mother'. Nehru, recalling his mother, writes, 'I had no fear of her, for I knew that she would condone everything I did, and because of her excessive and undiscriminating love for me, I tried to dominate over her a little.'[61] And Yogananda recollects, 'Father . . . was kind, grave, at times stern. Loving him dearly, we children yet observed a certain reverential distance. But mother was queen of hearts, and taught us only through love.'[62]

It needs to be noted here that this idealized image of the 'good mother' is largely a male construction. Women do not sentimentalize their mothers in this way. For daughters, the mother is not an adoring figure on a pedestal: she is a more earthy presence, not always benign but always *there*.

I have so far described the core of Indian personality in terms of confidence in the safeguarding supportiveness of others and trust in the fundamental benevolence of the environment. Mythological and religious representations of the 'good mother' as she is personified in the widely worshipped goddesses, Lakshmi, Sarasvati, Parvati or Gauri, allow us to elaborate on the Indian experience of this 'basic trust'. In Hindu mythology we find that the specifically oral aspect of maternal nurturing is represented by very minor deities such as Annapurna, portrayed as a fair woman standing on a lotus holding a rice bowl, or by the heavenly cow Surabhi who gives an eternal fountain of milk. But the central feature of the 'good mother', incorporated by every major goddess in the Hindu pantheon and dramatized either in her origins or in her function, is not her capacity to feed but to provide life-giving reassurance through her *pervasive presence*. Thus Lakshmi, the goddess of prosperity and good fortune, comes to *dwell* with men, while those in adversity are spoken of as being *forsaken* by her. Sarasvati, the goddess of learning, is identified as *Vak* (speech)—the mother soothing, consoling, talking to her infant. And Parvati, according to one of the Puranic accounts, came into existence to protect the gods against the distress caused by the demon Andhaka (born of Darkness), the representation of one of the elemental fears of childhood. The reassurance provided by the goddesses Sarasvati and Parvati against the terrific estrangements of infancy reminds me of Freud's account of the child who called out of a dark room, 'Auntie, speak to me! I'm frightened because it's so dark!' His aunt answered him, 'What good would that do? You can't see me.' 'That does not matter,' replied the child, 'if anyone speaks, it gets light.'[63]

This emphasis on a nurturing, fear-dispelling presence as the fundamental quality of the 'good mother' is unmistakable in the descriptions of the appearance of these goddesses: They *shine* 'with pearl and golden sheen', *glow* 'with splendour, bright as burnished gold' and *gaze* with faint smiles upon the worshippers.[64] Erikson has called this the 'numinous element, the sense of hallowed presence'.[65] This is the 'good mother', in earthly mothers and in maternal divinities, smiling down on the dependent infant, or on the devoted believer, who, each in his own way, yearns to be at one with that gracious presence. Shiva's lament at the loss of Parvati evokes the sense of intactness the mother's presence gives, as well as the dread of separation or abandonment: 'With thee I am almighty, the framer of all things, and the giver of all bliss; but without thee, my energy, I am like a corpse, powerless and incapable of action: how then, my beloved, canst thou forsake me? With smiles and glances of thine eyes, say something sweet as *amrita*, and with the rain of gentle words sprinkle my heart which is scorched with grief . . . O mother of the Universe! arise.'[66] The theme of isolation and its transcendence constitutes the core of the *moksha* ideal. This theme has its ontogenetic source in the specific form and quality of the interactions between mothers and infants in Indian society; and it is vividly elaborated in

Hindu mythology as the persistent nostalgic wish for the benevolent presence of the 'good mother' as she was experienced in infancy.

The preoccupation with the themes of loneliness and separation together with the strong unconscious desire for the confirming presence of the 'good (M)Other', stays with the individual in India throughout the course of his life. This is in striking contrast to most western cultures in which the yearning for a loved one and distress caused by her or his absence are often held to be 'childish' and 'regressive'. But as Bowlby, marshalling impressive evidence from clinical, empirical and ethological research, has demonstrated, the tendency to react with fear to the threat of being left alone is a natural one which has developed out of a genetically determined bias in man and has the character of an instinctive response.[67]

Yet in western culture on the whole, and especially in psycho therapy, '... little weight is given to the component of "being alone"'. Indeed in our culture for someone to confess himself afraid when alone is regarded as shameful or merely silly. Hence there exists a pervasive bias to overlook the very component of fear-arousing situations that a study of anxious patients suggests is most important![68] When a patient's suffering stems from certain phobias, or even when it involves free-floating anxiety, clinicians resort all too readily to complex explanations hinging on 'internal dangers'; no other anxiety-provoking situation is overlooked or camouflaged, either by the patient or by the clinician, as is the common fear of isolation and separation. In India, on the other hand, patients openly allude to, and even insist upon, the fear of being cut off from 'attachment figures' and the consequent threat of loneliness. This fear is acknowledged by family and society in India (however negligible it is to the clinician trained in the West); it has a cultural legitimacy which reinforces its vicissitudes in the course of an individual neurosis and hence merits serious consideration by clinicians. Indeed, in India the fear of isolation is projected on to the Creator himself: In one of the Hindu myths we are told that Creation began because Purusha, the soul of the universe, was alone and 'hence did not enjoy happiness'.[69]

The yearning for the confirming presence of the loved person in its positive as well as negative manifestation—the distress aroused by her or his unavailability or unresponsiveness in time of need—is the dominant modality of social relations in India, especially within the extended family. This 'modality' is expressed variously but consistently, as in a person's feeling of helplessness when family members are absent

or his difficulty in making decisions alone. In short, Indians characteristically rely on the support of others to go through life and to deal
with the exigencies imposed by the outside world. Some western as
well as Indian social scientists have chosen to interpret this as a
'weakness' in the Indian personality, the price to be paid for the indulgence enjoyed in infancy and early childhood. Statements like,
'Training in self-reliance and achievement are conspicuous by their absence. Children are not encouraged to be independent. They, like adults,
are expected to seek aid in difficulty,'[70] or, 'Family life tends to develop
an acute sense of dependence with a strong sense of security, and a clear
sense of responsibility without an accompanying sense of personal initiative or decision,'[71] are the rule in studies which touch on the
developmental aspects of Indian character. And this invariably carries
with it the general value implication that independence and initiative
are 'better' than mutual dependence and community. But it depends, of
course, on the culture's vision of a 'good society' and 'individual merit',
whether a person's behaviour in relationships approaches the isolation
pole of the fusion–isolation continuum, as postulated by the dominant
cultural tradition in the West today, or the fusion pole as maintained in
traditional Indian culture. To borrow from Schopenhauer's imagery, the
basic problem of human relations resembles that of hedgehogs on a cold
night. They creep closer to each other for warmth, are pricked by quills
and move away, but then get cold and again try to come nearer. This
movement to and fro is repeated until an optimum position is reached
in which the body temperature is above the freezing point and yet the
pain inflicted by the quills (the nearness of the other) is still bearable.
In Indian society the optimum position entails the acceptance of more
pain in order to get greater warmth.

The Indian resolution of the tension between the coldness of distance
and the price (in dependency) of nearness is not 'deviant', nor are the
consequences in patterns of social behaviour 'regressive'. Even in the
West, as Bowlby points out, a consensus is emerging among clinicians
of many theoretical persuasions that emotional maturity includes the
capacity to rely trustingly on others, and that true self-reliance is not
only compatible with the capacity for mutual dependence but grows out
of it and is complementary to it.[72] The capacity to be truly alone is
greatest when the 'Other', originally equated with the accepting, giving
'good mother', has become a constant and indestructible presence in the
individual's unconscious mind and is fused with it in the form of self-
acceptance. We have seen in an earlier chapter that this paradox also

underlines the Indian guru's meditation, his striving towards the attainment of *moksha*, wherein he attempts to reach the *sine qua non* of autonomy through the total introjection of the 'Other', the not-self. And, as ever, the imagery of Hinduism is uncompromising: Shiva, arch-ascetic and epitome of lonely self-sufficiency, is often portrayed in such close embrace with Shakti, the 'mother of the universe', that they are one, inseparable for the duration of a world–age.

THE 'BAD MOTHER'

I have suggested above that much of the so-called dependent behaviour observed in individuals and in social relations in India is a manifestation of the universal wish to avoid isolation and the need to share the responsibility for one's life with others. The apparent ubiquity of these needs in India, and their open, undisguised expression, reflect not so much a regressive striving or an 'oral fixation' as the cultural acceptance and even encouragement of such needs and behaviour, an acceptance that is itself rooted in an ideal model of human relationships which diverges sharply from the corresponding ideal in the West. Yet even if we can transfer the larger part of 'dependent' behaviour from the domain of the 'infantile' to that of the 'normal', the fact remains that anxiety around the theme of separation is much more common and intense in India than in western cultures. However, it is inappropriate to attribute the neurotic warp of an otherwise normative element in Indian identity to a prolonged infancy characterized by affectionate care. This theory of 'spoiling', which often crops up in discussions of personality development and psychopathology in India, rests on an uncritical acceptance of Freud's contention that an excess of parental love serves to magnify for the child the danger of losing this love, and renders him in later life incapable of either temporarily doing without love or accepting smaller amounts of it.[73] In spite of the widespread popularity of this hypothesis and its dogged influence on studies of character formation, there is little evidence to support it. In fact, all the available data[74] point in the opposite direction, namely, that a child becomes anxious and clinging if parental affection is insufficient or unreliable.

In India the anxiety that may fester around the theme of separation stems at least partly from that moment in later infancy when the mother may suddenly withdraw her attention and her presence from her child. And indeed, retrospective accounts of adults as well as anthropological observations of child-rearing practices suggest that this is a widely used method of disciplining young children in India. 'I don't remember my mother ever scolding me or hitting me. If I became too much for her she would become sad and start crying and would refuse to speak to me.' Or: 'She often told me that she would go away and leave me. If I was especially bothersome, she would say that the ghost living in the mango tree outside our courtyard would take me. I still cannot pass that mango tree without shivering a little inside.' These are typical recollections of patients in a culture where frightening a child with ghosts or · goblins, or locking him up alone in a dark room—in short, threats of abandonment and isolation—are deemed the most effective methods of socialization. These are the apprehensions that make an Indian child 'be good'; yet if these punishments are threatened or carried out in a context of reliable mothering and family affection they do not immobilize development, but recede into the depths of the psyche. a flickering trace of the dark side of the Indian inner world.

If there is disease in the mother–infant relationship (with its probable consequences in the formation of the Hindu psyche) it stems not so much from styles of maternal reprimand and punishment, and not from the duration or the intensity of the connection between mother and infant, but rather from the danger of inversion of emotional roles—a danger which all too frequently becomes a reality particularly in the case of the male child. By inversion of emotional roles I mean this: An Indian mother, as we have shown, preconsciously experiences her newborn infant, especially a son, as the means by which her 'motherly' identity is crystallized, her role and status in family and society established. She tends to perceive a son as a kind of saviour and to nurture him with gratitude and even reverence as well as with affection and care. For a range of reasons, the balance of nurturing may be so affected that the mother unconsciously demands that the child serve as an object of her own unfulfilled desires and wishes, however antithetical they may be to his own. The child feels compelled then to *act* as her saviour. Faced with her unconscious intimations and demands, he may feel confused, helpless and inadequate, frightened by his mother's overwhelming nearness and yet unable (and partly unwilling) to get away. In his fantasy, her presence acquires the ominous visage of the 'bad mother'.

Before I elaborate on the specific form the 'bad mother' theme takes in Hindu psyche and culture, it is necessary to emphasize that the 'bad' aspect of the mother is not unique to India. The 'bad mother' lives at the opposite pole from the 'good mother' in the fantasies of all of us.

As Erich Neumann has shown in an analysis of the myths of ancient cultures, and as clinical reports have demonstrated in contemporary society, a generative, nurturing and compassionate femininity has always had its counterpoint in the demanding, destroying and devouring maternal image.[75] And, in unconscious fantasy, the vagina as the passage between being and non-being is not only perceived as a source of life and equated with emergence into light, but also shunned as the forbidding dark hole, the entrance into the depths of a death womb which takes life back into itself. At this most fundamental level of the psyche, no one is entirely free from ambivalent feelings towards the mother. The theme of the 'bad mother' merits particular attention in the Indian context not just because it exists, but because it is characterized by a singular intensity and pervasiveness. Considered from this angle, the idealization of the 'good mother' doubtless betrays the intensity of emotion aroused by her during infancy and suggests a secondary repression of the anxious and hostile elements of these feelings.

Images of the 'bad mother' are culturally specific. To a large extent they are a function of the relationship between the sexes in any society. In patriarchal societies, moreover, they reflect the nature of the mother's own unconscious ambivalence towards the male child. Thus, for example, aggressive, destructive impulses towards the male child are a distinct probability in societies which blatantly derogate and discriminate against women. Traditional psycho-analytic theory compresses the abundant variety of affect and fantasy deriving from the basic duality of the sexes into the concept of penis envy, claims for it a stubborn prominence in the feminine unconscious, and concludes that this prevents women from finding the satisfaction of emotional and psycho-sexual needs in marriage and predisposes them to seek this satisfaction from their infant sons. The invariability of these propositions in individual lives is questionable; however, it is more than likely that erotic feelings towards the child will be more intense and closer to consciousness in a society such as India where a woman is expected and encouraged to find emotional fulfilment primarily in her relationship with her children.

In all societies the image of the 'bad mother' combines both the aggressively destroying and the sexually demanding themes. The question as to which of the two aspects, in any society, casts a longer shadow over the infant's earliest experience and thus contributes to the formation of a culturally specific image of the 'bad mother' depends upon the position and status of women within the society and also upon the means and circumstances of socially sanctioned feminine expression of aggressive and erotic impulses. It goes without saying that in this analysis I am speaking of the imagery that informs a collective fantasy of the 'bad mother', and necessarily setting aside individual variations, attributable to the life-historical fates of individual mothers within a given culture.

In Indian society as a whole, for reasons suggested earlier, the aggressive dimension of maternal feeling towards the male child is comparatively weak. Rather, it is in the sphere of unsatisfied erotic needs, a seductive restlessness, that the possibility of disturbance lies. By this I do not mean to imply that Indian women are without feelings of envy and hostility for the males among them; the castration fantasy of turning all men into eunuchs in the Arundhati myth, however much a patriarchal projection, is but one illustration of the ambivalence that governs relations between the sexes. Given the overwhelming preference in Indian society for the birth of male offspring, it would indeed give the psycho-analytic interpreter pause if such envy were non-existent or totally repressed. However, for the purposes of elaborating the imagery of the 'bad mother' in Indian personality development, we must shift our attention from the 'aggressive' sphere of rivalry and rage to the 'erotic' sphere of love and longing. We must attend to the outcome of female psychosexual development in traditional Indian society.

The fate of an Indian girl's sexuality is a socially enforced progressive renunciation. The birth of a child does not change this prescription; in fact, maternity often demands an even greater repudiation of a woman's erotic impulses. The familial and social expectation that she now devote herself exclusively to her child's welfare, the long periods of post-partum taboo on sexual intercourse in many communities, her increasing confinement to female quarters—these are a few of the social factors which dispose a young mother to turn the full force of her eroticism towards an infant son.

Here, it must be remembered that a mother's inner discontents are conveyed to her infant, wordlessly, in the daily intimacy of her contact with him, and that the relief of his mother's tension may become as important to the child as the satisfaction of his own needs. And indeed, clinical experience has consistently and convincingly demonstrated that the displacement of a woman's sexual longings from her husband to her son poses one of the most difficult problems for a boy to handle. At a certain point, the mother's touch and stimulation, whether or not her ministrations are deliberately seductive or overtly sexual, together with the unconscious erotic wishes that infuse her caretaking arouse an intensity of feeling in the male child which his still weak and unstructured ego cannot cope. The surge of unbidden and uncontrollable affect seems to threaten to engulf him while at the same time it arouses acute anxiety. The son's predicament is extreme: although he unconditionally needs the physical tending and emotional sustenance that at first only his mother provides,* he is profoundly wary of the intensity of his feelings for her (and of hers for him) and unconsciously afraid of being overwhelmed and 'devoured' by her. As the infant boy grows—cognitively, psycho-sexually and socially—as he develops the capacity to 'put it all together', he senses that he cannot do without his mother nor remove himself from her presence, but at the same time he is incapable of giving her what she unconsciously desires. 'Realizing' his inadequacy in this regard, he also begins to fear his mother's anger and the separation which her disappointment in him seems to forebode. In his fantasy, the mother's body and specially her genitals may assume an ominous aspect. As Philip Slater in his interpretation of child-rearing in ancient Greece has expressed: 'In so far as the child receives a healthy, non-devouring love from the mother he will regard the female genitalia as the source of life. But in so far as he fails to receive such love, or receive it at the price of living solely for the satisfaction of maternal needs, he will regard the female genitalia as threatening to his very existence.'[76]

In the child's fantasy, the menace implicit in the female genitalia may become concrete, magnified in horrific imagery—a chamber full of poison, causing death in the sexual act—or jaws lined with sharp teeth—the so-called *vagina dentata*. This ferocious motif, which occurs frequently in Indian legends and myths, is vividly illustrated in the following myth from the *Kalika Purana*: 'During a battle between the gods and the demons, Sukra, the guru of the demons, was able to revive all the demons who were slain. Siva knew that Sukra could not be killed because he was a Brahmin, and so he resolved to throw Sukra into the vagina of a woman. From Siva's third eye there appeared a horrible woman with flowing hair, a great belly, pendulous breasts, thighs like plantain tree trunks, and a mouth like a great cavern. There were teeth

---

*As we have noted on p. 30, the mother's primacy and the potential for a psychological 'clinch' between mother and son is prolonged well into childhood—and indeed into the whole life cycle.

and eyes in her womb. Siva said to her, "Keep the evil guru of the
demons in your womb while I kill Jalandhara [the chief of the demon
army], and then release him!" She ran after Sukra and grabbed him,
stripped him of his clothes and embraced him. She held him fast in her
womb, laughed and vanished with him.'[77]

Whereas the Sukra myth is a symbolic dramatization of the child's
helplessness in the face of the dreadful mother, another Siva myth from
the *Matsya Purana* manages to incorporate the child's own sexual
excitement and his fantasied revenge through the complementary motif
of *penis aculeatus*—the sharp phallus: Siva once teased Parvati about
her dark skin, and she resolved to perform *tapas* to obtain a golden skin.
As Parvati departed, she said to her son Viraka, 'My son, I am going to
do *tapas* [ascetic practices], but Siva is a great woman-chaser, and so I
want you to guard the door constantly while I am gone, so that no other
woman may come to Siva!' Meanwhile, Adi, the son of the demon
Andhaka, who had resolved to kill all the gods to revenge his father's
death, learned that Parvati had gone to do *tapas*. Adi did *tapas* and won
from Brahma the boon that he would only die when he had transformed
himself twice. Then he came to Siva's door and seeing Viraka there, he
changed himself into a serpent to delude him, forgetting the stipulation
about the manner of his death. Once inside the house, he took the form
of Parvati in order to deceive Siva, and he placed teeth as sharp as
thunderbolts inside her vagina, for he was determined to kill Siva.
When Siva saw him he embraced him, thinking him to be Parvati, and
Adi said, 'I went to do *tapas* in order to be dear to you and lovely, but
I found no pleasure there so I have returned to you.' When Siva heard
this he became suspicious, for he knew that Parvati would not have
returned without completing *tapas*, and so he looked closely for signs
by which to recognize her. When he saw that the illusory Parvati did
not have the mark of the lotus on the left side of her body, as the true
Parvati did, he recognized the magic form of the demon, and he placed
a thunderbolt in his own phallus and wounded the demon with it, killing
him.[78]

The figure of the mother is indeed omnipresent in the psyche of
Indian men. Yet what these typical myth fragments make clear is the
ambivalence with which she is regarded in fantasy: she is both nurturing benefactress and threatening seductress. The image of the 'bad
mother' as a woman who inflicts her male offspring with her unfulfilled, ominous sexuality is not just a clinical postulate, supported by
mythological evidence; it is indirectly confirmed by the staunch taboos

surrounding menstrual blood and childbirth throughout traditional India.[79] A menstruating woman may not prepare food, nor make offerings, nor participate in family feasts. She is forbidden to go into the temple, into the kitchen, into the granary or to the well. Men have a mortal horror of being near a woman during the time of menstruation. As with many other customs in India, the menstruation taboos have a hoary tradition. Manu is customarily blunt on the subject: 'The wisdom, the energy, the strength, the might and the vitality of a man who approaches a woman covered with menstrual excretions utterly perish.'[80]

Thus, underlying the conscious ideal of womanly purity, innocence and fidelity, and interwoven with the unconscious belief in a safeguarding maternal beneficence is a secret conviction among many Hindu men that the feminine principle is really the opposite—treacherous, lustful and rampant with an insatiable, contaminating sexuality. This dark imagery breaks through in such proverbs as, 'Fire is never satisfied with fuel, the ocean is never filled by the rivers, death is never satisfied by living beings and women are never satisfied with men.' In mythology, when Shiva destroys Kama, the god of sexual desire, Kama's essence enters the limbs of Devi, the great mother-goddess and archetypal woman. Or, the women in the Pine Forest, in their efforts to seduce Shiva, quote from a text which appears in several Upanishads and Brahmanas: 'The Vedas say, "Fire is the woman, the fuel is her lap; when she entices, that is the smoke, and the flames are her vulva. What is done within is the coals, and the pleasure is the sparks. In this Vaisvanara fire, the gods always offer seed as oblation." Therefore have pity. Hers is the sacrificial altar.'[81]

The anxiety aroused by the prospect of encountering female sexuality is also evident in the mildly phobic attitude towards sexually mature women in many parts of India. Dube's observations in a Hyderabad village—'Young people have a special fascination for adolescent girls "whose youth is just beginning to blossom." Young men who succeed in fondling "the unripe, half-developed breasts" of a girl and in having intercourse with one "whose pubic hair is just beginning to grow" easily win the admiration of their age-group . . . . Success—real or imaginary—with an adolescent girl is vividly described'[82]—illustrate the widespread preference for immature girls and the concomitant fear of mature female sexuality. The fantasy world of Hindu men is replete with the figures of older women whose appetites debilitate a man's sexuality, whose erotic practices include, for example, vaginal suction, 'milking the penis'. These fantastic women recall the Hindu son's primitive dread of the maternal sexuality that drains, devours and sucks dry. Here we may note that the common term of abuse, 'Your mother's penis', whose meaning puzzles Dube, stems from precisely this dark side of the Hindu male's emotional imagery of maternity; as Karen Horney has shown, the attempt in male fantasy to endow the woman with a penis is an attempt to deny the sinister female genitals—in India, those of the mother.[83]

The latent sexual dread of the mature female is also the main *psychological* reason for the unusual disparity in age between men and women at the time of marriage in India, although this difference in age rarely approaches the number contemplated by Manu as right and proper: namely, sixteen to eighteen years! Yet even a girl bride gets older, of course. She becomes an adult woman who, especially after childbirth, moves dangerously close to the sexually intimidating mother of infancy in her husband's unconscious fantasy. 'The most direct expression of this (generally unconscious) association in the male psyche is the myth of Skanda, the son of Shiva and Parvati: 'When Skanda killed Taraka [a demon who had been terrorizing the gods], his mother, Parvati, wished to reward him, so she told him to amuse himself as he pleased. Skanda made love to the wives of the gods, and the gods could not prevent it. They complained to Parvati, and so she decided she would take the form of whatever woman Skanda was about to seduce. Skanda summoned the wife of Indra [the king of gods], and then the wife of Varuna [the wind-god], but when he looked at each one he saw his mother's form, and so he would let her go and summon another. She too became the image of his mother, and then Skanda was ashamed and thought, "the universe is filled with my mother", and he became passionless.'[84] On the other side of the coin, the counterphobic attitude, the conscious seeking out of what is unconsciously feared, is expressed in the following passage from the *Yogatattva Upanishad*: 'That breast from which one sucked before he now presses and obtains pleasures. He enjoys the same genital organs from which he was born before. She who was once his mother, will now be his wife and she who is now wife, mother. He who is now father will be again son, and he who is now son will be again father.'[85]

One of the likely psycho-sexual consequences of this anxiety-provoking process of association in unconscious fantasy is a heightened fear, or the actual occurrence, of impotence. And indeed this is a phenomenon to whose ubiquity Indian psychiatrists as well as their traditional counterparts—the *vaids* and *hakims* to whom a majority of Indians turn with psychosomatic complaints—can bear witness. This anxiety is plainly in evidence in the advertisements for patent medicines plastered or painted on the walls enclosing the railway tracks in any of the larger Indian towns. Together with cures for barrenness, the major worry of Indian women, these remedies hold out the promise of sexual rejuvenation for men. Psycho-sexual development and problems of intimacy between Indian men and women suggest the vicious circle that spirals inward in the Indian unconscious: mature women are sexually threatening to men, which contributes to 'avoidance behaviour' in sexual relations, which in turn causes the women to extend a provocative sexual presence towards their sons, which eventually produces adult men who fear the sexuality of mature women.

Given the concurrence of these phenomena, we must conclude that the sexual presence of the 'bad mother' looms large in the unconscious experience of male children in India and is therefore critical to an understanding of the Hindu psyche. And indeed, as I attempt to show below, the mine of collective fantasy around this theme is unusually rich. Certainly all societies call upon witches, vampires, ghosts and other spectres to symbolize the forbidding, negative aspect of a real mother; these phantoms, along with other mother surrogates such as a stepmother and evil goddesses, are infused with meanings derived from archaic early childhood fears of the mother's emotional needs and fantasied threats. These are familiar figures in individual and collective fantasy across cultures, and the *dayans*, *jinns*, and *bhoots* who people the Indian night and the Hindu imagination in such profusion are unexceptional. Female vampires who suck the blood from the toe of a sleeping man suggest (even without an analysis of the obvious sexual symbolism) the fantasied rapacious mother as graphically as Ghitachi, Menaka, Rambha, Urvasi, Chitralekha and all the other *apsaras*, or 'heavenly damsels', who lure men from their practice of 'rigid austerities' and deprive them of their 'spiritual' life substance.

A vivid illustration of the collective male fantasy of the child's encounter with the sexual mother is the mythical meeting of Arjuna, a hero of the epic *Mahabharata*, with the *apsara* Urvasi, which is one of the most popular and frequently enacted subjects in Indian dance drama. As described in the *Mahabharata*, the episode has a dreamlike quality. It begins with the child's pleasurable feeling of wonderment at his mother's beauty and his desire for her presence, a tender expectancy which gradually changes into its opposite—anxiety about his inadequacy to fulfil her sexual needs. The conflict is resolved through a self-castration which appeases the mother. In fantasy, the mother takes the initiative and approaches the child: 'And when the twilight had deepened and the moon was up, that *Apsara* of high hips set out for the mansions of Arjuna. And in that mood, her imagination wholly taken up by thoughts of Arjuna, she mentally sported with him on a wide and excellent bed laid over with celestial sheets, and with her crisp, soft and long braids decked with bunches of flowers, she looked extremely beautiful. With her beauty and grace, and the charm of the motions of her eyebrows and of her soft accents, and her own moonlike face, she seemed to tread, challenging the moon himself. And as she proceeded, her deep, finely tapering bosoms, decked with a chain of gold and adorned with celestial unguents and smeared with fragrant sandal paste, began to tremble. And in consequence of the weight of her bosom, she was forced to bend slightly forward at every step, bending her waist exceedingly beautiful with three folds. And her loins of faultless shape, the elegant abode of the god of love, furnished with fair and high and round hips, and wide at their lower part as a hill, and decked with chains of gold and capable of shaking the saintship of anchorites, being decked with this attire, appeared highly graceful. And her feet with fair suppressed ankles, and possessing flat soles and straight toes of the colour of burnished copper and high and curved like a tortoise back and marked by the wearing of ornaments furnished with rows of little bells, looked exceedingly handsome. And exhilarated with a little liquor which she had taken and excited by desire, and moving in diverse attitudes and expressing a sensation of delight, she looked more handsome than usual.'

Urvasi enters Arjuna's palace. 'Upon beholding her at night in his mansion, Arjuna, with a fear-stricken heart, stepped up to receive her, but from modesty, closed his eyes. And Arjuna said, "O thou foremost of the Apsaras, I reverence thee by bending my head down. O lady, let me know thy commands. I wait upon thee as thy servant."' Without the circumlocution and hyperbole so dear to the Hindu, Urvasi expresses her sexual desire for Arjuna frankly and directly. But—'Hearing her speak in this strain, Arjuna was overcome with bashfulness. And shutting his ears with his hands, he said, "O blessed lady, fie on my sense of hearing, when thou speakest thus to me. For, O thou of beautiful face, thou art certainly equal in my estimation unto the wife of a superior. Even as Kunti [his mother] of high fortune or Sachi the queen of Indra [King of gods] art thou to me, O auspicious one . . . O blessed Apsara, it behoveth thee not to entertain other feelings towards me, for thou art superior to my superiors, being the parent of my race." ' Urvasi, however, insists, and Arjuna expresses the increasing helplessness of the child who desires the mother's comfort and care but instead is confronted with her sexuality: 'Return, O thou of the fairest complexion: I bend my head unto thee, and prostrate myself at thy feet. Thou deservest my worship as my own mother and it behoveth thee to protect me as a son.' The conflict now crescendos, for thus addressed, 'Urvasi was deprived of her sense by wrath. Trembling with rage, and contracting her brows, she cursed Arjuna saying that since he disregarded a woman who is pierced by shafts of Kama, the god of love, ". . . Thou shalt have to pass thy time among females unregarded, and as a dancer and destitute of manhood and scorned as a eunuch." '

As in all Hindu myths and legends, there is a benevolent power in the background who comes forward to mitigate the extreme consequences of the curse. In striking contrast to ancient Greek mythology with its blood-thirsty homicides, mutilations and castrations, in Indian fantasy the murderous impulses of parents towards children or of children towards their parents do not result in permanent injury or death. Even in the rare instance when an actor goes beyond the attempt to actual fulfilment, there is always a good figure, a god or goddess or ancestral spirit, who helps to undo the act that has been committed. Thus, Arjuna must live only one year in the castrated state as eunuch, a solution with which he 'experienced great delight and ceased to think of the curse'.[86]

The renunciation of masculine potency and prowess, mythically depicted in Arjuna's transient fate, is one of the principal unconscious defences of the male child against the threat posed by the mother's sexuality. This 'typical' defence is cartooned in yet another, less well-known myth: 'The demon Ruru with his army attacked the gods, who sought refuge with Devi. She laughed and an army of goddesses emerged from her mouth. They killed Ruru and his army, but then they were hungry and asked for food. Devi summoned Rudra Pasupati (Siva by another name) and said, "You have the form of a goat and you smell like a goat. These ladies will eat your flesh or else they will eat everything, even me." Siva said, "When I pierced the fleeing sacrifice of Daksa, which had taken the form of a goat, I obtained the smell of a goat. But let the goddesses eat that which pregnant women have defiled with their touch, and newborn children and women who cry all the time." Devi refused this disgusting food, and finally Siva said, "I will give you something never tasted by anyone else: the two balls resembling fruits below my navel. Eat the testicles that hang there and be satisfied." Delighted by this gift, the goddess praised Siva.'[87] Here, in spite of commendable efforts to dilute the elements of disgust and dread at the heart of the fantasy by adding such details as the multitude of goddesses, the goat, and so on, that maternal threat and the defence of self castration are unmistakable, although perceived and couched in the rapacious oral imagery of earliest infancy.

The fantasied renunciation of masculinity is but one resolution which the male child may resort to in his helplessness in this dilemma. Hindu mythology gives dramatic play to others—such as the unsexing of the 'bad mother'. Consider the myth of Surpanakha, sister of the demon-king Ravana. The giantess, 'grim of eye and foul of face', tells Rama that he should

> This poor misshapen Sita leave
> And me, thy worthier bride, receive.
> Look on my beauty, and prefer
> A spouse more like me than one like her;
> I'll eat that ill-formed woman there,
> Thy brother, too, her fate shall share.
> But come, beloved, thou shalt roam
> Through our woodland home.[88]

Rama staunchly refuses her advances. Thinking Sita to be the chief obstacle to her union with him, Surpanakha is about to kill her, but is forcibly prevented from doing so when Rama's brother cuts off Surpanakha's nose. In accordance with the well-known unconscious device of the upward displacement of the genitals, this becomes a fantasied clitoridectomy, designed to root out the cause and symbol of Surpanakha's lust.

Another 'defence' in the mythological repertoire against the sexually threatening 'bad mother' is matricide followed by resurrection and deification. Philip Spratt, summarizing the legends of twentynine popular goddesses locally worshipped in the villages of southern India, points out that nineteen of the women who were eventually deified had met first with a violent death; moreover, in fourteen of these legends the woman's forbidden sexual activity is the central theme.[89] Thus: 'Podilamma was suspected of sexual misconduct. Her brothers, who were farmers, threw her under the feet of their oxen. She vanished, and all they could find was a stone. Her spirit demanded that they [the villagers] worship the stone.' Or: 'A widow named Ramama had immoral relations with her servant. Her brother murdered them both. Cattle-plague broke out, and the villagers attributed it to her wrath and instituted rites to pacify her spirit.'[90] On the one hand, the fantasy underlying these legends aims to accomplish and gratify the sexual wishes of the mother, while on the other, the child revenges himself upon her for putting him, with his own unsettling 'wishes', his inexperience and his woeful lack of mature genital equipment, in this hopeless predicament. By the 'murder' of the sexual mother, however, the child's source of affirmation, protection and motherly love is also eliminated, thus arousing an unbearable sense of longing and guilt. To reclaim the filial relationship, to restore the forfeited mutuality, the mother must be resurrected as no less than a goddess.

Yet another defence in the male child's struggle against the 'bad mother' is the fantasy of having been born of a man, in which case one's existence has nothing whatsoever to do with the mother and is thus unquestionably masculine. This fantasy is expressed in one version of the birth of Ganesha, one of the most popular deities in the Hindu pantheon. Ganesha is usually portrayed as a short, corpulent god with an elephant's head and a large belly. His image, whether carved in stone or drawn up in a coloured print, may be found in almost any Hindu home or shop. Important matters of householding, whether in the sphere of the family or of business, whether the task at hand is the construction of a house or embarking on a journey or even writing a letter, are not undertaken without an invocation to Ganesha. In the particular version of his birth I have in mind here from the *Varaha Purana*, it is related that gods and holy sages, realizing that men are as liable to commit bad acts as good ones, came to Shiva and asked him to find a way of placing obstacles in the path of wrongdoing. While meditating on this request, Shiva produced a beautiful youth with whom all the heavenly damsels fell in love and who was charged by his father with the task of hindering evil. But Shiva's wife, the great mother-goddess Uma (also known as Durga, Parvati or Gauri), became extremely jealous of the youth's immaculate conception and incomparable beauty, and so she cursed him with a large belly and the head of an elephant.

Other accounts in Hindu mythology of the origin of Ganesha's incongruous physiognomy reflect the strikingly different sequential 'editions' of unconscious fantasy that inform infantile psycho-sexual development. Thus, in the version of the *Brahmavaivarta Purana*, it is narrated that Parvati who was very desirous of having a child was finally granted her wish after a long period of penance and prayer. All the gods come to Shiva's house to congratulate the couple and to admire the newborn. But Sani, the ill-omened Saturn, refuses to look at the baby, and keeps his gaze firmly fixed on the ground. When asked the reason for this discourtesy, Sani replies that he is cursed and that any child he looks upon will lose its head. Parvati, however, forces Sani to look at the infant, whereupon Ganesha's head is severed from his body and flies off Parvati's pitiful lamentations over her son's decapitation attract the sympathy of Vishnu who intercedes and finds an elephant's head which he joins to the infant's trunk. Thus Ganesha is resurrected.

In the sequence of developmental time within the individual psyche, these two versions of the Ganesha myth exist in close proximity. Without elaborating on the unconscious equation of genitals and head so prominent in Hindu fantasy, it is clear that each version of Ganesha's genesis threatens the son, symbolically, with the loss of his penis at the behest of the 'bad mother'. Moreover, when Ganesha's head is restored, we witness one of the psyche's marvellous compensations, for the replacement is not an ordinary human head, but the head of an elephant, with a trunk for good measure!

In the third version of the Ganesha story, which is from the *Shiva Purana*, the variation of the fantasy is more advanced; it condenses and reflects the dominant themes of a later, oedipal, stage of development. A new conflict arises out of the intrusive presence of the father, his claims on both mother and child, and the threat this poses to their earlier symbiosis. In this version of the myth, Siva has nothing to do with Ganesha's birth. Rather, the infant is said to have been fashioned solely by Parvati from the impurities of her own body and brought to life by being sprinkled with 'maternal water' from the holy river Ganges. Charged by Parvati to stand at the door and guard her from intruders while she is bathing, Ganesha refuses to let his father enter. In his anger at being kept from his wife, Shiva cuts off Ganesha's head. But when Parvati tells Shiva that her son was only carrying out her orders and when she proves inconsolable at the loss of her son, Shiva restores Ganesha to life by taking the head of a passing elephant and fitting it to the child's headless body.

The oedipal struggle in this version of the myth and the way the son resolves it, through castration by the father, is not my main concern here. I merely want to indicate, and stress, the various sequential transformations of fantasy from stage to stage in psychological development and their co-existence in the unconscious. Moreover, this may occur in relation to a *single* mythological figure, who thus comes to represent a plurality of psychic propensities. The enormous popularity enjoyed by Ganesha throughout India, a phenomenon of considerable puzzlement to Indologists, can thus be partially explained if we recognize Ganesha as a god for all psychic seasons, who embodies certain 'typical' resolutions of developmental conflicts in traditional Hindu society.

These, then, are the legendary elaborations of the Indian boy's encounters with the 'bad mother'. The evidence of popular myths, religious customs and anthropological observations converges to suggest that the modal resolution of the conflict is a lasting identification with the mother.[91] This process of identification contrasts with the earlier grateful incorporation of the 'good mother' into the infant's budding ego in that it contains an element of hostility, for the source of anxiety, the mother, is only eliminated by being taken inside oneself.

In psycho-sexual terms, to identify with one's mother means to sacrifice one's masculinity to her in order to escape sexual excitation and the threat it poses to the boy's fragile ego. In effect, the boy expresses his conviction that the only way he can propitiate the mother's demands and once again make her nurturing and protective is to repudiate the cause of the disturbance in their mutuality: his maleness. In myths, we witnessed this process in Arjuna's encounter with Urvasi, in Shiva's offer of his testicles, in Ganesha's losing his head because of Parvati's jealousy.[92] In the ancient and medieval tales collected, for example, in *Hitopadesha, Vikramaditya's Adventures* and *Kathasaritsagar*, the cutting off of one's own head (symbolic of self castration) as an act of sacrificial worship to the mother- goddess occurs frequently. Western readers may recollect Thomas Mann's treatment of the Indian tale, in *The Transposed Heads*, in which two friends caught in a sexually tempting and dangerous situation repair to the goddess Bhavani's temple and cut off their heads.

In its purely sexual sense, the puerile identification with the mother is even more explicit in the story of King Bhangaswana in the *Mahabharata*, who, after being transformed into a woman by Indra, wished to remain in that state. Refusing Indra's offer to restore his masculinity, the king contended that a woman's pleasure in intercourse was much greater than a man's.[93] Philip Spratt's painstaking collection of anthropological evidence—traditional village ceremonies in which men dress as women, the transvestite customs of low-caste beggars in Bellary, the possession of men of the Dhed community in Gujarat by the spirit of the goddess Durga, the simulated menstrual period among certain followers of Vallabhacharya—need not be further catalogued.[94] And although we may be tempted to view these phenomena as aberrant, as extreme manifestations of marginal behaviour, we must nevertheless acknowledge the possibility that, just as the 'sick' member may act out the unconscious conflict of the whole family, thereby permitting other family members to remain 'normal', so these marginal groups disclose the governing emotional constellations within Hindu society as a whole. Nor is this to deny that transvestism, like any aspect of behavioural style, is 'overdetermined'. As a re-enactment of a powerful infantile conflict, rituals such as these represent not only the boy's attempt to identify with his mother but also the man's effort to free himself from her domination. By trying to be like women—wearing their clothes, acquiring their organs, giving birth—these men are also saying that they do not need women (mothers) any longer. The counterpart of such extreme 'femininity' rituals among men are those rites, common in many parts of the world, in which men behave in a rigid, symbolic masculine way. Both extremes suggest a family structure in which the mother is perceived by the male child as a dangerous, seductive female presence during his early years. However compelling the sexual idiosyncrasies spawned by this childhood identification with the mother may be, our main concern is the broader question of its consequences on the evolution of Indian identity.

INFANCY AND EGO: ORIGINS OF IDENTITY IN A PATRIARCHAL CULTURE

We have been that minimal demands are placed on the Indian infant to master the world around him and to learn to function independently of his mother. The main emphasis in the early years of Indian childhood is avoidance of frustration and the enhancement of the pleasurable mutuality of mother and infant, not encouragement of the child's individuation and autonomy. By and large, an Indian child is neither pressed into active engagement with the external world, nor is he coerced or cajoled to master the inner world represented, temporarily at least, by his bodily processes. Thus, with respect to elimination, the toddler in India is exempt from anxious pressure to learn to control his bowel movements according to a rigid schedule of time and place. Soiling of clothes or floor is accepted in a matter-of-fact way and cleaned up afterwards by the mother or other older girls or women in the family without shame or disgust.

This does not of course mean that no attempts of any kind are made at training toddlers in cleanliness. A child may indeed be taken outside in the morning, seated on a hollow made by his mother's feet and coaxed to relieve himself. What is relevant here is that such attempts are not a matter of systematic instruction or *a priori* rules; therefore they rarely become occasions for a battle of wills in which the mother suddenly reveals an authoritarian doggedness that says her nurturing love is, after all, conditional. More often than not, an Indian child gradually learns to control his bowels by imitating older children and adults in the family as he follows them out into the fields for their morning ablutions. This relaxed form of toilet-training, as Muensterberger (among others) has observed,[95] can contribute to the formation of specific personality traits such as a relative feeling of timelessness, a relaxed conscience about swings of mood and a certain low-key tolerance of contradictory impulses and feelings not only in oneself but in others as well. Indians do tend to accept ambiguity in emotions, ideas and relationships, with little apparent need (let alone compulsion) to compartmentalize experience into good/evil, sacred/profane—or inner/outer, for that matter.

In India the process of ego development takes place according to a model which differs sharply from that of western psychologists. Indian mothers consistently emphasize the 'good object' in their behaviour. They tend to accede to their children's wishes and inclinations, rather than to try to mould or control them. Hindu children do not have a gradual, step-by-step experience of the many small frustrations and disappointments which would allow them to recognize a mother's limitations harmlessly, over some time. Rather her original perfection remains untarnished by reality, a part of the iconography of the Hindu inner world. Thus, the detachment from the mother by degrees that is considered essential to the development of a strong, independent ego, since it allows a child almost imperceptibly to take over his mother's functions in relation to himself, is simply not a feature of early childhood in India. The child's differentiation of himself from his mother (and consequently of the ego from the id) is structurally weaker and comes chronologically later than in the West with this outcome: the mental processes characteristic of the symbiosis of infancy play a relatively greater role in the personality of the adult Indian.

In these, the so-called primary mental processes, thinking is representational and affective; it relies on visual and sensual images rather than the abstract and conceptual secondary-process thinking that we express in the language of words. Primary-process perception takes place through sensory means—posture, vibration, rhythm, tempo, resonance, and other non-verbal expressions—not through semantic signals that underlie secondary-process thought and communication.[96] Although every individual's thinking and perception are governed by his idiosyncratic mixture of primary and secondary processes, generally speaking, primary-process organization looms larger in the Indian than the western psyche.[97] The relative absence of social pressure on the Indian child to give up non-logical modes of thinking and communication, and the lack of interest or effort on the part of the mother and the family to make the child understand that objects and events have their own meaning and consequences independent of his feelings or wishes, contribute to the protracted survival of primary-process modes well into the childhood years.

Compared with western children, an Indian child is encouraged to continue to live in a mythical, magical world for a long time. In this world, objects, events and other persons do not have an existence of their own, but are intimately related to the self and its mysterious moods. Thus, objective, everyday realities loom or disappear, are good or bad, threatening or rewarding, helpful or cruel, depending upon the child's affective state; for it is his own feelings at any given moment that are projected onto the external world and give it form and meaning. Animistic and magical thinking persists, somewhat diluted, among many Indians well into adulthood. The projection of one's own emotions onto others, the tendency to see natural and human 'objects' predominantly as extensions of oneself, the belief in spirits animating the world outside and the shuttling back and forth between secondary and primary process modes are common features of daily intercourse.

The emphasis on primary thought processes finds cultural expression in innumerable Hindu folk-tales in which trees speak and birds and animals are all too human, in the widespread Hindu belief in astrology and planetary influence on individual lives, and in the attribution of benign or baleful emanations to certain precious and semi-precious stones. The Indian sensitivity to the non-verbal nuances of communication—all that is perceived with the 'sixth sense' and the 'inner eye'—has been noted not only by western psychiatrists but also by western writers such as Hesse, Kipling and Forster with fascination or horror or both.

Traditionally, moreover, Indians have sought to convey abstract concepts through vivid concrete imagery. Whether we consider the instruction in political science by means of the animal fables of *Panchatantra*, or the abundance of parables in Upanishadic metaphysics, a good case can be made that symbolic imagery rather than abstract concepts, and teleology rather than causality, have historically played a prominent role in Indian culture. Causal thinking has never enjoyed the pre-eminence in Indian tradition that it has in western philosophy.

Clinically, the persistence of primary processes in an individual's thinking and perception has been associated with psychopathology, in the sense that it suggests the persistence in adult life of an 'infantile' mode of behaviour. As Pinchas Noy has pointed out, however, in many kinds of normal regression (such as reveries and daydreams), artistic activity and creative endeavour, primary processes govern in the sphere of thought without signs of regression in other aspects of the individual's life.[98] And though the supremacy of primary processes in an individual's mental life may indeed lead to distorted perceptions of outside reality or to an impaired ability to grasp the 'real meaning' of external events and relationships, these processes serve a fundamental human purpose, namely, preserving the continuity of the self in the flux of outer events and maintaining one's identity by assimilating new experiences into the self. Throughout our lives, we must deal not only with an outer world but also an inner one, and whereas the secondary processes of logical thought and reasoning govern our mastery of the outside world, the primary processes of condensation, displacement and symbolization—the language of children, dreams and poetry—contribute to the unfolding and enrichment of the inner world.

The western cultivation of secondary processes, by and large at the expense of primary processes, contributes (almost inevitably) to a sense of disorientation among westerners who confront Indian culture for the first time. This confusion has often resulted in a foreclosure of experience and explicit or implicit negative value judgements of the Indian mode of experiencing the world, rather than in a questioning of the basic cultural assumption. As Noy remarks:

The ability to represent a full experience, including all the feelings and ideas involved, is a higher achievement than merely operating with abstract concepts and words, and the ability to transcend time limits and organize past experiences with the present ones is a higher ability than being confined to the limitations of time and space . . . The schizophrenic, for example, tries to deal with reality by his primary processes, and accordingly tries to organize reality in terms of his own self. The obsessive–compulsive does the opposite—he tries to assimilate and work through his experience with the aid of secondary processes. He tries to 'understand' and analyse his feelings in terms of logic and reality. Both fail because you cannot deal with reality by self centred processes nor can you deal with your self by reality-oriented processes.[99]

The different emphases placed by western and Indian cultures on one or the other of the two basic modes thus reflect two diametrically opposed stances to the inner and outer worlds.

We can now appreciate that certain elements of the Hindu world image are strikingly consistent and reciprocal with the ego configuration generated in the developmental experience of Indian childhood. The widespread (conscious and pre-conscious) conviction that knowledge gained through ordering, categorizing, logical reasoning, is *avidya*, the not-knowledge, and real knowledge is only attainable through direct, primary-process thinking and perception ; the imperative that inspires the yogi's meditation and the artist's *sadhana* namely, that to reach their avowed goals they must enlarge the inner world rather than act on the outer one; the injunction inherent in the *karma* doctrine to accept and use outer reality for inner development rather than to strive to alter worldly realities; the indifferent respect given to eminent scientists and professionals, compared with the unequivocal reverence for Sai Baba, Anandamai, Tat Baba, Mehr Baba and the innumerable shamanic gurus who act as spiritual preceptors to Hindu families: these are a few of the indicators of the emphasis in Hindu culture on the primary processes of mental life.

Unless the social organization makes some special provision for it, however, no group can survive for long if its members are brought up to neglect the development of those secondary processes through which we mediate and connect outer and inner experience. An 'underdeveloped' ego in relation to the outer world is a risky luxury except under the most bountiful and utopian of natural conditions. Indian social organization traditionally 'took care' of the individual's adaptation to the outer world. That is, traditionally, in the early years, the mother serves as the child's ego, mediating his most elementary experiences, well into the years of childhood proper, until around the age of four. The ego's responsibility for monitoring and integrating reality is then transferred from the mother to the family-at-large and other social institutions. Thus, when making decisions based on reasoning through the pros and cons of a situation, the individual functions as a member of a group rather than on his own. With the help of traditional precedents and consensual (as opposed to adversary) modes of decision-making, based on the assumption that no two people have identical limits on their rationality, Indians cope effectively with their environment (if it does not change too fast). Similarly, as far as the environment of relationships is concerned, the myriad, detailed rules and regulations governing social interaction and conduct define the individual Hindu's interpersonal world in most conceivable situations and spell out appropriate behaviours. By making social interactions very predictable, these norms make it unnecessary (and usually imprudent) for each individual to assess the exigencies of a particular encounter or circumstance on his own, and encourage him to respond according to a tried-and-true traditional pattern.

The highly structured and elaborated social organization that seems oppressive to many westerners is functional in the sense that it strengthens and supplements the individual's basic ego fabric in which the world of magic and animistic projection looms large. In Indian society, this complementary 'fit' between ego and social organization remains functional only so long as the process of environmental change is a slow one, as it has been in the past, affording enough time for gradual, barely perceptible evolution of cultural ideals, social institutions and generational relationships. Difficulties arise when the pace of change quickens. Today, the outer world impinges on the Indian inner world in an unprecedented way. Harsh economic circumstances have resulted in higher social and geographical mobility, which has meant, in turn, that dealings with the outer world are more and more on an individual, rather than a social, footing. Under these 'modern' conditions, an individual ego structure, weak in secondary and reality-oriented processes and unsupported by an adequate social organization, may fail to be adaptive.

I have discussed the influence of the protracted intimacy between mother and infant in India—subsuming childhood, as it does—on the entrenchment of primary mental processes in the Hindu inner world. These processes, as we have seen, are supported by the structures of Hindu social organization and traditional cultural mores. The second lifelong theme in the Indian inner world (more actual for men by far than for women) that derives from the special psychosocial features of Indian motherhood is the simultaneous, often unintegrated presence in fantasy of images of the 'good' and the 'bad' mother.

These contradictory aspects of the maternal presence can coexist in the very young child's psyche without disturbing each other, for it is a feature of primary mental processes characteristic of infancy that contradictions do not cause urgent conflicts pressing for resolution. It is only later, when the ego gains strength and attempts to synthesize and integrate experience, that conflicts erupt and ambivalence comes into own, and that the negative, threatening aspects of earliest experience may be forcibly repressed or projected onto the external world.

Taken into the child's ego, the 'good mother's' maternal tolerance, emotional vitality, protectiveness, and nurturing become the core of every Indian's positive identity. Alongside this positive identity, however, and normally repressed, is its counterpart: the negative identity that originates in experiences with the demanding, sometimes stifling, all too present mother. Whatever the contours of the negative identity, they reflect certain defences against the 'bad mother' who may have been most undesirable or threatening, yet who was also most real at a critical stage of development.[100] In conditions of psychological stress and emotional turmoil, the negative identity fragments tend to coalesce in a liability to a kind of psychological self-castration, in a predisposition to identify with rather than resist a tormentor, and in a longing for a state of perfect passivity.

Although the inner world of Indian men is decisively influenced by both the 'good' and the 'bad' versions of the maternal–feminine, the adult identity consolidation of men is of course not to be cast exclusively in these terms. For identity is constituted not only out of early feminine identifications but also from later masculine ones, all of them rearranged in a new configuration in youth. Normally, the biological rock-bottom of maleness limits the extent to which a boy can or will identify with his mother as he grows up. The view advanced here, namely, that the length, intensity and nature of the mother–infant relationship in India, together with the sexualized nature of the threat posed by the mother to the male child in fantasy, contribute to the Hindu male's strong identification with his mother and a 'maternal–feminine' stance towards the worldly world, only makes sense in the light of these self evident reservations. The expression of the maternal–feminine in a man's positive identity is, however, neither deviant nor pathological, but that which makes a man more human. Its presence precludes that strenuous phallicism which condemns a man to live out his life as half a person, and it enhances the possibility of mutuality and empathic understanding between the sexes. Of course, in its defensive aspect, the maternal–feminine identification of men may serve to keep the sexes apart and may even contribute to discrimination against women. A precarious sense of masculine identity can lead to a rigid, all-or-nothing demarcation of sex roles; this kind of rigid differentiation is a means of building outer bulwarks against feared inner proclivities. The seeds of a viable identity, if they are not to mutate into plants of a 'false self', require the supportive soil of a compatible family structure and a corresponding set of cultural values and beliefs. In India, the child learns early that emotional strength resides primarily in his mother, that she is 'where the action is'. The cultural parallel to the principal actuality of infancy is the conviction that mother-goddesses are reservoirs of both constructive and destructive energy. The very word for energy, Shakti, is the name of the supreme mother-goddess. And although the spirit of the godhead is one, its active expression, worshipped in innumerable forms ranging from particular local village goddesses to the more or less universal manifestations of Mahadevi ('great goddess'), is decisively female. The male gods of the Hindu pantheon, Shiva, Vishnu, Brahma, may be more dignified beings, but the village deities, earthy, mundane, attuned to the uncertainties and troubles, the desires and prayers of daily life, are generally female. In south India, as Whitehead has shown, village deities are almost exclusively feminine; and the exceptional male gods, such as Potu-Razu in Andhra Pradesh, are not worshipped in their own right, but in conjunction (as brother or husband) with the local village goddess, the position of the male gods being often subordinate if not outright servile.[101]

Hindu cosmology is feminine to an extent rarely found in other major civilizations. In its extremity (for example) in Tantric beliefs, god and creation are unconditionally feminine; in *Mahanirvana Tantra*, even the normally male gods Vishnu and Brahma are portrayed as maidens with rising breasts. The essence of this deepest layer of Hindu religiosity is conveyed in the following prayer to the goddess Durga:

O thou foremost of all deities, extend to me thy grace, show me thy mercy, and be thou the source of blessings to me. Capable of going everywhere at will, and bestowing boons on thy devotees, thou art ever followed in thy journeys by Brahma and the other gods. By them that call upon thee at daybreak, there is nothing that cannot be attained in respect either of offspring or wealth. O great goddess, thou art fame, thou art prosperity, thou art steadiness, thou art success; thou art the wife, thou art man's offspring, thou art knowledge, thou art intellect. Thou art the two twilights, the night sleep, light, beauty, forgiveness, mercy and every other thing. And as I bow to thee with bended head, O supreme goddess, grant me protection. O Durga, kind as thou art unto all that seek thy protection, and affectionate unto all thy devotees, grant me protection![102]

The most striking illustration of the cultural acceptance and out-right encouragement of the passive feminine aspects of identity in Indian men is the *bhakti* cult associated with Lord Krishna. Its appeal is dramatically simple. Renouncing the austere practices of yoga, the classical Hindu means of attaining *moksha*, the Krishna cult emphasizes instead the emotional current in religious devotion. Personal devotion to Lord Krishna absorbs a devotee's whole self and requires all his energies. Depending on individual temperament and inclination, this devotional emotion—*bhava*—may express itself in a variety of modes: *santa*, awe, humility, a sense of one's own insignificances; *dasya*, respect, subservience and pious obedience; *vatsalya*, nurturing, protective (maternal) feelings of care; and so on.

The most intensely and commonly desirable feeling towards the god-head, a rudimentary prerequisite for the state of pure bliss, is held to be *madhurya bhava*, the longing of a woman for her lover, of the legendary *gopis* for their Lord. In an interview with Milton Singer, a Krishna devotee in the city of Madras articulates the systematic cultivation of this feminine-receptive stance and its transformation into a religious ideal:

The love of a woman for her husband or for her lover is very much more intense than any other sort of love in the world, and I mentioned the gopis, Radha, Ruk-mini, Satyabhama, and so forth, as instances in point. Their love was indeed transcendent. Even when the husband or lover is a man the woman's love for him is of a very high order and when the Lord Supreme is the husband or lover of a woman, you can find no other love excelling or surpassing this love. The ladies mentioned above can therefore be said to be the most blessed in the world. If we concede this, we can ourselves aspire for this kind of supreme love for God. We can imagine ourselves to be those women on at any rate ordinary women, imagine that the Lord is our husband or lover and bestow the maximum love on Him . . . Think constantly that you are a woman and that God is your husband or lover, and you will be a woman and God will be your husband or lover . . . You know the philosophy here that all men and women in the world are spiritually women, and the Lord alone is male—the Purusa. The love of the gopis, Radha, Rukmini, and Satyabhama explains the principle of the human soul being drawn to the Supreme Soul and getting merged in it.[103]

Fragments from the life history of the widely revered nineteenth-century Bengali saint, Sri Ramakrishna, further highlight the respect and reverence Indian society pays to the ontogenetically motivated, religiously sublimated femininity in a man. As a child, it is related, Ramakrishna often put on girl's clothing and sought to mimic the village women as they went about their daily chores. In adolescence, he would imagine that he was a forsaken wife or child-widow and would sing songs of longing for Krishna. In his quest for union with the god-head, he systematically practised *madhurya bhava*. For six months during his youth, he wore women's clothes and ornaments, adopted women's gestures, movements and expressions, and 'became so much absorbed in the constant thought of himself as a woman that he could not look upon himself as one of the other sex even in a dream'.[104]

If interpreted solely from an individual developmental viewpoint, Sri Ramakrishna's behaviour would seem deviant, the eruption of negative elements latent in Indian masculine identity. Yet the meaning of any thematic event or behaviour cannot be grasped in one dimension only. What appears to be an episode in Ramakrishna's life of 'psychopathological acting out' is, when viewed culturally and histori-cally, an accepted, representative phenomenon in the tradition of Krishna worship. It is profoundly consistent with the basic 'mood' of all schools of Hindu miniature painting and of the *bhajan, kirtan* and even *dadra* forms of vocal music. Finally, the feminine stance is con-sistent with the life style of certain specialized religious groups, and its aim dramatizes a cultural ideal of the whole society, namely, a receptive absorption rather than an active alteration and opposition.

To conclude, the primary themes of Indian identity, emerging from the infant's relationship with his mother, are inextricably intertwined with the predominant cultural concerns of Hindu India. These concerns, both individual and social, govern, inform and guide the Indian inner world in such a way that they reverberate throughout the identity strug-gles of a lifetime.

2

The Child in Indian Tradition

The maternity room in the southwest corner of the house, facing east, is light and airy. Two days ago, amid much ceremony—the trumpeting of conchshells, the playing of music and the beating of drums—the expectant mother entered this room accompanied by four older women of the family, all of them mothers of long standing. Together with the rest of the family, the women had worshipped the family priest and his apprentices before they had left for the room ritually prepared for imminent childbirth.

The room, its walls whitewashed and its floor freshly swept, is uncluttered. Simple mats, woven of bamboo reeds, are spread on the floor to be used as beds. Beside the expectant mother's mat, there is a clay pot containing the sacred *turyanti* plant, a jar of water, a mace, a spear and a sword—all of which help to ward off the evil spirits that threaten newborn infants, In one corner of the room, the *sutika* (impure) birth-fire burns brightly in a brazier; the flames fed with rice chaff and mustard seeds.

The woman reclines on her mat. As the labour pains begin, her limbs are massaged and rubbed with a herbal paste and she is addressed with comforting words of reassurance and practical instructions delivered in the calm voice of authority and experience. Outside, the rest of the family perform rites to ensure a safe delivery, and an apprentice priest goes around the house opening all the windows and doors and unlocking all the locks—practising sympathetic magic to loosen the foetus from its moorings in the womb. As the baby is born, one of the ministering women strikes stones near its ears while another dashes cold and warm water against its face to stimulate breathing. A third woman removes the mucus from the baby's mouth and throat with a lint of sterile cotton. *Ghee* and *Saindhav* salt are then given to the infant so that it will cough up any amniotic fluid it may have swallowed. The father now comes in to look at the baby's face. The paternal act of looking at a first-born son, the sacred texts assure him, will absolve him of all his debts to the gods and to the ancestors. But for a sensible man, and the father prides himself on being a sensible man, even the birth of a girl would have been only slightly less meritorious; her gift in marriage brings the father spiritual merit, and appreciably increases the store of his good *karmas*. Having seen the infant's face, the father goes out and takes a ritual bath. Accompanied by the priests and family elders, the father then re-enters the maternity room for the birth ceremonies. The room is getting quite crowded.

The first rite is designed to stimulate the newborn's mental development. While a priest holds aloft a cup of butter and honey, the father alternately dips a gold spoon and the fourth finger of his right hand into the mixture and touches it to the infant's mouth. While the father recites the sonorous Gayatri *mantra* with its prayer for the growth of talent and intellect, the infant screams away lustily, oblivious to the women's ineffectual efforts to hush it into a semblance of ceremonial seriousness. Ignoring the commotion, the father bends down and whispers the child's secret name (it will be known only to the parents) into the boy's ear. Prompted by the priest, he haltingly recites in verse examples of immortality—the immortality of the ocean, of nectar, of sacrificial fire, of ancient sages—so as to prolong the child's own life. His efforts are supplemented by the priests who stand around the child breathing forcefully and rhythmically—long-drawn out breaths intended to quicken and prolong the breath of life in the infant. The birth rites continue as the father kneels down on the floor and with folded hands says a prayer of thanks to the spot of earth where the birth took place. He turns toward the mother and, following the priest's lead, recites a verse thanking and praising her for having borne a strong son. The child is then washed and ceremoniously given to the mother.

The birth ritual is not yet over. Before the men leave the maternity room, the father places a jar of water near the pillow and says, 'O water, you watch with gods. As you watch with the gods, thus watch this our mother, who is confined, and her child'. The men now leave the room, the father taking away the birth-fire which he will place outside the room, ceremoniously fuelling it twice a day till the mother gets up from childbed and re-enters the family. Depending upon the mother's condition and the auspiciousness of the astrological constellations, this may happen on the tenth, twelfth, fifteenth or even the thirty-second postpartum day, and will be an occasion for yet another ritual. For the moment, at least, a relative quiet descends on the delivery room. The women busy themselves with various tasks while the mother sinks into an exhausted sleep with the baby snuggled against her breast. Outside, the sounds of the great feast in which family members, friends and community elders are taking part, slowly gather momentum and volume.[1]

Once the birth ritual has introduced the baby to the family and the community, we arrive at the starting point of this inquiry: what are the traditional conceptions of the nature of children and childhood in India that inform the behaviour of the newborn's caretakers and influence their interaction with this new human being in their midst ? Can we systematically identify a *cultural awareness* of the child that will help us to clarify our own adult attitudes toward the child before us? To answer these questions, I have looked at views of children expressed and reflected in various parts of the Indian cultural tradition. There are passages dealing with children in the law books, especially *The Laws of Manu*, and on the care and upbringing of infants and children in the three primary texts of traditional Indian medicine, *Ayurveda*. There are references to children and childhood in the *Ramayana* and the *Mahabharata* although I have only focused on the latter. And of course there are descriptions of childhood in ancient and medieval literature, although in this essay I have limited myself to the devotional poetry of Surdas and Tulsidas, which depicts the childhood of Krishna and Rama. The chief *samskaras* of childhood also contribute to the formation of an Indian consciousness and conception of childhood. These *samskaras* set temporal and behavioural limits to childhood and delineate childhood stages. In addition, their symbolic content and that of the traditional folk songs that accompany them, provide some indication of the chief characteristics of a given stage of childhood.[2] Perhaps I also need to mention at the outset that large parts of the Indian tradition of childhood are solely concerned with boys and ignore, if not dispossess, girls of their childhood.

THE CHILD IN LAW

In ancient Indian law, and here I specifically refer to the *Laws of Manu*, the child is located very near the bottom of a social pyramid at the apex of which stands the householder, an adult male belonging to one of the twice-born castes. At the bottom of the pyramid, the child finds himself in motley company: persons belonging to the lowest castes and those who have lost their caste by practising forbidden occupations, the mentally deficient and the mentally disturbed, slaves and hired servants, actors and vagrants, the old and the sick, newly-married women and those who are pregnant.[3] The lower social status of the child is also evident in Manu's mourning prescriptions: the younger the deceased, the shorter the mourning period, and the otherwise elaborate funeral rites are minimal in case of a child's death.[4]

A close examination of Manu's injunctions reveals a sharp line of cleavage through the social pyramid, a line that divides the lower orders into two clearly differentiated groups. Towards one of these groups, comprising the casteless and the lowest castes, the violators of Brahminical social ethics and the rejecters of a brahminical pietistic life style, Manu consistently takes an authoritarian and punitive stance. Children, however, belong to the second group—consisting of women, the aged, the sick and the infirm—who deserve society's protection and claim its indulgence. Thus, even before serving invited guests (and guests, as we know, are almost on a par with gods in the Hindu tradition) the householder is enjoined to feed pregnant women, the sick and the young.[5] Although a man may not quarrel with learned men, priests and teachers, he is also forbidden to speak harshly to the aged, the sick and children.[6] Whereas the king is within his rights to exact retribution on those who question his authority or inveigh against his person, he is required to forgive children (as also the old and the sick) who may be guilty of lese-majesty. Although punishments, including fines, are prescribed for anyone soiling the king's highways, children are specifically exempted; they are only to be reprimanded and required to clean up after themselves.[7]

The protective indulgence shown towards the child is manifested most clearly where it matters the most (at least to the child)—namely, in Manu's pronouncements on the chastisement of children. Children (and women) are only to be beaten with a rope or a bamboo stick split at the end. The split bamboo, as we may remember from circus clowns' mock fights, makes a loud noise without inflicting much pain. Moreover, even this punishment is to be carried out only on the back and never on a 'noble part'—that is, not on the head or the chest.[8] To those who hold progressive views of child discipline, the beating of children may hardly seem like 'protective indulgence'. However, the extent of this indulgence becomes strikingly clear when we compare Manu's *Laws* with legal texts of other ancient societies. For example, there is evidence in the law codes and digests of ancient Rome to suggest that brutal forms of child abuse were common mistreatment, which the more enlightened emperors attempted to mitigate;[9] it was only as late as AD 374 that infanticide was declared a capital offence in the Roman world.[10]

In short, though by modern standards Manu's *Laws* have been severely condemned as a repository of inequity, sanctioning the repression of the weak and the poor, their attitude toward children—one of protective nurturance—is unexceptionable. at least within the premises of the patriarchal society which gave the *Laws* their birth.

THE CHILD IN MEDICINE

The treatment of the child constitutes one of the eight branches of the traditional Ayurvedic system of Indian medicine. I hesitate to equate this branch of medicine (known as *Balanga* in *Ashtangahridya* and *Kumarbhrutya* in the *Caraka* and *Susruta Samhitas*) with modern pediatrics, primarily because child development in the Indian system is thought to begin not with birth but with conception. Observations and speculations on foetal development comprise a large portion of the Ayurvedic literature on the child. The pre-natal period is considered equally important (if not more so) as the period of childhood proper, for the physical and mental development of the individual. This concern with the psychological development of the foetus distinguishes the content of *Balanga* from that of modern embryology. Clearly, the Hindu worldview has played an important role in defining the scope and content of Indian medical specialization dealing with the child—as doubtless western images of the origins of life and the nature of man have informed the training of the modern pediatrician.

Since life is presumed to begin with conception, birth in the Indian tradition is a relatively later event that marks the end of the first stage of the life cycle rather than its beginning. According to the metaphysical doctrine of rebirth and transmigration of the soul, a doctrine shared by ancient Indian medics, it is at the moment of fertilization that the soul, in its 'subtle body' (which includes the mind) from previous life, enters the conceptus. The qualities of the sperm, the ovum, the *rasa* ('organic sap' or 'nutrition') and the soul's 'subtle body'—that is, its psychic constellation from its previous incarnation—are the determinants of the embryo's structural and functional growth.[11]

The critical period for the psychological development of the individual is said to commence from the third month of pregnancy (the fourth, in *Susruta Samhita*), when the latent 'mind' of the foetus becomes 'activated' or 'conscious' (*chetan*). In this stage of *dauhridaya* (literally, 'bi-cardiac'—where one heart belongs to the foetus and the other to the mother), the unborn child and the mother function psychologically as a unit mutually influencing each other. The feelings and affects of the foetus—a legacy from its previous birth—are transmitted to the mother through the channels of nutrition (*dhamanis*). For the future psychic well-being of the individual it is imperative—the texts are unanimous on this point—that the wishes and cravings of the pregnant woman be fully gratified and the unit of expectant mother and foetus be completely indulged. For these desires of the mother, Ayurveda claims, are but the mental strivings of the foetus, deflected and distorted through the prism of the mother's body and psyche. Of course, care should be taken while fulfilling the mother's desires that nothing is done or given to her which is harmful either to her or to her unborn child. If the pregnant woman's longing becomes overwhelming, it is better—the texts go so far in their indulgence—that she be given the desired object even if it is injurious to her health—care being taken to neutralize the object's baneful influence through appropriate countermeasures.[12] Finally, in the Ayurvedic tradition, the desires of the pregnant woman in *dauhridaya* are thought to contain clues to the unborn child's psychological predispositions and character.

For a student of human development, all this is quite fascinating, especially since Ayurveda claims, with much justification, to be a science of rational therapeutics based on the collected observations of a host of ancient doctors. Unfortunately, this claim to empirical validity cannot always be substantiated. Our credulity is strained, and the empirical likelihood of certain observations on child development becomes doubtful, when we read the predicted behaviour of the unborn child— predictions based on the longings of his mother during a particular period of pregnancy. Thus, for instance, the mother's desire to see a king means that the son will become rich and famous; her wish for the fine clothes and ornaments signifies that the child will have an aesthetic nature; her desire to visit a hermitage suggests that the child will be self-controlled; and so on. There is a long list of traits presumed to correlate with the expectant mother's culinary cravings—each craving presaging that the unborn individual will have the traits ascribed to that particular animal or bird. For instance, the expectant mother's wish to eat beef means that her child will grow up into a strong and hardy adult, the craving to eat partridge foretells a timid and fearful disposition, and so on. There are other lists too, cataloguing certain maternal activities and their influence on the foetus; many of the items on these lists have little or no possible basis in observation.

The hypothesized relationship between the feelings and behaviour of the expectant mother and those of her offspring seems closer to the omens, auguries, prophecies and soothsaying of the magical realm of thought. This mixture of genuine medical opinion based on observation and practice on the one hand, and speculations and attitudes deriving from the magico-religious realm on the other, are not only characteristic of the Ayurvedic literature on the child but are a feature of Ayurveda as a whole.[13] However, my purpose is not the evaluation of the scientific merit of Ayurvedic observations on child development. Rather, let me note two prominent Ayurvedic notions that contribute to the Indian *idea* of the child.

The first is that the child, as a subject of study or treatment, cannot be viewed in isolation but must be understood as part of a larger matrix in which the mother-child unit, epitomized in the *dauhridaya* stage of pregnancy, is fundamental. Measures to promote the child's growth or to alleviate its distress are thus to be directed towards this 'unit', whose centre shifts only gradually from the mother to the child. Thus, for example, even as late as the end of the first year after birth, while the child is still being breast fed, many of its diseases are apt to be diagnosed as due to the 'vitiation' of the mother's milk. Therapeutic measures, including the administration of drugs, are directed toward the mother to remove this 'vitiation'. Whatever the medical rationale for these practices, their symbolic and psychological thrust is unmistakable; they emphasize the symbiosis of the mother and child and express the conviction that during the foetal period and for a while after birth, the removal of the mother's tensions and diseases is the key to the child's well-being.[14]

The second central idea in 'Indian child development' is the belief that the basic contours of personality are laid down *in utero*. In contrast with the western, post-Freudian emphasis on early childhood as the vital period for psychological development, this period is relatively underplayed in the Hindu tradition, in favour of the embryonic period, especially the *dauhridaya* stage. It is not correct, however, that the Indian medical tradition has little to say about childhood proper. In fact, the Ayurvedic texts contain detailed and copious instructions on the care of the young child. These wide-ranging instructions—on such diverse topics as the time when a child should be encouraged to sit up or the specification of toys with regard to colour, size, shape and texture—reveal great solicitude concerning the period of infancy and early childhood. The voices of ancient doctors, in spite of the archaic language through which they reach us, sound strangely modern and positively Spockian as they expound on the relationship between child-rearing practices and personality development. The practice of persuading the child to eat or to stop crying by conjuring up threatening visions of ghosts, goblins and ferocious animals, they tell us, is to be avoided since it has a very harmful effect.[15] 'The child should not be awakened from sleep suddenly, they go on to say, nor should he be snatched or thrown up in the air. He should not be irritated, and he should be kept happy at all costs, as this is crucial for his psychological development and future well-being.[16]

In summary, Ayurvedic theory of optimal child development is an intriguing blend of the superstitious and the rational, the arcane and the modern. In its consistently humane attitude towards the child, however, ancient Indian medicine is irreproachable. With compassion and tenderness for the young, Ayurveda strives to develop the adult caretaker's capacity to comprehend the needs and emotions of the child—needs that are apt to be overlooked since they are articulated in voices that are frail and words that are indistinct.

CHILDREN IN THE MAHABHARATA

Of the three hundred and fifty odd references to children in the *Mahabharata*, many are mere records of birth, with perhaps a score having a supplementary verse that eulogizes the infant's physical and mental qualities. Later on in the epic, from the *Drona Parva* onward, 'children' are increasingly mentioned in the context of parental mourning as their sons die in the great war. In these descriptions, however, the child *qua* child is incidental—memories of his play and playfulness serving only to enhance the parents' grief at the loss of an adult son. Arjuna and Subhadra's distraught lamentations at Abhimanyu's death, Yudhishtira's grief when Ghatotkacha is killed, Dhritarashtra's poignant memories of the childhood of his sons, and many other instances of mourning are more evocative of the Hindu concept of death, and designed to help the survivors bear the death of their children with equanimity, rather than with giving us insight into the childhood of those who were slain in the battle.

For the rest, in the *Mahabharata* if there is one predominant child-related theme it is the importance attached to, and the intense longing expressed for, the birth of a son. A number of myths and didactic passages repeatedly emphasize that begetting a son is one of man's highest duties and the only way he can discharge the debt he owes to his ancestors.[17] Consider the story of Jaratkuru.

The renowned ascetic Jaratkuru, full of merit and great spiritual power derived from his sustained asceticism, was wandering around the world when one day he came across a deep pit. In this pit, the spirits of his ancestors—the *pitris*—were hanging head down, their feet tied to a tree trunk by a single skein of rope that was gradually being nibbled away by a large rat. It was evident that the *pitris* would fall down into the deep darkness of the pit. Moved by their pitiable condition, Jaratkuru enquired whether he could somehow save them from this fate, expressing his readiness to do so even if he had to give up all the rewards to which his great asceticism entitled him. 'Venerable *brahmacharin*', the *pitris* answered, 'thou desirest to relieve us! . . . O child, whether it is asceticism, or sacrifice, or whatever else there be of very holy acts, everything is inferior. These cannot count equal to a son. O child, having seen all, speak unto that Jaratkuru of ascetic wealth . . tell him all that would induce him to take a wife and beget children.'[18]

Similarly, the sage Agastya, having failed to procreate, beholds his *pitris* in a like predicament.[19] Another ascetic, Mandapala, is told in no uncertain terms that in spite of his most ascetic efforts, certain celestial regions will forever remain closed to him, for they can be reached only by those who have had children—'Beget children therefore!' Mandapala is instructed; 'Thou shalt then enjoy multifarious regions of felicity!'[20]

Sons in the *Mahabharata* are not only seen as instrumental in the fulfilment of a sacred *duty* which, however agreeable and meritorious, still carries the connotation of religious necessity and social imposition, they are also portrayed as a source of emotional and sensual gratification. Listen to Shakuntala asking Dushyanta to acknowledge his son: 'What happiness is greater than what the father feels when the son is running towards him, even though his body be covered with dust, and clasps his limbs ? Even ants support their own eggs without destroying them, then why shouldst not thou, virtuous as thou art, support thy own child? The touch of soft sandal paste, of women, of (cool) water is not so agreeable as the touch of one's own infant son locked in one's embrace. As a Brahmana is the foremost of all bipeds, a cow, the foremost of all quadrupeds, a protector, the foremost of all superiors, so is the son the foremost of all objects, agreeable to the touch. Let, therefore, this handsome child touch thee in embrace. There is nothing in the world more agreeable to the touch than the embrace of one's son.'[21]

In contrast to the joyous celebration at the birth of sons, girls generally receive a muted if not a totally cold reception. The religious merit reaped at the birth of a daughter is minimal; her entry into the world is accompanied by forebodings on the part of the parents Thus, Indra's charioteer Matali, father of the beauteous Gunakeshi, laments: 'Alas, the birth of a daughter in the families of those that are well-behaved and high-born and possess reputation and humility of character, is always attended with evil results. Daughters, when born in respectable families, always endanger the honour of these families, their maternal and paternal families and the family into which they are adopted by marriage.'[22] And though King Drupada, for very good reasons of his own, wishes for the birth of a son, he seems to go to ludicrous lengths to deny the sex of the daughter who is finally born, futilely begs Shiva to change her sex and (after her birth) conceals her real identity and performs the rites prescribed for a male child.[23]

We find that the random remarks on children scattered throughout the epic do not permit us to discern any single, consistent view of the child. In the rare passages where the ascetic mode prevails, the attitude towards the child, because of the child's strong association with the procreative act, is one of unrelieved disgust. 'In consequence of the keen desire that men entertain for women, offspring proceed from them, due to (the action of) the vital seed. As one casts off from one's body such vermin as take their birth there but as are not on that account any part of oneself, even so should one cast off those vermin of one's body that are called children, who, though regarded as one's own, are not one's own in reality. From the vital seed as from sweat (and other filth) creatures spring from the body, influenced by the acts of previous lives or in the course of nature. Therefore, one possessed of wisdom should feel no regard for them.'[24] As I have indicated above, however, such a life-negating and rejecting attitude towards children is a minor theme in the *Mahabharata*. Most references to children in the text are positive, full of acceptance and a joyous generativity that is actively solicitous and protectively caring of the next generation. Indeed in a few passages the child is thoroughly idealized as a creature 'without desires and aversions'—and thus nearer to God.[25] In other passages, where the Bhakti mode prevails, one of the attributes of God is that of his *being* a child: 'Salutations to thee that art of the form of the rising sun, and that art of the form of a child, that art the protector of attendants (Krishna's cowherds), all of whom are of the form of children.'[26]

On the familiar problem of whether heredity or environment exerts a greater influence on the child's personality, the *Mahabharata* comes down firmly in favour of heredity. Heredity, we must remember, in the *Mahabharata* as in the rest of Indian tradition, is not simply a matter of biology. Together with the father's 'seed', the *karmic* balance from the previous life gives the child certain predispositions that are all-determining in their impact on individual behaviour. The *Mahabharata* thus holds the contribution of 'nurture' during the impressionable childhood years to be negligible, when compared with the influence of 'nature' which it conceives of in terms of a metaphysical biology.

In contrast to the Ayurveda, which accords some recognition to the part played by the mother's 'ovum', the *Mahabharata* is patriarchically imperious in granting legitimacy only to the father's 'seed' in the formation of a son's personality. There are many passages in the text with an identical refrain : namely, that the father himself is born as the son, and with the placing of his seed in the womb he has placed his own self.[27] Child-rearing practices and the environment of the early years cannot alter the basic nature of the child, which has received this strong 'biological' stamp. This view comes through clearly in the story of Matanga, who was sired by a Shudra but adopted at birth by a Brahman. The Brahman brought Matanga up as his own son and with due performance of all the rites of infancy and childhood ordained for Brahmans. One day, Matanga was asked by his father to fetch some materials speedily for a sacrifice. Matanga set out on a cart drawn by a young ass, who, instead of obeying the carter, set out in the direction of its mother. Angry, Matanga began to strike the animal on its nose with a goad. On seeing these marks of violence on her offspring's nose, the she-ass said: 'Do not grieve, O child, for this treatment. A *chandala* it is that is driving thee . . . He is simply proving the order of his birth by conducting himself in this way. The nature which he hath derived from his sire forbids the rise of those sentiments of pity and kindness that are natural to the Brahmana.'[28]

We may then conclude that the *Mahabharata* elaborates and deepens our understanding of the two themes in the traditional Indian view of childhood encountered in ancient law and medicine. First, there is an intense parental longing for children, and their upbringing is characterized by affectionate indulgence. This 'child-centredness', however, as the *Mahabharata* makes clear, is limited to boys: the Indian tradition is indifferent, if not overtly hostile, to the developmental fate of girls. Secondly, the Indian tradition subscribes to an ideology that downgrades the role of the environment and nurture in the development of a child, and instead emphasizes a deterministic conception of mystical heredity. Whereas in Ayurveda this mystical heredity is still loose and composed of many factors, in the *Mahabharata* it is reduced to the *karmas* of the previous life and the attributes of the father (especially his caste) transmitted through his 'seed'.

THE CHILD IN LITERATURE

In classical Sanskrit literature, children rarely figure as individuals in their own right, with activities, reactions and feelings separate from those of their all-powerful parents. The child usually appears as a wish—that is, in the context of a couple's, or more often a father's, longing for offspring—or as the fulfilment of the wish—in descriptions of parental happiness when a child is born and in lyrical accounts of parental love, usually of a father for his son. Thus, to take two well-known examples, Bhavabhuti describes Rama's love for Lava and Kusha, while Banabhatta rhapsodizes over Prabhakarvardhan's love for his son, Harsha.[29] The greatest of all Sanskrit poets, Kalidasa, both follows and deviates somewhat from this pattern. He too is lyrical about the father's feeling for his child, for instance, in his descriptions of Dushyanta's feelings for his son Sarvadamana and of Dilip's love for Raghu in *Raghuvamsha*. Here is Dilip's response to Raghu's birth:

He went in immediately [on hearing the news] and as the lotus becomes motionless when the breeze stops, he gazed at his son's face with the same still eyes. Just as tides come into the ocean when it sees the moon, similarly the King [Dilip] was so happy on seeing his son that he could not contain the happiness in his heart.[30]

However, in addition, Kalidasa sensitively portrays, with much empathy, the sage Kanva's love for his *daughter* Shakuntala.

Classical Sanskrit literature is not a living tradition in the same sense that classical law and traditional medicine are; rather, its influence is indirect and hard to pin down. For an account of children and childhood in the Indian literary tradition, we must turn to the classics of the regional languages. Here, however, I will tap only one literary stream, the medieval Hindi literature associated with the Bhakti movement, and look especially at the poems and songs of Surdas and Tulsidas. My reasons for choosing Bhakti-inspired literature (in addition to its accessibility) are not hard to comprehend. First, this is the most powerful surviving literary tradition in the Hindi-speaking belt of northern and central India. Through the continuing popularity of its songs and poems, it has moulded folk consciousness in a way that is rare for *any* literature. Second, this literature in general, and the poems of Surdas in particular, are unique among the literary traditions of the world (as far as I know) in that children and childhood—Krishna's childhood in Surdas and Rama's childhood in Tulsidas—are placed close to the centre of poetic consciousness and creativity; rather than at its periphery. Surdas, in fact, composed five hundred verses on Krishna's childhood alone![31] Apart from their religious significance, these verses are a rich source for Hindu ideals of childhood and for delineating the topography of a culturally approved utopia of childhood.

A concept such as the 'utopia of childhood' suggests that I will treat the literary material on the child somewhat differently from similar material in legal and medical texts. Whereas with law and medicine the effort was to summarize and rearrange the scattered textual material on the child into unified and coherent constructs, here with the literature, I propose to add, and *consciously* emphasize, a point of view. This point of view is frankly psychological. It is based on the assumption that poetic descriptions of the infancy and childhood of Krishna and Rama also contain certain desires that both *relate* to, and *derive* from, the period of childhood. These desires, often not conscious, constitute the *fantasy* of childhood, which is not idiosyncratic to the poet–creators but instead, by virtue of being widely shared by audiences through the centuries, has acquired the status of an Indian child–utopia. Before we consider the main themes of this child–utopia, however, let us look at its genesis and position in the Bhakti literature more closely.

The religious poetry of the Bhakti—the devotional approach to the Divine—is chiefly of two types. In one, the poet (and through him, the devotee) places himself in relation to the Godhead as a child to his parent; he seeks forgiveness for transgressions and tries to evoke the parental response of nurturance. This is, of course, a common theme in the religious literatures of the world, although Indian Bhakti poetry differs from devotional literature in other societies by the fact that it conceives of the Divine in terms of a maternal rather than a paternal matrix. To give two brief illustrations : the first a short poem by Kabir (fifteenth century):

> Mother, I am your child
> Why not forgive my faults?
> The child misbehaves on many days.
> They are not the days the mother remembers.
> He catches her hair and hits her.
> She does not reduce her affection.
> Kabir says, it is evident.
> A child's unhappiness is the mother's pain.[32]

The second is by the Bengali religious poet Ramprasad (seventeenth century):

> O Mother! my desires are unfulfilled;
> My hopes are ungratified;
> But my life is fast coming to an end.
> Let me call Thee, Mother, for the last time;
> Come and take me in Thy arms.
> None loves in this world;
> This world knows not how to love;
> My heart yearns, O Mother, to go there,
> Where Love reigns supreme.[33]

Both these songs mirror a widespread, and perhaps universal, pattern of spiritual longing for a transcendence of separation from the Godhead. The attributes of the child (devotee) emphasized in this poetry are his yearning for infinite and unconditional love, the wish for a forgiving acceptance of his imperfections, and his search for the caretaker's responsive face.

The uniqueness of Bhakti poetry, however, lies more in its second school, where we find a surprising reversal. Here the poet (devotee) is as a mother towards God, who is the child. The celebration of the Divine, as in Surdas's poems of Krishna, takes place through the metaphor of celebration of the child. The aspects that are admiringly emphasized as divine attributes, as Kinsley has pointed out, are the child's freedom and spontaneity, his simplicity, charm and delight in self.[34]

> Krishna is singing in the courtyard.
> He dances on his small feet, joyous within.
> Lifting up his arms, he shouts for the black
>   and white cows.
> Sometimes he calls Nandbaba, sometimes he

goes in and out of the house.
Seeing his reflection, he tries to feed it.
Hidden, Yashoda watches the play that makes
  her so happy.
Surdas says, to see Krishna's play every day
  is bliss.[35]

Tulsidas sings:

Self-willed he [Rama] insists on having the moon.
He sees his shadow and is frightened.
Clapping his hands, he dances.
Seeing his child-play
All mother-hearts are brimming over with happiness.
Becoming angry, he is obstinate.
And remains stubborn till he gets what he wants.
Tulsidas says, the sons of the King of Ayodhya live
In the temple of his heart.[36]

In an adult-centred world that overvalues abstractions, prudence and reason, it is refreshing to find Bhakti poetry celebrating such childlike virtues as intensity and vivaciousness, capacity for sorrow and delight, mercurial anger and an equally quick readiness to forget and forgive injuries. In the Indian child–utopia these qualities are not seen as 'childish', to be socialized out of existence, but valuable attributes of human beings—of all ages—since they are but an expression of the Divine.

The second theme in the child–utopia of Bhakti poetry is the rapt play between mother and child. In poem after poem, we see Yashoda and Krishna, Kausalya and Rama, playfully, even blissfully, absorbed in each other. They are portrayed as oblivious to their surroundings, existing in a 'temporary world within the ordinary world, dedicated to the performance of an act apart'.[37] In this world, nothing exists for the mother but the child; the smallest expression of his being enhances the mother's erotic and affiliative leeway. Yashoda, for instance, is so full of joy at seeing Krishna's milk-teeth that, absorbed in her love for him, she loses consciousness of her own body. It is in these scenes of mother–child interplay that the Bhakti poets come into their own.
Surdas writes:

O Nanda's small Krishna, leave the butter-churn.
Again and again says Yashoda, Nanda's queen.

> Move to one side, my life, my wealth, I'll give
> you the butter.
> My priceless treasure, do not be obstinate.
> He [Krishna] who is meditated upon by all beings
> Is kissed on the face by Yashoda and lifted upon
> her shoulder:[38]

Similarly, Tulsidas:

> Queen Kausalya, with the beautiful Rama in her
> lap, is gracing the bed.
> Her eyes turned into *chakors*, they fly to Rama's
> face like the moon.
> Sometimes she lies down and gives him her breast.
> Sometimes she presses him to her heart.
> Singing of his child-play, she is happily absorbed
> in drinking the nectar of love.
> Behind the clouds, Brahma, Shiva, sages and the
> gods look on with happiness.
> Tulsidas says, no one but Kausalya ever had such
> bliss.[39]

Analogous to the mother child interplay, or rather as its extension, we find a third theme in Bhakti literature, in which the child is at the centre of an admiring circle of adults. If the mother is in the foreground, then the background consists of the adults in the community—the *gopis* of Gokul, the citizens of Ayodhya—milling around him. This particular theme reveals the child's primary need to be central to his world, rather than exist forlornly at its outskirts, to cause a glow in the eyes of adults rather than be looked at with indifference.

In medieval Bhakti literature, then, the child is truly an exalted being. To grow up at the centre of his human world, absorbed in interplay with the mother, admired for his spontaneity and self delight, seem to be the poet's conception of a child's 'birthright'—the utopia of Indian childhood.

STAGES OF CHILDHOOD IN THE INDIAN TRADITION

The conceptualization of the human life cycle unfolding in a series of stages, with each stage having its unique 'tasks' and the need for an orderly progression through the stages, is an established part of traditional

Indian thought, best exemplified in the well-known scheme of *ash-ramadharma*.[40] *Ashramadharma*, however, focuses largely on the period of youth and adulthood, and neglects to assign any formal importance to the stages of childhood. For an understanding of how these stages have been envisioned in the Indian tradition, we must turn to Ayurveda and the ritual literature that describes the childhood *samskaras*—the expressive and symbolic performances, including rites and ceremonies that are so to speak held over the child and mark his transition from one stage to another. Parenthetically, I should perhaps add that the concept of a child developing through a series of stages requiring differential treatment by his caretakers, a notion that some historians of western childhood consider 'modern', has always been a part of Indian folk-consciousness. It is expressed through such proverbs as 'Treat a son like a king for the first five years, like a slave for the next ten, and like a friend thereafter.'

The contribution of Ayurveda to the Indian image of childhood stages lies in its *formal* recognition of different periods of childhood and its assignment of 'appropriate' ages to each period. Consistent with the belief that life begins with conception rather than at birth, Ayurveda identifies five such childhood periods: (1) *Garbha*, or the foetal period; (2) *Ksheerda* (0-6 months), when the infant lives entirely on milk; (3) *Ksheerannada* (6 months-2 years), the period of early childhood in which weaning takes place; (4) *Bala* (2–5 years); and (5) *Kumara* (5–16) years.[41] As we shall see, this division of childhood is reflected and affirmed by ritual literature, in so far as the major rituals of childhood take place at ages that mark the transition from one period to another.

Looking at the timing and content of the various childhood *samskaras*, it appears that one of the major thrusts of these rituals is the gradual integration of the child into society, with the *samskaras*, as it were, beating time to a measured movement that takes the child away from the original mother-infant symbiosis into full-fledged membership in his community. Psychologically, through their periodic ritual reassurance of familiarity and mutuality, the *samskaras* seek to counteract the child's regressive longings and primal fears of abandonment and separation, which are invariably activated in the transition from one stage of life to another. By ceremoniously marking the transition points of a widening world of childhood and placing the child at the centre of rites that also command the intense participation of the whole family, the *samskaras* heighten a sense of both belonging and personal distinctiveness—that is, they strengthen the child's budding sense of identity.[42] Let us look at the major *samskaras* that mark the critical points of social development more closely.

A month after birth, in the naming rite of *namakarana*, the mother and infant emerge from the seclusion of the maternity room into the bustle of an expectant family, as the mother ceremoniously places the baby in the father's lap for the name-giving ceremony.[43] From the family, the mother and infant move into the wider world in the third or fourth month with the performance of *nishkramana*, the child's first outing or 'looking at the sun' and 'looking at the moon', as the texts poetically describe the infant's ritual introduction to the world and the cosmos. Between the sixth and ninth months, there is the important rite of *annaprasana*, the first time the child is given solid food, thus marking the onset of weaning and its psychological counterpart—the process of the child's individuation and separation from the mother.

If these rites are any guide, the process of individuation is deemed complete by the third year. At three, the child's 'psychological birth' is marked by the important rites of *chudakarana* or tonsure. The child is generally taken to the temple of a mother goddess (to the bank of a river in some regions) and his baby hair shaved and offered to the goddess. He is then dressed up in new clothes, which are a miniature replica of the clothes worn by adult members of his community. The symbolism of death and rebirth—in our terms, the death of the mother–infant symbiosis and the psychological birth of the child as a separate individual—is at the heart of the many rituals connected with *chudakarana*. Thus, for instance, in the Bhojpuri region of northern India, before the child's head is shaved and he is dressed in new clothes, the women of the family take the child to the Ganges and ceremoniously cross the river in a boat.[44] Moreover, the folk songs sung at the time of *mundan* (as the *samskara* is called in north India) are the *sohras*, the songs that are also sung at birth. In the popular tradition, it is only after the child's tonsure that he is considered ready for the process of discipline and the family's socialization efforts.

The rite of *vidyarambha* between the fifth and seventh years, when the child is supposed to be old enough to learn to read and write, is followed by the major *samskara* of *upanayana*. *Upanayana* marks the culmination, the grand end of childhood. Traditionally performed (depending upon the caste) anywhere between the eighth and twelfth year, *upanayana* initiates the child's 'social birth' into the wider community. As a text puts it, 'Till a boy is eight years old he is like one newly born, and only indicates the caste in which he is born. As long as his *upanayana* ceremony is not performed the boy incurs no blame as to what is allowed or forbidden.'[45] The initiation ceremony is elaborate, its preparatory rites designed to drive home the fact of the child's separation from his family and the final break with his mother. In its traditional version, the child is smeared with a yellowish paste and expected to spend the whole night in a pitch-dark room in absolute silence—a re-creation of the embryonic state—before he emerges the next morning for one of the most moving and poignant ceremonies of this *samskara*, the sharing of a meal with his mother, which is the last time the mother and son will ever eat together. Thus although as an initiation rite, *upanayana* contains many rituals symbolizing a hopeful beginning, it nevertheless also clearly marks the regretted end of a familial and familiar world—the world of childhood.

The question of the extent to which this traditional image of the stages of childhood remains part of modern consciousness is difficult to answer with any certainty. We do know that most of the childhood *samskaras*, especially those of birth, tonsure and initiation, are performed in the case of boys of the upper and intermediate castes in the same order and at approximately the same ages as outlined above.[46]

In fact, the omnibus reference to the 'child' in the discussion of the stages of childhood in the Indian tradition conceals two omissions: girls and children belonging to the lower castes have been largely excluded from this tradition—as indeed women and the lower castes have been excluded from most of the prescriptions and formulations of the Hindu tradition. To take just one example, the *sohras*—the joyous songs of celebration sung at the birth of a child in the Hindi-speaking belt—are almost never sung for newborn daughters. Indeed, many *sohras* express the mother's relief that this has not been the case and her worst fears have proven to be unfounded : 'As the *turiyan* leaf trembles with a gust of wind, my heart trembles at the thought that I may give birth to a daughter.'[47] With the proviso that 'child' primarily refers to a boy belonging to one of the upper castes and that the ages shown under each stage of childhood are only approximate or, more precisely, that they are the 'usual' ages,[48] the Hindu scheme of social development of the child can be schematically presented as in the chart below (see p. 81).

TRADITIONS OF CHILDHOAD: INDIAN AND WESTERN

Considering its fateful implications for the lives of children—and adults—the highlighting of a society's traditions of childhood, the historically derived pattern of deprivations and compensations offered to its children, becomes an important task. For this task to be properly fulfilled, one would also expect that the Indian tradition of childhood would be compared and contrasted with the childhood traditions of other societies. Such a comparative perspective, besides highlighting specific elements of one's own tradition, can also be socially therapeutic in so far as it shows us the range of human caretaking patterns that lie between the necessary minimum to keep the child physically and emotionally alive and the anxious maximum beyond which the child's development is apt to be stunted. Such a systematic comparison with other traditions cannot be attempted here, especially since for most societies (including the Indian) the histories of childhood still remain to be written. In conclusion, therefore, I shall content myself with noting a few impressions of the contrast between the Indian and western traditions of childhood.

Stages of Childhood: The Hindu Scheme of Social Development

Childhood period	Stage	Central mode of relationship	Rite marking transition into following stage
I. *Garbha*	1. Foetus	Symbiotic ('*dauhridya*')	*Jatakarma*
II. *Ksheerda*	2. Early infancy (0–1 month)	Dyadic intimacy	*Namakarana*
	3. Middle infancy (1–3/4 months)	Dyad in family	*Nishkramana*
	4. Late infancy (3/4–6/9 months)	Dyad in world	*Annaprasana*
III *Ksheeranna da*	5. Early childhood (6/9 months–2/3 years)	Dyadic dissolution (psychological birth)	*Chudakarana*
IV *Bala*	6. Middle childhood (2/3–5/7 years)	Familial	*Vidyarambha*
V *Kumara*	7. Late childhood (5/7–8/12 years)	Familial dissolution (social birth)	*Upanayana*

For an Indian, the most striking aspect of recent western scholarship on childhood is its depiction of an enduring ideological conflict between the rejecting and accepting attitudes towards the child[49] Some western scholars of childhood have discerned a definite movement within this conflict, a steady evolution that has made the western ideology of the child increasingly humane and nurturant.[50] In western antiquity and till perhaps the thirteenth century, adult attitudes toward children were generally dominated by an ideology that had little empathy for the needs of children. This ideology looked upon the child as a nuisance and an unwanted burden, perfunctorily tolerating brutal treatment of children by their parents as well as such associated phenomena as infanticide, the sale of children and their casual abandonment.[51] It is, however, also demonstrable that there has been a gradual progression in the western ideology of the child. From the earlier external suppression that permitted the grossest physical torture and when sexual abuse of children was commonplace, by the sixteenth and seventeenth centuries the ideological emphasis was decisively shifting towards an *internal* suppression in which child training and discipline were stressed. Here, for instance, is how an eminent scholar of the American family describes attitudes towards the child in colonial America: 'And what of the young in colonial America? There remain from the period various books and essays on the proper deportment of children, which convey some impression at least of what was expected. A central theme in these works—especially, but not exclusively, in the writings of the Puritans—is the need to impose strict discipline on the child virtually from the beginning of life. Here is the advice of Reverend John Robinson, a leading preacher among the Pilgrims just prior to their departure for America: "Surely there is in all children . . . a stubbornness and stoutness of mind arising from natural pride which must in the first place be broken and beaten down, so that the foundation of their education being laid in humility and tractableness, other virtues may in their time be built thereon." The key terms are "broken" and "beaten down". The child was regarded as coming into the world with an inherently corrupted and selfish nature, and this created *the* central problem for parents.'[52]

From parental efforts aimed at conquering the child's will, the western ideology of caretaking progressed further towards according the child a greater freedom, as in the nineteenth and twentieth centuries awareness of the sensibilities and needs of children increased appreciably. This movement towards the fostering attitude continues unabated. The spate of recent books on the rights of children, the effect of working mothers on the development of children, 'The Year of the Child' announced by the United Nations and so on, are some of the expressions of this progress: current manifestations of an old movement towards evolving an ideology of childhood which makes the child and its needs central to the caretaking process.

The conflict between the rejecting and fostering attitudes towards the child, so marked in the western tradition and which perhaps provides it with its evolutionary impetus, is simply not a feature of the Indian tradition. As we have seen in this essay, the evidence from textual sources is overwhelming that the child in Indian tradition is ideologically considered a valuable and welcome human being to whom the adults are expected to afford their fullest protection, affection and indulgence. Consider, for instance, the reflection of this ideology in linguistic usage where the notion of the child being autonomous and self-directing is much more pronounced than in English or German. In Hindi for example, what adults do to children is *palana–posana*—protecting–nurturing; they are not 'reared', 'brought up'. With its implications of training the child, teaching him to conform to social norms and 'channelling his impulses', the model of *socialization* (which governs contemporary western caretaking) is a logical next step in a historical evolution where the preceding model was that of disciplining and conquering the child's will. In its general orientation and focus, such a model is necessarily foreign to the Indian tradition that did not have to overcome an original burden of rejection of children. In fact, as we saw in our discussion of the child–utopia that is reflected in Bhakti songs and poems, there is a specific stream in the Indian tradition of childhood that values precisely those attributes of the child which have *not* been 'socialized'. In this tradition, it is the child who is considered nearest to a perfect, divine state and it is the adult who needs to learn the child's mode of experiencing the world. Here the proper form of interaction between adults and children is not conceived of in terms of socialization but *interplay*. Closer to that Indian tradition, interplay as a paradigm of growing up would emphasize the *adult–child unit,* concern itself with their *mutual* learning and mutual pleasure in each other. It would thus sharply differ from the socialization model that concentrates solely on the child and his movement towards adulthood.

Before losing ourselves in any self-congratulatory panegyrics, we must also note the gravest drawback of the Indian tradition—its relative rejection of girls. By rejection I do not mean to imply that the texts we have considered show any great hostility or contain instances of dramatic and overt violence towards female children. Even in the myths of abandonment of children in the *Mahabharata*, Menaka's abandonment of her new-born daughters Pramadvara and Shakuntala is counter-balanced by Kunti abandoning the infant Karna. It is more in its exaggerated emphasis on sons, in the joyous din at the birth of male children, that the silent rejection of female infants stands out so clearly and has had such grave consequences for Indian women and society. Again, by 'grave consequences' I am not alluding to the failure of Indian tradition to erect an ideological bulwark against female infanticide among certain castes at certain periods of history. Infanticide by sheer violence has probably always been exceptional all over the world. Rejection, or at best, ambivalence towards girls has always worked (and continues to do so) in a more subtle and insidious manner. It is reflected in statistics that show a higher rate of female infant mortality and underlies the crushed spirit of countless women for which no statistics but only folk-songs are available. Without the removal of this ambivalence towards the female child, without an ideological change that will ensure society's protection and nurturance to *all* its children, the Indian tradition of childhood, with all its dazzling 'achievement' remains gravely flawed.

3

The Revolutionary Yogi:
Childhood of Swami Vivekananda

To identify and understand those specific constellations in the Indian
inner world that help or hinder an individual's efforts to adapt to rapidly
changing historical circumstances, I intend to go back in history to the
nineteenth century and consider the life and work of Swami Vivekananda, a man who was both a passionate proponent of the traditional Hindu
world-image and a prophet of change in the modern western sense. In-
trospective yogi and activist monk, sensitive poet and fiery orator, a
religious philosopher who reinterpreted ancient Hindu thought to make
it more accessible to modern consciousness and who, at the same time,
was the dynamic organizer of the Ramakrishna Order of monks,
Vivekananda is one of the most fascinating figures in the history of
modern India. On the one hand, as a practising yogi and religious
teacher in the ancient Indian tradition of the sage–guru, he exhorted his
countrymen to make the traditional ideals of enhancement of the inner
world and fusion of 'I' and the 'Other' a living actuality in everyday
life. Yet, on the other hand, he was also a firm believer in the value of
activity directed towards necessary social change, a dedicated advocate
of furthering scientific and technical education among Indians and the
founder of an order of monks who not only took the traditional vows of
personal striving for *moksha* but gave a new, unprecedented pledge of
service to the Indian masses, a pledge that was carried out in mundane
activities such as the running of schools, orphanages, dispensaries and
relief campaigns during famines and epidemics.

In the political sphere, Vivekananda synthesized apparent cultural
contradictions in a new nationalism that combined both religious and
political ideals; redemption from alien subjection became both a

patriotic and religious duty, the means to immediate independence and ultimate salvation too. A western disciple, Sister Nivedita, described Vivekananda thus:

In his consciousness, the ancient light of the mood in which man comes face to face with God might shine, but it shone on all those questions and all those puzzles which are present to the thinkers and workers of the modern world. . . . I see in him the heir to the spiritual discoveries and religious struggles of innumerable teachers and saints in the past of India and the world, and at the same time the pioneer and prophet of a new and future order of development.[1]

From all accounts, those of disciples, contemporaries and biographers, the man himself must have had a tremendous—there is no other word for it—*presence*. As in descriptions of all charismatic leaders credited with this quality of magnetic presence, Vivekananda's counterplayers emphasize that particular aspect of his personality that is most meaningful in the context of their own lives, while aware that the essence of the man's charisma is indefinable. Thus some stress Vivekananda's vigour and vitality, others his tenderness and serenity; some talk of the luminous profundity of his eyes, others of a Savonarola-like fearless outspokenness; some marvel at his power and lucid intellectuality while others admire his spirituality.

In historical retrospect, Vivekananda stands out as a leader of prodigious faith and scepticism, a catalyst of India's national consciousness. In psychological terms, Vivekananda created, as he represented, an early version of modern Indian identity. In the last part of the nineteenth century, as Indian society began to recover from its first intoxication with the West and to resist the political domination of Britain, Vivekananda's speeches and writings provided a rudder of self-respect and intellectual *explication* for the emerging militant nationalist movement. Because of its roots deep within the Indian tradition and because of its implications for the future shape of Indian polity, the ideology of nineteenth-century nationalism is more significant, in a psycho-historical sense, than the disintegration of its political organization soon after Vivekananda's death. The development of the ideology of militant nationalism, the religious basis of patriotism, the concept of the nation as an organic spirit, the importance of popular identification with the nation and mass participation in its self assertion, psychological and cultural self confidence as a necessary prelude to political action and finally, the qualified legitimacy of revolutionary violence: this is Vivekananda's legacy.[2]

In Vivekananda's view, the development of a modern Indian identity had only one legitimate basis: the traditional Hindu world-image. The past, he believed, had to be retrieved, in fact essentially rediscovered, before a modern Indian national identity could emerge and take shape and become powerful in the world of nations, In a speech at Madras, on his triumphant return from the United States in 1897, he stated this conviction with passion:

Each nation, like each individual, has one theme in this life which is its centre, the principal note around which every other note comes to form the harmony. If any one nation attempts to throw off its national vitality, the direction which has become its own through the transmission of centuries, that nation dies . . . In one nation political power is its vitality, as in England. Artistic life, in another, and so on. In India religious life forms the centre, the key-note of the whole music of the national life. And therefore, if you succeed in the attempt to throw off your religion and take up either politics or society, the result will be that you will become extinct. Social reform and politics have to be preached through the vitality of your religion. . . . Every man has to make his own choice; so has every nation. We made our choice ages ago.[3]

Vivekananda was passionately convinced that the regeneration of religious vitality required a massive effort in raising cultural consciousness so that the Hindu world-image would come to pervade every form of individual and social endeavour, which in turn called for elementary measures of economic and sheer physical emancipation. Religion cannot be preached to empty bellies, he asserted. Or, as Bertolt Brecht would later put it, '*Erst kommt das Fressen und dann die Moral*' ('Eating comes first, morality later'). The Indian masses had to become strong, had first to gain pride and faith in themselves; the energy that had for so long gone into the mortification of the body needed now, to meet modern tests, to be directed towards the development of physical strength:

No more is this the time for us to become soft. This softness has been with us till we have become like masses of cotton. What our country now wants is muscles of iron and nerves of steel, gigantic will, which nothing can resist, which can accomplish their purpose in any fashion, even if it means going down to the bottom of the ocean and meeting death face to face. That is what we want, and that can only be created, established, and strengthened by understanding and realizing the ideal of Advaita, that ideal of the oneness of all. Faith, faith, faith in ourselves! . . . Not the English; it is we who are responsible for all our degradation. Our aristocratic ancestors went on treading the common masses of our country underfoot till they became helpless, till under this torment the poor, poor people nearly forgot that they were human beings. They have been compelled to be merely hewers of wood and drawers of water for centuries, so that they are made to believe that they are born as slaves, born as hewers of wood and drawers of water.[4]

Vivekananda's answer to Indian dependence was activism:

We want that energy, that love of independence, that spirit of self-reliance, that immovable fortitude, that dexterity in action, that bond of unity of purpose, that thirst for improvement checking a little the constant looking back to the past, we want that extensive vision infinitely projected forward; and we want that intense spirit of activity (*Rajas*) which will flow through every vein, from head to foot.[5]

In periods of emotional strain—and intense, 'altered' mental states were a recurring feature of his life—Vivekananda's assertive imagery of struggle directed outward would give way to that of acceptance, passivity and turning inward. In the aftermath of these periods of emotional crisis, he was wont to maintain that the ideas of activity and progress were delusions. Things never got better; they remained as they were. Only individuals grew better through the changes they made in themselves: 'The musk deer, after vain search for the cause of the scent of the musk, at last will have to find it in himself.'[6] After an especially severe crisis at the age of thirty-five, four years before his death in Calcutta, Vivekananda gravely informed his disciples that he had been all wrong and that his patriotism and zeal as a nationalist reformer had completely vanished. Two years later, in a letter to a friend, he could write: 'And work? What is work? Whose work? Whom to work for? I am free. I am Mother's* child. She works, She plays. Why should I plan? What shall I plan? Things came and went, just as She liked, without my planning, in spite of planning. We are Her automata. She is the wire-puller.'[7]

A great man's contradictions are an integral part of his greatness; they may indeed fuel his historic initiatives. As Erikson in his biography of Luther, another *homo religiosus*, emphasizes, the state of inner repose, a simple enjoyment of life, an ordinary decency and conflict-free sense of purpose and direction are not the lot of intensely creative men with a sense of their own historical destiny.[8] Although I reject the pathographic approach which would diagnose Vivekananda as a 'classic' manic-depressive, the hagiographic adulation of his direct and indirect disciples, Nivedita and Nikhilananda, and admirers like Romain

---

*The Great Goddess.

Rolland, who explain Vivekananda's heightened propensity for emotional conflict, his mystical visions and intense mental experiences as
an expression of the Divine, the manifestation of a spiritual 'supra-
consciousness', doesn't tell us much either. Rather, I intend to bring the
insights of psycho-analytic psychology to bear on some aspects of
Vivekananda's life and to try to weave a pattern of meaning (not
causality) from the tangled threads of conflict and contradiction. My
purpose is threefold: first, to identify the principal motivational themes
of Vivekananda's life and thus to show that the divergent facts of his
personality do indeed have a core of psychological consistency; second,
to trace in a concrete life history some of the themes I have suggested
are characteristic of a modal Indian personality; and third, to illustrate
the psychological dilemma of modernization in the life of a charismatic
Indian leader.

Narendranath*—or Naren, as he was affectionately called as a boy—
was born in Calcutta in January, 1863 in a Bengali upper-middle class
family belonging to the Kayastha community. The Kayasthas, one of
the higher castes of Hindu society, are mentioned in early Sanskrit texts
as hereditary government officials, although the community probably
crystallized as a separate *jati* around the thirteenth century. Staffing the
bureaucracies of the princely states through the many upheavals of Indian history, the Kayasthas proved to be an adaptable people, capable
and willing to adopt the mores and even the language of the rulers they
successively (and successfully) served—whether they were Muslim or
British. Thus, whereas in the period of Muslim rule, they had diligently
learned Persian, when the British conquered Bengal the Kayasthas
quickly became proficient in English. Given the nature of their occupation and their access to those who ruled, the Kayasthas were always in
the front lines of the cultural confrontation that attends imperial conquest. In the eighteenth and nineteenth centuries, the Kayasthas were
one of the first Hindu communities to be exposed to the new social and
ethical philosophies emanating from the West. Together with the other
communities of Bengal's traditional intelligentsia, the Brahmins and the
Vaidyas, the Kayasthas reacted strongly to the British cultural penetration of a conservative society, as ever larger numbers experienced the
inner conflicts aroused by cultural and social dislocation. The first
response of many was a revolt against the restraining norms of Hindu

*Vivekananda's real name.

tradition and an indiscriminate acceptance of all things British. Caught in the cultural cross-current and uniquely sensitive to it, this traditional intelligentsia initiated the early movements to reform the conservative Hindu social order. In fact, as early as the 1850s, one of Naren's uncles was writing pamphlets on such subjects as the education of Indian women and the unequal distribution of land and wealth—causes which Vivekananda later adopted and 'radicalized'.

During Naren's childhood in the latter part of the nineteenth century, the conflict between the old, Brahmin-dominated Hindu orthodoxy and the new, British-inspired liberalism championed by many members of his community was at its peak. As his brother writes, 'He was born when Hindu society was again on the road to regain its dynamism. In his own Kayastha community the blow fell terribly. Parents and sons, husbands and wives used to be separated because the son either has changed his religion or has become a reformer or has gone to England for study.'[9] Many of the more progressive members of the community who had not identified with the British in India, nevertheless saw in the western scientific and rationalist world-view a means of purging Indian social institutions of the dead weight of tradition. But once the seeds of self criticism had been sown among these sensitive Bengali intellectuals, it was not long before their uncritical emulation of the British developed into hypercritical ambivalence, then rejection, and finally into a revival of hyperbolic reverence for the Hindu tradition. Thus, to understand Naren's intellectual and psychological development fully, we must bear in mind the ideological instability (perhaps chronic to Bengal) of his time which manifested itself acutely—paradigmatically—among the members of his community.

Naren's father, Vishwanath Datta, was a lawyer practising at the Calcutta High Court. He was westernized and 'modern', a man well-versed in Persian and English literature, agnostic in religious outlook, and a *bon vivant* who is said to have thoroughly enjoyed the good things of this world. I have an impression of him as the prototype of the modern Indian who moves in the professional and business circles of large Indian cities, although one hundred years ago this new class of westernized Indians was confined to small oases in Calcutta, Bombay and Madras. Viswanath Datta was a member of India's new professional class, which was beginning to provide civil servants, military and police officials, engineers, doctors, teachers and other professionals, the vanguard of modernization.

Naren's mother, Bhuvaneshwari Devi, was a traditional Hindu

woman. Deeply religious, steeped in Puranic mythology and lore she took her cosmology and values from the ideals of the *Ramayana* and *Mahabharata*, the repository of Hindu culture. Indeed, she could recite large portions of the beloved epics from memory. Bhuvaneshwari Devi, with her religious piety, steadfast devotion to tradition and calm efficiency in running the household, typified in the eyes of her sons the ideal of Indian womanhood. This combination of a westernized father and a traditional Hindu mother is not uncommon in the higher castes and upper-middle classes of India even today; it is a striking fact that many of India's leaders during the nationalist movement and since independence are the offspring of this parental combination.

Naren was born into an extended family in which his father's uncle was the *pater familias*. In addition to Vishwanath, his wife and children, the family included the large families of the uncle's two sons (Vishwanath's cousins). Naren's mother's place in this family was that of the outsider with manifold obligations to other family members and very few rights or enjoyments. She was necessarily a dutiful and compliant daughter-in-law and her husband was not a son but a nephew of the family. Her status in the family hierarchy was minimal, and she suffered a great deal under the strict regimen of her husband's aunt, the female head of the family.[10] Before Naren's birth, his mother had borne one son and four daughters, but the son and two daughters had died in infancy. Given these circumstances, it is not difficult to imagine her longing for a son during this, her sixth, confinement. We are told that while Naren was still in the womb, Bhuvaneshwari Devi, as other pious Hindu mothers then and since, took religious vows, prayed and fasted that she might be blessed with a son. Especially she prayed to Shiva; and it is reported that 'one night she dreamt that this supreme Deity aroused himself from his meditation and agreed to be born as her son. When she awoke she was filled with joy.'[11] We cannot know of course whether the dream is a fact, or one of those adventitious legends that grow up around the 'birth of a hero'. Apocryphal or not, it reveals the mother's devotional attitude and emotional investment in the infant Naren. She named him Vireshwara at first, after Shiva, a name the family later changed to Narendranath. To Bhuvaneshwari Devi; her eldest living son was a special object of maternal affection and ministration. In later life, Vivekananda too rarely talked about his father but often of his mother's 'unselfish love and purity', maintaining that his mother was the one being in the world, if any, whom he loved.

Naren's unique position among Bhuvaneshwari Devi's many

children comes through clearly in a biography of Vivekananda written by his younger brother, Bhupendranath. Although the purpose of this book is to highlight Vivekananda's contributions to modern India, its reminiscences reveal something of the younger brother's rivalry and envy towards the mother's favourite. Thus, after a stint in jail for his revolutionary activity against the British, which had been given wide press coverage, Bhupendranath 'jokingly' remarks to his mother, 'You never got any recognition for being Vivekananda's mother, but you got public reception for being my mother'.[12] On another occasion, when Vivekananda's American disciples ask to meet his mother, Bhupendranath prohibits such a meeting, exclaiming to her angrily, 'As half of your body falls in my share, I will cut you into two with a see-saw [*sic*] if your eldest son insists about it.'[13]

'A man who has been the indisputable favourite of his mother' Freud once remarked, 'keeps for life the feeling of a conqueror, that confidence of success that often induces real success.'[14] Even as a child, Naren had this conquistador feeling; he assumed as a matter of course that in the game of 'king and the court' he would be the monarch who assigns the roles of ministers and courtiers to the other playmates who would accept his right to do so without question and submit meekly to his dictates. Later, this same charismatic authority informed his leadership of the Ramakrishna order, and even when he deviated from traditional ideals of monkhood in the United States, his brother-monks accepted as a matter of course his plans, proposals, and even his whims as the natural prerogatives of the 'chosen one'.

This sense of being chosen as the bearer of a superior destiny never left Vivekananda, even in his 'dark nights of the soul'. As he once wrote in a piece of perceptive self-analysis:

There are two sorts of persons in the world—the one strong-nerved, quiet, yielding to nature, not given to much imagination, yet good, kind, sweet, etc. For such is this world—they alone are born to be happy. There are others, again, with high-strung nerves, tremendously imaginative, with intense feelings—always going high, and coming down the next moment. For them there is no happiness. The first class will have almost an even tenor of happiness. The second will have to run between ecstasy and misery. But of these alone geniuses are made. There is some truth in a recent theory that genius is a sort of madness.

Now persons of this class, if they want to be great, must fight to be so—clear the decks for battle. No encumbrance—no marriage—no children, no undue attachment to anything except the one idea, and live and die for that. I am a person of this sort.[15]

Although it clearly originated in his earliest relationship with his devoted mother, Naren's indelible sense of superior mission was reinforced by his family. His paternal grandfather, after the birth of Naren's father Vishwanath, had renounced the world and put aside his responsibilities as a *grihastha* to lead a monk's life. Many thought that Naren's striking resemblance to this grandfather 'proved' that he had been reborn in the child, or, in other words, that the child Naren was his father's father. If we add to this Naren's dominance over his playmates, his leadership in school, his intellectual and rhetorical gifts that in college won him universal praise and admiration from his teachers, his being chosen at the age of eighteen by Ramakrishna as his foremost disciple and spiritual heir, it is not difficult to argue that Naren's environment conspired—he was an unconsciously willing co-conspirator—to maintain and enhance the intra-psychic construction of archaic grandiosity ('I am great'). Whereas the 'reality testing' of most children gradually reveals their limitations and sooner or later they lose their original sense of primacy, of 'specialness', Naren's encounters with the real world simply confirmed his sense of special destiny.

The sense of being the bearer of a superior destiny can generate in a child an inner drivenness to become 'great' and thereby fulfil his parents' expectations as well as the imperatives of his own self image. Yet this unconscious conviction of superiority *vis-à-vis* parents and the other adults around him can also be a source of great conflict and psychological tension for a young child. For one thing, his fantasied grandiosity is not matched by the realities of his physical stature and stage of ego development; the precocity of the small boy's unconscious wishes and ideals contrasts starkly with the anxious self doubt and confusion that all too easily can overwhelm the still tentative identity. The conflict between the fantasies of greatness and the reality of dependence upon parents, and other adults in the family makes its appearance in Vivekananda's earliest memory, a 'cover memory' in the psychoanalytic sense, for it condenses a continuing and pervasive childhood conflict in a single dramatic scene:

When I was only two years old, I used to play with my *syce* (coachman) at being *vairagi* (monk, renunciant,) clothed in ashes and *kaupina*. And if a *sadhu* came to beg, they would lock me in, upstairs, to prevent my giving too much away. I felt that I *was* this [a holy *vairagi*),and that for some mischief I had to be sent away from Shiva. No doubt my family increased this feeling, for when I was naughty they would say, 'Dear, Dear! So many austerities, yet Shiva sent us this demon after all, instead of a good soul.' Or when I was very rebellious they would empty a can of water over me, saying 'Shiva! Shiva!' Even now, when I feel mischievous, that word keeps me straight. 'No!' I say to myself, 'not this time!'[16]

Such a scene not only reflects the 'chosen' child's deep sense of hurt and humiliation at being treated so unceremoniously *by his mother*[17] but also the guilty fear that his budding initiative and curiosity might lead to some kind of exile from his mother and home as he was once sent away from Shiva. The remembered scene also suggests the contrapuntal role assumed by Naren's mother in their relationship, namely, she idealizes her son and yet rejects his somewhat cocky display of independence and initiative, or what she calls his 'rebelliousness'. The inner tension created by a mother who mistrusts or mocks her son's actual behaviour even as she elicits his ambitions and stretches his expectations is at the heart of a child's (and for that matter, vestigially, of an adult's) unstable self-concept and fluctuations in self-esteem.

The struggle to free himself from his mother and the advocacy of a thoroughly masculine courage and initiative (both in personal relations and on the collective plane of nationalist politics) were lifelong themes in Vivekananda's inner world, and in adulthood the maternal counterplayer would be Kali, the Divine Mother. Vivekananda was aware of this inner struggle; indeed, he believed it enhanced and befitted a man: 'Yes, let the world come, the hells come, the gods come, let Mother come. I fight and do not give in. Ravana got his release in three births by fighting the Lord himself! It is glorious to fight Mother.'[18] The struggle manifested itself in his historic mission to infuse Indian nationalism with a militant revival of tradition, to bring resolute 'manly' activity and radical social transformation to 'that awful mass of conservative jelly-fish',[19] that 'nation of women',[20] as he characterized the India of his time. And the same inner struggle would immobilize him during those frequent 'spells' in which he repudiated this ideal and denied his mission.

When a boy's early years have been characterized by intense emotional attachment and identification with his mother, the struggle for individuality and potence is an unremitting one. The unconscious dynamics of the struggle are these: the attempt to separate himself arouses guilt that not only dims the benevolent mother imago, but threatens the sense of one's own uniqueness of which she was the original guarantor. The 'bad mother' may then become magnified and stifle the pretension to greatness. The internal psychological 'work' of restitution thus becomes necessary; the threatening 'bad mother' must be propitiated by the child's renouncing any claim to independence and by claiming once again protection from Putana and Agasur, the maternal monsters who, in the deepest recesses of the inner world, are as alive as the 'good' Bhuvaneshwari Devi. This swinging back and forth between an 'agentic' adult manliness and the dependency of childhood was a recurrent feature of Vivekananda's life. In fact, the years of his greatest success and achievement, years when his name became a household word all over India, coincided with severe personal crises.

I want to quote at length here from a disciple's eye-witness account of the 'culminating' crisis in Vivekananda's life (in 1897),not only because it illuminates his personal conflict but also because it reflects a fundamental constellation in the Hindu inner world:

In some imperceptible way, at all events, the Swami's attention appeared to shift, during the month of August, from Shiva to the Mother. He was always singing the songs of Ram Prasad,* as if he would saturate his own mind with the conception of himself as a child. He told some of us once, that wherever he turned he was conscious of the presence of the Mother, as if she were a person in the room. It was always his habit to speak simply and naturally of Mother, and some of the older members of the party caught this, so that such phrases as 'Well, well! Mother knows best!' were a constant mode of thought and speech amongst us: when, for instance, some cherished intention had to be abandoned.

Gradually, however, his absorption became more intense. He complained bitterly of the malady of thought, which would consume a man, leaving him no time for sleep or rest, and would often become as insistent as a human voice. He had constantly striven to make clear to us the ideal of rising beyond the pair of opposites, beyond pain and pleasure, good and evil alike—that conception which forms the Hindu solution of the problem of sin—but now he seemed to fasten his whole attention on the dark, the painful, and the inscrutable . . . 'The worship of the Terrible' now became his whole cry. Illness or pain would always draw forth the reminder that 'She is the organ. She is the pain. And she is the Giver of pain, Kali! Kali! Kali!!'

His brain was teeming with thoughts, he said one day, and his fingers would not rest till they were written down. It was the same evening that we came back to our houseboat from some expedition, and found waiting for us, where he had called and left them, his manuscript lines on 'Kali the Mother'. Writing in a fever of inspiration, he had fallen on the floor, when he had finished—as we learnt afterwards—exhausted with his own intensity.

*Eighteenth century singer and poet whose songs of longing for the Mother are very popular in Bengal.

KALI THE MOTHER

The stars are blotted out
The clouds are covering clouds
It is darkness vibrant, sonant.
In the roaring, whirling wind,
Are the souls of a million lunatics,
Just loosed from the prison house,
Wrenching trees by the roots
Sweeping all from the path.
The sea has joined the fray
And swirls up mountain waves,
To reach the pitchy sky.
The flash of lurid light
Reveals on every side
A thousand, thousand shades
Of death, begrimed and black.
Scattering plagues and sorrows,
Dancing mad with joy,
Come, Mother, Come!
For terror is Thy name.
Death is Thy breath.
And every shaking step
Destroys a world for e'er.
Thou 'Time' the All-Destroyer!
Come, O Mother, come!
Who dares misery love,
Dance in destruction's dance.
And hug the form of death,—
To him the Mother comes.

About this time, he had taken the boat away from our vicinity, and only a young Brahmo doctor, who was also living in Kashmir that summer—and whose kindness and devotion to him were beyond all praise—was allowed to know where he was, and to inquire about his daily needs. The next evening the doctor went as usual, but finding him lost in thought, retired without speaking, and the following day, September the thirteenth, he had gone, leaving word that he was not to be followed, to Kshir Bhowani, the coloured springs.* He was away, from that day till October the sixth.

In the afternoon of that day we saw him coming back to us, up the river. He stood in front of the *dunga*, grasping with one hand the bamboo roofpole, and with the other holding yellow flowers. He entered our houseboat—a transfigured presence and silently passed from one to another blessing us, and put-

*There is a well-known ruined temple of Kali at this spot.

ting marigolds on our heads. 'I offered them to Mother', he said at last, as he ended by handing the garland to one of us. Then he sat down. 'No more "Hari Om!" It is all "Mother" now!' he said, with a smile. We all sat silent. Had we tried to speak, we should have failed, so tense was the spot, with something that stilled thought. He opened his lips again. 'All my patriotism is gone. Everything is gone. Now it's only "Mother, Mother!"'

'I have been very wrong', he said simply, after another pause. 'Mother said to me, "What, even if unbelievers should enter My temples, and defile My images! What is that to you? Do you protect Me? Or do I protect you?" So there is no more patriotism. I am only a little child!'[21]

Symbolically, Vivekananda had the hair on his head shaved off. With uncanny insight, he connected his physical symptoms (among them, severe asthmatic attacks) with his mental conflict; while the mood seemed to deepen and grow upon him that he was a child, 'seated in the Mother's lap and being caressed by her . . . the thought came to us, unspoken, that these Her kisses might make themselves known to mind and nerves as anguish, yet be welcomed with rapture of recognition.'[22]

To do full justice to Vivekananda's 'encounter' with Kali, we must view his crisis against the backdrop of Indian culture in which mother-religions and the worship of Kali in her many manifestations, especially in Bengal, form the deepest layer of Hindu religiosity. Without going into detail, I would only stress that the rapture of recognizing (and being recognized by) the mother's affirming presence together with the ambivalent anguish in response to her individuality-destroying embrace are the complementary affects evoked and condensed in the worship of Kali. In her gracious (*sundarmurti*) manifestations of world-mother (*jagadamba*) and world-nurse (*jagaddhatri*), Kali awakens an intense nostalgia for the abundance and benevolence of maternal nurturing, approval and reassurance. At the same time, in her hideous (*ghorarupa*) form, as the bone-wreathed lady of the graveyards, quaffing a skull full of seething blood, Kali symbolizes the ominous dimension in every Hindu's maternal imagery. Through the sanctioned rituals of her religion and the collective sharing of a symbol hallowed by generations of worship, Kali provides her devotees with a powerful symbolic and ritual integration of the two faces of Hindu motherhood, the trust and the dread, the rapturous sense of being cared for and the formidable fear of annihilation in that care.

At the time of the Hindu son's second birth, which coincides with the oedipal period of psycho-sexual development, the grandiose infantile self usually becomes somewhat dented as the child comes up against the world of men. In Naren's case, this developmental transition was complicated by his fantasy (somewhat corroborated by other family members) of being his father's father, if not the father-of-them-all, Shiva. In a boy's unconscious fantasy, to feel or imagine himself superior to his father means to replace that father, to have the power to annihilate him, a psychic process laden with enormous guilt. Most boys succeed in reducing this guilt through idealization and gradual identification with their father; the oedipal conflict is typically resolved within the everyday realities of the family and family relationships. For an uncommon child such as Naren, adored by his mother and intensely attached to her, determined almost involuntarily to maintain his original superiority and sense of greatness intact, convinced early on that he was 'chosen' to fulfil a special destiny, the way of idealization and identification with the father seems to have been difficult, especially since his father, according to the testimony of Naren's younger brother, was a 'weak' man.[23] That is, Vishwanath had low status among the Dattas; he was completely subservient to the wishes of his uncle, the head of the extended family. In spite of the cruel treatment meted out to his wife, Bhuvaneshwari Devi, who for a long time had only one sari to clothe her, Vishwanath had neither the temerity to protest nor the wherewithal to break away from the joint family to whose economic maintenance he contributed the lion's share. More or less passively accepting the decisions affecting the welfare of his wife and children, Vishwanath sought refuge from family tensions and quarrels in a wide circle of friends whom he was in the habit of entertaining lavishly. That he was a sensitive and gifted man who loved his eldest son dearly is beyond question; it is reported that when young Naren wanted to go to England to study law, he was not permitted to do so because Vishwanath could not bear to be separated from his son. Yet Vishwanath can scarcely be called a rock of strength, a father to be unconditionally idealized and identified with, a means of safe passage out of the mother's ambivalently consequential embrace. I do not mean that Naren did not identify with his father at all but I am suggesting that this identification must have been a tenuous one that required inward vigilance and constant struggle to maintain. For in spite of the availability of other adult males in his extended family, manliness and the clear sanction for it that are normally absorbed by a boy in his unconscious identification with his father remained emotionally charged issues in

Vivekananda's life: individuation as a man, separate from the maternal presence, remained the central, unresolved life task.

Again and again, as a grown man and nationalist leader, Vivekananda comes back to India's (and his own?) need for manliness as the all-encompassing cure for the country's ills, the means of political development and independence. 'Who cares for your *bhakti* and *mukti*?' he would retort angrily to brother monks who chided him on his western activist ideas so different from those of their guru Ramakrishna. 'Who cares what your scriptures say? I will go into a thousand hells cheerfully if I can rouse my countrymen, immersed in *tamas* (darkness), to stand on their own feet and be *men* inspired with the spirit of Karma yoga.'[24] Or : '. . . the older I grow, the more everything seems to me to lie in manliness. This is my new gospel. Do even evil like a man! Be wicked, if you must, on a grand scale,'[25] Or: 'No more weeping, but stand on your feet and be men. It is a man-making religion that we want. It is man-making theories that we want:'[26] 'I want the strength, manhood, *kshatravirya* or the virility of a warrior . . .'[27] And: 'O Thou Mother of the Universe, vouchsafe manliness unto me! O thou Mother of Strength, take away my weakness, take away my unmanliness, and— *Make me a Man!'*[28]

This obsession with manliness carried over into an admiration for India's conquerors, the Muslims and the British. Vivekananda often proclaimed that he wanted to build an India with a Muslim body and a Vedantist brain, and maintained that no race understood as the British did 'what should be the glory of a man'.[29] For the young men of India who were Vivekananda's primary constituency, this was (and still is) a powerful call for freedom from the conflicting embrace of the Great Mother—the appeal of this kind of masculinist campaign touching a deep current of potential militance and aggressive activity in Indian society.

As a child, Naren's solution to the early version of the conflict over 'manly' individuation was to withdraw from the world around him, to become (and remain) wholly self-absorbed. Symbolically, this withdrawal from reality to fantasy is condensed in a striking incident. Following his mother's example, Naren had obtained for himself images of Rama and Sita, bedecked them with flowers and ritually, regularly worshipped these deities, who are the idealized parental couple of Hindu India. At the age of four or five, he discarded the couple and installed in their place an image of Shiva, the self-sufficient god of renunciation. Apparently, Naren, oblivious of the world around him, would sit for hours 'meditating' before Shiva's image, sometimes opening his eyes to see whether his own hair, like that of fabled holy men who meditate for years at a stretch, had grown long and entered the earth.

Yet internal pressures cannot be held at bay indefinitely, no matter how intricate and 'successful' the fantasies, no matter how grand the self-image. In moments of stress, and whenever the watchfulness of the ego is relaxed, the elation of 'I am All' can give way to the despair of 'I am Nothing' : deeply buried knowledge of the 'rebellious' boy who might be banished from his mother's presence, or of the presumptuous son who might provoke dire punishment should he outdo his father in any way (even in fantasy) presses insistently from within. I believe Vivekananda's long-time presentiment that he would meet his death in a Shiva temple, the ultimate vengeance of the father–god for the son's oedipal hubris, and his fainting before the ice phallus of Shiva in the cave at Amarnath when he was thirty-four, reveals the anxiety accompanying the claims of the grandiose self. In Vivekananda's adult life, states of depression invariably followed when he was unable to repress the ever restless, unresolved childhood anxieties, 'If I become an independent man my mother will abandon me' and 'If I am greater than my father I will be punished.' He struggled against depression by escaping into transient mental states in which grandiose fantasy took over completely. 'Black and thick are the folds of sinister fate,' Vivekananda would write in one period, 'but I am the master. I raise my hand, and lo, they vanish! All this is nonsense and fear. I am the Fear of fear, Terror of terror. I am the fearless, secondless One! I am the Ruler of destiny, the Wiper-out of fact.'[30] Or, in another letter:

'He whose joy is only himself, whose desires are only in himself, he has learnt his lessons. This is the great lesson we have to learn, through myriads of births and heavens and hells: There is nothing to be sought for, asked for, desired beyond one's self. I am free therefore I require none else for my happiness. Alone through eternity because I was free, am free and shall remain free for ever . . . Yes, I am. I am free—Alone. I am the One without a second . . . if the universe tumbles round my ears, what is that to me? I am Peace that passeth understanding. Understanding only gives us good or evil. I am beyond—I am Peace.'[31]

At other times, in response to the same inner pressure, the fantasy of complete isolation, of being 'One without a second', would be replaced by its opposite, the 'regressive' imagery of the fervent wish for fusion with the mother. Here, the lonely splendour of Shiva would become transformed into the infant Krishna's longing for unconditional acceptance and peace that beloved sons find in the 'good mother's' embrace. In these periods of vulnerability, Vivekananda inadvertently made use of standard contemporary psycho-analytic techniques of retracing early psychological experience in order to recover the past creatively. His letters at these times have the flavour of free associations in psychotherapy:

I am drifting again, with the bright warm sun ahead and masses of vegetation around, and in the heat everything is so still, so calm, and I am drifting, languidly, in the warm heat of the river. I dare not make a splash with my hands or my feet for fear of breaking the wonderful stillness, stillness that makes you feel it is an illusion! Behind my work was ambition, behind my love was personality, behind my purity was fear, behind my guidance was a thirst for power. Now they are vanishing and I drift. I come, Mother, I come, in Thy warm bosom, floating wheresoever Thou takest me, in the voiceless, in the strange, in the wonderland, I come, a spectator, no more an actor.

Oh, it is so calm; my thoughts seem to come from a great, great distance in the interior of my own heart. They seem like faint distant whispers, and peace is upon everything, sweet, sweet peace . . . [32]

This alternation of vivid fantasies of isolation and fusion by means of which Vivekananda dealt with conflict reflects one of the dominant cultural concerns of India. In his relatively conflict-free periods of initiative and political leadership, this underlying polarity provided the energy and the direction for his historic achievements. For whereas most people are likely to be incapacitated by the relentless (and illusory) claims of a poorly integrated grandiose self, the ego of a gifted person may be pushed to its utmost capacity by such pressure and embark on objectively outstanding achievements. [33] In a charismatic leader such as Vivekananda, the importance of this turn towards the self in childhood and the drive (beset with anxiety and guilt, to be sure) to realize his superior destiny, cannot be underestimated. The turn towards the self gave him a central focus inside, an internal audience in the psyche, which might severely disapprove or enthusiastically applaud, but which gave Vivekananda the ability to act according to an inner light, independent of the judgements of others as to the 'realism' of a particular course of action. By carrying within him a sense of his own psychological inviolacy, coupled with a stubborn will that held to the self chosen course in the face of all outer obstacles, Vivekananda could, when the time came, project his vision with a passionate conviction capable of striking such a responsive chord in his audience that action on a large scale and resistance to the status quo (political and cultural) became possible. Yet this activist potential was never fully realized, and Vivekananda's vision of India's rejuvenation never became a mass movement. For one thing, the 'contents' of his vision were ultimately dissonant with the prevailing direction of political organization and anti-British resistance; but more important, the very nature of his conflict led him intermittently to withdraw from (if not reject outright) the responsibilities of ideological and organizational leadership against a foreign 'enemy' to a deeply private region where his psychic energies were fully deployed in combating or appeasing the demons within.

In 1870, at the age of seven, Naren entered school where his exceptional intelligence was quickly recognized by both teachers and classmates. In contrast with the brooding moodiness of his early childhood at home, the *leitmotif* of the so-called latency stage, which extended in Naren's case well into adolescence, was boundless activity and inexhaustible energy, especially of the locomotor kind. He organized a gymnasium and an amateur theatrical company, took lessons in the 'manly' sports of fencing, rowing and wrestling, and was the leader of a gang of mischievous youngsters who climbed the neighbourhood trees to pluck fruit and flowers, to the indignant (and apparently futile) remonstrances of tree-owners. Shiva and Kali, Rama and Sita, the *vairagis* and the meditating holy men whose hair took root in the earth, were apparently 'forgotten', and the dreamy maternal cosmos of his early years appears to have been temporarily superseded by the fascinations of the 'world of men', as the boy constructed models of the gas works and aerated-water factory lately introduced to Calcutta— much as an American boy today might make space-ship models in preconscious homage to the dominant technological image of our time.

With the advent of adolescence, however, 'forgotten' childhood themes were reactivated and Narendra's ego controls, the psychosocial gains of middle childhood, were buffeted by the renewed instinctual pressures of this stage. Once more, he found he could not always cope with the claims of archaic grandiosity and the anxiety and guilt associated with its breakthrough. Increasingly, he experienced periods of hypomanic excitement; once, on a journey with his parents to a small town in Madhya Pradesh when he was fifteen, they passed through a narrow pass surrounded on both sides by lofty peaks, and it is reported that Narendra 'spied a large bee-hive in the cleft of a giant cliff and suddenly his mind was filled with awe and reverence for the Divine Providence. He lost outer consciousness and lay thus in the cart for a long time.'[34] There were repeated *déjà vu* experiences as childhood repressions were momentarily lifted; on occasions he would, trance-like, break into song extolling divine glories, much to the astonishment of his college friends. It was as if the youth Narendra, whom Vivekananda would later look back upon as something of a fanatic, lived simultaneously in several *personas*. He was the activist patriot, convinced that his country's future depended upon the acquisition of a modern identity and that his own supreme task lay in promoting and hastening this process. At other times, he was the young man with 'burning eyes', prone to ecstasies, in search of a guru. He apparently went from one eminent religious teacher to another, asking each (much to their embarrassment) whether he had ever really seen God face to face. And there were others in what we might call his 'identity repertoire': the ascetic young man with a 'passion for purity' who had repudiated the demands of his sexual nature; the son who refused to marry and settle on a professional career in law as his parents desired. And from childhood, the unconscious selves of the 'great one', the *vairagi* and the father's father, made their own insistent demands. To put it briefly, more than most other youths, Narendra's identity was a fragmented one; he was looking for someone to provide him with a single integrated image of himself and the world, of himself *in* the world, someone to whom he could offer his complete devotion and who, in return, would make him whole.

This 'someone' was of course the remarkable Ramakrishna Paramahansa, whom millions of Hindus believe to have been an *avatar*,* the ultimate tribute paid in India to a liberated man. Ramakrishna's struggle to persuade his chosen spiritual heir to accept the Great Mother in whom lies the perfect synthesis of 'good' and 'bad' mother imagery as the fundamental reality of his inner cosmos; and the intimate, quasi-therapeutic relationship that developed between the patient, loving and motherly teacher and his imperious, stubborn disciple who openly mocked his guru's childlike *bhakti*-religiosity—these are subjects that would take us beyond the boundaries of our present study. Perhaps it is enough to note here that during the last two years of his six-year apprenticeship to Ramakrishna, and after the death of his father when he was twenty-one years old, Narendra was under intense mental strain, highly vulnerable and suggestible. Ramakrishna stepped

---

*Incarnation of the godhead.

into the void his pupil's inner world had become—indeed, he was already at home there—and serving as a mighty mentor, he helped to set the inner stage for the emergence of Vivekananda, the revolutionary monk and one of the greatest men India has produced in the last one hundred years.

For much of his adult life, Vivekananda managed successfully to integrate his divergent strivings for individuation as a man with the yearning for fusion with some ultimate divine matrix in the propagation of a specifically Indian form of nationalism that captured the imagination of his countrymen. By combining elements of an activist, self-assertive manhood with those of emotional and religious mysticism, Vivekananda equated patriotism with an identification with Mother India; his powerful oratory stirred the masses with its appeal to *their* pride and *their* tradition, and used symbols meaningful to *them*. The theme of phallic grandiosity was as much a part of his appeal as the bliss inherent in the imagery of a strong, bounteous and fertile Motherland—his reassurance that the skull-garlanded Kali 'of blackest gloom' could be transformed into the resplendent Durga if only her sons would come back to her and to their ancient *dharma*. Vivekananda ultimately failed politically in that he was unable to sustain or substantiate the religious-emotional identity he purveyed with a tight, efficient political organization. As Pamela Daniels puts it, 'Religious and political ideals briefly and powerfully combined under the banner of militant nationalism, but the alliance was not sustained. The politicians went their way, and the mystics theirs.'[35] The task of fashioning the tools of power with which to effect nationalist aspirations was left for Vivekananda's more pragmatic successors, for men such as Gandhi, Nehru and Patel. I have suggested above that Vivekananda's 'failure' was rooted in the same psychic constellation that gave his message its powerful appeal, in the vestiges of the archaic narcissism of Hindu childhood. For to the extent that an individual or a movement succeeded in consolidating a vigorous sense of existential or political independence and in exalting the good mother, that very success brought in its wake the *alter imago* of the bad mother—the dark Kali who allows neither individuation nor a blissful union but only permits an anxious abject surrender. A profound ambivalence towards manhood and its representations such as Shiva and the British *raj*, towards the 'good mother' and her symbols—Durga and the motherly Ramakrishna—cast a long shadow on the Indian independence movement.

Let us step back to consider the validity of this sketch of

Vivekananda's emotional development. How far is this rough chart of his inner territory 'true' and how much of it is mere conjecture? This is a recurring question in the psycho-biographical study of historical figures in that the modification, extension or revision of preliminary hypotheses on the basis of the subject's responses, corrections and questions is not possible. Nevertheless, this rough map strikes me as probable in that it connects and integrates a series of (sometimes contradictory) episodes in Vivekananda's life history, it is consistent with psycho-analytic theory and, especially in the biographer's own empathic reactions towards his subject—his 'countertransference'—persists in having a ring of truth.

II

CULTURE AND HEALING

4

Lord of the Spirit World

Two hundred and fifty miles south of Delhi, the Balaji temple is best reached by taking a bus from the nearest town of Bharatpur, a town described in tourist brochures as 'the eastern gateway to Rajasthan.' Founded by the Jat chieftain Suraj Mal, who carved out a kingdom of his own in the eighteenth century in the twilight of the Moghul empire, Bharatpur is not unlike other north Indian towns. Except for the presence of Suraj Mal's dilapidated fort and a group of palaces, cannily turned by his descendants into a luxury hotel for tourists, the ecology of Bharatpur's bazaars is universal. In summer, there are the usual flies in dense clusters on the overripe fruit and sweets and the dust that steams and not infrequently smells of horse urine once the monsoon comes. There are the irate tonga drivers cursing their scrawny horses, apparently lifeless but for their running sores; the placid oxcarts plodding unhurriedly through crowded bazaars, overloaded with everything from hay to steel girders; the Sikh drivers, strands of hair defying the purpose of their dirty turbans, two feet on the accelerator and two hands on the horns of their ancient trucks. There are the dank eating places with grime-covered clay ovens, radios blaring the latest film songs and the all-pervasive smell of frying onions and hot curries.

If the impression I have given of Bharatpur is one of sweltering discomfort, an unrelieved drabness, then I should hasten to correct it. For during the four or five months of cold weather at least, Bharatpur is transformed. These months are a feast of brilliant color and sharp smells, patches of wild bougainvillaea and strings of red chillies drying under the wintry sun. It is the season for fresh spices and the bazaars abound in heaps of gnarled turmeric roots and rich brown tamarind stocked in front of the shops. The air is crisp and the intervening haze of dust no longer dulls the clear sky, which has only a few wisps of gray to mar its blinding blue symmetry. The Ghana bird sanctuary, three miles from the town, lies on the great migratory route to the warm south and is a resting place for the birds from north and central Asia, the Siberian cranes, the gray-legged geese and countless others that are the ornithologist's delight. In fact, on our first trip to the Balaji temple in the middle of November, it was the variety of birds in the countryside outside Bharatpur that made the strongest impression on me. Families of peacocks pecking their way through the plowed furrows, sleek blue kingfishers swooping down gracefully to find a sure perch on the telegraph wires that run parallel to the road, flights of parrots and flamingos, were a common sight.

At least for the first few miles outside Bharatpur, the visual impressions one receives as the bus clatters past the villages lining the road are ones that are familiar from the rest of the Indo-Gangetic plain. They are registered as a succession of snapshots: a buffalo, immersed up to its neck in a pond thickly carpeted with green slime, motionless except for the occasional movement of its primeval head; a little girl, wrapped up in a yellow *chudder*, trying to move a recalcitrant ox by pulling at the string that runs through the animal's nose; the deeply pitted mud wall of a hut, plastered with flat cowdung cakes drying in the sun. Gradually, however, as we move deeper into Rajasthan and approach Balaji, the landscape begins to change. Squat hills, with thorny bushes and eroded topsoil that exposes the underlying rock, become more frequent. Some of the hills are crowned by the ruins of equally squat fortresses that loom above the road and once guarded this old invasion route to the medieval Rajput kingdoms to the south. The countryside is sparsely populated. Miles and miles of barren land, dotted with olive-green scrub and scarred by dried-out gullies and narrow ravines, stretch out on either side of the road. It is as if the vast Rajasthan desert, still hundreds of miles to the south, is sending out intimations of its inexorable existence, an impression enhanced by the increasing number of camel carts coming from that direction.

The temple of Balaji lies between two hills in the middle of just such a desolate landscape, three miles off the main road to Jaipur. After a twenty-minute tonga ride through a sun-drugged silence, broken only by the sound of the horse's hooves rhythmically striking against the metalled road, the sudden din on reaching the lane that leads up to the temple comes as something of a shock. In fantasy, I had envisioned the temple having been built in the tradition of the classical Hindu temples—those of Bhubaneshwar or Puri, for instance. I had pictured it being lovingly hewn out of rock by ancient guilds of anonymous craftsmen, strong in their simple faith and devotion. I had thought of it standing in a solitary if somewhat decayed splendor in the middle of jungle scrub and rocky hills. Except for the scrub and the hills, the reality does not bear the faintest resemblance to the imaginary product. Flat-roofed, the temple is a simple two-storied structure at the end of a long lane which is lined on both sides by shops and a number of *dharmashalas*, the free boardinghouses for pilgrims erected by the pious. The temple can be distinguished from its neighbours only by the fact that its facade has been painted a bilious green. In spite of the fluted columns, small arched windows and stone latticed balconies typical of the Rajasthani style of architecture, the building still manages to convey a general impression of shabbiness, enhanced by the patches of green paint peeling off the underlying stucco. There is a total absence of any atmosphere of sanctity both in and around the temple premises. The space in front of the steps that lead into the temple (as also the steps themselves) are littered with banana skins, orange peels, crushed marigolds and other assorted refuse. The sides of the temple are crowded by eating places, small provision stores and hawkers selling fruit, vegetables, gaudy posters and painted clay images of the temple deities as well as prayer books and other holy bric-a-brac. The shop on the right side of the temple displays the signboard of an R.M.P.— registered medical practitioner—and the good doctor, a stout unshaven man with a roll of fat bulging out between the end of his undervest and the top string of his pajamas, can be seen reclining on a cot, thoughtfully paring his nails as he waits for customers who might have cause to be disappointed with the healing powers of the gods inside the great temple. In Balaji at least, medicine exists as a poor relation to religion, obsequious and faintly disreputable.

Like the ancient Greek temples of Asclepius at Epidaurus, Pergamon and Cos, the temple of Balaji at Mehndipur has acquired more than local prominence as a shrine of healing. To the large number of patients from all over northern India who approach it in 'a spirit of service, faith and devotion,' the temple promises a quick relief from many afflictions, including 'obstacles raised by *bhuta–preta* [malignant spirits], madness, epilepsy, tuberculosis, barrenness and other diseases.' The overwhelming number of patients I interviewed had come to Balaji because of certain bodily symptoms and alterations in behaviour that were diagnosed, by their neighbourhood exorcist (*sayana*) or by knowledgeable elders in the family and community, as manifestations of a mental illness caused by spirit possession. It is its promise of cure from mental illness caused by malignant spirits, illness that has proved intractable to the best efforts of modern doctors and traditional shamanic healers, which gives the temple its distinctive reputation.

The malignant spirits of which I speak here are collectively known as *bhuta-preta*, though Hindu demonology distinguishes between the various classes of these supernatural beings. The *bhuta*, for instance, originates from the souls of those who meet an untimely and violent death, while a *preta* is the spirit of a child who died in infancy or was born deformed.[1] A third class, that of *pishacha*, derives from the mental characteristics of the dead person: a *pishacha* being generally the ghost of a man who was either mad, dissolute or violent-tempered. In addition, to complete the malignant pantheon, there are a few female spirits of which the best known is the *churel*—the ghost of an unhappy widow, a childless woman or, more generally, of any woman who lived and died with her desires grossly unsatisfied. It is emphasized by both laymen and experts alike that a common characteristic of most malignant spirits is the fact that they are souls of persons who could not live out their full life and potential. In other words, they are all *atripta* spirits—*ghosts of unsatisfied desires*—and this of course makes them of professional interest not only to the exorcist but also to the psychoanalyst.

The *bhuta–preta* are said to exist in a halfway house between the human world and the world of ancestral spirits (*pitri–lok*). Until they have been judged, have paid their Karmic debts and are allowed into the world of ancestral spirits, the *bhuta–preta* continue to yearn for a human body which they can enter and contrive to make sick through their nefarious activity. I was, however, struck by the fact that both the individual's guarded apprehensiveness in relation to the malignant spirits and his longing for guidance from the benign ancestral spirits had an underlying tone of easy familiarity. In his relationship with these spirits, the person did not seem to feel the terror and the awe often evoked by the village and local deities; nor did he have the feelings of reverence that are due to the major gods such as Ganesha and Hanuman, and he certainly had none of the distant devotion with which the great gods and goddesses (and their incarnations) are apt to be regarded. Perhaps this psychological proximity is due to the fact that these spirits, occupying the lowest rungs in the Hindu hierarchy of supernatural beings, are closest to the human state. Whatever the reason, both the *bhuta–preta* and the *pitri* are a tangible, living presence for most people. They seem to populate a mental region that is contiguous and has open borders with the land of ordinary consciousness in which normal everyday life takes place. Persons may occasionally have encounters with the spirit world without these encounters being necessarily regarded as auditory or visual hallucinations of the pathological kind.

THE LEGEND OF THE DIVINE HEALER

Balaji, the chief deity of the temple, is better known throughout India as Hanuman, the monkey god who was Rama's main assistant in his epic battle against Ravana. The myth goes that Balaji was born of Anjana, a heavenly nymph who married a noble monkey and was cursed by the gods with a simian form. One day, while standing on top of a mountain, lost in a pleasant reverie, Anjana was ravished by Vayu, the god of the winds. Balaji was the offspring of this forced union. Like Bhima, the mighty warrior of the *Mahabharata* and another son of Vayu, Balaji was distinguished right from the start by great strength and gargantuan appetites. As an infant, he was perpetually hungry. Once he ran after the sun with all intentions of swallowing the orb to appease his hunger pangs. This caused great consternation among the gods and elicited vociferous protests from Rahu, whose right to periodically swallow the sun and cause the solar eclipse was being so insolently violated. In anger, Indra, the king of gods hurled his thunderbolt at the greedy infant, who fell down on a mountain top, breaking his jaw or *hanu*; hence also his name of Hanuman. The father Vayu picked up his unconscious son, retired into a cave and in sorrow and protest over the treatment meted to his offspring refused to carry out his assigned tasks. With Vayu on strike, there was a sudden absence of the ten forms of wind (*prana, apana, samana, udana*, etc.) and thus a stoppage of such functions as breathing, elimination, digestion, sleep and so on, with the result that creation ground to an abrupt halt. Thrown into a panic, the gods came rushing to the grieving Vayu's cave, begging for forgiveness and offering to make the necessary amends. As a first step, each god blessed Balaji with a special power. At the end of this process, Balaji had not only become immortal and invulnerable but also the very personification of all the powers—mental and physical—of the gods. Perhaps the most important blessing given to him, at least from our viewpoint of tracing his status as a divine healer for those afflicted with possession by malignant spirits, was Brahma the Creator's blessing of total *fearlessness*. Indeed these are the two qualities—power and freedom from fear—that Balaji displayed in abundance in his later exploits on behalf of Rama.

From this point onward, the all-India myth of Balaji gets diverted into a local channel to become the legend of the temple at Mehndipur.[2] In the local legend the Vedic gods and the masculine preoccupations with power and fearlessness are given short shrift as the legend chooses to focus on Balaji's mother. For while the father gods are fighting the infant, grudgingly relinquishing their powers to him and otherwise acting out the unconscious script of an immemorial paternal fantasy toward sons, the mother is longing to reclaim her darling boy. As the local legend has it, the mother waited at a spot between two hills (yes, the spot where the present temple is located) and was beside herself with joy when she could finally take Balaji in her lap. She 'kissed his face repeatedly, gave him both her breasts to drink from and then after seating him in her lap, both mother and son were soon absorbed in their spiritual practices.'[3] Here, it seems to us, the local additions and elaborations of the original myth intuitively recognize the fact that the worship of Balaji as a god of power and fearlessness alone makes him much too masculine and distant to fulfill ideally the role of the divine healer. Like the female members of Asclepius's family to whom prayers for cure could be addressed,[4] the local legend recognizes the need to surround Balaji with the feminine–maternal principle and the 'feminine' powers of nurturance, warmth, concern, intuitive understanding and relatedness which, many psychotherapists claim, are essential in every healing encounter and for the success of the healing process.[5]

For millions of years and many world ages, the legend goes on, Balaji sat here in the lap of his mother, accessible only to the gods who approached him for removal of their troubles. Then one day, a thousand years ago, a young prince was murdered at the spot where the temple now stands. His soul, taking the form of a *preta*, cried out for justice and clamored for liberation into the world of ancestral spirits. Moved by the *preta*-prince's plight and seeing that the *bhuta–preta* were a source of such misery to mankind, Balaji decided to make his 'court' (*darbar*) accessible to troubled human beings. He sent a vision to a young priest of Mehndipur village, intimating this decision and requiring that a temple be built. The descendants of this priest are even today the priests of the Balaji temple.

To help him in his task of bringing order in the chaos of the spirit world and in regulating the relations between humans and the *bhuta–*

preta, Balaji invited two other deities to take up their abode in the temple. The first god who accepted the invitation and moved to the Balaji temple with his own court was Preta-raja ('lord of the *preta*'), which is another name of Dharma-raja, the god of death and the guardian of *dharma*. As lord of the *preta*s, Preta-raja is expected to consider the problems and difficulties of a *preta* before deciding upon his fate, determine the *preta*'s proper quantum of punishment and decide the time when its soul is to be liberated from the *preta* order into the next order of the spirit world. The second deity to take up his residence within the temple was Mahakal Bhairav, an incarnation of Shiva, who was entrusted with the task of administering the punishments.

Following the inexorable laws of bureaucracy which seem to apply impartially to both the human and the divine worlds, the original trio of gods has since then mushroomed into a whole department of spirits. The three chief gods have added on assistants who specialize in different functions relating to the *bhuta–preta* and some of whom have further acquired assistants of their own. The origins of these minor gods and how they became a part of the temple are unknown, even to the temple priest, who expressed his frank bafflement at the proliferation of deities. It is, however, indisputable that people have allotted these minor gods temple space and rituals of their own and that these deities take a vigorous part in the healing process and in the life of the temple: in fact, there are many patients whose cures would not be complete without the full collaboration of these suprahuman functionaries. Here, I am specifically thinking of *bhangiwara*, a minor god in the court of Preta-raja who specializes in dealing with the Muslim *bhuta* and those belonging to the untouchable castes. When a patient comes out of the *bhangiwara* enclosure after having exorcised one of these *bhuta*s, it is imperative that he take a ritual bath to rid himself of the pollution. Otherwise it is held that if the patient touches someone else after his *bhangiwara* sojourn, it is almost certain that his *bhuta* will be transferred to the other person.

THE TEMPLE AND THE HEALING RITUALS

The shabbiness of the temple's surroundings and its unimpressive architecture become of minor importance once we enter the temple premises. The moment one steps inside the halls and courtyards of Balaji there is little time and even less inclination for contemplating aesthetic issues. The senses are taken hold of violently and wrenched out of their normal grooves by strange sights and unfamiliar sounds and smells, embedded in a whirling crowd of pilgrims, patients and their families in various stages of self-absorption. If I look back to my own first impressions before the bizarre became the familiar, I am struck by the wide gulf in the range of behaviour permitted and encouraged in a healing space—in this case, the court of the Lord of the Spirit World— as compared to rooms and spaces where everyday life is carried on.

Passages from the journal of a colleague describing his first visit to the temple vividly illustrate the drama of the healing process and the colourfulness of the surroundings in which it takes place.

'Climbing up the temple steps to enter the outer courtyard, I am greeted by an unfamiliar aroma. It takes me a few seconds to identify the sweet, smoky smell coming from the direction of the main hall as being produced by burning rice, grain, sugar crystals, coconut and other offerings that the patients are required to make to Balaji. The courtyard is crowded, mostly by young women, many of them sitting or lying on the floor in odd, contorted postures. A young girl, perhaps eighteen years old, quite attractive despite the unnatural pallor of her face, is lying on her back. Her loose hair is spread around her head which is violently jerking from one side to another as expressions of pain flit across her face. Her lips move in an inaudible murmur, interspersed by full-throated shouts of 'Baba, Baba, I won't go, I won't go!'—the *bhuta* (a male to judge by the timbre of his voice and the gender he uses in the verbs) expressing his refusal to vacate her body. My attention is caught by another young girl. She is crouching on her knees, her hips thrust back, the pelvis moving provocatively to both invite and repel an unseen violator. 'Get away! Get away from me, leave me!' she is crying out in a strong voice. She then bursts into deep moans of 'Oh, Baba! Oh, Baba!' her tightly closed eyes shutting out the world from her private struggles with the possessing spirit. I look around but no one else seems to be noticing the girl and my gaze slides off incurious eyes. Another girl, barely into her teens, is standing on her head against the wall. I hear a swishing movement and a shoulder brushes against the back of my legs. I turn around to see a girl bounding away in high, leaping somersaults; the acrobatic somersaults taking her from one end of the courtyard to another and then back again.

'From the outer courtyard, I step into the main hall. This room is much larger, squarer in shape, and the grilled roof at the top makes it bright and airy. On the left side, beyond the columns of the temple, there is a narrow, dark corridor from where I get a good view of what is happening in the main hall. As my eyes get accustomed to the darkness I notice that I am not alone. An old woman is squatting next to me, surrounded by the paraphernalia needed for the ritual worship. There are two copper pots in front of her, both of them filled with water. She is counting beads from a rosary in her lap and with every count she dips a spoon into one of the pots, takes out a spoonful of water and pours it into the second pot. I suddenly notice the presence of yet another person. This is another old woman, with a dark-complexioned face that almost merges into the surrounding darkness. As I move nearer, I am startled to see an unusually long and purple tongue protruding out of her mouth. She is being Kali, I tell myself, and reflexively bow to her. The woman raises a withered hand in benediction and I could almost swear that she has pushed her tongue out a little more for my benefit. Feeling somewhat uneasy I quickly move back into the main hall and step into the path of a dog who swerves to avoid me. The dog is hurrying toward the front of the hall to the dense crowd pressing against an iron grill behind which lie the food offerings heaped into a mound. A part of the offerings is being burned by a priest in a large brass lamp, producing sacred ash and the thick acrid smoke which I had smelled at the temple entrance. Through the smoke, the squares of the iron grill and over the heads of people clamoring to get nearer, I can see the idol of Balaji, which is in fact a triangular piece of stone, vaguely reminiscent of the shape of a human head, painted in ochre and silver colours and with two large black eyes painted on it to give it the appearance of a face.

'On the right side of the main hall, there is another corridor in which the temple of Mahakal Bhairav is located. The god of punishment is again represented by a large round stone, enclosed in a protective grill, painted the same ochre and silver colours and with eyes drawn on the surface of the stone. Next to the grill there is a circular cavity in the floor, barely six inches deep and little bigger than a man's head in circumference. An old man, noticing my show of interest, enlightens me as to the cavity's purpose. 'This is where the hangings take place. If you are here for some days you must see a hanging.' Later in the evening I would indeed get a chance to witness a 'hanging.' In fact it was the old Kali woman of my earlier encounter. She had put her head in the cavity and with the help of a female companion who held up her legs, she stood on her head for a full thirty minutes. Her muffled groans of pain indicated both the *bhuta*'s distress and her own physical discomfort, which must have been considerable indeed: 'It's enough, Baba,' she kept on repeating during her ordeal. 'Forgive me now!' 'Don't let him go, Baba,' her companion would shout back. 'Leave him only after you have choked him to death.'

'In the open courtyard I join a group of five women and a boy sitting around an elderly man. The man's eyes are closed, a faint smile plays around the corners of his mouth, and the whole atmosphere is charged with a suppressed merriment that is very different from the solemnity of a modern psychotherapist's office. The elderly man, whom they call 'Panditji,' is supposedly in a trance and the women seem to be enjoying themselves as they engage his *bhuta* in an animated conversation. 'O *re Mussulman!*' one of them says. 'Tell us quickly from where you have come.' Panditji murmurs something in reply and the woman repeats it aloud for our benefit. 'He says he is a Sayyad [a particularly strong Muslim *bhuta*],' and then turning to Panditji she says, 'Just now you were telling us that you want to eat kababs. Don't you know that you won't get any kababs as long as you are on this pandit? Do you understand? Run along now!'

'Panditji is now distinctly agitated. His head moves up and down vigorously and his voice is stronger, though it has the quality of a stubborn child, 'I'll eat kababs; I'll eat kababs! I'll certainly eat kababs! I have been hungry for three years. This idiot pandit has neither eaten kababs himself nor has he given me some to eat.' Panditji's wife, who is sitting next to him, takes umbrage at the *bhuta*'s rude tone and starts scolding him, but I'm more interested in the women's conversation. 'These *Mussulmans!* They have ruined our *dharma*,' says one of the women, referring to the *bhuta*. 'I don't know where they all come from!' 'First check up whether he is a *Mussulman* at all,' the second woman retorts, and she is supported by another one: 'Perhaps he is trying to fool us. Sometimes he says he is a Rajput, sometimes he says he is a *Mussulman*.' As I muse over the fact that Muslim *bhutas* are considered to be the strongest and the most malignant of evil spirits, indicating perhaps the psychological depths of the antipathy between Hindus and Muslims, I hear Panditji speak: 'I *am* a *Mussulman*. My home is the shrine of Islaudin. Burn an oil lamp for me there every day or I won't leave.' I ask one of the women about Panditji's problems. 'Panditji stays at our boardinghouse,' she confides in me without hesitation. 'His whole family has the *sankat* [lit. stress, predicament]. Sometimes Panditji also gets possessed by a *Mussulman* who asks to be fed kababs and then we bring him here.' *Sankat* or distress, I have gathered by now, is the word used in Balaji to describe possession by a malignant spirit.

'It's almost three in the afternoon when I leave the group and climb up the staircase to the second floor where the 'court' of Preta-raja is being held. Since the 'King of the Spirits' is most intimately involved in the affairs of *bhuta–preta*, the second-floor hall is crowded and humming with a suppressed energy. Most people are sitting in an orderly fashion, their prayer books open in front of them, singing hymns in praise of Preta-raja's miracles. The singing is led by a boy of fifteen, under the approving eyes of the priest sitting in front of Preta-raja's stone representation and enclosed by the inevitable iron fence that prevents the patients from touching the stone. The singing is full of devotional excitement, punctuated by the sound of dull thuds produced by patients who are hitting their backs rhythmically against the walls. I go up to the back of the hall, which has three iron gates, similar in appearance to those that bar prison cells. I lean back against one of the gates and notice that the space in front of the other two is already occupied by two girls whose legs are chained to the iron bars. A couple of yards to my right, a woman is lying on her face with heavy stones piled on her back. She lifts up her head and calls me in a pleading voice, asking me to shift one of the stones, which is hurting her. With some effort I lift the heavy stone and put it down on the floor. 'Who told you to remove that stone?' she asks angrily. 'Put it back at once!' A couple of men and a woman—her family, I presume—loudly reproach me at my effrontery and the older of the two men seems very annoyed. I try to explain my action but he is shaking his head angrily muttering abuses against 'good-for-nothing interferers.' Noticing my consternation, a kindly man explains the situation. 'Actually when the girl called you, her *bhuta* was in considerable pain. If you had not lifted the stone he might have perhaps confessed his origin and his wishes. The family has been waiting here for three months for the *bhuta*'s confession.' I sulkily retire to my place, warning myself never to interfere again and to be on my guard against expressing any human impulse of sympathy and fellow feeling.

'The chained girl beside me, whom I have studiously ignored so far, is getting noisier. She is rattling her chains loudly and occasionally she starts shouting in a hoarse voice, 'Stop it! Shut up and stop this nonsense or I'll reduce you all to ashes.' Some people in the crowd who hear her turn their heads but hurriedly look away as she grimaces at them and makes obscene gestures. She then calls her husband, a young man who is desperately trying to ignore her and concentrate on his hymn singing. She loudly asks him to have intercourse with her right away and then attempts to lift up her *sari*. This produces the desired result since the husband rushes to her side to stop her. As if she had been waiting for this, the girl catches hold of her husband's arm and sinks her teeth into his forearm. The husband gives her a hard slap which sends her sprawling against the gate. 'I am fed up,' the young man is saying, addressing no one in particular. 'I don't know what happens to her. Rot here for all I care! Show everyone your dramas, I am going home!' The girl, recovered from the blow, is sitting up and laughing delightedly.

'Looking out of the gate, I see the high cliffs against which the temple nestles. In fact it has been carved out of the hillside. There are big stone steps leading to the top of the cliffs. Names of *pretas* who have been exorcised and have joined Preta-raja's court as his servants and helpers are chiseled in these stone slabs. Next to the first step there is a raised platform, on which boiled rice, dhal and other edibles from the offerings made by the devout are heaped. Stray dogs and street urchins are gathered around the heap, rushing in to snatch the delicacies—*burfis* or *laddoos*—when a fresh offering is added to the growing mound. Dogs, I learn, are Mahakal Bhairav's mount and are thus sacrosanct within the temple precincts. Slightly higher than the platform and toward its left, there is a small water cistern which is supposed to be the home of another god known as Kundi Wale Baba. The dirty water of the cistern (it is a favourite bathing place of the dogs) is drunk by those whose spirit proves to be particularly stubborn.'

The direct attack on the possessing spirit takes place through a series of temple rituals that seem to be patterned after judicial procedures. The first step is called the 'application' (*darkhwast*), in which a patient makes an offering of rice and dhal worth one and a quarter rupees and gives two *laddoos* to an attendant every morning and evening before the start of the temple service. During these services, a priest touches the *laddoos* to a part of Balaji's idol and then gives them back to the patient to eat. It is believed that with the eating of the *laddoos* the power of Balaji goes into the patient and forces the *bhuta* to make his 'appearance' in the court (*peshi*)—the dramatic high point of the healing rituals. If the application is unsuccessful and the spirit does not appear, then the patient can make a 'petition' (*arzi*) in which the 'court costs' are seventeen and a quarter rupees' worth of *laddoos* for Balaji, boiled rice for Preta-raja and boiled *urad* for Mahakal Bhairav. If the *bhuta* proves to be stubborn and does not appear even once during the morning and evening services for Balaji or in the afternoon service for

Preta-raja, then the petition money is raised to twenty-one and a quarter rupees (*badi arzi*).* In addition, the patient may be asked to make offerings of sweets to various minor deities such as *bhangiwara*. Meanwhile, the family members too have been active. Many of them are asked by the priest to chant specific mantras or to read aloud certain passages from the Ramayana and the Hanuman Chalisa. Others are found in the temple halls, chanting mantras over spoonfuls of water that they keep transferring from one pot to another. The mantras supposedly impart divine energy to the water, which is later drunk by the patient, presumably to the further dismay of the possessing spirit. It is quite understandable that the *bhuta* is rarely able to withstand the concerted onslaught of so many 'divine energies.' In secular language we would say that the application and petition rituals incorporate the awesome authority of the gods in their demand that the patient go into the trancelike state of *peshi*. The demand is reinforced by the expectations of the priests and family members and is encouraged by the contagious effect of observing other patients having their *peshi* in the midst of approving groups.

The start of a *peshi* is marked by well-defined signs of which the rhythmic swaying of the upper half of the body and the violent sideways shaking of the head are the surest evidence of the *bhuta*'s 'appearance.' Beating of the floor with hands, hitting the back against the wall, lying down on the floor with heavy stones piled on the back, and other acts of self-punishment are further signs of *peshi*. In essence, *peshi* is a trancelike, altered state of consciousness (not of unconsciousness) where the focus of the patient's awareness of the environment is radically narrowed but not completely erased. In this state, technically known as dissociation, the patient can generally carry out a conversation with members of the audience, though the conversation is often subject to later amnesia. He is careful not to cause himself serious injury in his acts of self-punishment and the *peshi* stops automatically with the end of the temple service. If the *peshi* is interrupted for any reason, patients report a fullness in their chests and a choking sensation in their throats 'as if something wanted to come out.'

---

*In Hindu ritual, the number of quantities ending in quarters, *i.e.*, broken numbers, denotes the magnitudes of misfortunes transferred to the gods.

In many patients, the next phase of *peshi* is marked by a struggle between the patient's *bhuta* and one of the temple's presiding deities. 'You have called me here,' the spirit may challenge the god, 'but if you had any courage you should have come to me and then I'd have shown you my strength!' The people around the patient try to provoke the spirit by shouting slogans in praise of the god. Excited, the spirit often becomes angry and abusive, hurling obscenities at the god and mocking the piety of the onlookers. The torrent of aggressive abuse, especially when it is issuing out of the otherwise demure mouths of frail young girls and women, leaves little doubt that we are witnessing a convulsive release of pent-up aggression and a rare rebellion against the inhibiting norms and mores of a conservative Hindu society of which its gods are the most obvious representatives. Temporarily, some of the patients even opt out of the Hindu fold by their *bhuta* claiming that it is a Muslim, a *Sayyad* in fact, who is as powerful as Balaji and would never admit defeat. The excitement crescendoes as the community now brings its full weight to bear upon the rebellious and wayward spirit, 'You'd fight Baba, will you?' the audience shouts. 'Baba, give it a good thrashing, otherwise this villain will not listen!' Indeed the patient begins to hit himself, which simultaneously increases the volume of his spirit's protesting screams, 'I shall not submit! I'll see you and all of them [the audience] in hell first!' After some time, the patient, patently tired, stops beating himself and the spirit admits defeat: 'Fine, you have won. You starved me and you thrashed me, but after all you are my father. I'll obey you.' There is obvious relief among the onlookers at the reestablishment of the normal cosmic order and the patient's acceptance of old values and old authorities. Many begin to laugh, 'Baba, this is a clever one! Just because you thrashed him, he recognizes you as his father.' The ritual now goes into its next phase of 'statement' (*bayan*), where the spirit begs for forgiveness and, at the urging of the crowd, identifies itself. The spirit then promises to leave the patient alone and to throw itself at the mercy of the god. Sometimes the god might send a reformed, benign spirit—the *duta*—to protect the patient against the onslaught of other malignant spirits; the coming of the *duta* is signaled by a short trancelike state in which the patient repeatedly prostrates himself before the idol.

THE PATIENTS AND THEIR ILLNESSES

As I attempted to enter the inner world of the patients, reflecting on their life histories and observing the possessing spirits at close quarters, many of the *bhuta*s turned out to be familiar acquaintances from clinical psychoanalytic work; the happenings that seemed so mysterious on the first visit gradually lost their sense of the strange and the uncanny. Perhaps a few case histories will not only add to our understanding of possession illness from a dynamic psychoanalytic viewpoint—as distinguished from the more psychiatric, sociological and cultural contributions of other writers[6]—but also highlight certain kinds of culturally unacceptable behaviour and make vivid the psychic stresses to which the individual is subjected in Indian society.

1. Shakun's Aunt

Shakun was a nineteen-year-old girl from a small town in Bihar who came to Balaji with her mother and her three brothers. A shy and pretty girl, Shakun was sixteen when she was first possessed by a *bhuta*. One afternoon she had gone out to the courtyard to urinate and had called to her mother to help her with her underwear since she had freshly dyed her hands with henna, a cosmetic primarily used by girls on the eve of their wedding. On the same night, after everyone had gone to bed, the family heard Shakun's frightened screams. It seems that in the hypnogogic state before falling asleep, Shakun 'saw' a laughing woman come up to her. The girl was frightened and claimed that the woman then danced on her head, giving her a violent headache. The dancing woman's visitations and Shakun's consequent headaches and severe anxiety states occurred at regular intervals for the next three years. The diagnosis of the family and the exorcists brought in for consultation was unanimous in attributing Shakun's state to possession by a female *bhuta*. Since the local exorcist's efforts at exorcism proved fruitless (though in one of the rituals the *bhuta* had identified herself as the spirit of Shakun's father's brother's wife), it was decided that the girl be taken to Balaji.

In contrast to Shakun, who was painfully self-conscious and reticent, her mother willingly provided details of her daughter's illness. The dead aunt—Shakun's possessing spirit—the mother said with an air of conspiratorial secrecy, had committed suicide when Shakun was only three years old. 'Surely Shakun was too young to remember her,' the mother said. The suicide of the aunt, who was married to the elder brother of Shakun's father and who lived in the same household, had taken place in scandalous circumstances and the mother's salacious delight was unmistakable as she went on to describe the exciting details. The aunt, it seemed, was quite promiscuous and took her lovers indiscriminately from among all comers, including the low-caste labourers who worked in the family's small cigar-making enterprise. Though everyone else in the family knew and strongly disapproved of the aunt's affairs— Shakun's father had forbidden his wife even to talk to the woman—the husband had proverbially remained unaware of his wife's amorous adventures to the very end. One day, however, he caught his wife in *flagrante delicto* with one of his labourers and there was a violent quarrel between the couple. The aunt committed suicide on the same night. 'But, of course, Shakun doesn't know anything about her aunt. We haven't even mentioned her name in Shakun's presence,' the mother repeated.

Here, I am afraid, I must disagree with Shakun's mother. I cannot imagine that the three-year-old child, at a stage of life when curiosity is at its highest, remained unaware and unaffected by an exciting yet also violently disapproved-of aunt who died in such mysterious circumstances. At that time (and even later), there must have been whispered conversations between her parents and other family elders—conversations that simultaneously reflected their condemnation and vicarious sexual excitement—and which would suddenly cease when the child came within hearing distance of the adults. There must have been many references to the family tragedy, which Shakun overheard, and explicit taunts by other children which left Shakun in little doubt about the aunt's promiscuity and its disastrous fate. For Shakun, the memory of her aunt must have remained vividly alive in the unconscious, becoming involved with all that is both strongly forbidden and overwhelmingly exciting, harboring that 'secret of life' which every child yearns to unravel.

The aunt, I am suggesting, gradually became the personification of the growing girl's *negative identity*[7]—all that Shakun 'knew' she should never be but feared she might become, especially when her sexual impulses started asserting themselves during the tumult of adolescence. Changing from the Eriksonian to the Jungian idiom, one would say the aunt is the *shadow*, the inferior, dark part of the personality which is repressed to the unconscious and consists of all those forbidden desires that are incompatible with the values and strivings of the conscious persona. Shakun's *bhuta* is, then, a figure of her unconscious, an iconic representation (in the form of the aunt) of the girl's own sexual (even homosexual?) wishes. Because of the social standards of her community but especially because of the horrible fate of the aunt who gave in to *her* sexual wishes, Shakun, I believe, has struggled desperately to keep these desires from becoming conscious. At sixteen, a time of heightened sexual impulses, the repression failed for the first time, resulting in a psychological possession that led to great anxiety as this inhibited girl's ego fought desperately against being overwhelmed by the feared unconscious content.

2. Asha and her Spirits

Asha was a twenty-six-year-old woman from a lower-middle-class family in Delhi who had come to Balaji accompanied by her mother and her uncle. A thin, attractive woman with sharply chiseled features and a dusky complexion, Asha had a slight, girlish figure that made her look younger than her age. She had suffered from periodic headaches ever since she could remember, though her acute distress began two and a half years ago when a number of baffling symptoms made their first appearance. Among these were violent stomachaches that would convulse her with pain and leave her weak and drained of energy. Periodically, she had the sensation of ants crawling over her body, a sensation that would gradually concentrate on her head and produce such discomfort that she could not bear even to touch her head. There were bouts of gluttony and fits of rage in which she would break objects and physically lash out at anyone who happened to be near her. 'Once I even slapped my father during such a rage,' Asha told us. 'Can you imagine a daughter hitting her father, especially a father who I have loved more than anyone else in this world?'

Treatment with drugs (her uncle was a medical doctor) and consultations with an exorcist did not make any appreciable difference to her condition, but what really moved Asha to come to Balaji was her discovery, six months after her father's death, that her skin had suddenly turned dark. This caused her intense mental anguish, since she had always prided herself on her fair complexion. Asha now felt that she had become very unattractive and toyed with the idea of suicide.

After coming to Balaji, Asha's *peshi* was immediate. She had barely finished eating the two *laddoo*s in Balaji's 'court' when she fell down on the floor and revealed that she was possessed by two spirits. The first spirit, who caused the stomachaches, stated that it was sent by Asha's brother's wife. Its name was Masan, it said, a ghost that inhabits cemeteries and cremation grounds and whose 'specialty' is the eating of unborn babies in the womb. The second spirit admitted its responsibility for the sensation of crawling ants and for Asha's rages, and further revealed that it had been sent by the elder brother of Asha's fiancé. After their first confession, both the spirits were silent and did not make any further statements. On subsequent occasions Asha's *peshi* was a gentler affair consisting of a dreamy swaying of the body from which Asha emerged with a feeling of heightened well-being and the conviction that her skin had become lighter. Asha, it seems, had become addicted to *peshi*. She was not overly concerned with the punishment of her *bhuta* and indeed seemed indifferent to the prospects of her cure. If for any reason the *peshi* did not take place for more than two to three days, Asha's eyes screwed up into narrow slits, her headaches became worse and she inevitably had one of her fits of rage. In a more theoretical formulation, Asha was attempting to exchange her possession symptoms, a pathological reaction to individual conflict, for the ritual trance of *peshi*, a socially sanctioned psychological defense.[8]

Though Asha was anything but secretive and talked animatedly about her life and her problems, the talk was mostly diffused and scattered. She flitted from one experience to another, from the present to the past and back to the present again so that a chronological piecing together of her life history became a difficult task. Dramatic impressions and nostalgic memories, described with elaborate gestures and in a theatrical voice, succeeded each other with bewildering rapidity, making it difficult to sift facts from impressions, reality from fantasy.

As the youngest child in the family and the only daughter after a succession of five boys, Asha had always been her father's favourite. The memories of her childhood were pervaded by images of a father–daughter closeness and of their delight in each other that had excluded other members of the family from their charmed circle. The first thing the father did on coming home from the office every evening was to ask for his beloved daughter and play with her till it was time for dinner. Even when she was twenty, Asha remembers that her father inevitably brought her sweets in the evening, and then, lifting the now not-so-little girl upon his shoulders, he would romp around the house, often exclaiming, 'O my darling daughter, what would I do when you get married and leave this house! My life would be ever so empty!'

The only discordant note in the 'idyllic' father–daughter relationship occurred when Asha was fifteen. She fell in love with a young college student who had been engaged as her tutor. When her father came to know of their budding romance, he was furious and packed Asha off to her aunt in Saharanpur. Here she was so closely watched that she could neither write nor receive letters. For one year the girl pined away in virtual imprisonment and came back to Delhi only when her father fell sick and refused to be nursed by anyone except his favourite daughter. Asha devotedly nursed him back to health and the subject of the young tutor was never mentioned by either one of them; in fact, the episode seemed to have brought the father and daughter even closer.

The sequence of events that led to Asha's possession by the two spirits seems to have been as follows. Three years before, Asha's favourite brother had got married, and according to Asha, under the influence of his wife he became quite indifferent to his sister. Asha felt very unhappy at her brother's 'betrayal' but continued to perform all her sisterly duties. Once, when she had gone to her brother's house for a short stay—her sister-in-law was pregnant—Asha found some of her own clothes in her sister-in-law's cupboard, which made her very upset at her 'thieving' sister-in-law. Her stomachaches started shortly afterward.

It was during this time that a young man from the neighbourhood began to take a pronounced romantic interest in Asha. Every day the man dropped in at the clinic where Asha helped her uncle in his work and would talk to her for hours. Asha was uninterested in her ardent suitor, she claims, but this did not faze the young man in the least. In their long and frequent conversations the man openly declared his love for the girl. When Asha's father came to know of the young man's pursuit of his daughter, he was, once again, furious. Accompanied by two of his sons, the father went to the man's house to remonstrate with his family. The man's mother persuaded Asha's father and her brothers that Asha should be married into their family and it was decided (it was not clear how and by whom) that Asha would marry not her suitor but his younger brother instead. Asha felt very unhappy at this arrangement but her father fell sick and she could not give vent to her feelings as that might have worsened his cardiac condition. Once again she devotedly nursed her father through his illness, even 'holding and cleaning the organ which a girl never holds in her hand.'

The elder brother of her fiancé had now become bolder and even more insistent in his sexual advances toward the girl. He seemed unmoved by Asha's repeated plea that since she would soon become the wife of his younger brother he should, like a good Hindu, begin to look upon her as his daughter. It was during this period that Asha was attacked by her second spirit for the first time. She had gone to her mother-in-law's house for a visit but found that everyone was out except her lovelorn admirer. He had asked her to come up to his room and Asha had fainted. Her rages, the sensation of crawling ants and the headaches began soon afterward.

As a psychoanalyst, trying for the moment to understand the basic underlying psychic processes rather than the cultural significance of Asha's behaviour and symptoms, I would say that apart from its Indian stage and Punjabi middle-class setting, Asha's case seems to be a part of the same genre that is often encountered in the early psychoanalytic literature on young women who fell ill while caring for an older, sick relative. Torn between her duty and her love for her father and her own unacknowledged sexual wishes towards another man, Asha's conflict is similar to that of many girls in the European bourgeoisie society of the late nineteenth century—that of Freud's patient Elisabeth von R., for instance.[9] With her need for intense closeness to her father, Asha seems to have had little choice but to deny the hostile .component of her feelings toward him—as she must have denied her rage during her first, abortive love affair with the tutor. Given the present stressful circumstances—her father's illness, her engagement and the man's importunate demands—Asha's defense of denying her aggressive and sexual wishes was no longer sufficient but needed to be supplemented by having these wishes split off from consciousness and attributed to the machinations of a *bhuta*. Naturally, the spirit was 'sent' by the lovelorn swain who is unconsciously held to be responsible for the conflicting emotions that constantly threaten to overwhelm her. Asha's other distressful symptom of a darkening of her skin, I would say, springs from her identification with her father, since we learn that just before the father died, *his* skin had turned blue-black in colour. Such an identification is not only intended as a compensation for the loss of the beloved father but can also be the expression of Asha's vain attempt to free herself from him. Asha's other *bhuta*—the embryo-eater Masan—too represents a similar symbiosis of destructive and sexual wishes. Her stomachaches, I would suggest, are an expression of her unconscious pregnancy fantasy, created by means of an identification with the 'fortunate rival,' the sister-in-law. The ghost killer of unborn babies then symbolizes the idea, 'It is not I who would like to destroy my sister-in-law's unborn baby but she who wants to kill my [fantasied] baby." Asha's bouts of gluttony would seem to reinforce this interpretation. As many creative writers have also known, neurotic greed is the reflection not of the need for food but of unconscious wishes that cannot be satisfied, and thus can never be assuaged by eating. In his novel *Two*

Women, for instance, Balzac in describing a pregnant woman's passion for rotten oranges intuitively recognizes the cannibalistic nature of her wishes directed against the child in her body.

I have suggested above that Asha (but also Shakun) has much in common with Freud's women patients from the Viennese bourgeoisie. The similarity does not lie in their symptoms but in the underlying *hysteric personality* which they share. The elements of this 'ideal type' hysteric personality are well known: an intense, erotic attachment to the father and an unresolved Oedipal conflict, a fear of sexuality accompanied often by a strong but hidden interest in it, overly great concern with conventional values and social proprieties, an impressionistic way of experiencing the world, dramatized and exaggerated behaviour, a capacity for multiple identifications and so on. Indeed, a majority of the patients interviewed at Balaji—fifteen out of twenty-eight, eleven of whom were women—evidenced such a core hysteric personality. Significantly, though many of the other patients did not have a *peshi* in the temple, nor did their *bhuta* appear to make a 'statement,' in the case of all the fifteen hysterical patients the possessing *bhuta*s appeared without exception to give their 'statements.' Although possession is more than hysteria, the hysterical personality seems to make the best use of possession states.

Where Asha and other Indian hysterical personalities differ from their European counterparts is in the display of a rich, dramatic and concrete imagery of the *bhuta*s, this kind of visual imagery being diffuse, if not completely absent, in the recorded cases of *la grande hystérie* in the West. Here, the culture comes in. The rich mythological world, peopled by many gods, goddesses and other supernatural beings, in which the Indian child grows up, his early experiences of multiple caretakers, all contribute to the imagery of possessing spirits. Hysteria, as Alan Krohn has pointed out, is uniquely a neurosis that takes on the colouring of a specific historical and cultural setting.[10] 'Vapors,' fainting fits, inexplicable paralyses and convulsions in the Victorian era, the devil or a witch wresting control of the body to use it for its own purposes in the Middle Ages, are some of the many costumes that the hysterical personality has worn in its time in the West. In fact, the hysterical personality is probably unique in aligning itself with what Krohn calls the prevailing 'myth of passivity' of its culture. I am the 'passive' vehicle of gods, or of the devil, of my twitchings, or my *bhuta*s, which make me do these things, not my own desires.

It may well be that the hysterical personality has not largely disappeared in the West but has merely adapted itself to the culture's present myth of passivity. 'To be the helpless victim of one's society, the stars, one's unconscious, or mental disease,' Krohn writes, 'are now our culturally sponsored myths of passivity and this forms the basis of current hysterical alternatives.'[11] In any event, for an Indian psychoanalyst, Freud's libido theory, derived from his studies of hysteria, which often tends to be relegated these days to the realm of an aesthetic metaphor, is still central to much of his clinical work. In spite of the newer theoretical developments, such as Heinz Kohut's 'psychology of the self,' which may preoccupy his colleagues in the West, for the Indian analyst psychoanalysis remains preeminently the child of a hysterical woman.

We saw above that the single largest category of patients, comprised mostly of young women who come to Balaji in search of healing, are suffering from a hysterical disorder; or, if one prefers to use the traditional idiom, they are possessed by the ghosts of forbidden sexual and aggressive wishes. Though the individual variations in all these cases are of great interest from the clinical angle, the wide prevalence of hysterical personality among Indian women and their use of this particular cultural myth of passivity, are also reflections of certain social conditions prevailing in the society. In other words, there is no individual anxiety that does not also reflect a latent concern common to the group, a fact that Erik Erikson pointed out long ago but which we clinicians often tend to underplay in our pursuit of the uniquely individual in case history.[12] For in going through my Balaji case histories, especially of rural women, I am struck by their accumulated and repressed rage, the helpless anger of young women at the lack of their social emancipation being the canvas on which the individual picture of hysterical illness is painted.[13] Let us look at another case which illustrates this clearly.

3. Urmilla's rage

Urmilla is an attractive eighteen-year-old from a village in Rajasthan who had come to Balaji with her husband. A couple of years ago, immediately after her marriage, she started complaining of body aches accompanied by difficulties in breathing. Shortly thereafter she began to get into uncontrollable fits of rage. During these fits of rage she would heap abuse on everyone who came near her, though reserving her choicest epithets for her husband, toward whom she often became physically violent. 'She gets such strength at these times that it takes two or three strong men to restrain her', the husband reported with grudging admiration. 'She also gets so hungry that she'd eat up the food cooked for the whole family and so thirsty that she'd drink up a full bucket of water.' 'Yes, Doctor Sahib,' Urmilla confirmed her young husband's account. 'Before marriage I did not get angry even once. But when the *bhuta* comes I don't remember what happens to me. Later, they tell me the filthy abuses I have used against my husband but I have no memory of such a shameful act.'

Urmilla was possessed not only by a malignant *bhuta* but also by a benign spirit—that of her dead father—who would come to protect her when her *bhuta*-inspired rages threatened to cause grievous injury. The father had died when Urmilla was five years old and had the reputation of being a short-tempered man. The father's spirit, though also hot-tempered, was perceived by Urmilla as a guiding and benevolent *pitri* and it was at *his* advice that the couple had made the pilgrimage to Balaji. The couple had been in Balaji for some time now and though the *bhuta* came often he had yet to confess his origins and his wishes. The husband was getting impatient to go home but Urmilla insisted that she would not go back till her father's spirit instructed her to do so. When the husband insisted, Urmilla became possessed by her father's spirit and roundly abused her husband, threatening to break his legs for even daring to think of leaving his daughter behind. The spirit also told everyone in the boardinghouse where the couple was staying that the man was perhaps planning to take a second wife and that he (Urmilla's father) would see to it that he was severely punished. Occasionally, Urmilla also got possessed by another benevolent spirit—that of her dead mother-in-law—who complained of the family's neglect in carrying out the proper rituals for the welfare of her soul and ordered them to make up the deficiencies.

For the past few days, Urmilla had increasingly got the feeling that her *bhuta* was leaving her. One day she announced that they would all go to a nearby temple of the Mother Goddess Vaishno Devi—two miles from Balaji—where the Mother (the goddess) would come to possess her and tell them whether the *bhuta* had really left or whether he was playing one of his tricks for which the *bhuta*s are so notorious. Next morning, a small group consisting of Urmilla, her husband and another couple from a neighbouring village went up to the temple and waited for the Mother in the small room where the idol was kept. Urmilla went on staring at the Mother's face while the others kept up a rhythmical shouting of 'Victory to the Mother!' Urmilla's breathing was becoming faster and expressions of pain and anger flitted across her face in quick succession. Suddenly we noticed a transformation on her face, which became quite still and devoid of all expression; the Mother had come. In a loud and confident voice, Urmilla began to speak rapidly. Urmilla: 'What do you want? Speak. What do you want? Why have you called me?'

The husband (in a low, respectful tone): 'Please tell us if we should leave on Saturday.'

Urmilla: 'Yes, go away. Leave.'

The husband: 'Please also tell us whether her distress is over. Sometimes she is fine but sometimes she starts getting angry again.'

Urmilla (in an excited tone): 'Haven't I told you to leave? We'll look after the girl there. Have faith. We are with her.'

The husband: 'One more favour . . . the *bhuta*'s name—' This sentence was left incomplete since Urmilla thundered back angrily: Why do you want to know the name, you villain? We'll tell the names when we go back. The whole family is torturing this poor girl! How many names do you want?'

The husband was intimidated and mumbled his assent. Urmilla sought to confirm her domination by ordering him to rub his nose on the floor, the sign of abject surrender. The husband caught the lobes of his ears with his hands and bowing down before the idol rubbed his nose three times on the ground. The other woman who was sitting with folded hands now addressed Urmilla, 'Mother, tell me something about myself too.'

Urmilla (speaking very rapidly): 'The villain eats babies in the womb. Has ruined this poor woman. But everything will be fine. Say "Victory to the Mother." I'll take care of the *Mussulman*.'

The woman bowed to her and after a couple of minutes Urmilla came to herself. She looked exhausted but at the same time her face glowed with satisfaction at her recent experience. As they walked back to the boardinghouse, Urmilla told us that they would leave Balaji this Saturday. There was no fear of the *bhuta* returning, she said, since the Mother had decided to be with her and she could protect Urmilla even better than the spirit of her father.

The evidence is strong that Urmilla harboured within her a violent rage, which she suppressed till her marriage, until finally her inability to control the rage provoked the mysterious aches and the motor discharge in possession states. In these states, assured of the protection afforded by the clouding of consciousness and the subsequent amnesia, Urmilla was able to give an otherwise forbidden satisfaction to her pent-up fury. Under the pretext that she herself was not the subject of the rages, she could refuse to acknowledge them as her own and split herself off from her other 'selves'—the *bhuta*, the father spirit, the mother-in-law spirit and the Mother Goddess. The question then arises: what was the cause of Urmilla's rage and against whom was it aimed, since such rages can be directed not only against actual persons but also against parental images and other inner figures from childhood? As I do not have enough information on Urmilla's past, I can only look at her present circumstances and suggest that Urmilla's expression of rage against her husband and his family is also a rage against her feelings of powerlessness. It is indeed a striking fact that her identifications are with the powerful figures of the father, the mother-in-law and the Mother Goddess. In a Rajput village community where the young daughter-in-law is expected to be completely subservient and not even think angry thoughts about her husband's family and especially about her 'lord and master,' possession by spirits who behave otherwise seems to be one way for a young girl to express and yet not acknowledge the resentment against the powerlessness of her condition. Anger against 'superior' family members seems to be particularly difficult to express. Even 'She hates me,' as in the case of Asha and her sister-in-law, is not easy to acknowledge, while one has to be terribly ill and possessed by all manners of spirits to be able to express 'I hate him [or her].' The coin that depicts the *Bharatiya nari*—the 'Indian woman'—in all her sentimentalized chasteness and calm fortitude on one side, shows the same woman engaged in a desperate struggle with her inner demons on the other.

4. *Sushil's possession*

Whereas powerlessness is the social denominator of female hysteria— the cumulative trauma of Indian women, so to speak—the demands of autonomous functioning and anxiety at the prospect of individuation seem to be the social correlates of male hysteria. Instead of reproducing detailed individual case histories in support of this contention, perhaps a vignette will serve the purposes of illustration.

Sushil was a twenty-seven-year-old man who was possessed by a spirit when he was twenty-two. A year earlier, after Sushil graduated from his college in Agra, his father had set him up in a small pharmaceutical business which he expected his son to manage on his own. Things had gone well for a couple of months till Sushil was married. A few days after the marriage, Sushil found that he had lost all interest in business. Instead of going to the shop in the mornings, Sushil would wander around in the bazaar in a daze. Then one day, in this dazed state, Sushil 'saw' his younger brother—who had died in an accident when Sushil was ten—walk toward him, his school bag swinging from a thin, jaunty shoulder. From that day onward Sushil frequently became possessed by his younger brother's spirit. In these possession states, which he did not find unpleasant, Sushil's voice changed into a childish treble, his vocabulary dwindled to that of an eight-year-old and his whole demeanor took on a pronounced childish cast in which his renunciation of independent adulthood was complete.

In the *timing* of his illness, Sushil's case was identical with that of other male hysterics who also had invariably suffered their first attack of possession a few days after their marriage. It was as if they had experienced the sexual activity and the demand of establishing a close emotional bond with a strange woman as the first truly individual act of their lives in which the family could not participate and which had threatened to isolate them from the web of their familial and group emotional ties.

HEALING AT BALAJI: PSYCHOTHERAPEUTIC PERSPECTIVES

In the West, a big step in the treatment of mental disorders was taken at the end of the last century with the realization—primarily attributed to Charcot and Freud—that hysterical 'illnesses' were the symbolic expression of a definite emotional content; that the person's bodily symptoms could be seen as bits of behaviour intended to convey a message. In other words, the essential and distinctive feature of a hysterical disorder was the substitution of a bodily state for a personal problem which enabled the individual to ignore and escape the anxiety caused by the personal problem. Moreover, Freud demonstrated that the roots of the personal, emotional problem lay in the individual's past of which he or she was normally unconscious. The psychoanalyst's task was to foster a self-reflective attitude in the patient toward his bodily signs or symptoms so as to facilitate their translation into ordinary language. As Thomas Szasz has aptly put it, those who want to deal with so-called hysterical patients must therefore learn not how to diagnose or treat them but how to understand their special idiom and how to translate it into ordinary language.[14] The assumption of psychoanalysis is that by helping a person to decode his symptoms and become explicitly aware of past events that have influenced their genesis, the persistent effects of these events in his future can be mitigated and indeed radically modified.

This approach to the cure of hysteria later became the dominant psychoanalytic paradigm for dealing with other types of mental illness. In short, psychoanalysis and western psychotherapies influenced by psychoanalysis concentrate on what I would call the *text* of the mental illness—on its understanding, translation and genesis. In contrast, as we shall see below, the healing rituals of the Balaji temple follow radically different principles of therapy. They seem to be more concerned with the *context* of the illness. In traditional therapy, the special idiom under-lying the visitations of Shakun's aunt, Asha's spirits and Urmilla's rages is left at the symbolic level without any attempt at translation. Instead, the healing efforts seem to be directed more toward changing the con-text of the problem by changing the person's feelings about himself or herself. Basically, the healing rituals seek to connect (or reconnect) the individual with sources of psychological strength available in his or her life situation and thus counteract the more or less conscious feelings of despair, shame, guilt, inferiority, confusion and isolation in which the 'illness' is embedded. Let me illustrate the essentials of the contextual approach to healing through an analysis of the healing process at Balaji.

Typically, a patient whose illness started with disturbing bodily and mental symptoms has exhausted all the local resources before he makes the decision to come to Balaji. He has tried out home remedies, con-sulted doctors—both of traditional and of modern medicine—and has perhaps undergone the exorcism ritual of one or more exorcists. The decision to go to Balaji is then an admission, both by the patient and by his family, that things are seriously wrong and that the temple repre-sents perhaps the last chance of a cure. The journey to Balaji then acquires an added emotional significance and given the considerable distance a patient and his family must travel, with all the attendant in-convenience and hardship, the long trip to Balaji becomes a sacred journey, a pilgrimage in search of healing. From the medical metaphor of illness, the patient has shifted to a religious-spiritual, metaphor of the pilgrim's progress toward wholeness. All of this represents a strong emotional investment by both the patient and the family in the success of the pilgrimage. We find this increased investment in dreams that some patients had before they came to Balaji. The dreams typically involved a personal summons from the divine healer, either through the god speaking directly in the dream or through the dream image of one or more monkeys—the symbol of Hanuman. Thus even before they embarked on the healing journey, some patients had begun to send themselves messages of reassurance from the unconscious depths, increasing their hope and confidence in the success of the healing mission. Many other patients reported that once the decision was made, their *bhuta*, knowing of his imminent demise, began to raise obstacles which the patient had to overcome before he could come to Balaji. Obviously such a patient no longer feels himself as a passive recipient of healing ministrations—whether the doctor's medicines or the exorcist's incantations—but has become a more active participant in the process of his own cure.

Expectations and hope are greatly strengthened by the culture prevailing in the Balaji community. Patients and their relatives constantly extoll the powers of the divine healer and describe to each other (and especially to the newcomers) the details of miraculous cures that have taken place over the years. The fact that these cures are neither ephemeral nor hearsay is underlined by the presence of a large class of ex-patients. Many of these ex-patients come to Balaji at periodic intervals or on special festive occasions in order to sustain their link with the healing temple and to remain free from distress. Others come to fulfill their commitment of *sava–mani* in which a patient promises to feed the poor with food weighing fifty kilograms after he has been cured. All these former sufferers are living witnesses and reinforcers of the patient's growing faith that the temple healing really 'works.'

A second important characteristic of the temple's healing culture is the involvement and integration of the patient's relatives in the healing process. According to the temple rules a patient can stay in a boardinghouse only if he is escorted by at least one caretaker. In practice there are often three or four family members who accompany the 'sick' person on his pilgrimage. Many rituals that need to be carried out in the temple require the active participation of these family members. Accompanying the patient from morning till late in the evening through the various healing rituals and living in an environment where *sankat* (and its vicissitudes) is the central theme of community life, the distinction between a 'sick' and a 'normal' member of the family is gradually eroded. There were many cases where a person who had come to Balaji with a possessed relative soon discovered that he too was in distress from a *bhuta* and in need of healing. Another bridge between the 'normal' and the 'sick' is through the concept of *sankat* transfer. According to this belief, if a close relative of the patient prays to Balaji that he is ready to take on the distress then the *bhuta* often leaves the patient and possesses the supplicant. However, in the three cases of *sankat* transfer that I observed, the family member began to show signs of *bhuta* possession without any corresponding relief for the original sufferer.

The importance of the wall between 'sickness' and 'health' becoming porous and the blurring of the distinctions between 'normal' and 'possessed' lies in the fact that it helps the patient considerably to overcome his feelings of isolation and moral worthlessness. Even though possession by a *bhuta* is not culturally alien to the patient, who has seen and heard of many others who have been similarly afflicted, possession by a malignant spirit nevertheless isolates and bars the individual from sources of collective strength residing in his or her group and community. The feeling of isolation is attributable to the fact that possession is also seen as a stigma, a kind of leprosy of the character that cuts off the individual from members of his immediate and extended community. This becomes evident when we read of the kinds of people that Hindu culture considers especially susceptible to possession by *bhuta–preta*. These are 'the impotent, the lustful, the lately widowed, bankrupts, sons and brothers of whores, convicts, the idle, the brooders on the unknowable, gluttons and starvers. . . . Intelligent and educated men and healthy intelligent women are free from spirit attacks.'[15]

The temple regulations, verbally communicated to the patient by the priest and available in a printed brochure, lay considerable stress on the patient's achieving a state of purity before any appeal to the deities can be made. These rules enjoin a strict observation of celibacy during the whole of his or her stay at Balaji, prohibit the use of spices, onion, garlic and other impure foods and require daily morning baths and a fresh change of clothes every time the patient enters the temple precincts. Elsewhere, I have suggested that the feeling of being dirty and polluted is the Indian form of experiencing guilt. The purification rituals, then, with their washing and cleansing the inner 'filth,' seem to be directed toward a symbolic expiation of the patient's feeling of guilt, while at the conscious level they prepare the patient to receive the superior power of the god.

Yet another quality of Balaji's communal culture is the openness with which *sankats* are discussed. Patients (and their families) exchange detailed case histories within and outside the temple premises and when two patients encounter each other in the street, 'How is your *sankat* doing?' is both an acceptable greeting and a mode of inquiry about the other's well-being. The possible responses to such an inquiry—'There is no change,' 'It is turning out well'—are very much like the matter-of-fact exchanges between two graduate students in physics on the progress of their experiment. The point is that possession illness and the presence of *bhuta–preta* are accepted in a plain, uncomplicated way. In the boardinghouses, after their gates are closed for the night, patients and their families spontaneously form into small groups to discuss each other's distress. In such therapeutic group sessions, the most intimate details of the individual's distress are revealed, speculations on the probable origins of the spirit are advanced and the possible outcome of a particular healing ritual debated. Besides lessening any residual feelings of shame, the public sharing of the illness certainly makes the malignant spirits lose their private terrors. Anxious and fearful emotions that we would normally expect to be associated with the *bhuta–preta* are quite conspicuous by their absence as the patients begin to address their possessing spirits derisively with the diminutive '*bhutra*'. What one's *bhutra* did on a particular day during the healing ritual in the temple is related to others in an indulgent manner, as if the *bhuta* were a naughty child whose antics had to be suffered patiently. This marks a distinct change in the individual's attitude toward the illness, for it is no longer the *bhuta* who is possessing the patient but the patient who has to bear with the *bhuta*. From our own clinical experience, we can appreciate the difference it makes (and the big step it constitutes toward cure) when a person begins to feel he has the neurosis instead of the earlier feeling that the neurosis has him. We can now understand better how a 'standard ritual'—as Obeyesekere in his excellent study of exorcism in Sri Lanka has called such healing practices[16]—can help patients who are suffering from various kinds of mental illnesses. Ignoring the different texts of the illness, the standard ritual works chiefly through the context in which the feelings aroused by the illness are embedded. This approach 'works' since the context is also the nexus for those universal human strengths whose restoration in the individual makes for his wholeness.

Of the multiple perspectives on mental illness—illness as an expression of alienation from the bodily order, illness as an alienation from the self and illness as alienation from the social order—we see from the above description that healing at Balaji lays an emphasis on ending the patient's alienation from his social (and cosmic) order. The judicial court of the god recognizes two parties who are clamouring for the possession of the individual: his or her cut-off 'selves' (the *bhuta*s) and the representatives of the family and community. The judicial (and therapeutic) task, in the judgement of the court, is not only, or even primarily, the reintegration of the cut-off parts of the self, as in western psychotherapy, which therefore demands that an isolated neurotic be put into an isolated setting under a treatment dominated by a scientific theory. Instead, the 'court' also sees as its task the reintegration of the individual with his community. This requires a polyphonic social drama that attempts a ritual restoration of the dialogue, not only within the patient but with the family. By participating in rituals together with the patient, and especially by having the patient's *sankat* transferred onto themselves, the family members too seem to be accepting their share of the blame for the patient's problems.

As far as the cut-off parts of the self are concerned, the therapy proceeds along two separate lines. One, the individual's tolerance of the *bhuta* is sought to be increased by lessening the spirit's fearsomeness. The spirit's potentially benign nature—the *bhuta* being replaced by a *duta*, the god's 'messenger'—is pointed out and it is reemphasized that malignant spirits are only unfortunate *pitri*s or ancestral spirits deserving compassion rather than anxious reactions. In other, psychoanalytic words, the unconscious content of the psyche is considered neither fixed and immutable nor malignant and threatening, as in the notion of the psychoanalytic id, but as fundamentally capable of a benign transformation. And we must remember that the *bhuta–preta* are only defendants in Balaji's court and not outside the pale of society. Pretaraja, after all, is as much a defense lawyer who must look after the *bhuta–preta*'s interests, as a judge who must punish them.

Second, *peshi* ritual attempts to transform the patient's belief into a conviction that his bad traits and impulses are not within but without; that they are not his own but belong to the *bhuta*. The fact that fifteen out of twenty-eight patients were possessed by a Muslim spirit indicates the extent of this projection in the sense that the Muslim seems to be *the* symbolic representation of the alien in the Hindu unconscious. Possession by a Muslim *bhuta* reflects the patient's desperate efforts to convince himself and others that his hungers for forbidden foods, tumultuous sexuality and uncontrollable rage belong to the Muslim destroyer of taboos and are farthest away from his 'good' Hindu self.

Like every other system of therapy—western or eastern—which can help some but not all of its clients, the temple healing finds reasons for not being as universally effective as it would like or as its adherents might claim.[17] In cases where a patient has successfully gone through the complete course of 'application,' 'appearance' and 'statement' and yet retains many of his original symptoms, he is declared to have multiple *sankat*s, with more than one possessing spirit being involved. In such cases, the patient is expected to go through the complete ritual all over again and to repeat it as many times as the number of *bhuta*s that possess him. The record is held by a man who had twenty-one possessing spirits! In other cases, where the patient is obviously relieved of his symptoms but falls ill soon after he gets back home, the relapse is attributed to the inherently deceitful nature of the *bhuta*, who has sneakily reneged on its solemn promise to Balaji. For more severe disorders where in spite of all efforts the *peshi* is at best limited to a swaying of the body, without the dramatic struggles between Good and Evil and without the *bhuta* making the 'statement,' the solution offered is 'imprisonment' of the spirit for a year at the temple. The patient may then go about his normal affairs, but must return to Balaji before the end of the year to once again go through the healing rituals. As a direct suggestion to the patient to remain well for at least a year, the *sankat* imprisonment seems like a last desperate measure and has correspondingly little success.

In conclusion, without going into a comparison of the effectiveness of the temple healing *vis-à-vis* modern psychotherapy in the treatment of the various classes of mental disorder, I would only like to underline their radically different assumptions. The assumptions underlying western psychotherapy are also the highest values of modern individualism. They are epitomized in psychoanalysis (in Kenneth Keniston's words) as 'its almost limitless respect for the individual, faith that understanding is better than illusion, insistence that our psyches harbour darker secrets than we care to confess, refusal to promise too much, and a sense of the complexity, tragedy and wonder of human life.'[18] The underlying values of the traditional temple healing, on the other hand, stress that faith and surrender to a power beyond the individual are better than individual effort and struggle, that the source of human strengths lies in a harmonious integration with one's group, in the individual's affirmation of the community's values and its given order, in his obedience to the community's gods and in his cherishing of its traditions.

5

The Guru as Healer

The contemporary images of the Indian guru, the sacred centre of Hindu religious and philosophical traditions, are many. He is that stately figure in spotless white or saffron robes, with flowing locks and beard, to all appearances the younger brother of a brown Jehovah. To be approached in awe and reverence, he is someone who makes possible the disciple's fateful encounter with the mystery lying at the heart of human life. He is also the Rasputin look-alike, with piercing yet warm eyes, hypnotic and seductive at once, a promiser of secret ecstasies and radical transformations of consciousness and life. The guru is also the venerable guardian of ancient, esoteric traditions, benevolently watchful over the disciple's experiences in faith, gently facilitating his sense of identity and self. He can also be (to use the imagery of Pupul Jayakar, the biographer of the Indian sage Jiddu Krishnamurti), 'the silent, straight-backed stranger, the mendicant who stands waiting at the doorways of home and mind, holding an invitation to otherness,' evoking 'passionate longings, anguish and a reaching out physically and inwardly to that which is unattainable.'[1]

In the above snapshots we find little trace of the old polarity which characterized the guru image. This polarity consisted of the worldly, orthodox teacher guru at one end representing relative, empirical knowledge, and the otherworldly, mystic guru at the other pole who was the representative of esoteric, existential knowledge. In Hindu terms, the dominant image of the guru seems to have decisively shifted toward the *moksha* (liberation) guru rather than the *dharma* (virtue) guru, toward the *bhakti* (devotional) guru rather than the *jnana* (knowledge) guru or, in Tantric terms, toward the *diksha* (initiation) guru who initiated the novice into methods of salvation rather than the *shiksha* (teaching) guru who taught the scriptures and explained the meaning and purpose of life.[2]

This was, of course, not always the case. In Vedic times (1500–500 BC), when man's encounter with the sacred mysteries took place through ritual, the guru was more a guide to their correct performance and an instructor in religious duties. A teacher deserving respect and a measure of obedience, he was not yet a mysterious figure of awe and the venerated incarnation of divinity.

In the later Upanishadic era (800–500 BC), the polar shift begins in earnest as the person of the guru starts to replace Vedic rituals as the path to spiritual liberation. He now changes from a knower and dweller in Brahman to being the only conduit to Brahman. Yet the Upanishadic guru is still recognizably human—a teacher of acute intellect, astute and compassionate, demanding from the disciple the exercise of his reason rather than exercises in submission and blind obedience. When, in the seventh century AD, the great Shankara, in his project of reviving the ancient Brahminical tradition, seeks to resurrect the Upanishadic guru, he sees in him a teacher who 'is calm, tranquil, childlike, silent and free from distracting motivations. Although learned he should be as a child, parading neither wisdom, nor learning, nor virtue itself. . . . He is a reservoir of mercy who teaches out of compassion to the multitude. He is sympathetic to the conditions of the student and is able to act with empathy towards him.'[3] In the disciple's spiritual quest, Shankara's guru places reason on par with scriptural authority and constantly exhorts the student to test and verify the teachings through his own experience. Every student needs to discover anew for himself or herself what is already known, a spiritual patrimony which has to be earned each time for it to become truly one's own. Here, the ideal of the Hindu guru was not too far removed from the Buddhist master who, too, constructed near-experience situations to illustrate a teaching and who saw the master–disciple relationship as one of perfect equality in self-realization, with radical insight as its goal. The relationship between the guru and disciple was of intimacy, not of merger. Both the guru and disciple were separate individuals, and potential equals, though striving for ever-greater closeness.

From the seventh century onwards, the swing away from the teacher image of the guru received its greatest momentum with the rise of the *bhakti* cults in both north and south India. Devotional surrender on the part of the disciple, with such features as ritualistic service to the guru, the worship of his feet, bodily prostration and other forms of veneration, and divine grace (*prasada*) on the part of the guru, mark the guru–disciple relationship. 'Guru and Govind [i.e. Lord Krishna] stand before me,' says the 15th-century poet-saint Kabir, and asks, 'Whose feet should I touch?' The answer is, 'The guru gets the offering. He shows the way to Govind.'[4] The operative word is now love rather than understanding. To quote Kabir again:

Reading book after book, the whole world died
And none ever became learned
He who can decipher just a syllable of 'love'
is the true learned man (pandit)[5]

With the spread of *tantric* cults around AD 1000, the guru not only shows the way to the Lord, but is the Lord. 'There is no higher god than guru,' *tantric* texts tell us, 'No higher truth than the guru.' 'The guru is father, the guru is mother, the guru is the God Shiva. When Shiva is angry, the guru is the Saviour. But when the guru is angry, there is no one who can save you.'[6] The guru is now an extraordinary figure of divine mystery and power, greater than the scriptures and the gods, and all that the disciple requires to realize his own godlike nature, his extraordinary identity as Lawrence Babb puts it, is to merge his substantial and spiritual being with that of the guru.[7] The ambiguities of thought and the agonizings of reason can be safely sidestepped since the way is no longer through a complete and wilful surrender—the offering of *tana, mana,* and *dhana* (body, mind, and wealth) in the well-known phrase of north Indian devotionalism. The responsibility for the disciple's inner transformation is no longer that of the disciple but of the guru. 'One single word of the guru gives liberation,' says a tantric text. 'All the sciences are masquerades. Only the knowledge flowing out of the guru's mouth is living. All other kinds of knowledge are powerless and causes of suffering.'[8]

The combined forces of the *bhakti* and *tantra* pushed toward an ever-increasing deification of the guru, a massive idealization of his mystery and power. The 13th-century Marathi saint Jnaneshvara writes of the guru:

As for his powers,
He surpasses even the greatness of Shiva,
With his help,
The soul attains the state of Brahman;
But if he is indifferent,
Brahman has no more worth than a blade of grass.[9]

Complementary to the movement of the guru from man to god is the

144 / *Culture and Healing*

shift in the disciple from man to child. The favoured, the ideal disciple is pure of heart, malleable of character, and a natural renouncer of all adult categories, especially of rational inquiry and of the sexual gift. These images of the guru and disciple and their ideal relationship pervades the Hindu psyche to a substantial extent even today. 'Guru is Brahma, guru is Vishnu, guru is Maheshwara,' is a verse not only familiar to most Hindus but one that evokes complex cultural longings, that resonates with what is felt to be the best part of their selves and of the Hindu tradition.

Let me not give the impression that the triumphant procession of the liberation / salvation guru in Hindu tradition has gone completely unchallenged. In traditional texts there are at least two instances questioning the need for a guru, admittedly an insignificant number compared to hundreds of tales, parables, and pronouncements extolling him. The first one is from the *Uddhavagita* in the sixth-century text of *Bhagvata Purana* where Dattareya, on asked to account for his self-possession and equanimity, lists elements of nature, the river, certain animals, and even a prostitute (from whom he learned autonomy from the sensual world) as his 24 gurus. The parable of Dattareya ends with the exhortation, 'Learn, above all, from the rhythms of your own body.' The second incident is an episode from the *Yogavasistha*, a text composed between the ninth and 12th-centuries in Kashmir, wherein Princess Cudala, setting out on her inner journey of self exploration, deliberately eschews all gurus and external authorities, and reaches her goal through a seven-stage self-analysis.

In more recent times, beginning in the 19th-century, there have been reformers who have sought to revive Vedic rituals and Upanishadic religion. They would at the most sanction the teacher guru, such as the socially engaged intellectual swami of the Ramakrishna Mission or of the 19th-century reformist movement, Arya Samaj. There have been also reluctant gurus, such as Krishnamurti, who vehemently denied the need for a guru and in fact saw in him the chief obstacle to spiritual liberation. For him and some modern educated Indians the guru institution as it exists today is a focus of all the anti-intellectual and authoritarian tendencies in Hindu society.[10] Yet for the great mass of Hindus, the mystical, charismatic, divine guru image continues to be a beacon of their inner worlds. The all-pervasiveness of this image is due to more complex reasons than the mere victory of irrationality over reason, servility over autonomy, or of a contemporary dark age over an earlier golden era.

What I am suggesting here is that the shift from the teacher to the master image is inevitable given the fact that perhaps a major, if not the most significant, role of the guru is that of a healer of emotional suffering and its somatic manifestations. This psychotherapeutic function, insufficiently acknowledged, is clearly visible in well-known modern gurus whose fame depends on their reported healing capabilities, rather than deriving from any mastery of traditional scriptures, philosophical knowledge, of even great spiritual attainments. Of course, in cases of international gurus, the healing is tailored to culture-specific needs. In India there will be more miracles and magical healing, while in the West there will be a greater use of psycho-religious methods and techniques which are not unfamiliar to a psycho-therapeutically informed population.[11]

The importance of the healing guru comes through clearly in all available accounts. Ramakrishna's disciple-biographer writes:

The spiritual teacher has been described in the *Guru-Gita* and other books as the 'physician of the world-disease.' We did not at all understand that so much hidden meaning was there in it before we had the blessing of meeting the master. We had no notion of the fact that the guru was indeed the physician of mental diseases and could diagnose at first sight the modifications of the human mind due to influence of spiritual emotions.[12]

Perhaps the most vivid recent account of the therapeutic encounter between a guru and a disciple is contained in Pupul Jayakar's moving description of her first one-to-one meeting with Krishnamurti. The narration could very well also have been of an initial interview with a good analyst. In her early 30s, outwardly active and successful, yet with intimations of something seriously wrong with her life, Jayakar is apprehensive and tries to prepare for the meeting. She begins the interview by talking of the fullness of her life and work, her concern for the underprivileged, her interest in art, her desire to enter politics. As the first flow of words peters out, Jayakar gradually falls silent.

I looked up and saw he was gazing at me; there was a questioning in his eyes and a deep probing. After a pause he said, 'I have noticed you at the discussions. When you are in repose, there is a great sadness on your face.'

I forgot what I had intended to say, forgot everything but the sorrow within me. I had refused to allow the pain to come through. So deep was it buried that it rarely impinged on my conscious mind. I was horrified of the idea that others would show me pity and sympathy, and had covered up my sorrow with layers of aggression. I had never spoken of this to anyone—not even to myself had I acknowledged my loneliness; but before this silent stranger all masks were swept away. I looked into his eyes and it was my own face I saw reflected. Like a torrent long held in check, the words came.[13]

Jayakar talks of her childhood, of a sensitive lonely girl, 'dark of complexion in a family where everyone was fair, unnoticed, a girl when I should have been a boy.' She talks of her pregnancies, in one case the baby dying in the womb, in other the birth of a deformed child, a girl who dies in childhood. She tells Krishnamurti of the racking pain of her beloved father's death and the tearing, unendurable agony she feels as she talks. 'In his presence the past, hidden in the darkness of the long forgotten, found form and awakened. He was as a mirror that reflected. There was an absence of personality, of the evaluator, to weigh and distort. I kept trying to keep back something of my past but he would not let me. He said, "I can see if you want me to." And so the words which for years had been destroying me were said.'[14]

Krishnamurti is one of the most 'intellectual' of modern gurus, with a following chiefly among the most modern and highly educated sections of Indian society. It is nonetheless the news of his 'miracle' cures—deafness in one instance, an acute depression in another—which spreads like wildfire through the *ashram*s all over the country. Crowds of potential disciples gather at his talks, striving to touch his hand, to share in his benediction. 'These incidents and the vastness of his silent presence impressed people tremendously,' Jayakar writes somewhat ruefully. 'The teaching, though they all agreed it was grounded in a total nonduality, appeared too distant and too unattainable.'[15]

In my own work with gurus and disciples, I found that many of the latter shared a common pattern in their lives that had led them to a search for the guru and to initiation in his cult.[16] Almost invariably the individual had gone through one or more experiences that had severely mauled his sense of self worth, if not shattered it completely. In contrast to the rest of us, who must also deal with the painful feelings aroused by temporary depletions in self esteem, it seems that those who went to gurus grappled with these feelings for a much longer time, sometimes for many years, without being able to change them appreciably. Unable to rid themselves of the feelings of 'I have lost everything and the world is empty,' or 'I have lost everything because I do not deserve anything,' they had been on the lookout for someone, somewhere, to restore the lost sense of self worth and to counteract their hidden image of a failing, depleted self—a search nonetheless desperate for its being mostly unconscious. This 'someone' eventually turned out to be the particular guru to whom the seekers were led by events—such as his vision—

which in retrospect seemed miraculous. The conviction and the sense of a miracle having taken place, though projected to the circumstances that led to the individual's initiation into the cult, actually derived from the 'miraculous' ending of a persistent and painful internal sate, the disappearance of the black depressive cloud that had seemed to be a permanent feature of the individual's life. Perhaps a vignette from a life history will illustrate this pattern more concretely.

Harnam was the youngest of four sons of a peasant family from a north Indian village who had tilled their own land for many generations. As the 'baby' of the family, Harnam had been much indulged during his childhood, especially by his mother. She had died when he was 18, and ever since her death, he said, a peculiar *udasinta* (sadness) had taken possession of his soul. Though he had all the comforts at home, enough to eat and drink, and an abundant measure of affection from his father and elder brothers, the *udasinta* had persisted. For 15 long years, he said, his soul remained restless, yearning for an unattainable peace. His thoughts often dwelt upon death, of which he developed an exaggerated fear, and he was subject to crippling headaches that confined him to the darkness of his room for long periods. Then, suddenly he had a vision in a dream of the guru (he had seen his photograph earlier), who told him to come to his *ashram* to take initiation into the cult. He had done so; his sadness had disappeared as did his fear and headaches, and he felt the loving omnipresence of the guru as a protection against their return.

Besides cultural encouragement and individual needs, I believe there are some shared developmental experiences of many upper caste Hindu men which contribute to the intensification of the fantasy of guru as healer. In an earlier work, I have described the male child's experience of 'second birth,' a more or less sudden loss of a relationship of symbiotic intimacy with the mother in late childhood and an entry into the more businesslike relationships of the world of men.[17] Two of the consequences of the 'second birth' in the identity development of Hindu men are first, an unconscious tendency to 'submit' to an idealized omnipotent figure, both in the inner world of fantasy and in the outside world of making a living, and second the lifelong search for someone, a charismatic leader or a guru, who will provide mentorship and a guiding worldview, thereby restoring intimacy and authority to individual life. I would interpret the same phenomena more explicitly in terms of self psychology. Since I believe some of the concepts of self psychology to be of value in illuminating the healing process in the guru–disciple relationship, these concepts may first need a brief elucidation.

The major focus of the Kohutian psychology of the self is what he called a self-object.[18] One exists as a person, a self, because a significant other, the self-object, has addressed one as a self and evoked the self experience. Self-objects, strictly speaking, are not persons but the subjective aspect of a function performed by a relationship. It is thus more apt to speak of self-object experiences, intrapsychic rather than interpersonal, which evoke, maintain, and give cohesion to the self.[19] The very emergence and maintenance of the self as a psychological structure, then, depends on the continued presence of an evoking–sustaining–responding matrix of self-object experiences. Always needed, from birth to death, the absence of these experiences leads to a sense of fragmentation of the self, including, in extreme states of narcissistic starvation, the terrors of self dissolution.

The mode of needed self-object experiences, of course, changes with age from the simple to the more complex. In a child, the required self-object experience occurs primarily, though not exclusively (remember the importance of the glow in the mother's eye and of the affirmative timbre in her voice), through physical ministrations. In the adult, symbolic self-object experiences supplied by his culture, such as religious, aesthetic, and group experiences, may replace some of the more concrete modes of infancy and childhood. In the language of self psychology, the guru is the primary cultural self-object experience for adults in Hindu tradition and society. For everyone whose self was weakened because of faulty self-object relations during crucial developmental phases or for those who have been forced into defensive postures by the self's fragility where they are cut off from all normal sustaining and healing self-object responses, the guru is the culture's irresistible offer for the redressal of injury and the provision of self-object experiences needed for the strengthening of the self.

It is the immanence of the healing moment in the guru–disciple relationship which inevitably pushes the guru image toward that of a divine parent and of the disciple toward that of a small child. Western psychiatrists have tended to focus more on the pathology and the malevolent regression unleashed by the psychic shifts in the images of the self and the guru when therapeutic expectations of the disciples take firm hold.[20] They have talked of the extreme submissiveness of the disciples, of a denial of strong unconscious hostility, of the devotee's deepest desire being of oral dependence on the mother, and so on.

I believe the western psychiatric emphasis on the pathological and regressive—'bad' regressive—aspects of the guru–disciple relationship does it injustice. However one may prefer the Enlightenment virtues of reason and ideological egalitarianism, the universal power exercised by what I would call the guru fantasy is not to be denied. By guru fantasy I mean the existence of someone, somewhere, who will heal the wounds suffered in the original parent–child relationship. It is the unconscious longing for the curer of the 'world-disease,' a longing which marks all potentially healing encounters whether they are or not officially termed as such. This fantasy invariably exerts its power in changing the self image of the seeker and of the healing Other in the directions I have described above.

My own profession, psychoanalysis, in its theories of cure has not escaped from the ubiquitous power of this fantasy. Patients, of course, have always approached analysis and analysts with a full-blown guru fantasy. Analysts, on the other hand, tended at first to believe with Freud that healing took place through knowledge and an expansion of conscious awareness. Yet beginning with one of the most original of the first generation of analysts, Sandor Ferenzci, there has been a growing body of opinion which holds the person of the analyst and his interaction with the patient, in which the analyst counteracts the specific pathogenic deficit of the parent–child relationship, as the prime carriers of the healing moment. Franz Alexander was perhaps the most outright advocate of the analyst adopting corrective postures, but the stress on the role of the analyst as someone who makes up in some fashion or other for a deficient nonempathic parent is met with again and again in analytical literature, especially in the school of object relations. Winnicott, for instance, believed that with patients who suffered from not-good-enough early maternal environment, the analytic setting and the analyst, more than his interpretations, provided an opportunity for the development of an ego, for its integration from ego nuclei. Kohut's self psychology with its stress on the curative powers of the analyst's empathy moves further in the same direction. As Ernst Wolf states the self psychological position, 'It is not the content of the information conveyed to the patient, not the substance of the interpretations and interventions made, not the correctness of the therapist's conjectures, not even the therapist's compliance with demands to "mirror" the patient or to be his or her ideal that is pivotal: It is decisive for the progress of the therapeutic endeavour that the patient experience an ambience in which he or she feels respected, accepted and at least a little understood. . . . The person who is the therapist then becomes as crucial a variable as the person who is the patient.'[21]

Many years earlier, Sacha Nacht had captured this shift in the psychoanalytic view of healing when he said 'It is of more value from the curative point of view, to have a mediocre interpretation supported by good transference than the reverse.'[22] In interviews with devotees, the unconscious expectation that the guru will counteract specific parental deficits becomes manifest in the way an individual selects a particular guru. It seems to be a fact that often the Master who is experienced as an incarnation of the Divine by his own disciples leaves other seekers cold. In the politics of gurudom, reverence and worship by your own devotees does not ensure that you are not a figure of indifference, even of derision and contempt, to other gurus and members of *their* cults. Let me illustrate.

Amita, a 30-year-old woman who is a lecturer in Hindi in a local college, is one of the closest disciples of a contemporary female guru, Nirmala Devi. Born into an orthodox middle-class Brahmin family, she has been engaged in the 'search' ever since childhood. 'My mother used to worship 560 million gods every day,' she says in a bitter, contemptuous voice, 'but it didn't change her a bit. She was a hot-tempered, dried-up woman with little human sympathy or kindness. So what was the use of observing all the rites and praying to the gods?' As Amita talks of her past, it is clear that she has been in a hostile clinch with her mother all her life. Amita went to see many gurus but was dissatisfied with every one of them till one day, a few years ago, she attended one of Mataji's public meetings. Her conversion was instantaneous and she has remained a devoted disciple ever since. 'Mataji is like the cloud that gives rain to everyone,' she says. I am struck by the juxtaposition of her imagery in which mother is dry while Mataji brims over with the rain of iove.

For Amita, then, Mataji's parental style has elements of both the familiar and the strange. The familiarity is in Mataji's fierceness, the 'hot temper'; the difference, and this is indeed crucial, is in the preponderance of warmth and love in Mataji as compared to Amita's early experience of the indifference of her mother's style.' A guru like the late Maharaj Charan Singh of the Radhasoami sect, I would suggest, is too remote from Amita's central conflict, while the late Bhagwan Rajneesh, of Oregon and Pune fame, would be too threatening to the moral values of a girl brought up in an orthodox, middle-class Brahmin family. Mataji's parental style, on the other hand, dovetails with Amita's self-object needs and social experience.

That the guru–disciple relationship is in important ways an extension of the parent–child relationship, constituting a developmental second chance for obtaining the required nutrients for the cohesion, integration, and vigorousness of the self, is implicit in some of the older devotional literature and is often explicitly stated by modern gurus. Basava, the 12th-century founder of the Virsaiva sect, identifies the guru god with a particular aspect of the mother:

> As a mother runs
> Close behind the child
> With his hand on a cobra
>   or a fire
> The lord of meeting rivers
>   Stays with me
> Every step of the way
> And looks after me.[23]

In his instructions to disciples, a contemporary guru, Swami Satyanand Saraswati, tells us, 'Now in relation with the guru, the disciple chooses one *bhava* (emotional state) for himself, according to his personality and needs, and develops that to its fullest potential. If he feels the need for a friend, he should regard the guru as his friend. Or, if he has been lacking parental love, the guru can be his father and mother. . . . It all depends on your basic needs and which area of your personality is the most powerful. Sometimes in adopting a certain *bhava* toward the guru, the disciple tends to transfer his complexes and neurosis too. If he has become insecure due to the suffering meted out to him by harsh parents, then in relationship with the guru too, he feels insecure.'[24]

Swami Satyanand's remarks also tell us of the difficulties in the path of *surrender* to the guru, an emotional experience which is indispensable for mutative changes in the disciple's self.

If there is one demand made by the guru on the disciple, it is of surrender, an opening up and receptivity of the latter's psyche which is sometimes sought to be conveyed through (what men imagine to be) the imagery of female sexual experience. Saraswati writes, 'When you surrender to the guru, you become like a valley, a vacuum, an abyss, a bottomless pit. You acquire depth, not height. This surrender can be felt in many ways. The guru begins to manifest in you; his energy begins to flow into you. The guru's energy is continuously flowing, but in order to receive it, you have to become a womb, a receptacle.'[25]

Surrender of the self is, of course, ubiquitous in the religious traditions of the world. In his *The Varieties of Religious Experience*, William James called it regeneration by relaxing and letting go, psychologically indistinguishable from Lutheran justification by faith and the Wesleyan acceptance of free grace. He characterized it as giving one's private convulsive self a rest and finding that a greater self is there. 'The results, slow or sudden, great or small, of the combined optimism and expectancy, the regenerative phenomenon which ensues on the abandonment of effort, remain firm facts of human nature.' He added, . . . 'You see why self surrender has been and always must be regarded as the vital turning point of religious life. . . . One may say the whole development of Christianity in inwardness has consisted in little more than greater and greater emphasis attached to this crisis of self surrender.'[26]

In Sufism, too, surrender to the master is a necessary prerequisite for the state of *fana fil-shaykh* or annihilation of oneself in the master. Of the *iradah*, the relationship between the Sufi master and his disciple, the Sufi poet says: 'O heart, if thou wanted the Beloved to be happy with thee, then thou must do and say what he commands. If he says, "Weep blood!" do not ask "Why?"; if He says, "Die!" do not say "How is that fitting?"'[27]

In terms of self-psychology, surrender is the full flowering of the idealizing transference, with its strong need for the experience of merging into a good and powerful, wise and perfect self-object—the guru. 'This is the secret of the guru–disciple relationship,' says one guru. 'The guru is the disciple, but perfected, complete. When he forms a relationship with the guru, the disciple is in fact forming a relationship with his own best self.'[28] The disciple, in experiencing his or her self as part of the guru's self, hearing with the guru's ears, seeing with the guru's eyes, tasting with the guru's tongue, feeling with the guru's skin, may be said to be striving for some of the most archaic self-object experiences.

Ramakrishna, the arch example of the Indian penchant for using narrative form in construction of a coherent and integrated world, of his preference for the language of the concrete, of image and symbol over more conceptual and abstract forms, tells us the following parable.

One day while driving with Arjuna (the warrior hero of the epic *Mahabharata*), Krishna (who is both God and Arjuna's guru) looked at the sky and said, 'See, friend, how beautiful is the flock of pigeons flying there!' Arjuna saw it and immediately said, 'Yes, friend, very beautiful pigeons indeed.' The very next moment Krishna looked up again and said, 'How strange, friend, they are by no means pigeons.' Arjuna saw the birds and said, 'Quite so, my friend, they are not pigeons at all.' 'Now try to understand the matter,' Ramakrishan exhorts us. 'Arjuna's truthfulness is unquestionable. He could have never flattered Krishna in agreeing with him both the times. But Arjuna's devotional surrender to Krishna was so very great that he actually saw with his own eyes whatever Krishna saw with his.'[29]

Devotees come to the guru, as do patients to the analyst, in a conflicted state. On the one hand, there is the unconscious hope of making up for missing or deficient self-object responses in interaction with the guru. On the other hand, there is the fear of evoking self-fragmenting responses through the same interaction. The omnipresence of fears of injury to the self and of regression into early primitive states of self-dissolution is what forces the devotee to be wary of intimacy. It prevents the desired surrender to the guru, however high the conscious idealization of the values of surrender and letting go might be. Gurus are of course aware of the conflict and in their various ways have sought to reassure the disciples about their fears. Muktananda, for instance, writes, 'There are only two ways to live: One is with constant conflict, and the other is with surrender. Conflict leads to anguish and suffering. . . . But when someone surrenders with understanding and equanimity, his house, body and heart become full. His former feeling of emptiness and lack disappears.'[30] And one of his disciples puts it in a language which the modern self-psychologist would have no hesitation in acknowledging as his own: 'We live in countless fleeting relationships, always seeking, finding and losing again. As children and adults, we learn through these relationships. We learn by taking into ourselves our loved ones' thoughts and voices, absorbing our loved ones' very presence along with their knowledge.'[31] Gurus, gurus have always emphasized, are not human beings, not objects in the inelegant language of psychoanalysis, but functions. They are the power of grace in spiritual terms and intense self-object experiences in the language of self-psychology.

The psychological term 'intense self-object experience' of course transfers the location of the fount of 'grace' from the person of the guru to the psyche of the devotee. It is a grace we have all experienced as infants when the mother's various ministrations transformed our internal world from states of disintegration to one of feeling integrated, from dreaded intimations of fragmentation to blissful experiences of wholeness. The persistent search for this inner metamorphosis in adult life is what makes the guru in India—to use Christopher Bollas' concept—a primary 'transformational object.'[32] He is the culturally-sanctioned addressee of a collective request for the transforming experience which goes beyond healing in its narrow sense. The guru's grace is, then, the devotee's recollection of an earlier transformed state. It is a remembrance, Bollas reminds us, which does not take place cognitively but existentially through intense affective experience, even when the latter is not on the same scale as in early life. The anticipation of being transformed by the guru inspires the reverential attitude toward his person, an attitude which in secular man, especially in the West, is more easily evoked by the transformational objects of art than those of religious faith.

The idealizing transference, leading to the merging experience, is thus the core of the healing process in the guru–disciple relationship. The healing is seen in terms of an alchemical transformation of the self: 'When iron comes in contact with the philosopher's stone, it is transmuted in gold. Sandalwood trees infuse their fragrance into the trees around them.'[33] Psychoanalysts, of the object relations and self-psychology schools, will have no quarrel with this formulation of the basis of healing. Their model of the healthy person, however, requires an additional step—of re-emergence; the drowning and the resurfacing are both constituents of psychological growth, at all developmental levels. In Kohut's language, healing will not only involve an ancient merger state but a further shift from this state to an experience of empathic resonance with the self-object.

Gurus are generally aware of the dangers of self-fragmentation and the disciple's defences against that dreaded inner state. Modern gurus, like Muktananda, talk explicitly about the agitation and anxiety a disciple may feel when he is close to the guru. The training required en route to surrender is hard and painful. Merger experience, they know, takes place not at once but in progressive stages as, for instance, depicted in Jnaneshvara's description of the unfolding of the guru–disciple relationship in the imagery of bridal mysticism.[34] They are aware of the resistances and the negative transferences, the times when the devotee loses faith in the guru, and doubts and suspicions tend to creep in. Do not break the relationship when this is happening, is the general and analytically sound advice. The development of inimical feelings toward the guru are part of the process of healing transformation. What is important about the feelings toward the guru is their strength, not their direction. Whether devoted or hostile, as long as the disciple remains turned toward the guru, he will be met by total acceptance. Muktananda describes the ideal guru's behaviour: 'A true guru breaks your old habits of fault-finding, of seeing sin, of hating yourself. He roots out the negative seeds that you have sown as well as your feelings of guilt. . . . You will never hear the guru criticize you. Instead, when you are in his company, you will never be found guilty in the guru's eyes. You will find in them only the praise of your hidden inner God.'[35]

The 'ambience of affective acceptance' provided by the guru and his establishment, the *ashram*, will, the master knows, make the disciple feel increasingly safe, shifting the inner balance between need and fear toward the former. Old repressed and disavowed self-object needs will reawaken and be mobilized, making the transference more and more intense. Or, put simply, as the conflict between need and fear recedes, the guru, like the analyst, will become the focus for the freshly released, though old, capacities for love, which push strongly toward a merger with the beloved.

If there is a second word besides surrender with which the guru-disciple relationship can be captured, it is intimacy. As Lawrence Babb remarks of his interviews with the devotees of Sai Baba, 'What emerges as one general theme in these accounts is the same kind of visual, tactile and alimentary intimacy that is so central to devotional Hinduism in general. The devotees long to see him, to hear him, to be near him, to have private audiences with him, to touch him (especially his feet) and to receive or consume, or use in other ways, substances and objects that have been touched by him or that originate from him.'[36] This striving for intimacy not only marks the disciple's response to the devotional, but also to the knowledge, guru. Pupul Jayakar, in talking of her response to the 'intellectual' Krishnamurti, says 'I was driven by the urge to be with him, to be noticed by him, to probe into the mysteries that pervaded his presence. I was afraid of what would happen, but I could not keep away.'[37]

The sought-for intimacy is of an archaic nature, before the birth of language which separates and bifurcates. In the intimacy scale of the 16th-century north Indian saint Dabu:

> The guru speaks first with the mind
> Then with the glance of the eye
> If the disciple fails to understand
> He instructs him at last by word of mouth

> He that understands the spoken word is a common man
> He that interprets the gesture is an initiate
> He that reads the thought of the mind
> Unsearchable, unfathomable, is a god.[38]

In the desired preverbal intimacy with the guru, Jnaneshvara highlights the devotee's infantile quiescence.

> To say nothing is your praise
> To do nothing is your worship
> To be nothing is to be near you.[39]

Analysts are, of course, familiar with the regressive movements in the patient's psyche occasioned by the growing transference toward the analyst. The regression gives the patient a double vision, both in relation to himself and to the analyst. Within the transference, he 'sees' the analyst as a parental self-object; in the real relationship as a helpful doctor. The two images, in flux over time, constantly condition each other. Because of the copresence of the patient's adult self, the illusion in relation to the analyst, though it waxes and wanes, remains more or less moderate.[40]

The patient's illusion of the analyst corresponds to another illusion in relation to the self. Patients in analysis often report feeling childlike, even childish, also outside the analytic setting. They imagine themselves at times to be smaller and more awkward than their actual adult selves. The infantile and the adult in relation to the self shape each other and are often in a state of partial identity. In the guru–disciple relationship, the identity between the actual and the infantile selves of the disciple on the one hand and the real and parental representations of the master on the other overlap to a much greater extent and for longer periods of time than in psychoanalysis. The double vision in relation to both self and guru representations tends to become monocular. In other words, the guru–disciple interaction touches deeper, more regressed layers of the psyche which are generally not reached by psychoanalysis. The devotee, I believe, is better (but also more dangerously) placed than the analysand to connect with—and correct—the depressive core at the base of human life from which a self first emerged and which lies beyond words and interpretations.

The healing techniques of the guru are thus designed to foster deeper regressions than those of the analyst. Elsewhere, I have talked of the importance of looking and being looked at as a primary technique of the master–disciple intercourse.[41] I discussed the identity-giving power of the eyes that recognize, that is, of their self-evoking and self-sustaining functions. Taken in through the eyes, the guru as a benign self-object opens the devotee's closed world of archaic destructive relationships to new possibilities. The technical word, used in scriptural descriptions of the initiation process, is *darshanat*, 'through the guru's look' in which, as Muktananda observes, 'you are seen in every detail as in a clear mirror.'[42] To the utter clarity of the look he might have added its absolute love and complete forgiveness. To adapt Dostoevski's remark on the lover's vision, in *darshanat* the devotee is looked at, and is enabled to look at himself or herself, as God might have. Even gurus with thousands of disciples, whose devotees might conceivably doubt that a one-to-one recognition by the guru is taking place at regular intervals, are at pains to confirm the operation of *darshanat* in spite of the large numbers involved. To quote Muktananda again: 'Many people become angry with me out of love. They say "Baba did not look at me," or "When Baba looked at me, he didn't smile!" People who say these things do not understand that when I sit on my chair I look at everyone once, silently and with great joy. . . . True love has no language. If I look at someone, silently emitting a ray of love, that is sublime. This is true and should be understood: love is a secret ray of the eyes.'[43]

What about the guru's words, the discourses to which the devotees listen with such rapt attention? To someone reading such a discourse or listening to it apart from a devotee group, it may seem trite, repetitious, and full of well-known homilies. The power of the guru's speech, however, lies not in its insight, but has a different source. 'I did not understand but I came away with the words alive within me' is a typical reaction.[44] The psychological impact of the words is not through their literal meaning but their symbolic power, through the sound which conveys the experience of the guru's presence within the psyche. They are a form of early human contact, much as the experience of a child who is soothed by the mother's vocalizations even when he is physically separated from her and cannot feel her arms around him. In psychoanalysis, a patient will sometimes comment on the quality of the therapist's voice when he feels it as a psychological bridge which joins the two or when he feels it as distancing and evoking a self fragmenting response. Susan Bady has suggested that it is not only the psychological reaction to the therapist's voice but its virtual ingestion by the patient in a concrete way which is significant.[45] Taken into one's vocal chords, the pattern and rate of breathing, the movement of the diaphragm, the relaxed and self-assured voice of the therapist or the guru will calm his agitation, infuse hope and courage into his own timid and hesitant voice.

The concrete physical and psychic manifestations of the guru's speech and sound are immeasurably enhanced by the group setting in which a disciple normally hears his words. To quote from my own experience of listening to a guru in a large crowd: 'At first there is a sense of unease as the body, the container of our individuality and the demarcator of our spatial boundaries, is sharply wrenched from its habitual mode of experiencing others. For as we grow up, the touch of others, once so deliberately courted and responded to with delight, increasingly becomes ambivalent. Coming from a loved one, touch is deliciously welcomed; with strangers, on the other hand, there is an involuntary shrinking of the body, their touch taking on the menacing air of invasion by the other. But once the fear of touch disappears in the fierce press of other bodies and the individual lets himself become a part of the crowd's density, the original apprehension is gradually transformed into an expansiveness that stretches to include the others. Distances and differences—of status, age and sex—disappear in an exhilarating feeling (temporary to be sure) that individual boundaries can indeed be transcended and were perhaps illusory in the first place. Of course, touch is only one of the sensual stimuli that hammer at the gate of individual identity. Other excitations, channelled through vision, hearing and smell, are also very much involved. In addition, as Phyllis Greenacre has suggested, there are other, more subliminal exchanges of body heat, muscle tension and body rhythms taking place in a crowd. In short the crowd's assault on the sense of individual identity appears to be well-nigh irresistible; its invitation to a psychological regression—in which the image of one's body becomes fluid and increasingly blurred, controls over emotions and impulses are weakened, critical faculties and rational thought processes are abandoned—is extended in a way that is both forceful and seductive.'[46]

Other techniques employed in the guru–disciple interaction perform a similar function of psychic loosening and fostering deep regression—an increasing surrender to the self-object experience of the merging kind. The taking in of *prasada*, food offerings touched or tasted by the guru, drinking of the water used to wash his feet, helps in a loosening up of individual bodily and psychic boundaries, transforming the experience of the guru from that of a separate Other to one of co-mingling with a self-object. Gurus and devotees have always known that meditation on the guru's face or form or the contemplative use of his photograph, as required in some cults, will contribute to and hasten the merging experience. As Muktananda observes: 'The mind that always contemplates the guru eventually becomes the guru. Meditation on the guru's form, immerses the meditator in the state of the guru.'[47]

In a sense, my use of the term guru–disciple interaction has been a misnomer since it has had the disciple's rather than the guru's inner state as its focus. Perhaps this is as it should be given the fact that ostensibly the disciple is the one in search of healing, and that we know infinitely more about the inner processes of disciples than those of the gurus. Yet an analyst has to wonder how a guru deals with the massive idealizing transferences of so many disciples. Negative transferences and malignant projections are of course easier to handle since they cause severe discomfort, compelling us to reject them by discriminating inside between what belongs to us and the alien attributes that have been projected onto us. This painful motivation for repelling the invasion of the self by others does not exist when projections are narcissistically gratifying, as they invariably are in case of the adoring followers.

The problem is further complicated by the fact that for the self-sustaining and self-healing responses to be evoked in the follower (or in the patient), the guru (and the analyst) must accept being the wiser, greater, and more powerful parent. To accept and yet not identify with the disciple's parental representation demands the guru remain in touch with his own infantile self. The best of the gurus, as we saw in the case of Ramakrishna, clearly do that; their own relationship to the Divine keeps intact self-representations other than those of the omniscient parent. But for many others, I would speculate, the temptation to identify with the disciple's projected parental self is overwhelming. As the parent and the stronger figure in the parent–child relationship, it is easier to unload one's conflicts and the depressives self onto the child. In the case of the analyst's counter-transference, as Michael Moeller points out, the identification with the parental role is a source of twofold relief: one, in the transferential repetition of the relationship with the patient the analyst is the stronger and the less incriminated parent, and two, in reality he is not that parent at all.[48] The empirical finding on the antidepressive effect of the psychoanalytic role also applies to the guru. His calm, cheerful, loving mien is perhaps a consequence rather than a cause of his role as the healer.

I have mentioned above that the dangers of the guru role lie in the disciples' massive parental projections which the guru must process internally. Although the guru shares this danger with the analyst, or more generally, with any healer, the intensity of these projections, their duration, and the sheer number of devotees involved are vastly greater than in the case of his secular counterparts. These idealizing projections are subversive of the guru's self-representation, constitute an insidious assault which a few gurus—again like some therapists—are not able to successfully resist. A regression to an omnipotent grandiosity is one consequence, while in the sexual sphere a retreat into sexual perversion has been reported often enough to constitute a specific danger of the guru role. It is sad to hear or read reliable reports about 70-year-old gurus who become Peeping Toms as they arrange, with all the cunning of the voyeur, to spy on their teenaged female disciples (generally western) undressing for the night in the ashram. The promiscuity of some other gurus, pathetically effortful in the case of elderly bodies with a tendency to flag, is also too well-known to merit further repetition.

The sexual aberrations, however, have not only to do with pathological regression in stray individual cases, but are perhaps also facilitated by the way the fundamentals of healing are conceptualized in the guru-devotee encounter. For instance, given the significance of a specific kind of intimacy, there is no inherent reason (except cultural disapproval) why intimacy between guru and devotee does not progress to the most intimate encounter of all and be seen as a special mark of the guru's favour; why the merger of souls does not take place through their containers, the bodies. If substances which have been in intimate contact with the guru's body are powerful agents of inner change when ingested by the devotee, then the logic of transformation dictates that the most powerful transforming substance would be the guru's 'purest' and innermost essence—his semen.

6

The Body Image

The human body occupies a unique position in creation as the only object that is part of both our inner and our outer worlds.[1] The body distinguishes itself from other parts of the universe by the fact that it is perceived simultaneously through two types of sensation. On the one hand we perceive our bodies through the inner, 'proprioceptive' sensations of depth sensibility while on the other hand the body is also perceived by external, 'sensoriperceptive' sensations, mainly tactile and visual. Our earliest inner sensations, the beating of the heart, the contractions and expansions of the lungs as we breathe, the abdominal sensations associated with feeding and evacuation; are the central crystallization point for the 'feeling of self' around which a 'sense of identity' will be later established. The external perception of the body's central and peripheral parts will help the infant gradually work out the distinction between the self and the not-self and contribute to the differentiation of the self from the world of objects. The integration of these two kinds of processes, of our bodily feelings and the unconscious fantasies about the body's processes and contents on the one hand with the relevant visual, auditory and kinesthetic data on the other, yields our individual *body image*. Shimmeringly hazy at the beginning of life, the contours of the body image in our 'prehistory' change ceaselessly like the bed of a capricious monsoon stream. Sometimes its parts are surrealistically distorted, while at others a part may disappear altogether like the extra-smile anatomy of the Cheshire cat. It is only after the quasi-bodily experimentation starting from the end of the first year of life, when touching and the visual taking in of the bodily parts—one's own and those of others—help the child in the construction and drawing of the body together in a central gestalt, that the body image gradually becomes stable, its boundaries differentiated more firmly from all that is not the self.

Of course, this body image, the nucleus of an individual's identity and the guarantor of his separation from the object world, does not coincide with the objective body. The proportions of different limbs are apt to be distorted, while the images of bodily processes can be truly fantastic. In certain psychotic episodes, we find the regressed individual expressing the feeling that his body has expanded (or contracted) or that his face has become 'different'; sometimes he might feel that one of his organs does not belong to him or even that it is inexplicably absent. In other, more 'normal' , the body image may include articles of clothing or even an amputated limb. There are mature women whose body image consists of the vagina of a little girl that will get torn and damaged in the sexual act, while the fat man or woman with a sylphlike body image has been a familiar and poignant object of many literary efforts, both tragic and farcical.

Perhaps, as Phyllis Greenacre has suggested, each individual needs constantly to reinforce the sense of his own body through an association with others of predominantly similar appearance.[2] Even at a mature age, the individual may need at least one other person similar to himself, to look at, speak to and to 'take in,' in order to accentuate his own body image and thus safeguard the core of his sense of identity. The isolation and avoidance of human contact sought by many aspiring and adept yogis—the 'withdrawal to the Himalayas' syndrome—may indeed have its roots in a systematic effort to diminish the clarity of the personal body image. In turn, this diminution temporarily dissolves the laboriously built-up sense of identity and undoes the differentiation of the self from the nonself. Little wonder that the body—'the temple of the living god'—is of such vital significance in mystical rituals, practices and symbolism, since it is preeminently our body (or more precisely our body image) that holds us back from the mystical goals of nonduality, nonseparation and dissolution of individual identity in a larger 'cosmic' identity.

I have discussed the body image in terms of individual development and emphasized both its universal and idiosyncratic elements. Each person's body image, however, also has a strong cultural component. I would go so far as to suggest that, given the body's central position in human life, the cultural variations in the body image lead to radically different ways of experiencing the world and organizing this experience. Let me illustrate this through a comparison of some aspects of the Indian body image with my impressions of the 'modal' body image in western—mainly North American and northern and central European—societies.

The Indian image of the body, I have pointed out earlier, emphasizes its intimate connection with the cosmos. As a nineteenth-century Bengali text on the body puts it, 'In this universe a great wheel of transformative power (*maya-chakra*) is spinning ceaselessly. The small individual wheels of transformative power in the bodies of living things are connected with that wheel. Just as, when some great steam-driven wheel turns like the prime mover, then all of the components of the machinery move together in coordination and smoothly accomplish their tasks, similarly the small wheels of transformative power that turn through their connection with the great wheel, within the bodies of individual living things, help accomplish such bodily activities as regulating the flow of blood in the body, digesting food, inhaling and exhaling, and moving back and forth.'[3] The Indian body image stresses an unremitting interchange taking place with the environment, simultaneously accompanied by ceaseless change within the body. As Francis Zimmermann writes, 'There is no map nor topography of the body but only an *economy*, that is to say fluids going in or coming out, residing in some *asrya* (recipient) or flowing through some *srotas* (channels):'[4] It is the imagery from the vegetable kingdom, such as the plant's drawing of nourishment through the roots, the rising of the sap, and the milky exudation of the resinous trees, that provides models for the image in Ayurveda. Indeed, as Wendy O'Flaherty has shown in her discussion of some Vedic and post-Vedic myths, fluidity and the transaction of fluids—between humans, between gods and between humans and gods—are central Hindu preoccupations.[5]

The Hindu body imagery gives rise to a whole class of diseases, which Obeyesekere has called *cultural diseases*, where a person falls ill because of his conviction that an inordinate loss of a bodily substance—essentially a fluid—has taken place. The most obvious example of such a cultural disease is *svapanadosha* (lit. 'dream fault') in which young men complain of body aches and headaches, increasing enervation and feelings of unreality about the body scheme because of the loss of semen in nocturnal emissions. Clinically, the complaint involving substance loss may resemble the hypochondriacal sensations at the beginning of schizophrenia where the body image is perceived to be altered and the body, or some of its parts, are felt to be not quite the same as usual. Substance-loss anxieties, however, are clearly not schizophrenic but the natural (though pathological) outcome of a cultural vision of the body in ceaseless flux.

I do not mean to imply that such a vision protects the members of the culture against the universal anxiety felt at the threat of loss of individual boundaries and identity. In fact, the presence of this cultural body image, though increasing the tolerance of the anxiety associated with the danger of identity dissolution, also keeps this anxiety closer to the surface of consciousness. The traditional preoccupation of Hindu culture with the question of identity, with 'Who am I?' then needs to be viewed against this backdrop, *i.e.* the Hindu stress on the vision of an unchanging human core—the *atman*—may (among other things) also be a cultural defence against the fundamental anxiety aroused by an image of the body in unflagging transformation.

The western image is of a clearly etched body, sharply differentiated from the rest of the objects in the universe. This vision of the body as a safe stronghold with a limited number of drawbridges that maintain a tenuous contact with the outside world has its own particular cultural consequences. It seems to me that in western discourse, both scientific and artistic, there is considerable preoccupation with what is going on *within* the fortress of the individual body. Preeminently, one seeks to explain behavioural processes through psychologies that derive from biology—to the relative exclusion of the natural and the metanatural environment. Let me give an illustration.

For many years, research on child development has focused on what is happening within the child as it grows up. There has been much interesting work on the 'unfolding' of a child's capacities and the construction of a number of sophisticated tests and benchmarks of intellectual and cognitive development. In contrast, the work done on a systematic conception and differentiation of the environment in which the child's development takes place has been minimal. At most, the environment has been conceived of in nutritional and human terms; for instance, in finding out the effects of maternal deprivation on the development of the child. The natural aspects of the environment—the quality of air, the quantity of sunlight, the presence of birds and animals, the plants and the trees—are *a priori* viewed, when they are considered at all, as irrelevant to intellectual and emotional development. Given the western image of the body, it is understandable that the more 'far-out' Indian beliefs on the effects of the natural world on the human body and psyche, for example, the effects of planetary constellations, earth's magnetic fields, seasonal and daily rhythms, precious stones and metals—are summarily consigned to the realm of fantasy, where they are of interest solely to a 'lunatic fringe' of western society.

Similar to the Indian body image which holds out the threat of a dissolution of individual identity and thus encourages a cultural preoc-cupation with questions of identity and the unchanging part of the self, the western body image too contains an intrinsic threat. The danger here is of a complete isolation and the cutting off of the self from its human and natural moorings. This, in turn, encourages a (defensive) cultural preoccupation with the question of man's 'alienation' and the ecological issue of man's relationship with his environment.

Another central aspect of the Indian body image is the very high amount of emotional investment in the body. To a westerner, the atten-tion that the texts expect a person to devote to his body appears more appropriate to a doting mother's care of her newborn infant than to an adult's relationship with his body. The efforts to increase the body's strength, beauty and grace and to preserve its youthfulness against the ravages of age may even be seen as an expression of 'bodily narcissism' in a neutral and relativistic sense since the rejection of the body in the West for long periods of its history has loaded the word with a negative value orientation.

Beginning with the eyes, the *Caraka Samhita* recommends the ap-plication once in every five nights of a collyrium made of copper and a daily application of a collyrium of antimony to soothe the eyes and enhance their natural luster.[6] Nasal drops made from *anu taila* (an oil made by boiling twenty-four different herbs and plants with rainwater and then with goat's milk and oil) are to be administered three times a day for seven days during the autumn, spring and rainy seasons. This ensures that 'his (the user's) hair and beard never become white or grey; he never experiences hair fall; they grow luxuriantly. . . . His face be-comes cheerful and plump; his voice becomes sweet, stabilized and stentorious.'[7]

I have already mentioned the tongue-scraping part of oral hygiene. In addition, chewing of various spices and nuts is recommended for the clarity, taste and good smell of the mouth, and gargling with *til* oil for the strength of the jaws, depth of voice and—a peculiarly Hindu ideal of masculine beauty—'plumpness of the face.'[8] Regular oiling of the hair and the ears and periodic oil massages are a part of the normal body care; the latter is suggested to make the physique smooth, strong and charming and to prevent the onslaught of aging.[9] The use of scents and garlands of flowers 'stimulate[s] libido, produce[s] good smell in the body, enhance[s] longevity and charm,' while the 'wearing of gems and ornaments adds to prosperity, auspiciousness, longevity, grace, prevents dangers of snakes, evil spirits, etc.'[10] Even sexuality is pressed into the service of bodily narcissism; frequent intercourse is recommended in winter to keep up the body's vigour, while complete sexual abstention is prescribed for the duration of the summer.[11] Somehow, it seems quite appropriate that India's national bird is the peacock!

In contrast, the legacy of rejection of the body in the West persists in the unconscious fantasy of the body as a dirt-producing factory. As Lawrence Kubie has pointed out in an original and stimulating paper, there exists an unconscious image 'of the body as a kind of animated, mobile dirt factory, exuding filth at every aperture and that all that is necessary to turn something into dirt is that it should even momentarily enter the body through one of these apertures.'[12] Kubie's remarks on this ubiquitous fantasy perhaps apply more to the North American and northern and central European societies than to Mediterranean ones, and he may well be correct in identifying a widespread western assumption that the insides of the body are in fact a cistern, that all apertures of the body are dirty avenues of approach, dirty holes leading into dirty spaces, and that everything which comes out of the body, with the possible exception of tears, is for that reason alone dirty.

Speaking as an Indian, I must say that I too have been struck by the North American and European taboo on body apertures, a taboo which at the most permits the wiggling of an itching ear but not a digging into it with a finger; nasal acrobatics but not a boring in the nostril with a finger to remove an uncomfortably lodged mucus. In contrast to the relative unconcern in India with public hawking, belches and farts, the western taboo forbids noises or smells to emanate from an aperture that may draw attention to the opening and thus to the dirt factory humming behind it. By extension, a cavity, a cleft or a pit in the body carries the presumption of dirt, whose smells must be disguised—to the considerable satisfaction and profit of the deodorant industry and the media that thrive on the dirt fantasy. I do not mean to imply that the dirt fantasy is absent in the Indian context. There is certainly a horror of the dirt of others (though perhaps a great tolerance of one's own dirt) that is expressed in the preoccupation with purity and pollution. What makes the dirt fantasy in India different is its relatively greater access to consciousness; the fascination and revulsion with dirt, as we saw in the Tantra chapter, are neither disguised nor displaced to the extent they are in the West.

7

Clinical Work and Cultural Imagination*

The perennial question of the cross-cultural validity of psychoanalysis actually has two parts: Is psychoanalysis at all possible in a traditional non-western society with its different family system, religious beliefs and cultural values? Is the mental life of non-western patients radically different from that of their western counterparts?

Over the years, in my own talks to diverse audiences in Europe and the United States, the question of trans-cultural validity of psychoanalysis has invariably constituted the core of animated discussion. The sharp increase in scepticism about this particular question has in recent years been correlated with the rise of relativism in the human sciences. Intellectually, the relativistic position owes much of its impetus to Foucault's powerful argument on the rootedness of all thought in history and culture—and in the framework of power relations. Adherents of this perspective are not a priori willing to accept why psychoanalysis, a product of nineteenth-century European bourgeois family and social structure, should be an exception to the general rule of the incapacity of thought to transcend its roots. In this paper, I propose to discuss the issue of the cultural rootedness of psychoanalysis with illustrations from my own clinical practice in India.

Ramnath was a 51-year-old man who owned a grocery shop in the oldest part of the city of Delhi. When he came to see me some eighteen years ago, he was suffering from a number of complaints, though he desired my help for only one of them—an unspecified 'fearfulness'.

*First published in *Psychoanalytic Quarterly*, 64, 1995. Reprinted with permission.

This anxiety, less than three years old, was a relatively new development. His migraine headaches, on the other hand went back to his adolescence. Ramnath attributed them to an excess of 'wind' in the stomach, which periodically rose up and pressed against the veins in his head. Ramnath had always had a nervous stomach. It is now never quite as bad as it was in the months following his marriage some thirty years ago, when it was accompanied by severe stomach cramps and an alarming weight loss. He was first taken to the hospital by his father, where he was X-rayed and tested. Finding nothing wrong with him, the doctors had prescribed a variety of vitamins and tonics which were not of much help. Older family members and friends had then recommended a nearby *ojha*—'sorcerer' is too fierce a translation for this mild-mannered professional of ritual exorcism—who diagnosed his condition as the result of magic practised by an enemy, namely, his newly acquired father-in-law. The rituals to counteract the enemy magic were expensive, as was the yellowish liquid emetic prescribed by the *ojha*, which periodically forced Ramnath to empty his stomach with gasping heaves. In any event, he was fully cured within two months of the *ojha*'s treatment, and the cramps and weight loss have not recurred.

Before coming to see me about his 'fearfulness', Ramnath had been treated with drugs by various doctors: by allopaths (as western-style doctors are called in India) as well as homeopaths, by the *vaids* of Hindu medicine as well as the *hakims* of the Islamic medical tradition. He had consulted psychiatrists, ingested psychotropic drugs, and submitted to therapy. He had gone through the rituals of two *ojhas* and was thinking of consulting a third who was highly recommended.

His only relief came through the weekly gathering of the local chapter of the Brahmakumari (literally 'Virgins of Brahma') sect which he had recently joined. The communal meditations and singing gave him a feeling of temporary peace and his nights were no longer so restless. Ramnath was puzzled by the persistence of his anxious state and its various symptoms. He had tried to be a good man, he said, according to his *dharma*, which is both the 'right conduct' of his caste and the limits imposed by his own character and predispositions. He had worshipped the gods and attended services in the temple with regularity, even contributing generously toward the consecration of a Krishna idol in his native village in Rajasthan. He did not have any bad habits, he asserted. Tea and cigarettes, yes, but for a couple of years he had abjured even these minor though pleasurable addictions. Yet the anxiety persisted, unremitting and unrelenting.

Since it is culture rather than psyche which is the focus of this presentation, let me essay a cultural—rather than a psycho—analysis of Ramnath's condition. At first glance, Ramnath's cognitive space in matters of illness and well-being seems incredibly cluttered. Gods and spirits, community and family, food and drink, personal habits and character, all seem to be somehow intimately involved in the maintenance of health. Yet these and other factors such as biological infection, social pollution, and cosmic displeasure, all of which most Hindus would also acknowledge as causes of ill health—only point to the recognition of a person's simultaneous existence in different orders of being; of the person being a body, a psyche and a social being at the same time. Ramnath's experience of his illness may appear alien to Europeans only because, as I have elaborated elsewhere (Kakar, 1982), the body, the psyche, and the community do not possess fixed, immutable meanings across cultures. The concept of the body and the understanding of its processes are not quite the same in India as they are in the West. The Hindu body, portrayed in relevant cultural texts, predominantly in imagery from the vegetable kingdom, is much more intimately connected with the cosmos than the clearly etched western body which is sharply differentiated from the rest of the objects in the universe. The Hindu body image stresses an unremitting interchange taking place with the environment, simultaneously accompanied by ceaseless change within the body. The psyche—the Hindu 'subtle body'—is not primarily a psychological category in India. It is closer to the ancient Greek meaning of the 'psyche', the source of all vital activities and psychic processes, and considered capable of persisting in its disembodied state after death. Similarly, for many Indians, the community consists not only of living members of the family and the social group but also of ancestral and other spirits as well as the gods and goddesses who populate the Hindu cosmos. An Indian is inclined to believe that his or her illness can reflect a disturbance in any one of these orders of being, while the symptoms may also be manifested in the other orders. If a treatment, say, in the bodily order fails, one is quite prepared to reassign the cause of the illness to a different order and undergo its particular curing regimen—prayers or exorcisms, for instance—without losing regard for other methods of treatment.

The involvement of all orders of being in health and illness means that an Indian is generally inclined to seek more than one cause for illness in especially intractable cases. An Indian tends to view these causes as complementary rather than exclusive and arranges them in a hierarchical order by identifying an immediate cause as well as others that are more remote. The causes are arranged in concentric circles, with the outer circle including all the inner ones.

To continue with our example: Ramnath had suffered migraine headaches since his adolescence. Doctors of traditional Hindu medicine, Ayurveda, had diagnosed the cause as a humoral disequilibrium—an excess of 'wind' in the stomach which periodically rose up and pressed against the veins in his head—and prescribed Ayurvedic drugs, dietary restrictions as well as liberal doses of aspirin. Such a disequilibrium is usually felt to be compounded by bad habits which, in turn, demand changes in personal conduct. When an illness like Ramnath's persists, its stubborn intensity will be linked with his unfavourable astrological conditions, requiring palliative measures such as a round of prayers (*puja*). The astrological 'fault' probably will be further traced back to the bad karma of a previous birth about which, finally, nothing can be done—except, perhaps, the cultivation of a stoic endurance with the help of the weekly meetings of the Virgins of Brahma sect.

I saw Ramnath thrice a week in psychoanalytic therapy for twenty-one sessions before he decided to terminate the treatment. At the time, although acutely aware of my deficiencies as a novice, I had placed the blame for the failure of the therapy on the patient or, to be more exact, on the cultural factors involved in his decision. Some of these were obvious. Ramnath had slotted me into a place normally reserved for a personal guru. From the beginning, he envisioned not a contractual doctor-patient relationship but a much more intimate guru–disciple bond that would allow him to abdicate responsibility for his life. He was increasingly dismayed that a psychoanalyst did not dispense wise counsel but expected the client to talk, that I wanted to follow his lead rather than impose my own views or directions on the course of our sessions. My behaviour also went against the guru model which demands that the therapist demonstrate his compassion, interest, warmth and responsiveness much more openly than I believed is possible or desirable in a psychoanalytic relationship. I did not know then that Ramnath's 'guru fantasy', namely the existence of someone, somewhere—now discovered in my person—who will heal the wounds suffered in all past relationships, remove the blights on the soul so that it shines anew in its pristine state, was not inherent in his Indianness but common across many cultures. Irrespective of their conscious subscription to the ideology of egalitarianism and a more contractual doctor–patient relationship, my European and American patients too approached analysis and the analyst with a full-blown guru fantasy which, though, was more hidden and less accessible to consciousness than in the case of Ramnath.

More than Ramnath's expectations, it was the disappointment of mine, I now realize, on which the analysis floundered. I had expected Ramnath to be an individual in the sense of someone whose consciousness has been moulded in a crucible which is commonly regarded as having come into existence as part of the psychological revolution in the wake of the Enlightenment in Europe. This revolution, of course, is supposed to have narrowed the older, metaphysical scope of the mind, to mind as an isolated island of individual consciousness, profoundly aware of its almost limitless subjectivity and its infantile tendency to heedless projection and illusion. Psychoanalysis, I believed, with some justification, is possible only with a person who is individual in this special sense, who shares, at some level of awareness and to some minimum degree, the modern vision of human experience wherein each of us lives in his own subjective world, pursuing personal pleasures and private fantasies, constructing a fate which will vanish when our time is over. The reason why in most psychoanalytic case histories, whether in western or non-western worlds, analysands, except for their different neurotic or character disturbances, sound pretty much like each other (and like their analysts), is because they all share the post-Enlightenment world-view of what constitutes an individual. In a fundamental sense, psychoanalysis does not have a cross-cultural context but takes place in the same culture across different societies; it works in the established (and expanding) enclaves of psychological modernity around the world. We can therefore better understand why psychoanalysis in India began in Calcutta—the first capital of the British empire in India where Indians began their engagement and confrontation with post-Enlightenment western thought—before extending itself and virtually limiting itself to Bombay which prides itself on its cosmopolitan character and cultural 'modernity'. It is also comprehensible that the clientele for psychoanalysis in India consists overwhelmingly—though not completely—of individuals (and their family members) who are involved in modern professions like journalism, advertising, academia, law, medicine and so on. In its sociological profile, at least, this clientele does not significantly differ from one that seeks psychoanalytic therapy in Europe and America.

Ramnath, I believed, was not an individual in the sense that he lacked 'psychologically modernity'. He had manfully tried to understand the psychoanalytic model of inner conflict rooted in life history that was implied in my occasional interventions. It was clear that this went against his cultural model of psychic distress and healing wherein the causes for his suffering lay outside himself and had little to do with his biography—black magic by father-in-law, disturbed planetary constellations, bad karma from previous life, disturbed humoral equilibrium. He was thus not suitable for psychoanalytic therapy and perhaps I had given up on him before he gave up on me. But Ramnath, I realized later, like many of my other traditional Hindu patients, had an individuality which is embedded in and expressed in terms from the Hindu cultural universe. This individuality is accessible to psychoanalysis if the therapist is willing and able to build the required bridges from a modern to a traditional individuality. The Indian analyst has to be prepared, for instance, to interpret the current problems of such a patient in terms of his or her bad karma—feelings, thoughts and actions—not from a previous existence but from a forgotten life, the period of infancy and childhood, his or her 'pre-history'. Let me elaborate on this distinction between traditional and modern individuals who both share what I believe is the essence of psychological modernity.

Psychological modernity, although strongly associated with post-Enlightenment, is nevertheless not identical with it. The core of psychological modernity is internalization rather than externalization. I use internalization here as a sensing by the person of a psyche in the Greek sense, an animation from within rather than without. Experientially, this internalization is a recognition that one is possessed of a mind in all its complexity. It is the acknowledgement, however vague, unwilling or conflicted, of a subjectivity that fates one to episodic suffering through some of its ideas and feelings—in psychoanalysis, murderous rage, envy, and possessive desire seeking to destroy those one loves and would keep alive—simultaneously with the knowledge, at some level of awareness, that the mind can help in containing and processing disturbed thoughts—as indeed can the family and the group as well (Bollas, 1992). In Hindu terms, it is a person's sense and acknowledgement of the primacy of the 'subtle body'—the *sukshmasharira*—in human action and of human suffering as caused by the workings of the five passions: sexual desire, rage, greed, infatuation and egotism. Similarly, Buddhists too describe human suffering as being due to causes internal to the individual: cognitive factors such as a perceptual cloudiness causing mis-perception of objects of awareness but also affective causes such as agitation and worry—the elements of anxiety, and greed, avarice and envy which form the cluster of grasping attachment. This *internalization* is the essence of 'individuation', and of psychological modernity, which has always been a part of what Hindus call the 'more evolved' beings in traditional civilizations. The fact that this core of individuation is expressed in a religious rather than a psychological idiom should not prevent us from recognizing its importance as an ideal of maturity in traditional civilizations such as Hindu India; it should also give us pause in characterizing, indeed with the danger of pathologizing India or any other civilization as one where some kind of familial self (Roland, 1990) or group mind (Kurtz, 1992) reigns in individual mental life. The 'evolved' Hindu in the past or even in the present who has little to do with the post-Enlightenment West, thus interprets the *Mahabharata* as an account of inner conflict in man's soul rather than of outer hostilities. The 'evolved beings' in India, including the most respected gurus, have always held that the guru, too, is only seemingly a person but actually a function, a transitional object in modern parlance, as are all the various gods who, too, are only aspects of the self. 'The Guru is the disciple, but perfected, complete,' says Muktananda (1983). 'When he forms a relationship with the guru, the disciple is in fact forming a relationship with his own best self' (p. ix). At the end of your *sadhana*, burn the guru, say the Tantriks; kill the Buddha if you meet him on the way, is a familiar piece of Zen Buddhist wisdom. All of them, gurus or gods (as also the analyst), have served the purpose of internalization—of a specific mode of relating to and experiencing the self, and are dispensable.

Psychological modernity is thus not coterminous with historical modernity, nor are its origins in a specific geographical location even if it received a sharp impetus from the European Enlightenment. My biggest error in Ramnath's case was in making a sharp dichotomy between a 'Hindu' cultural view of the interpersonal and transpersonal nature of man and a modern 'Western' view of man's individual and instinctual nature and assuming that since Ramnath was not an individual in the latter sense, he was not an individual at all. Although suggestive and fruitful for cultural understanding, the individual/relational differences should not be overemphasized. Even my distinction between traditional and modern individuality is not a sharp one. In reference to his satori or enlightenment, occasioned by the cry of a crow, Ikkyu, a fifteenth-century Zen master, known for his colourful eccentricity, suggests the presence of a 'modern' biographical individuality when he writes:

ten dumb years I wanted things to be different furious proud I
still feel it
one summer night in my little boat on lake Biwa
caaaawwweeeee
father when I was a boy you left us now I forgive you

(Berg, 1989, p. 42).

In spite of the cultural highlighting of the inter- and transpersonal I found my traditional Indian patients more individual in their unconscious than they initially realized. Similarly, in spite of a western cultural emphasis on autonomous individuality, my European and American patients are more relational than *they* realize. Individual and communal, self and other, are complementary ways of looking at the organization of mental life and exist in a dialectical relationship to each other although a culture may, over a period of time, stress the importance of one or the other in its ideology of the fulfilled human life and thus shape a person's *conscious* experience of the self in predominantly individual or communal modes. It is undeniable that Indians are very relational, with the family and community (including the family of divinities) playing a dominant role in the experience of the self. It is also undeniable, though less evident, that Indians are very individualistic and, at least in fantasy, are capable of conceiving and desiring a self free of *all* attachments and relationships.

In positing some shared fundamentals for the practice of the psychoanalytic enterprise, I do not mean to imply that there is no difference between analysands from Bombay, Beirut or Birmingham. The middle-class, educated, urban Indian although more individualized in his experience of the self and closer to his western counterpart on this dimension, is nevertheless not identical with the latter. Contrary to the stance popular among many anthropologists of Indian society, the traditional Hindu villager is not the only Indian there is with the rest being some kind of imposters or cultural deviants. The urban Indian analysand shares with others many of the broader social and cultural patterns which are reflected in the cultural particularities of the self. One of these particularities, frequently met with in case histories and a dominant motif in Hindu myths and other products of cultural imagination, is the centrality of the male Hindu Indian's experience of the powerful mother (Kakar, 1978; 1990). Let me first illustrate this more concretely through a vignette.

Pran, a thirty-five year old journalist, came to analysis suffering from a general, unspecified anxiety and what he called a persistent feeling of being always on the 'edge'. Until March of that year, Pran's 320 sessions have been pervaded by his mother to a degree unsurpassed in my clinical work. For almost two years, four times a week, hour after hour, Pran would recollect what his mother told him on this or that particular occasion, what she thought, believed or said, as he struggles to dislodge her from the throne on which he has ensconced her in the deepest recesses of his psyche. She was a deeply religious woman, a frequenter of discourses given by various holy men, to which Pran accompanied her and which contributed significantly to the formation of his traditional Hindu world view. In contrast to the mother, Pran's memories of his father, who died when he was eleven, are scant. They are also tinged with a regret that Pran did not get a chance to be closer to a figure who remains dim and was banished to the outskirts of family life when alive. He is clearly and irrevocably dead while the mother, who died ten years ago, is very much alive. The father was a man about town, rarely at home, and thoroughly disapproved of by the mother who not only considered herself more virtuous and intelligent, but also implied to the son that the stroke which finally killed his father was a consequence of his dissolute, 'manly' ways.

Pran's memories of his closeness to his mother, the hours they spent just sitting together, communing in silence, a feeling of deep repose flowing through him, are many. He remembers being breast-fed till he was eight or nine, although when he thinks about it a little more, he doubts whether there was any milk in the breasts for many of those years. In any event, he distinctly recollects peremptorily lifting up her blouse whenever he felt like a suck, even when she was busy talking to other women. Her visiting friends were at times indulgent and at other indignant, 'Why don't you stop him?' they would ask his mother. 'He does not listen,' she would reply in mock helplessness.

Pran slept in his mother's bed till he was eighteen. He vividly recalls the peculiar mixture of dread and excitement, especially during the adolescence years, when he would manoeuvre his erect penis near her vagina for that most elusive and forbidden of touches which he was never sure was a touch at all, where he never knew whether his penis had actually been in contact with her body. Later, his few physical encounters with women were limited to hugging, while he awkwardly contorted the lower part of his body to keep his erection beyond their ken. For a long time, his sexual fantasies were limited to looking at and touching a woman's breasts. As his analysis progressed, his most pleasurable sexual fantasy became one of the penis hovering on the brink of the labial lips, even briefly touching them, but never of entering the woman's body.

After his studies, at which he was very good, Pran joined a newspaper and became quite successful. The time for his marriage had now arrived and there began the first open though still subdued conflicts with his mother on the choice of a marriage partner. His mother invariably rejected every attractive woman he fancied, stating bluntly that sons forget their mothers if they get into the clutches of a beautiful woman. Pran finally agreed to his mother's choice of a docile and plain-looking woman. For the first six months, he felt no desire for his wife. (The fact that his mother slept in the room next to the bridal couple and insisted that the connecting door remain open at all times except for the hours of the night, did not exactly work as an aphrodisiac.) When the family used the car, the wife would sit at the back, the mother not holding with new-fangled modern notions which would relegate her to the back seat once the son had brought a wife home. Even now his sexual desire for his wife is perfunctory and occasional. He feels excited by women with short hair who wear make-up and skirts rather than a long-tressed Indian beauty in the traditional attire of *salwar kameez* or sari. Such a woman is too near the mother. For many years, Pran has been trying to change his wife's conservative appearance, so reminiscent of the mother's, toward one which is closer to the object of his desire.

It was only after his mother's death that Pran experienced sexual intercourse with his wife as pleasurable. Yet after intercourse there is invariably a feeling of tiredness for a couple of days and Pran feels, as he puts it, that his body is 'breaking'. His need for food, especially the spicy-sour savouries (*chat*) which were a special favourite of the mother and are popularly considered 'woman's food', goes up markedly. In spite of his tiredness, Pran can drive miles in search of the spicy fare.

The need for sleep and spicy food, together with the feeling of physical unease, also occurs at certain other times. A regular feature of his work day is that after a few hours of work, he feels the need for something to eat and a short nap. The physical unease, the craving for food and sleep increase dramatically when he has to travel on business or to take people out for dinner. It is particularly marked if he ever has a drink at a bar with friends.

Relatively early in his analysis, Pran became aware of the underlying pattern in his behaviour. Going to work, travelling, drinking and, of course, sexual intercourse, are 'manly' activities to which he is greatly drawn. They are, however, also experienced as a separation from the mother which give rise to anxiety till he must come back to her, for food and sleep. He must recurrently merge with her in order, as he put it, to strengthen his nervous system. The re-establishment of an oral connection with the mother is striking in its details. Pran not only hankers after the mother's favourite foods but feels a great increase in the sensitivity of the lips and the palate. The texture and taste of food in the mouth is vastly more important for the process of his recuperation than is the food's function in filling his belly. His sensual memories of his mother's breasts and the taste of her nipples in the mouth are utterly precise. He can recover the body of the early mother as a series of spaced flashes, as islands of memory. The short naps he takes after one of his 'manly' activities are framed in a special ritual. He lies down on his stomach with his face burrowed between two soft pillows, fantasizes about hugging a woman before he falls asleep, and wakes up fresh and vigorous.

It took longer time for Pran to become aware of the terror his mother's overwhelming invasiveness inspired in the little boy and his helpless rage in dealing with it. He railed, and continues to do so, at her selfishness which kept him bound to her and wept at memories of countless occasions when she would ridicule his efforts to break away from her in play with other boys, or in the choice of his workplace, clothes, or friends. She has destroyed his masculinity, he feels. As a boy, she made him wash her underclothes, squeeze out the discharge from her nipples, oil her hair and pluck out the grey ones on an almost daily basis. The birth of his four daughters, he felt, was due to this feminization which had made his semen 'weak'. He realized that all his 'manly' activities were not only in pursuit of individuation as a man, or even in a quest for pleasure but also because they would lacerate the mother. 'I always wanted to hurt her and at the same time I could not do without her. She has been raping me ever since I was born,' he once said.

Often, as he lies there, abusing the mother, with a blissful expression on his face reflecting her close presence, I cannot help but feel that this is *nindastuti*, worship of a divinity through insult, denigration and contempt, which is one of the recognized relationships of a Hindu devotee with a divinity.

I have selected this particular vignette from my case histories because in its palette of stark, primary colours and in its lack of complex forms and subtle shades, it highlights, even caricatures, a dominant theme in the analysis of many male Hindu Indians. Judged by its frequency of occurrence in clinical work and in its pre-eminence in the

178 / *Culture and Healing*

Hindu cultural imagination, the theme of what I call maternal enthrallment and the issue of the boy's separation from the overwhelming
maternal–feminine—rather than the dilemmas of Oedipus—appears to
be the hegemonic (to use the fashionable Gramscian term) narrative of
the Hindu family drama (Kakar, 1989). It is the cornerstone in the architecture of the male self. The reason why I mention cultural
imagination in conjunction with clinical work when advancing a
generalized psychoanalytic proposition about the Indian cultural context, is simple. Clinical psychoanalysis is generally limited to a small
sample from three or four large Indian metropolises. It cannot adequately take into account the heterogeneity of a country of eight hundred
million people with its regional, linguistic, religious and caste divisions.
Clinical cases can, at best, generate hypotheses about cultural particularities. The further testing of these hypotheses is done (and remains
true to psychoanalytic intention and enterprise) by testing them in the
crucible of the culture's imagination.

The kind of maternal enthrallment and the prolonged mother–son
symbiosis I have described in this particular vignette, including the
peek-a-boo, was-it-or-was-it-not incest, would ordinarily be associated
with much greater pathology in analytic case conferences in Europe and
North America. Pran's level of functioning, however, is quite impressive in spite of his many inhibitions and anxieties, especially sexual. I
wonder how much of this kind of psychoanalytical expectation that
Pran is sicker than what I believe to be actually the case, is due to a
cultural contamination creeping into the clinical judgement of his
sexual differentiation and separation–individuation processes. For instance; is the psychoanalytic evaluation of Pran's undoubted
feminization and a certain lack of differentiation also being influenced
by a western cultural imagination on what it means to be, look, think
and behave like a man or a woman? This becomes clearer if one thinks
of Greek or Roman sculpture with their hard, muscled men's bodies and
chests without any fat at all and compares it with the sculpted representations of Hindu gods or the Buddha where the bodies are softer,
suppler and, in their hint of breasts, nearer to the female form.

I have no intention of relativizing Pran's pain and suffering out of
existence. I only wish to point out that between a minimum of sexual
differentiation that is required to function heterosexually with a
modicum of pleasure, and a maximum which cuts off any sense of empathy and emotional contact with the other sex which is then
experienced as a different species altogether, there is a whole range of

positions, each occupied by a culture which insists on calling it the only one that is mature and healthy.

Compared to a modal western analysand, then (and one needs to postulate such a being if civilizational comparisons are to be made) his Hindu counterpart highlights different intra-psychic issues and places different accents on universal developmental experiences. Yet, perhaps because of an underlying similarity in the psychoanalytic clientele across cultures, discussed earlier, cultural otherness does not spring the psychoanalytic framework, made increasingly flexible by a profusion of models. Clinical work in India is thus not radically different from that in Europe and America. An analyst from outside the culture, encountering the strangeness of the cultural mask rather than the similarity of the individual face, may get carried away into exaggerating differences. However, if he could listen long enough and with a well-tuned ear for the analysand's symbolic and linguistic universes, he would discover that individual voices speaking of the whirling of imperious passion, the stabs of searing, burdensome guilt, the voracious hungers of the urge to merge, and the black despair at the absence of the Other, are as much evident here as in the psychoanalysis of western patients.

Clinical work in another culture, however, does make us aware that because of the American and European domination of psychoanalytic discourse, western cultural (and moral) imagination sometimes tends to slip into psychoanalytic theorizing as hidden 'health and maturity moralities', as Kohut (1979, p. 12) called them. Cultural judgements about psychological maturity, the nature of reality, 'positive' and 'negative' resolutions of conflicts and complexes often appear in the garb of psychoanalytic universals. Awareness of the cultural contexts of psychoanalysis would therefore contribute to increasing the ken and tolerance of our common discipline for the range of human variations and a much greater circumspection in dealing with notions of pathology and deviance.

SUMMARY

Based on clinical experience with Hindu patients in India, this essay tries to address the question of the cross-cultural validity of psychoanalysis, namely whether psychoanalysis is possible with culturally traditional individuals in non-western societies and if so, whether there is a radical difference in the mental life of these patients. A core requirement for psychoanalysis, it is argued, is the presence of psychological modernity, an awareness at some level in the individual that to a large extent both emotional suffering and its healing have their sources in what may be called a mind, which is internal to the individual. Psychological modernity, the essence of individuation and individuality, is not limited to any particular historical period or geographic location but is also found in traditional non-western civilizations such as the Hindu or the Buddhist. Psychoanalysis is therefore eminently possible with persons who do not share the modern western version of psychological modernity but subscribe instead to their own traditional concept of individuation. This does not mean that there are no differences at all between, say, European and Hindu patients. We find the mental life of the latter often highlighting themes—such as the theme of 'maternal enthrallment'—which, because of its different salience (as compared, for example, to the oedipal motif) in western cultural imagination, may tend to be too easily or too quickly pathologized in western analytical discourse.

8

The Maternal–Feminine in Indian Psychoanalysis*

On 11 April 1929, Girindrasekhar Bose, the founder and first president of the Indian Psychoanalytical Society, wrote to Freud on the difference he had observed in the psychoanalytic treatment of Indian and western patients:

Of course I do not expect that you would accept offhand my reading of the Oedipus situation. I do not deny the importance of the castration threat in European cases; my argument is that the threat owes its efficiency to its connection with the wish to be female [Freud in a previous letter had gently chided Bose with understating the efficiency of the castration threat]. The real struggle lies between the desire to be a male and its opposite, the desire to be a female. I have already referred to the fact that castration threat is very common in Indian society but my Indian patients do not exhibit castration symptoms to such a marked degree as my European cases. The desire to be female is more easily unearthed in Indian male patients than in European . . . The Oedipus mother is very often a combined parental image and this is a fact of great importance. I have reason to believe that much of the motivation of the 'maternal deity' is traceable to this source.

Freud's reply is courteous and diplomatic: 'I am fully impressed by the difference in the castration reaction between Indian and European patients and promise to keep my attention fixed on the opposite wish you accentuate. The latter is too important for a hasty decision' (Sinha, 1966, p. 66).

In another paper, Bose (1950) elaborates on his observations and explains them through his theory of opposite wishes:

*First published in *International Review of Psychoanalysis*, 16(3), 1989. Reprinted with the permission of the Institute of Psychoanalysis, London.

During my analysis of Indian patients I have never come across a case of castration complex in the form in which it has been described by European observers.
This fact would seem to indicate that the castration idea develops as a result of
environmental conditions acting on some more primitive trend in the subject.
The difference in social environment of Indians and European is responsible for
the difference in modes of expression in two cases. It has been usually proposed
that threat of castration in early childhood days, owing to some misdemeanour,
is directly responsible for the complex, but histories of Indian patients seem to
disprove this (p. 74).

Bose then goes on to say that though the castration threat is extremely common—in girls it takes the form of chastisement by snakes—the
difference in Indian reactions to it is due to children growing up naked
till the ages of 9 to 10 years (girls till 7) so that the difference between
the sexes never comes as a surprise. The castration idea which comes
up symbolically in dreams as decapitation, a cut on a finger or a sore
in some parts of the body has behind it the 'primitive' idea of being a
woman.

Indeed, reading early Indian case histories, one is struck by the
fluidity of the patients' cross-sexual and generational identifications. In
the Indian patient the fantasy of taking on the sexual attributes of both
the parents seems to have relatively easier access to awareness. Bose,
for instance, in one of his vignettes (Bose, 1948) tells us of a middle-
aged lawyer who, with reference to his parents, sometimes

took up an active male sexual role, treating both of them as females in his unconscious and sometimes a female attitude, especially towards the father, craving for a child from him. In the male role, sometimes he identified himself with
his father and felt a sexual craving for the mother; on the other occasions his
unconscious mind built up a composite of both the parents toward which male
sexual needs were directed; it is in this attitude that he made his father give birth
to a child like a woman in his dream (p. 158).

Another young Bengali (Bose, 1949), whenever he thought of a particular man, felt with a hallucinatory intensity that his penis and testes
vanished altogether and were replaced by female genitalia. While
defecating he felt he heard the peremptory voice of his guru asking,
'Have you given me a child yet?' In many of his dreams, he was a man
whereas his father and brothers had become women. During intercourse
with his wife he tied a handkerchief over his eyes as it gave him the
feeling of being a veiled bride while he fantasized his own penis as that
of his father and his wife's vagina as that of his mother.

In my own work, fifty years after Bose's contributions of which till
recently I was only vaguely aware, I am struck by the comparable pat-

terns in Indian mental life we observed independently of each other, and this in spite of our different emotional predilections, analytic styles, theoretical preoccupations, geographical locations and historical situations. Such a convergence further strengthens my belief, shared by every practising analyst, that there is no absolute arbitrariness in our representation of the inner world. There is unquestionably something that resists, a something which can only be characterized by the attribute 'psychical reality' which both the analyst and the analysand help discover and give meaning to.

It is the ubiquity and multiformity of the 'primitive idea of being a woman', and the embeddedness of this fantasy in the maternal configurations of the family and the culture in India, which I would like to discuss from my observations. My main argument is that the 'hegemonic narrative' of Hindu culture as far as male development is concerned is neither that of Freud's Oedipus nor that of Christianity's Adam. One of the more dominant narratives of this culture is that of Devi, the great goddess, especially in her manifold expressions as mother; in the inner world of the Hindu son. In India at least, a primary task of psychoanalysis, the science of imagination or even (in Wallace Stevens' words) 'the science of illusion'—*Mayalogy*—is to grapple with *Mahamaya*, 'The Great Illusion', as the goddess is also called. Of course, it is not my intention to deny or underestimate the importance of the powerful mother in western psychoanalysis. All I seek to suggest is that certain forms of the maternal–feminine may be more central in Indian myths and psyche than in their western counterparts. I would then like to begin my exposition with the first ten minutes of an analytic session.

The patient is a 26-year-old social worker who has been in analysis for three years. He comes four times a week with each session lasting fifty minutes and conducted in the classical manner with the patient lying on the couch and the analyst sitting in a chair behind him. He entered analysis not because of any pressing personal problems but because he thought it would help him professionally. In this particular session, he begins with a fantasy he had while he was in a bus. The fantasy was of a tribe living in the jungle which unclothes its dead and hangs them on the trees. Mohan, the patient, visualized a beautiful woman hanging on one of the trees. He imagined himself coming at night and having intercourse with the woman. Other members of the tribe are eating parts of the hanging corpses. The fantasy is immediately followed by the recollection of an incident from the previous evening.

Mohan was visiting his parents' home where he had lived till recently when he married and set up his own household. This step was not only personally painful but also unusual for his social milieu where sons normally brought their wives to live in their parental home. His younger sister, with her three-year-old son, was also visiting at the same time. Mohan felt irritated by the anxious attention his mother and grandmother gave the boy. The grandmother kept telling the child not to go and play outside the house, to be careful of venturing too far and so on. On my remarking that perhaps he recognized himself in the nephew, Mohan exclaimed with rare resentment, 'Yes, all the women [his mother, grandmother, his father's brother's wife and his father's unmarried sister who lived with them] were always doing the same with me'.

Beginning with these ten minutes of a session, I would like to unroll Mohan's conflicts around maternal representations and weave them together with the central maternal configurations of Indian culture. Because of his particular objective, my presentation of further material from Mohan's analysis is bound to be subject to what Donald Spence (1986) has called 'narrative smoothing'. A case history, though it purports to be a story that is true, is actually always at the intersection of fact and fable. Its tale quality, though, arises less from the commissions in imagination than from omissions in reality.

Born in a lower-middle-class family in a large village near Delhi, Mohan is the eldest of three brothers and two sisters. His memories of growing up, till well into youth, are pervaded by the maternal phalanx of the four women. Like his mother, who in his earliest memories stands out as a distinct figure from a maternal–feminine continuum to be then reabsorbed into it, Mohan, too, often emerges from and retreats into femininity. In the transference, the fantasies of being a woman are not especially disturbing; neither are the fantasies of being an infant suckling at a breast which he has grown on to my exaggeratedly hairy chest. One of his earliest recollections is of a woman who used to pull at the penises of the little boys playing out in the street. Mohan never felt afraid when the woman grabbed at his own penis. In fact, he rather liked it, reassured that he had a penis at all or at least enough of one for the woman to acknowledge its existence.

Bathed, dressed, combed and caressed by one or the other of the women, Mohan's wishes and needs were met before they were even articulated. Food, especially the milk-based Indian sweets, was constantly pressed on him. Even now, on his visits to the family, the first question by one of the women pertains to what he would like to eat. For a long time during the analysis, whenever a particular session was stressful because of what he considered a lack of maternal empathy in my interventions, Mohan felt compelled to go to a restaurant in town where he would first gorge himself on sweets before he returned home.

Besides the omnipresence of women, my most striking impressions of Mohan's early memories is their diurnal location in night and their primarily tactile quality. Partly, this has to do with the crowded, public living arrangements of the Indian family. Here, even the notions of privacy are absent, not to speak of such luxuries as separate bedrooms for parents and children. Sleeping in the heat with little or no clothes next to one of his caretakers, an arm or a leg thrown across the maternal body, there is one disturbing memory which stands out clearly. This is of Mohan's penis erect against the buttocks of his sleeping mother and his reluctance to move away struggling against the feelings of shame and embarrassment that she may wake up and notice the forbidden touch. Later, in adolescence, the mothers are replaced by visiting cousins sharing mattresses spread out in the room or on the roof, furtive rubbings of bodies and occasional genital contact while other members of the extended family were in various stages of sleep.

Embedded in this blissful abundance of maternal flesh and promiscuity of touch, however, is a nightmare. Ever since childhood and persisting well into the initial phases of the analysis, Mohan would often scream in his sleep while a vague, dark shape threatened to envelop him. At these times only his father's awakening him with the reassurance that everything was all right helped Mohan compose himself for renewed slumber. The father, a gentle, retiring man who left early in the morning for work and returned home late at night, was otherwise a dim figure hovering at the outskirts of an animated family life.

In the very first sessions of the analysis, Mohan talked of a sexual compulsion which he found embarrassing to acknowledge. The compulsion consisted of travelling in a crowded bus and seeking to press close to the hips of any plump, middle-aged woman standing in the aisle. It was vital for his ensuing excitement that the woman have her back to him. If she ever turned to face Mohan, with the knowledge of his desire in her eyes, his erection immediately subsided and he would hurriedly move away with intense feelings of shame. After marriage, too, the edge of his desire was often at its sharpest when his wife slept on her side with her back to him. In mounting excitement, Mohan would rub against her and want to make love when she was still not quite awake.

If, however, the wife gave intimation of becoming an enthusiastic partner in the exercise, Mohan sometimes ejaculated prematurely or found his erection precipitately shrivel.

It is evident from these brief fragments of Mohan's case history that his desire is closely connected with some of the most inert parts of a woman's body, hips and buttocks. In other words, the desire needs the woman to be sexually dead for its fulfillment. The genesis of the fantasy of the hanging corpse with whom Mohan has intercourse at night has at its root the fear of the mothers' sexuality as well as the anger at their restraint on his explorations of the world. My choice of Mohan's case, though, is not dictated by the interest it may hold from a psychoanalytical perspective. The choice, instead, has to do with its central theme, namely the various paths in imagination which Mohan traverses, in face of many obstacles, to maintain an idealized relationship with the maternal body. This theme and the fantasized solutions to the disorders in the mother-son relationship are repeated again and again in Indian case and life histories. Bose's observation on the Indian male patient's 'primitive idea of being a woman' is then only a special proposition of a more general theorem. The wish to be a woman is one particular solution to the discord that threatens the breaking up of the son's fantasized connection to the mother, a solution whose access to awareness is facilitated by the culture's views on sexual differentiation and the permeability of gender boundaries. Thus, for instance, when Gandhi (1943) publicly proclaims that he has mentally become a woman or, quite unaware of Karen Horney and other deviants from the orthodox analytic position of the time, talks of man's envy of the woman's procreative capacities, saying 'There is as much reason for a man to wish that he was born a woman as for woman to do otherwise', he is sure of a sympathetic and receptive audience.

In the Indian context, this particular theme can be explored in individual stories as well as in the cultural narratives as we call myths, both of which are more closely interwoven in Indian culture than is the case in the modern West. In an apparent reversal of a western pattern, traditional myths in India are less a source of intellectual and aesthetic satisfaction for the mythologist than of emotional recognition for others, more moving for the patient than for the analyst. Myths in India are not part of a bygone era. They are not '*retained* fragments from the infantile psychic life of the race' as Karl Abraham (1913, p. 72) called them or '*vestiges* of the infantile fantasies of whole nations, secular dreams of youthful humanity' in Freud's words (Freud, 1908, p. 152). Vibrantly alive, their symbolic power intact, Indian myths constitute a cultural idiom which aids the individual in the construction and integration of his inner world. Parallel to pattern of infant care and to the structure and values of family relationships, popular and well-known myths are isomorphic with the central psychological constellations of the culture and are constantly renewed and validated by the nature of subjective experience (Obeyesekere, 1981). Given the availability of the mythological idiom, it is almost as easy to mythologize a psychoanalysis, such as that of Mohan, as to analyse a myth; almost as convenient to elaborate on intrapsychic conflict in a mythological mode as it is in a case–historical narrative mode.

Earlier, I advanced the thesis that the myths of Devi, the great goddess, constitute a 'hegemonic narrative' of Hindu culture. Of the hundreds of myths on her various manifestations, my special interest here is in the goddess as mother, and especially the mother of the sons, Ganesha and Skanda. But before proceeding to connect Mohan's tale to the larger cultural story, let me note that I have ignored the various versions of these myths in traditional texts and modern folklore—an undertaking which is rightly the preserve of mythologists and folklorists—and instead picked on their best-known, popular versions.

The popularity of Ganesha and Skanda as gods—psychologically representing two childhood positions of the Indian son—is certainly undeniable. Ganesha, the remover of obstacles and the god of all beginnings, is perhaps the most adored of the reputed 330 million Hindu gods. Iconically represented as a pot-bellied toddler with an elephant head and one missing tusk, he is represented proportionately as a small child when portrayed in the family group with his mother Parvati and father Shiva. His image, whether carved in stone or drawn up in a coloured print, is everywhere: in temples, homes, shops, roadside shrines, calendars. Ganesha's younger brother Skanda or Kartikeya, has his own following, especially in South India where he is extremely popular and worshipped under the name of Murugan or Subramanya. In contrast to Ganesha, Skanda is a handsome child, a youth of slender body and heroic exploits who in analytic parlance may be said to occupy the phallic position.

Ganesha's myths tell us one part of Mohan's inner life while those of Skanda reveal yet another. Ganesha, in many myths, is solely his mother Parvati's creation. Desirous of child and lacking Shiva's cooperation in the venture, she created him out of the dirt and sweat of her body mixed with unguents. Like Mohan's fantasies of his femininity, Ganesha too is not only his mother's boy but contains her very essence. Mohan, even while indubitably male like Skanda, is immersed in the world of mothers which an Indian extended family creates for the child. Skanda, like Mohan, is the son of more than one mother: his father Shiva's seed being too powerful could not be borne by one woman and wandered from womb to womb before Skanda took birth. Mohan's ravenous consumption of sweets to restore feelings of well-being has parallels with Ganesha's appetite for modakas, the sweet wheat or rice balls which devotees offer to the god in large quantities, 'knowing' that the god is never satisfied, that his belly empties itself as fast as it is filled (Courtright, 1986, p. 114). For, like the lean Mohan, the fat god's sweets are a lifeline to the mother's breast; his hunger for the mother's body, in spite of temporary appeasements, is ultimately doomed to remain unfulfilled. Mohan is further like Ganesha in that he too has emerged from infancy with an ample capacity for vital involvement with others.

In the dramatization of Mohan's dilemma in relation to the mother, brought to a head by developmental changes that push the child towards an exploration of the outer world while they also give him increasing intimations of his biological rock-bottom identity as a male, Ganesha and Skanda play the leading roles. In a version common to both south India and Sri Lanka (Obeyesekere, 1984) the myth is as follows:

A mango was floating down the stream and Uma (Parvati), the mother, said that whoever rides around the universe first will get the mango [in other versions, the promise is of *modakas* or wives). Skanda impulsively got on his golden peacock and went around the universe. But Ganesha, who rode the rat, had more wisdom. He thought: 'What could my mother have meant by this?' He then circumambulated his mother, worshipped her and said, 'I have gone around my universe.' Since Ganesha was right his mother gave him the mango. Skanda was furious when he arrived and demanded the mango. But before he could get it Ganesha bit the mango and broke one of his tusks (p. 471).

Here Skanda and Ganesha are personifications of the two opposing wishes of the older child on the eve of the Oedipus complex. He is torn between a powerful push for independent and autonomous functioning and an equally strong pull toward surrender and re-immersion in the enveloping maternal fusion from which he has just emerged. Giving in to the pull of individuation and independence, Skanda becomes liable to one kind of punishment—exile from the mother's bountiful presence, and one kind of reward—the promise of functioning as an adult, virile man. Going back to the mother—and I would view Ganesha's eating of the mango as a return to and feeding at the breast, especially since we know that in Tamil Nadu the analogy between a mango and the breast is a matter of common awareness (Egnor, 1984, p. 15)—has the broken tusk, the loss of potential masculinity, as a consequence. Remaining an infant, Ganesha's reward, on the other hand, will be never to know the pangs of separation from the mother, never to feel the despair at her absence. That Ganesha's lot is considered superior to Skanda's is perhaps an indication of the Indian man's cultural preference in the dilemma of separation–individuation. He is at one with his mother in her wish not to have the son separate from her, individuate out of their shared anima (Kakar, 1987).

For Mohan, as we have seen, the Ganesha position is often longed for and sometimes returned to in fantasy. It does not, however, represent an enduring solution to the problem of maintaining phallic desire in the face of the overwhelming inner presence of the Great Mother. Enter Skanda. After he killed the demon Taraka who had been terrorizing the gods, the goddess became quite indulgent towards her son and told him to amuse himself as he pleased. Skanda became wayward, his lust rampant. He made love to the wives of the gods and the gods could not stop him. Upon their complaining to the goddess, she decided she would assume the form of whatever woman Skanda was about to seduce. Skanda summoned the wife of one god after another but in each saw his mother and became passionless. Finally thinking that 'the universe is filled with my mother' he decided to remain celibate for ever.

Mohan, too, we saw, became 'passionless' whenever the motherly woman he fancied in the bus turned to face him. But, instead of celibacy, he tried to hold on to desire by killing the sexual part of the mother, deadening the lower portion of her trunk, which threatened him with impotence. Furthermore, the imagined sexual overpoweringness of the mother, in the face of which the child feels hopelessly inadequate, with fears of being engulfed and swallowed by her dark depth, is not experienced by Mohan in the form of clear-cut fantasies but in a recurrent nightmare from which he wakes up screaming. Elsewhere, I have traced in detail the passage of the powerful, sexual mother through Hindu myths, folk beliefs, proverbs, symptoms and the ritual worship of the goddess in her terrible and fierce forms (Kakar, 1978). Here, I shall only narrate one of the better-known myths of Devi, widely reproduced in her iconic representations in sculpture and painting, in order to convey through the myth's language of the concrete, of image and symbol, some of the quality of the child's awe and terror of this particular maternal image.

The demon Mahisasura had conquered all the three worlds. Falling in love with the goddess, he sent a message to make his desire known to her. Devi replied that she would accept as her husband only someone who defeated her in battle. Mahisasura entered the battlefield with a vast army and a huge quantity of fighting equipment. Devi came alone, mounted on her lion. The gods were surprised to see her without even an armour, riding naked to the combat. Dismounting, Devi started dancing and cutting off the heads of millions and millions of demons with her sword to the rhythm of her movement. Mahisasura, facing death, tried to run away by becoming an elephant. Devi cut off his trunk. The elephant became a buffalo and against its thick hide Devi's sword and spear were of no avail. Angered, Devi jumped on the buffalo's back and rode it to exhaustion. When the buffalo demon's power of resistance had collapsed, Devi plunged her spear into its ear and Mahisasura fell dead.

The myth is stark enough in its immediacy and needs no further gloss on the omnipotence and sexual energy of the goddess, expressed in the imagery of her dancing and riding naked, exhausting even the most powerful male to abject submission and ultimately death, decapitating (i.e. castrating) millions of 'bad boys' with demonic desires, and so on. The only feature of the myth I would like to highlight, and which is absent both in Mohan's case vignette and in the myths narrated so far is that of the sword- and spear-wielding Devi as the phallic mother. In the Indian context, this fantasy seems more related to Chasseguet–Smirgel's (1964) notion of the phallic mother being a denial of the adult vagina and the feelings of inadequacy it invokes rather than allowing its traditional interpretation as a denial of castration anxiety. In addition I would see the image of the goddess as man–woman (or, for the matter, of Shiva as *ardhanarishwara*, half man–half woman) as incorporating the boy's wish to become a man without having to separate and sexually differentiate from the mother, to take on male sexual attributes while not letting go the female ones.

The myth continues that when Devi's frenzied dancing did not come to an end even after the killing of the buffalo demon, the gods became alarmed and asked Shiva for help. Shiva lay down on his back and when the goddess stepped on her husband she hung out her tongue in shame and stopped. Like Mohan's gentle and somewhat withdrawn father who was the only one who could help in dissipating the impact of the nightmare, Shiva too enters the scene supine yet a container for the great mother's energy and power. In other words, the father may be unassuming and remote, yet powerful. First experienced as an ally and a protector (or even as a co-victim), the father emerges as a rival only later. The rivalry too, in popular Indian myths and most of the case histories, is not so much that of Oedipus, where the power of the myth derives from the son's guilt over a fantasized and eventually unconscious parricide. The Indian context stresses more the father's envy of what belongs to the son—including the mother—and thus the son's persecution anxiety as a primary motivation in the father–son relationship. It is thus charged with the fear of filicide and with the son's castration, by self or the father, as solution to father–son competition, Shiva's beheading of Ganesha who on the express wish of his mother stood guard at her private chambers while she bathed, and the replacement of his head by that of an elephant, the legends of Bhishma and Puru, who renounced sexual functioning in order to keep the affections of their fathers intact, are some of the better known illustrations (Kakar and Ross, 1987). But the fate of fathers and sons and families and daughters are different narratives; stories yet to be told, texts still to be written.

The importance of the Oedipus complex in classical psychoanalysis lies not only in it being a dominant organizing pattern of a boy's object relations but also in it being the fulcrum of Freud's cultural theory. Freud considered the myth of Oedipus as a hegemonic narrative of all cultures at all times although enough evidence is now available to suggest that its dominance may be limited to some western cultures at certain periods of their history. In other words, the Oedipus complex, in one variation or the other, may well be universal but not equally hegemonic across cultures. Similarly, I suggest, the Ganesha complex discussed in this essay together with its myth, is equally universal at a certain stage of the male child's development. It is a mythologem for relations between mother and child at the eve of Oedipus before any significant triangulation has taken place. The Ganesha complex, I have tried to show, is also the hegemonic developmental narrative of the male self in Hindu India. In another of its variations as the Ajase complex, it has also been postulated as the dominant narrative of the male self in Japan.

CULTURE AND HUMAN DEVELOPMENT

Cultural ideas and ideals, manifested in their narrative form as myths, are the innermost experience of the self. One cannot therefore speak of an 'earlier' or 'deeper', of the self beyond cultural reach. As a 'depth psychology', psychoanalysis dives deep but in the same waters in which the cultural rivers too flow. Pre-eminently operating from within the heart of the western Myth, enclosed in the *mahamaya* of Europe—from myths of ancient Greece to the 'illusions' of the Enlightenment—psychoanalysis has had little opportunity to observe from within, and with empathy, the deeper import of other cultures, myths in the workings of the self.

The questions relating to the 'how' of this process are bound up with the larger issue of the relationship between the inner and outer worlds which has been of perennial psychological and philosophical interest. It is certainly not my intention to discuss these questions at any length. I would only like to point out that apart from some notable exceptions, such as Erik Erikson (1950) who both held aloft and significantly contributed to a vision of a 'psychoanalysis sophisticated enough to include the environment', the impact of culture on the development of a sense of identity—in the construction of the self, in modern parlance—has been generally underestimated. Freud's 'timetable' of culture entering the psychic structure relatively late in life as 'ideology' of the superego (Freud, 1922) has continued to be followed by other almanac makers of the psyche. Even Heinz Kohut, as Janis Long (1986) has shown, does not quite follow the logical implications of his concept of 'selfobject'. These are, of course, the aspects of the other which are incorporated in the self and are experienced as part of one's own subjectivity. Kohut, too, follows Freud in talking of a 'culture selfobject' of later life (Kohut, 1985), derived in part from cultural ideas and ideals, which helps in maintaining the integrity and vitality of the individual self. Yet the idea of selfobject which goes beyond the notion of a budding self's relatedness to the environment, to the environment's gradual transmutation into *becoming* the self implies that '*what* the parents respond to in a developing child, *how* they respond and what they present as idealizable from the earliest age' (Long, 1986, p. 8)—surely much of it a cultural matter—will be the raw material for the child's inner construction of the self. In other words, a caretaker's *knowing* of the child, a knowing in which affect and cognition are ideally fused, is in large part cultural and forms the basis of the child's own knowing of his or her self. The notion that the construction and experience of the self is greatly influenced by culture from the very beginning does not imply that there is no difference between individual faces and cultural masks, no boundary between inner and outer worlds. The tension between the two is what gives psychoanalysis and literature much of their narrative power. What I seek to emphasize here is that this boundary cannot be fixed either in time or psychic space. It is dynamic, mobile and constantly subject to change.

SUMMARY

Interweaving myths and case history, this paper argues that given the non-western nature of the family environment in India, certain aspects of the powerful mother (-goddess) have a great impact on the development of the male child. Defensively the Hindu boy copes with this figure of intense import in certain culturally favoured ways, e.g. by remaining tied to the infantile position, celibacy or impotence as a defence against phallic licence, retaining a degree of potency by deadening the mother, identification with the mother and so on. Moreover, the role of the father too has a specific cultural configuration. The paper further argues that the construction and experience of the self are influenced by culture from the very beginning of life and that analysts have generally placed its influence too late in the developmental timetable.

III

Erotic Love

Erotic Love

9

The Cloistered Passion of Radha and Krishna

A psychoanalytic patient, a passionate man of twenty-four, found himself avoiding more and more the pleasure of intercourse with his girlfriend. Yet another of his symptom was his inability to weep, much to his consternation, denting his image of himself as a romantic.

A dream brought to light one level of his terror, and desire. In it the patient dived with other children into a great gulf. He emerged as if uncertain of his body—of what lay beneath the neck—and found himself crossing his old school's soccer field, making his way not to the boy's but rather to the girl's changing room. In his associations he talked of the eerie feeling that, with penetration, he was welded to his lover, as if their pubic hair were somehow squashed, almost glued together. Her breasts, so delightful in their spongy roundness, seemed to seep into his chest and become his own. Upon climaxing he felt, in an almost altered state of consciousness, that he was taking in her moistened vagina with his penis and found himself fighting off unnamed fears, becoming chilled and anxious. All of a sudden he remarked on his inadvertent refusal to weep, equating the watering of his eyes with the lubrication of a woman's genitals.

The analysand at last discovered and voiced what seemed his 'most secret' of wishes. He wanted to be as beautiful and bountiful as his lover; he wished to be a woman. Tasting the illusion, satisfying this surprising desire in the safety of the analytic space, he wondered whether he would re-emerge from a woman as a man—ambitious, powerful, rich?

After a pause the patient comforted himself with thoughts about the ubiquity of what had seemed an altogether idiosyncratic perversity. Perhaps his analyst 'knew' women in much the same way as he did. Had not the self-revelatory hero of Janet Malcolm's *The Impossible Profession*, the dreamy workman-like amalgam portrayed by her as the 'typical' psychoanalyst, confessed the source of his failure to speak or write more? To do so, the hero of the book lamented, would be to symbolically fulfil a treasured but shameful wish—to parade before the gaze of others as a 'beautiful woman', and this before analysts who 'saw into people's souls'.

Another patient, in imitating an illicit love affair with the wife of a businessman for whom he worked, had crossed daunting social barriers of caste and class. The couple had secretly met on three occasions but had not yet become sexually intimate. His illness was preceded by a dream about the long desired moment of consummation. In it, as the would-be lovers finally embrace, he discovers to his excited horror that the woman has grown a penis which is rubbing against the wet lips of his newly formed vagina in a welter of unknown but exquisite sensations. Soon he felt strange changes taking place in his body: parts of it becoming soft and delicate like a woman's while others became even stronger and muscular. His terror began mounting when he began having 'visions' of Hindu gods and goddesses—Shiva and Parvati, Krishna and Radha, Rama and Sita—in amorous embrace. The sensations and feelings of the gods and goddesses in intercourse, he felt, were being manifested in his own person, succeeding each other with a frightening rapidity.

It is some secrets of these patients—and of many 'normal' others—which we now address in the paradigmatic love story of Hindu India.

For an Indian—or, more exactly, a Hindu—the love of Radha, the beautiful cowherdess who later became a goddess for some cults, and Krishna, the youthful dark god who is the object of widespread devotion, is less a story remembered than a random succession of episodes seen and heard, sung and danced. Over the centuries their liaison has been portrayed in thousands of exquisite miniature paintings which have fixed the lovers in separation and union, longing and abandonment. The story is heard whenever we listen to the great vocalists of Indian classical music—from Kumara Gandharva to Pandit Jasraj—sing the devotional songs of medieval saints who in their poems sometimes watch and at others participate in the love-making as Krishna's beloved. The story grips our imagination every time we behold the animated expressions, flashing eyes and sinuous movements of an Indian dancer who (as Radha) dances her anger at Krishna's infidelities or (as Krishna) begs forgiveness for his impetuous dalliance. The affair is recreated each time a Krishna devotee participates in the communal singing of an episode from the story in a temple, and especially when he or she, possessed by the spirit of one of the lovers, feels impelled to get up and ecstatically dance the god or his beloved.

The Radha–Krishna legend, then, is not a narrative in the sense of an orderly progression whose protagonists have a shared past and are progressing towards a tragic or happy future. It is more an evocation and elaboration of the here-and-now of passion, an attempt to capture the exciting, fleeting moments of the senses and the baffling ways in which pleasures and pains are felt before the retrospective recollection which, in trying to regain a lost control over emotional life, edits away love's inevitable confusions. It is not tragic but tender, and, ultimately, cheerful.

The sybaritic tenderness enveloping the cameos of the lovers is striking. A long line of bards and balladeers, most of them indebted to the twelfth-century Sanskrit poet Jayadeva, who decisively shaped the legend's outlines, have often described the setting of their meetings. A Hindu needs only to close his eyes and 'remember' to see Vrindavan, an Indian garden of Eden, spring into existence. In the perpetual sunshine of the myth, distinct from the mists of history, a forest thicket of the banks of the river Yamuna awakens to life on a tropical spring day. The mustard fields at the edge of the forest, with their thick carpet of dazzling yellow flowers, stretch far into the distance. The air is redolent with the perfume of the pollen shaken loose from newly blossomed jasmine and bunches of flame-coloured mimosa flowers hanging round and heavy from the trees. The ears are awash with the humming of bees, the cries of cuckoos and the distant tinkling of bells on the necks of grazing cattle. The call of Krishna's flute comes floating through the forest thicket, further agitating the already unquiet senses, making for an inner uprising and an alien invasion. The story, aiming to fix the essence of youthful ardour, has an amorous rather than geographical landscape as its location; its setting is neither social nor historical but sensuous.

In the falling dusk, Nanda, Krishna's foster father and the chief of a community of cowherds, asks Radha to escort Krishna home through the forest. On the way, in a grove, their 'secret passion triumphs'. Radha's thoughts come to be absorbed by Krishna who, however, is unfaithful to her as he sports with other cowherdesses—hugging one, kissing another and caressing yet another dark beauty.

When he quickens all things to create bliss in the world
His soft black sinuous lotus limbs
Begin the festival of love
And beautiful cowherd girls wildly
Wind him in their bodies.
Friend, in spring young Hari [Krishna] plays
Like erotic mood incarnate.[1]

Radha is jealous as she imagines the 'vines of his great throbbing arms circle a thousand cowherdesses'. But more than that, she is infused with all the confusing emotions of a proud, intense woman who feels deserted by her lover.

My heart values his vulgar ways,
Refuses to admit my rage,
Feels strangely elated,
And keeps denying his guilt.
When he steals away without me
To indulge his craving
For more young women,
My perverse heart
Only wants Krishna back
What can I do?

Solitary grief and images of love betrayed and passion lost, recreated in reverie, alternate and reinforce each other but seem somehow benign.

My eyes close languidly as I feel
The flesh quiver on his cheek,
My body is moist with sweat; he is
Shaking from the wine of lust.
Friend, bring Kesi's sublime tormentor to revel with me!
I've gone mad waiting for his fickle love to change.

The power of Radha's yearning works a change in Krishna. Of all the *gopis* (cowherdesses), interchangeable suppliers of pleasure and feelings of conquest, Radha begins to stand out in Krishna's mind as someone special who is desired in her uniqueness. In Maurice Valency's formulation, from the 'heroic lover' for whom no woman is exceptional and who simply desires a variety of amatory dalliances, Krishna becomes the 'romantic lover' impelled towards a single irreplaceable mistress.[2] The unheeding pursuit of pleasure, a bewildered Krishna dis-

covers, had been brought to a halt by pleasure's worst enemies—
memory and attachment.

> Her joyful responses to my touch,
> Trembling liquid movement of her eyes,
> Fragrance from her lotus mouth,
> A sweet ambiguous stream of words,
> Nectar from her red berry lips—
> Even when the sensuous objects are gone,
> My mind holds on to her in a trance.
> How does the wound of her desertion deepen?

Having been the god who strove to please himself alone, Krishna has
become a man for whom the partner's well-being assumes an importance easily the equal of his own. He discovers, that he would rather
serve and adore than vanquish and demand. As a tale of love this transformative moment from desire's sensations to love's adoration gives the
story of Radha and Krishna its singular impact.

It is a remarkable coincidence that three of the world's best-known
works of romantic love which occupy pivotal positions in their respective cultures—Beroul's *Tristan and Isolde* in Europe, Nizami's *Layla
and Majnun* in the Islamic world and Jayadeva's *Gitagovinda* in
India—were all produced roughly at the same time: in the twelfth century. Whether this represents happenstance, coincidence, or springs
from sociohistorical trends coalescing across the globe is beyond our
scope in this more *life* historical endeavour. However, it is striking that
the poetry of passion should predate and possibly prefigure important
cultural-historical changes in Europe, India and the Middle East. It is as
if the unfolding discovery of each other portrayed in the love story
sheds light on what is fundamental to the human spirit.

To continue the story: hearing of Krishna's remorse and of his attachment to her, Radha, dressed and ornamented for love, awaits
Krishna at their trysting place in the forest. She lingers in vain for
Krishna does not come. Radha is consumed by jealousy as she imagines
him engaged in an amorous encounter with a rival. When Krishna finally does appear, Radha spurns him angrily:

> Dark from kissing her kohl-blackened eyes
> At dawn your lips match your body's colour, Krishna
> Damn you Madhava! Go! Kesava leave me!
> Don't plead your lies with me!

> Go after her, Krishna!
> She will ease your despair.

But, in separation, Radha and Krishna long for each other with a mounting sense of desolation. Eventually, Radha's friend persuades her to abandon her modesty and pride and go to her lover.

> Your full hips and breasts are heavy to bear.
> Approach with anklets ringing!
> Their sound inspires lingering feet.
> Run with the gait of a wild goose!
> Madhu's tormentor
> Is faithful to you, fool.
> Follow him, Radhika!

In the full throes of a sexual excitement—when even her 'modesty left in shame'—Radha rushes to meet an equally ardent (and repentant) lover, Krishna sings:

> Throbbing breasts aching for love's embrace are hard to
>   touch.
> Rest these vessels on my chest!
> Queen love's burning fire!
> Narayana [Krishna) is faithful now. Love me Radhika!
> Offer your lips' nectar to revive a dying slave, Radha!
> This obsessed mind and listless body burn in love's
>   desolation,
> Narayana is faithful now. Love me, Radhika!

Once the ecstatic love-making has subsided momentarily in an orgasmic release, a playful Radha asks Krishna to rearrange her clothes and her tousled hair:

> Paint a leaf on my breasts!
> Put colour on my cheeks!
> Lay a girdle on my hips!
> Twine my heavy braid with flowers!
> Fix rows of bangles on my hands
> And jewelled anklets on my feet!
> Her yellow-robed lover
> Did what Radha said.

Jayadeva, legend has it, hesitant to commit sacrilege by having the god touch Radha's feet—the usual sign of a submissive lower status—was unable to pen the last lines and went out to bathe; when he returned he found that Krishna himself had completed the verse in his absence!

The fascination of Jayadeva's creation is, of course, also due to its musical form. Jayadeva set each canto of the love poem to a different musical mode (*raga*) and rhythm (*tala*). It is a work which succeeding generations have regarded a marvel of music as much as of language and meaning. And music, we know, that fine-tuned language of the. senses, best captures the Dionysian—or rather, in our context, the 'Krishnanian'—spirit and sensual spontaneity of the erotic. The great Persian poet Rumi has aptly described the house of love as having doors and roof made of music, melodies and poetry. The sensibilities and pulse of lovers, and of others with either the potential for love or its haunting memory, can be reproduced in music with greater fidelity than in words since there is a direct rather than signified correspondence between musical forms and the forms of emotional life. Love is not *about* something: it *is*. Jayadeva seems to have intuitively known that (in Kierkegaard's words) 'the sensual wood is too heavy and too dense to be sustained by speech; only music can express it.'

The story of Radha and Krishna, as it has come down to us today, differs from Jayadeva's version in only one significant respect. Jayadeva merely hints at the illicit nature of their love when he has an older Radha change from young Krishna's protective escort to become his lover, thereby also defying the authority and instructions of the chief of cowherds:

> 'Clouds thicken the sky.
> Tamala trees darken the forest.
> The night frightens him.
> Radha, you take him home!'
> They leave at Nanda's order,
> Passing trees in thickets on the way,
> Until secret passions of Radha and Madhava
> Triumph on the Jamuna riverbank.

Later poets, notably Vidyapati, who tend to focus more on Radha and her love than on Krishna, gave the illicit in the story a more concrete cast and a specific content. Radha is another man's wife and her liaison with Krishna, whatever its meaning in mystical allegory, is plainly adulterous in human terms. Radha is certainly not a paragon of womanly virtues detailed in Hindu texts; not does she come close to any of the 'good' or 'bad' mother-goddesses of Indian mythology and religion.

She is a more sophisticated character, more rounded and complex than a toddler's (or a Majnun's) dichotomous imagery would allow for. Radha is, indeed, a figure of the imagination of the boy just as he begins to discover his and his mother's sexuality. Rivals have just begun to enter the scene and have not yet beer recreated as internal inhibitions, jaundicing any delight in the mother's eroticism. There is an unobstructed joy to the sensuality of this all-too brief era, a lack of self-consciousness about experimenting with its variations. In her passionate craving for sexual union with her lover and in her desperate suffering in his absence, Radha is simply the personification of *mahabhava*, a 'great feeling' that is heedless of social proprieties and unbounded by conventions.

Before continuing in our own interpretation of the *mahabhava* of the legend, we must first briefly locate the love of Radha and Krishna in its cultural-historical context. As various scholars have pointed out, many different Indian traditions—religious and erotic, classical literary and folk—have converged and coalesced in the poetical renditions of the myth, especially Jayadeva's *Gitagovinda*, to give that particular work an allure that extends over large parts of the subcontinent.[3]

In India 'passion love' first appeared in the court poetry and drama of the so-called classical period of Hindu civilization, spanning the first few centuries of the Christian era. Earlier, in the epics of *Mahabharata* and *Ramayana*, love was usually a matter of straightforward desire and its gratification[4] This was especially so for the man for whom a woman was an instrument of pleasure and an object of the senses (*indriyartha*)—one physical need among many others. There is an idealization of marriage in the epics, yes, but chiefly as a social and religious act. The obligation of conjugal love and the virtue of chastity within marriage were primarily demanded of the wife, while few limits were set on a husband who lived under and looked up at a licentious heaven teeming with lusty gods and 'heavenly' whores—otherworldly and utterly desirable at once, and most eager to give and take pleasure. Their Hindu pantheon is not unlike the Greeks' Olympus where gods and goddesses sport and politic with a welcome absence of moralistic subterfuge.

The Buddhist domination of Indian society which followed brought with it Buddhism's sombre view of life, in which the god of love was identified with Mara or Death. The new cosmology it imposed was not particularly conducive to developing a literature of passionate love. Nor did love enter through the backdoor of erotic mysticism. In the Therigatha, or psalms of notable sisters of the Buddhist order, marked by dutiful daughterly sentiments towards the Buddha, there is none of the eroticism of their medieval Christian counterparts who in their passionate outpourings conceived of Christ as a youthful bridegroom.

All this seems to have changed radically with the dawn of the classical period that spanned the first six to seven centuries of the present era. In the poetry and drama flourishing at the courts, love became a predominant theme, indeed one overshadowing every other sentiment. It is a love that is both deeply sensual and moulded by mutual passion. The woman is as ardent as the man and initiates the wooing quite as often. Masculinity is not equated with seduction and conquest. Indeed the surviving poems of the few women poets show them to be even freer in their expression than their male counterparts.

Yet, though one's 'ego' or self is not at stake, the verse depicts an eroticism that is narcissistic in spirit, more hedonist than impassioned. The Sanskrit poems and dramas are characterized by a playful enjoyment of love's ambiguities, a delighted savouring of its pleasures and a consummately refined suffering of its sorrows. Spontaneity, fervid abandon and exaltation are generally absent from this poetry. Apart from one or two notable exceptions, the rendering of love is on a miniature scale; corresponding to the paintings for which the culture is known. Short stanzas seek to freeze one or another of love's emotions; they are cameos yielding glimpses into arresting erotic moments. What is considered important—and this is the core of the Indian theory of aesthetics—is to capture the *rasa*, literally, 'flavour' or 'essence' or the mood, of a particular passionate instant, which can then be relished by the poetically cultivated connoisseur. The intensity of the mood is not enhanced through psychological depth but by the accumulation of sensuous detail.

Blurring the boundaries between internal feeling and external sensation, the poet seldom treats love as something ethereal or lifts from it a sentiment to be evaluated. Rather it is equated with a definite sensation or a feeling in its concrete bodily manifestation. As Barbara Miller remarks in relation to the *Gitagovinda*:

Passion is made palpable through the sensuous descriptions of movements and physical forms. Seasonal changes in nature and bodily signs of inner feelings are colored richly to create a dense atmosphere of passion.[5]

The emphasis, replete with developmental resources in the 'early genital stage' and its revival in pubescence, is on sexual self-discovery. The 'other' is a source of excitement and delight, enlivening the senses and the body with her image and aura. This 'other' is to be explored thoroughly, in enormous detail, and therefore she is not quickly abandoned. Yet her inner life or her past and future are not subjects of the entrancement; the impulse is not one of fierce monogamy.

For most modern readers who have an affinity for the personal and the subjective, the emphasis of classical Indian literature on love as a depersonalized voluptuous state, while delighting the senses, does not touch the heart. For those whose sensibility has been moulded by romanticism and individualism it is difficult to identify with the impersonal protagonists of Sanskrit and Tamil love poems. These are not a particular man or woman but man and woman as such—provided he is handsome, she beautiful, and both young. The face of the heroine, for instance, is always like a moon or lotus flower, eyes like waterlilies or those of a fawn. She always stoops slightly from the weight of her full breasts, improbable fleshy flowers of rounded perfection that do not even admit a blade of grass between them. The waist is slim, with three folds, the thighs round and plump, like the trunk of an elephant or a banana tree. The navel is deep, the hips heavy. These lyrical yet conventional descriptions of body parts seem to operate like collective fetishes, culturally approved cues for the individual to allow himself to indulge erotic excitement without the risk of surrender or merger.

Now, a facet of the beloved woman's beauty is certainly impersonal in the sense that it is nature's gift, especially to youth, and its minimal presence is necessary for the glance to become a gaze, for the poet to wax lyrical. As Auden remarks, 'A girl who weighs two hundred pounds and a woman of eighty may both have beautiful faces in the personal sense, but men do not fall in love with them'.[6] For our tastes, however, the part played by impersonal beauty is receding in favour of a personal beauty which is more an individual than a natural or cultural creation. To borrow from the Brontës, 'beauty lies in the eye of the beholder', whose scrutiny sees in lustrous eyes windows to the soul and reflections of the whole. The lust evoked by looking at a woman in parts—and at the parts of a woman, as in most traditional Indian poetry—is for a mature modern man no longer solely determined by her conformity to a uniform cultural model. Rather it also resides in a feeling for her uniqueness in which even her flaws are cherished. It is now the fleeting yet characteristic trivialities—the narrowing of her eyes in a quizzical smile, the nibbling of the fleshy part of the lower lip when engrossed in thought—which fascinate and enthral the lover, the flash of aesthetic admiration superseded by the wave of adoration. In the verses of Shakespeare's great sonnet:

> My mistress' eyes are nothing like the sun;
> . . . .
> My mistress, when she walks, treads on the ground.
> And yet, by heaven, I think my love as rare
> As any she belied with false compare.[7]

A woman is a woman not out of her predictable construction but because she is herself, her limbs and features moved by her destined femininity. Appreciating her individuality goes hand in hand with what Jung, and later Mahler, termed the lover's individuation. Its attainment, relatively speaking, is a developmental milestone that brings to a close the early dyadic struggles of infancy and introduces the growing child to a world of 'whole objects or person', each with his or her complex attributes. Loving these people, a child or the adult proceeds beyond the self and its sensations for their own reflexive sake. To do otherwise, to reify sybaritics, is to deny the regressive and progressive thrusts of genuine passion.

Indian poetry becomes inaccessible, even boring, when its early freshness begins to wilt under scholastic dictates, which become more and more compelling in the later centuries. Not unlike the cataloguing efforts of modern sexologists, Sanskrit poetics and 'erotics' began to define, analyse and categorize the many moods and situations of love. Lovers—men and women—were stereotyped according to the ways they approached and reacted to love. They were further divided and subdivided according to rank, character and circumstances, as well as by the different shades of their feelings and gestures. An initial revolutionary aesthetic fervour gave way to the bureaucratization of beauty. With its insistence on the 'appropriate' combination of types, feelings and situations, the scholastic steamroller gained momentum and, in its way, crushed the creative expression of passionate love as effectively as epic indifference or Buddhist disapproval.

From the sixth century onwards, first in the south and then in the north, another auspicious shift took place which led to a re-emergence of passionate love. As with most things Indian, the change originated in the religious sphere but then expanded to influence Hindu culture and sensibility in such a profound way that its reverberations are still felt today. Scholars have called the shift *bhakti*, the rise of devotional religions in rebellion against the petrification of contemporary Hindu practice. Drawing on conventions of the classical literature of love and using an existing pan-Indian stock of symbols and figures of speech, the *bhakti* poets none the less strive for spontaneous, direct, personal expression of feeling rather than a rarified cultivation of aesthetic effect and the 'emotion recollected' preferred by Sanskrit poets.[8]

Although linked to the heroine and hero of classical love poetry in many ways, the figures of Radha and Krishna are primarily products of the *bhakti* movement, whose principal mood has always been erotic. Here the culture has imprinted its particular stamp upon the sensual experience—in contrast to much western poetry of sexual mysticism— though Radha and Krishna are not figures of erotic allegory. *Bhakti* extols possessing and being possessed by the god. For it sexual love is where the fullest possession, the 'closest touch of all', takes place. With this the creators and audiences of *bhakti* poetry seek to project themselves into Radha's love for Krishna through poems that recount all its passionate phases. *Bhakti* is pre-eminently feminine in its orientation, and the erotic love for Krishna (or Shiva as the case may be) is envisioned entirely from the woman's viewpoint, or at least from her position as imagined by the man. The male devotees, saints, and poets must all adopt a feminine posture and persona to recreate Radha's responses in themselves. Radha's passionate love for Krishna, raised to its highest intensity, is not an allegory for religious passion but *is* religious passion.[9] Jayadeva thus does not need to make a distinction or choose between the religious and the erotic when he introduces the subject matter of his poem by saying:

> If remembering Hari [Krishna] enriches your heart,
> If his arts of seduction arouse you,
> Listen to Jayadeva's speech
> In these sweet soft lyrical songs.

Befitting his status as the *adi-guru* (first teacher) of Radhakrishna cults, Jayadeva, *knows* that the enrichment of the heart and the arousal of senses belong together. Moreover, this coincidence of knowledge and feeling is intimately tied to an illusion, or at least a crossing over, of genders.

The augmentation of passion, or, more specifically, the heightening of sexual excitement, is then the 'great feeling', the *mahabhava*, that pervades the Radha–Krishna legend. Radha incarnates a state of per-

manent amorous tension, a here-and-now of desire that caries within itself a future expectation of pleasurable release but . . . oh, not yet! Her
concern is not with 'lineaments of gratified desire' but with their anticipation. Radha personifies an enduring arousal that does not seek
orgasmic resolution, an embodiment of ideals elsewhere put into Tantric
practices. Hers is an effort to reach the very essence of eroticism. As
she herself says in one of Vidyapati's songs:

> Through all the ages he [Krishna] has been clasped
> To my breast,
> Yet my desire never abates.
> I have seen subtle people sink in passion
> But none came so close to the heart of the fire.[10]

In her interviews with the temple-dancers of Orissa the
anthropologist Frédérique Marglin highlighted the fact that when these
women talk of the love (*prema*) of Radha and other cowherdesses they
do not mean a chaste, platonic love. Rather they refer specifically to the
fantasy—conscious in this case but unconscious in many others—of unending and sustained sexual excitement.[11] The absence of *kama* or lust
in Radha's love for Krishna does not mean an absence of desire, but
simply of orgasm. The dancers, who seek to enact for themselves the
tension and intensity of the mythical cowherdesses, explicate the distinction by stating that one of Krishna's names is *Acyuta*, 'the one
whose seed does not fall.' Marglin writes:

What is the meaning of Krishna's retention of his seed? My informant
delineated several levels of meaning. First, there is the testimony of everyday
experience, in which sexual pleasure is only momentary. After orgasm the
pleasurable erotic tension is gone; in such a manner one attains only temporary
pleasure or happiness (*kshanika sukha*). Furthermore, by ejaculating one loses
one's strength and becomes old. In this world, the world of *samsara*, pleasure
is brief and one begets children whereas in the divine play of Krishna there
is continuous (*nitya*) pleasure and no children. The *gopis* are not impregnated.
. . . The shedding of the seed has ulterior consequences, i.e. a birth. Krishna's
erotic dalliances with the *gopis* has no ulterior purpose or consequence. It exists
for itself, in itself.[12]

It is indeed a dwelling in the immediacy of excitement, a locking in of
body and mind in total involvement.

Using classical conventions in which sexual excitement is denoted
by certain bodily manifestations such as sweating and the bristling of
hair (the mention of sexual organs and genital sensations were always

crude and unacceptable), poem after poem seeks to convey the *rasa* of
Radha's arousal. In giving central place to the body in the depiction of
erotic passions—which are, after all, ideas which the mind would not
entertain unless it were united to the body and dependent on it for its
survival—the *bhakti* poets seem to intuitively recognize and affirm the
truth of Auden's assertion that 'Our bodies cannot love: / But, without
one / what works of love could we do.'[13] In Radha's excitement,
produced by the anticipation of intercourse,

> She bristles with pain, sucks in breath
> Cries, shudders, gasps,
> Broods deep, reels, stammers,
> Falls, raises herself, then faints.
> When fevers of passion rage so high,
> A frail girl may live by your charm.[14]

While in the sensuous fervour of foreplay.

> There was a shudder in her whispering voice.
> She was shy to frame her words.
> What has happened tonight to lovely Radha?
> Now she consents, now she is afraid.
> When asked for love, she closes up her eyes
> Eager to reach the ocean of desire.
> He begs her for a kiss.
> She turns her mouth away
> And then, like a night lily, the moon seized her.
> She felt his touch startling her girdle.
> She knew her love treasure was being robbed.
> With her dress she covered up her breasts.
> The treasure was left uncovered.'[15]

At first perusal the large number of Radha–Krishna poems that
describe the near harrowing effects of their separation on Radha do not
seem to support the contention that sexual excitement is the central
emotion and its generation their chief object. Much of the content of the
separation poems, however, consists of Radha's recollections of their
erotic pleasure—an effort to retain expectancy through reminiscence.
Further, in romantic literature around the world, the division of lovers
has been a well-known device for whetting erotic hunger. In life, as in
art, turnings in the path of love's fulfilment have always been found
necessary to swell the libidinal tide. Separateness and union are not dif-

ferent categories of love, as the convention of Indian poetics would have it, but are merely different phases of the cycle of love, both intimately connected through the workings of desire. The lover's and the poet's dwelling on apartness represents his or her renouncing a possession that would deflate desire. Erotic passion, in de Rougemont's anthropomorphic formulation, always invents distance in order to exult itself more completely.[16] Below the surface sadness lies the lover's *need* to create impediments to the enjoyment of their love, to *deliciously* postpone delight, to suspend ecstasy in time, make it all last forever.

Sexual excitement is also a mental state, the product of those fantasies wherein, as Robert Stoller has pointed out, one oscillates between an anticipation of danger and the expectation of replacing danger with pleasure.[17] The major fantasies, largely unconscious, which are reflected in the trembling attraction of Radha's love for Krishna, are decisively formed and coloured by the theme of a forbidden crossing of boundaries.

First, in the pervasive presence of the adulterous in the narrative there is an illicit transgression of moral limits. Second, in striving to entertain the erotic feelings and sensations of the other sex, a lover would violate his primal sexual demarcation as a male. Furthermore, the arousal provoked by these fantasies is both preserved and brought to pitch by the stealth and secrecy in which the crossing of such bounds takes place.

The most obvious manifestation of the illicit, involving the crossing of boundaries set by social mores and norms, is found in the adulterous and later accounts which saddle Radha with a husband, throwing in a mother-in-law for good measure. These persistently underline the adulterous nature of her love for Krishna. There was, of course, much theological uneasiness regarding this circumstance. Some commentators went to great lengths to explain why, since Krishna is god, he could not have actually coveted the wife of another. Others strained to prove the contrary, explaining that precisely because Krishna is god he is not bound by normal human restrictions. In the end, and perhaps inevitably, the community's quest for pleasure triumphed over its theological scruples in firmly demanding that the mythical lovers be accepted as unambiguously adulterous.

The identification of the adulterous with the thrilling and romantic is common enough in the western literary tradition, evident in the etiquette of Aquitaine and the novels of our own day. But in the Indian context the link is possessed of a special resonance since there the dichotomy between the conjugal and the adulterous had remained sharp and charged with tension over many centuries.[18]

In the ritual sphere the god and goddess of sexual love have always been segregated from deities who preside over marriage and fertility. Even today in India the so-called 'love marriage', almost a contradiction in terms and the subject of much excited gossip when it occurs, is mostly met with in the fantastical world of movies and is generally deemed a daring western import of the urbanized and presumably licentious upper classes.

As far as legalities are concerned both the conventions and the laws about adultery have been and remain extremely strict. The epics considered adultery as one of the five great sins for which there is no atonement—the others are the murder of a Brahmin, the slaying of a cow, unbelief and living off a woman—and warned against its frightful consequences:

In all castes a man must never approach the wife of another. For there is nought in the world which so shortens life as that the man on earth should visit the wife of another. As many pores as are on women's bodies, so many years will he sit in hell. . . . He that touches another man's wife is born as a wolf, as a dog, as a jackal, then born as a vulture, a snake, a heron, as also a crane.'[19]

In mythology, too, the adulterous woman at least, rarely escapes the consequences of her actions. Ahilya, the wife of a sage, who was more a victim of Indra's (the king of the gods') lechery and less an enthusiastic participant in their short-lived revel, paid dearly for her unwitting lapse. Parshuram, commanded by his father, killed his own mother who, when out bathing, caught sight of a handsome king sporting with his wives and was 'unfaithful in her heart.' Even today we know from clinical practice that in most sections of Indian society adultery is rarely a matter of casual, commonplace liaison. Its mere contemplation is a momentous psychological event for a woman, provoking moral dread.

In contrast the poets and litterati of the classical period, who have exercised a great influence on subsequent cultural attitudes and sentiments, at least of the upper castes, generally scorned the Hindu marriage as a pre-eminently social and religious duty. They saw in marriage a deadly foe of the great feeling to which they—as indeed most poets—have always aspired. In writing with nostalgia of scenes of love unhampered by matrimony, or in lamenting the disappearance of love with marriage, the poet's scorn of conjugal love was unremitting.

> Where the moon is not inveighed against
> And no sweet words of the messenger are heard
> Where speech is not choked with tears
> And the body grows not thin;
> But where one sleeps in one's own house
> With he who owns subservient to one's wish ;
> Can this routine of household sex,
> This wretched thing, deserve the name of love?[20]

The poets, then, and especially the females of this artistic species—Vidya and Bhavakadevi for example—idealized the rapture of the illicit liaison.[21] In counterpoint to the damnation heaped upon her in religious and legal texts, the adultress was assured of the poet's admiration.

In the poetic and dramatic conventions, for instance, there are three kinds of women: the courtesan (*veshya*), the wife (*svakiya*), and the 'other woman' (*parakiya*). The other woman is further subdivided into two kinds: the unmarried young girl (*kanyaka*) and the married woman (*parodha*). In an obvious 'oedipal' allusion, it is the *parodha*, the other man's wife, who best embodies the principle of eros (since, risking much, she has the most to lose) and is therefore considered the most desirable lover. As one Sanskrit poet writes:

> So there are
> women who attract with
> their loose ways
> prostitutes
> and there is the deep shyness
> of one's own wife
> the most beautiful and most
> graceful showing
> her love
> opening flower
> but who in this world can
> fill one with joy
> like another man's wife
> loving with naked breast.

In contrast to classical poets who stressed the frank elation, the incomparable 'joy' of loving another man's wife, the *bhakti* cults gave more exalted reasons for making Radha an adulterous *parakiya*. For them the adulterous was symbolic of the sacred, the overwhelming moment that denies world and society, transcending the profanity of everyday convention, as it forges an unconditional (and unruly) relationship with god as the lover. Stirring our sense of the essential instabilities and disorderliness of passionate love, Radha would sing:

> At the first note of his flute
> down came the lion gate of
> reverence for elders,
> down came the door of *dharma*,
> my guarded treasure of modesty was lost,
> I was thrust to the ground as if by
> a thunderbolt.
> Ah, yes, his dark body
> poised in the *tribhanga* pose
> shot the arrow that pierced me;
> no more honour, my family
> lost to me,
> my home at Vraja
> lost to me.
> Only my life is left and my life too
> is only a breath that is leaving me.[22]

In imparting adulterous love elements of the divine, the *bhakti* poets went even further than the troubadours of medieval Europe who had equated it with 'true' love. In the legendary decision taken at the so-called Court of Love in Champagne in 1174 it was maintained:

We declare and affirm, agreeably to the general opinion of those present, that love cannot exercise its powers on married people. The following reason is proof of the fact; lovers grant everything, mutually and gratuitously, without being constrained by any motive of necessity. Married people, on the contrary, are compelled as a duty to submit to one another's wishes, and not to refuse anything to one another. For this reason, it is evident that love cannot exercise its powers on married people.[23]

Both the Indian sanctification and the European romanticization of extra-marital love distract attention from its 'real' fascination: its obviation of many factors that promote sexual anxiety and consequently inhibit desire. The structure of the adulterous, so far removed from the mundane, the long-term 'dream of safety' and dependability of the conjugal relationship, may not be so easily subject to the steady erosion wrought by oedipal taboos which, in a marriage, often come to attach themselves to the partner. In other words, lacking in defensiveness, the adulterous relationship is relatively free of those instances of impotency or frigidity in marriage that involve a transference to the spouse of unconscious sexual attitudes and prohibitions entertained earlier towards the parent of the opposite sex. Freed of inner taboos the adulterous situation yet partakes of its delightful excitement, with the betrayed spouse serving as an *outside* impediment, both regulating erotic intensity and, in so far as he or she is an obstacle, enhancing it. Reliving the thrills of oedipal fantasy, the adulterous lover does not confront the parent's image or injunctions in the person to whom he or she makes love. In this adventure taboos have been cast by the wayside and are not everyday matters.

In the Indian case there is an additional consideration. The hierarchical dictates of the family call for male supremacy within marriage. The adulterous, in contrast, is free of all distinctions of relative status between man and woman. Radha can address Krishna as '*tu chora*' (You thief!), which would be unthinkable for a wife, who is constrained to use the most respectful form of second person address when speaking to her husband—a proscription which is hardly conducive to sexual abandon in the 'master['s] bedroom'. Furthermore, the clandestine life of the adulterous is composed of snatches of stolen time, rather than long periods of coexistence. This mitigates demands for intimacy on levels other than the sexual. The body, shackled by social and moral restraints and enmeshed in a web of unconscious expectations and attitudes from the past, glimpses in the adulterous a promise of newfound emancipation and expansiveness. Therein it is liberated by the spontaneous, vivid, if transient, encounter.

Besides the adulterous overthrow of social convention, indeed facilitated by this very circumstance, the crossing of individual sexual boundaries provides the other major source of erotic excitement in the artistic treatment of Radha and Krishna. We are either men or women, after all. We have known this to be an intractable fact of life since we were two and a half years of age when our core gender identity becomes fixed. Thereafter we grow up in an established social milieu which affixes to gender sex roles that seem to emanate from our bodies, our penises and wombs, and all those secondary sexual characteristics that go along with them. Can all this be changed, should it—when it is the distinctions of sex that impel and permit man and woman to come together? To these questions the Indian love poetry and art respond with a resounding yes. And they do this within an elaborate mythological tradition rather unknown to the West, whose deities have always tended to be more prosaically human than otherwise.

In painting, the depiction of this crossing ranges from the portrayal of the lovers in the traditional Orissa school, where they appear as one androgynous entity, to some of the paintings from the Himalayan foothills where Radha and Krishna are dressed in each other's clothes, or Radha is seen taking the more active 'masculine' role in coitus. In poetry, Sur Das would speak in Radha's voice:

You become Radha and I will become Madhava, truly Madhava; this is the reversal which I shall produce. I shall braid your hair and will put [your] crown upon my head. Sur Das says: Thus the Lord becomes Radha and Radha the son of Nanda.[24]

The inversion of sexual roles is all the more striking in the depiction of their intercourse. The poet Chandi Das praises as beautiful 'the deliberate, sensuous union of the two / the girl playing this time the active role / riding her lover's outstretched body in delight,'[25] while Jayadeva gives voice to what are normally regarded as 'feminine masochistic' sexual wishes when he has Krishna sing:

> Punish me, lovely fool!
> Bite me with your cruel teeth!
> Chain me with your creeper arms!
> Crush me with your hard breasts!
> Angry goddess, don't weaken with joy!
> Let Love's despised arrows
> Pierce me to sap my life's power![26]

It was only under the influence of nineteenth-century western phallocentricity, one of the dubious intellectual 'blessings' of British colonial rule, that many educated Indians would become uneasy with this accentuation of femininity in a culture hero. The great Bengali writer Bankim Chandra Chatterji, the proponent of a virile nationalism, would write of the *Gitagovinda*:

From the beginning to the end, it does not contain a single expression of manly feelings—of womanly feelings there is a great deal—or a single elevated sentiment. . . . I do not deny his [Jayadeva's] high poetical merits in a certain sense of exquisite imagery, tender feeling, and unrivalled powers of expression, but that does not make him less the poet of an effeminate and sensual race.[27]

In the *bhakti* cults, where the worshipper must create an erotic relationship with Krishna, the transcendence of boundaries of gender becomes imperative for the male devotee, who endeavours to become as a woman in relation to the Lord. In his case the violation of the biblical injunction 'The woman shall not wear that which pertaineth unto a man, neither shall a man put on a woman's garments' is far from being an 'abomination unto the Lord thy God.' In *bhakti* Krishna not only demands such a willing reversal from his male worshippers but is himself the compelling exemplar. Consequently, tales of Indian saints who have succeeded in feminizing themselves are legion. To give only two illustrations: the fifteenth-century Gujarati saint Narsi Mehta writes,

I took the hand of that lover of *gopis* [Krishna] in loving converse. . . . I forgot all else. Even my manhood left me. I began to sing and dance like a woman. My body seemed to change and I become one of the *gopis*. I acted as go-between like a woman, and began to lecture Radha for being too proud. . . . At such times I experienced moments of incomparable sweetness and joy.[28]

A. K. Ramanujan tells us that the voice of the Tamil saint-poet Nammalvar, who wrote 370 poems on the theme of love, was always that of a woman: Krishna's beloved, the girl friend who consoles and counsels, or 'the mother who restrains her and despairs over her daughter's lovesick fantasies'.[29] Nammalvar's love poems alternated with other subjects and a thirteenth-century commentary explained these shifts: 'In knowledge, his own words; in love, a woman's words'.[30] A legend has it that Amaru, one of the earliest and greatest Sanskrit poets of love, was the hundred and first incarnation of a soul which had previously occupied the bodies of a hundred women.

Narsi Mehta, Nammalvar, and countless other unknown devotees of the Radha–Krishna cults, bear testimony to the primal yearning of men, ensheathed and isolated by their 'phallic' masculinity, to yield their heroic trappings and delight in womanliness, woman's and their own. These universal wishes are distinct from the pathological cases where similar fantasies and feminine behaviour might well be a manifestation of 'homosexual libido', a retreat from phallic masculinity into anal eroticism. In other words some of the devotees may indeed be closer to Freud's history of the paranoid Schreber, the psychotic German judge who was convinced that he was being transformed into a woman in order to become God's wife and give birth to a whole new race of men.[31] Like Schreber, these devotees too may be defending against their fear and unconscious belief that they have been emasculated and consoling themselves with femininity as a compensation.

Yet for most of the worshippers and the saints, as for the rest of us, the wish to be a woman is not a later distortion of phallic strivings but rather another legacy from our 'prehistoric' experience with our mothers. Indeed this ambisexuality, the play of masculine and feminine, probably represents the acme, the climax of pre-oedipal development before castration anxiety and guilt enter to limit and dull the sexual quest.

The mother has figured early on as the omnipotent force of a parental universe, making things, including fathers and other males, materialize as if at will. It is she whose breast and magic touch have long ago soothed the savage instinctual imperatives, she whose fecund womb seemed the very fount of life. Such maternal and feminine powers are earthly yet mysterious and transcendent, undiminished by the utter sensuousness in which they are manifest. As the little boy grows towards manhood and assumes his predestined masculine role in society, he may come to exaggerate the brittle and rather obvious puissant attributes of the phallus and disparage those who do not possess it. Notwithstanding what has been termed his 'masculine protest', what he, does not have gnaws at a boy, at a man. In the veil of night, or in the veil drawn over consciousness in the ecstasy of religious possession, he would gratefully surrender his penis to the vagina and the woman who possesses it—that is, so long as he does not lose it forever.

Krishna's erotic homage to Radha conveys something of the aching quality of the man's fantasy of surrender at the height of sexual excitement. He longs to be smothered and penetrated by the woman's breasts as he himself willingly shrinks in his mind's eye. Every genital fibre is attuned to the welcoming wetness his eyes cannot see nor know from within, straining even as he finally expels his seed from his self, an emissary journeying deep into the lover's internal dark continent, still forbidden to him. The thrusting penis, man realizes once again, can never take or hold the woman. It merely enters her territory and touches her portals, only to shrivel and all too rapidly to be withdrawn. Did it not provide a recurrent bridge to her, man would gladly cede his crude organ and castrate himself to be one with the beloved—at least for a moment of bliss. The 'secret of men', gods included, to borrow from Bruno Bettelheim, is that they want to be that which they cannot have: Woman.

The profusion of the imagery of darkness and night—in the meetings of Radha–Krishna—as indeed in the trysts of Romeo and Juliet and of Layla and Majnun (or, for that matter, Tristan and Isolde)—underscores the secret nature of these fantasmagoria and illusions of the soul. The paintings show Radha and Krishna surrounded by darkness while they themselves are lit by a sullen glare from the sky. They portray the lovers enclosed in a triangle of inky night while around them the rest of Vrindavan's inhabitants unconcernedly go about the day's tasks. These are visual metaphors for a sensualism which is simultaneously hidden from the world and from the lovers' awareness. For Radha, as for Juliet, night and darkness are excitement's protectors, silence and secrecy its friends. Shrill disturbances to these servants of nature's erotic cycle are to be avoided: 'Leave your noisy anklets! They clang like traitors in love's play / Go to the darkened thicket, friend! Hide in a cloak of night!'[32] In a Basholi painting from *Rasmanjari* the text describes the seated lovers thus: 'Fear of detection does not permit the eager lovers' gaze to meet. Scared of the jingling sound of armlets they desist from embracing. They kiss each others' lips without the contact of teeth. Their union is hushed too'.[33] Many other portraits of Radha reveal that it is not only other people who must remain unaware of her sexual arousal. Radha, too, when in a state where 'love's deep fantasies / struggle with her modesty'[34], would fain ignorance of her true condition, as if it were a secret another part of her self must not admit to knowing. It is given to the poet to perceive correctly her struggle.

> Words of protest filled with passion
> Gestures of resistance lacking force,
> Frowns transmuted into smiles,
> Crying dry of tears—friend,
> Though Radha seeks to hide her feelings
> Each attempt betrays her heart's
> Deep love for demon Mura's slayer.[35]

Identifying with Radha's pounding breast as she steals out at night to meet Krishna, other poets graphically describe her fear while merely hinting at the suppressed thrill of her sortie, her arousal sharpened by the threat of discovery. They give us images of storm, writhing snakes, scratched and burning feet.

> O Madhava, how shall I tell you of my terror?
> I could not describe my coming here
> If I had a million tongues.
> When I left my room and saw the darkness
> I trembled:

I could not see the path,
There were snakes that writhed round my ankles!

I was alone, a woman; the night was so dark,
The forest so dense and gloomy,
And I had so far to go.
The rain was pouring down—
Which path should I take?
My feet were muddy
And burning where thorns had scratched them.
But I had the hope of seeing you,
None of it mattered,
And now my terror seems far away . . .
When the sound of your flute reaches my ears
It compels me to leave my home, my friends,
It draws me in the dark toward you.[36]

We imagine that, on hearing Radha's plaint, Krishna, whose gaze into the recesses of the human heart is as penetrating as it is compassionate, smiled to himself in the dark. He would have surely known that the strains of his flute, like that of Pan's before him, are the perennial and irresistible call of the human senses caught up in the throes of love.

And what do darkness and night mean to Krishna as he passively offers himself to Radha's embraces? Here, too, only under the cloak of night does the Lord reveal the deepest 'secret of man'—that he, too, would be a woman. In the night, in the jungle, visual and discrete modes of perception are replaced by the tactile, the visceral, and the more synesthetic forms of cognizance. Representations of the self and beloved fade and innermost sensate experience comes to the fore. As the illusion of bodies fused, hermaphroditic, it fostered, the fantasies around womanliness and sexual excitement feed each other, and Krishna 'knows' Radha not with the eye but with the flesh.

Night's curtains never completely part in this gentler story, whose protagonist, moreover, is a god able to withstand and transcend such protean changes. Hence the lovers survive, and tragedy is averted. Undiscovered, they remain unseen by the eyes of inner vigilance—by castration terror, by ambivalence, or, worst of all, by guilt.

10

Gandhi and Women

Continuing my search for facets of the man–woman relationship in India, I turn to the autobiographical writings of one of the greatest men of the 20th century. Although my task of psychoanalytic deconstruction, the activity of taking a text apart by bringing out its latent meanings, remains the same, Gandhi's fame and status as a culture hero makes this enterprise both easier and more difficult.

The task is easier in that the retrospective narrative enrichment engaged in by every autobiographer—who consciously or otherwise selects and orders details of his life so as to create a coherent and satisfying story, explaining and indeed justifying his present situation for the particular audience he has in mind—is capable of correction and modification through the accounts of other actors involved in the hero's epic.[1] The inconsistencies and the omission of vital details which may otherwise mar the symmetry of the hero's unconscious myth about himself, are easier to detect in the case of a man like Gandhi who has attracted so much biographical attention, both contemporary and posthumous. I may, though, add here that Gandhi's autobiographical writings, *The Story of My Experiments With Truth* the foremost among them, are marked by a candour and honesty which, if not unique, are certainly rare in the annals of self narration. In his quasi-mystical preoccupation with 'truth,' the blame for any distortions in the story of his self-revelation can be safely laid at the door of the narrator's unconscious purposes rather than ascribed to any deliberate efforts at omission or concealment.

The work of deconstruction is made more difficult as Gandhi is the foremost culture-hero of modern India. For an Indian child, the faces of Gandhi and other heroes like Nehru and Vivekananda are identical, with the masks crafted by the culture in order to provide ideals for emulation and identification. Every child in India has been exposed to stock narratives that celebrate their genius and greatness, the portraits utterly devoid of any normal human blemish such as envy, anger, lust, ordinariness, pettiness, or stupidity. The Indian analyst, also a child of his culture, is thus bound to have a special kind of 'counter-transference' towards the culture-hero as a biographical subject. In other words, the analytic stance of respectful empathy combined with critical detachment, difficult enough to maintain in normal circumstances, becomes especially so in the case of a man like Gandhi. His image is apt to merge with other idealized figures from the biographer's own past, who were loved and admired yet secretly rebelled against. The analytic stance must then be charted out between contradictory hagiographic and pathographic impulses that seek constantly to buffet it.

For the analyst, the story of a man's relationship with women inevitably begins ('and also ends,' sceptics would add) with his mother. Yet we know the mother–son dyad to be the most elusive of all human relationships. Located in the life space before the birth of language, the effort to recapture the truth of the dyad through words alone can give but teasing intimations of the hallucinatory intensity of a period when the mother, after giving the son life, also gave him the world. With some exceptions, like that of Nabokov, a mother cannot speak to her son through memory alone.[2] *Her* truth lies in the conjunction, indeed confabulation of imagination, symbols and reality through which she was earlier perceived and through which she may be later conjured, the latter being a rare artist's gift. For others, including Gandhi, the truth of the dyad we once built with our mothers is but fragmentarily glimpsed in various maternal proxies—from inanimate objects ('part' or 'transitional' objects in analytic parlance) which a child endows with her vital spirit, to the woman who will later attract and hold him. Like all mothers, Putlibai, whose favourite, Gandhi, was by virtue of his being the youngest child, and whose special object of care and concern he remained because of his sickly constitution, is an abiding yet diffuse presence in her son's inner life, an intensely luminous being albeit lacking definition. We will discover her chimerical presence in Gandhi's relationships with various other women in whom she was temporarily reincarnated, his wife Kasturbai the foremost among them.

In his autobiography, written over a five-year period during his mid-50s, Gandhi begins the account of his sexual preoccupations and struggles with his marriage at the age of thirteen. He had been betrothed to Kasturbai Nakanji, the daughter of a well-to-do merchant in his hometown of Porbandar, since they were both seven years old. Now, with the two children entering puberty, the families decided that the time for the nuptials had finally arrived.

In Kathiawar, on the west coast of India, the region where Gandhi grew up and where his father was the prime minister of a small princely state, such child marriages were the norm rather than the exception. Writing 43 years after the event, Gandhi could still recall the details of the marriage festivities. His elder brother and a cousin were to be married at the same time in one big ceremony and young Mohandas was excited by the prospect of new clothes, sumptuous wedding feasts, and the evenings and nights full of music and dance During the ceremony itself, whenever the couple was required to hold hands for a particular rite, Mohandas would secretly give Kasturbai's hand a squeeze which she, in turn, eagerly reciprocated.

The excitement of the wedding was marred by one jarring incident. On his way to the celebrations, Mohandas's father had a serious accident when the horse-carriage he was travelling in overturned, and he arrived late for the ceremony, with bandages covering his arms and back. The young boy was much too excited by what was happening to him to pay attention to the injured father, a fact that the older man notes with shame 'I was devoted to my father but I was equally devoted to sensuality. Here by sensuality I do not mean one organ but the whole realm of sensual enjoyment.'[3]

Looking back at his younger self, Gandhi feels that sex became an obsession with the adolescent Mohandas. At school, his thoughts were constantly with his wife, as he impatiently waited for the night to descend when he could go to her. He was also consumed by a raging jealousy. He wanted to know of every move his wife made in his absence and would forbid her to go out alone to the temple, on household errands or to meet girlfriends. Kasturbai was not the sort of girl to accept such unreasonable restrictions and accusations based on unfounded jealousy with any degree of equanimity. Small in stature, she was an attractive girl with glossy black hair, large dark eyes set deep in an oval face, a well-formed mouth, and a determined chin. She was by no means a female creature subservient to male whims and could easily be self-willed and impatient with her young husband. They had violent quarrels, dissolved in the love-making of the night, only to reemerge with the light of day.

Later in life, Gandhi, regretting his treatment of Kasturbai during the first 15 years of their married life, gave two causes for his jealousy. The first was the projection of his own turbulent sexual wishes and fantasies onto his wife—'I took out my anger at her for my own weakness'— while the second was the influence of Sheikh Mehtab, the intimate friend of his youth. Physically strong, fearless, and rakishly handsome, while Mohandas was none of these, Sheikh Mehtab has been portrayed by Gandhi as his evil genius, the tempter whose blandishments Mohandas was incapable of resisting. The breacher of taboos and values Mohandas held dear, Sheikh Mehtab introduced the vegetarian lad to the guilt-ridden pleasures of eating meat, and was the organizer of their joint visit to a brothel. Mehtab constantly fueled Gandhi's suspicions with regard to Kasturbai's fidelity. Reading about their youthful transgressions a hundred years later, to us Mehtab does not appear especially evil. He is neither more nor less than an average representative of the world of male adolescence, with its phallic displays and the ethic of a devil-may-care bravery. For a 13-year-old (and from all accounts, including his own) 'mama's boy,' dealing with the sexual upsurge of adolescence at the same time as the demand for establishing an emotional intimacy with a strange girl, Sheikh Mehtab must have been a godsend. He provided Mohandas with the adolescent haven where young men can be both dismissive and fearful of women and heterosexual love, where in the vague homoeroticism of masculine banter and ceaseless activism a youth can gradually come to terms with the femininity within and without him. Little wonder that, in spite of the family's strong disapproval and Mohandas's own conscious view of their relationship as one between a reformer and a rake, their friendship remained close and lasted for almost 20 years. During his sojourn in England, Gandhi sent Mehtab money from his meagre allowance, voluntarily sought him out again after his return to India and later took his friend with him when he sailed for South Africa.

Two circumstances, Gandhi writes, saved him from becoming an emotional and physical wreck during the initial phase of his marriage. The first was the custom among the Hindus, wisely aware of the consuming nature of adolescent passion, of separating the husband and wife for long periods during the first years of marriage. Kasturbai was often away on extended visits to her family and Gandhi estimates that in the first six years of their married life they could not have lived together for more than half of this period.

The second saving circumstance was Gandhi's highly developed sense of duty, both as a member of a large extended family, with an assigned role and definite tasks, and as a son who was especially conscientious and conscious of his obligation to an ageing and ailing father. After coming home from school, Gandhi would first spend time with his father, massaging his legs and attending to his other needs. Even when he was thus engaged, his mind wandered as he impatiently waited for the filial service to come to an end, his fantasies absorbed by the images of his girl-wife in another room of the house. As all readers of his autobiography know, the conflict between sexual desire and his sense of duty and devotion to the father was to load the marriage, especially its physical side, with an enormous burden of guilt. We shall briefly recapitulate the incident that has often been reproduced either as a cautionary moral tale or as a choice text for psychoanalytical exegesis.

Gandhi's father had been seriously ill and his younger brother had come to look after him, a task he shared with the son. One night around 10:30 or 11:00, while Gandhi was massaging his father's legs, his uncle told him to rest. Happily, Gandhi rushed off to the bedroom to wake up his pregnant wife for sexual intercourse. After a few minutes, a servant knocked at the bedroom door and informed the couple that the father had expired. Gandhi talks of his lifelong feeling of remorse that blind lust had deprived him of the chance of rendering some last service to his father and thus missing the patriarch's 'blessing' which was instead received by the uncle. 'This is the shame I hinted at in the last chapter,' he writes,

my sexual obsession even at the time of service to my father. Till today I have not been able to wash away this dark stain. I cannot forget that though my devotion to my parents was boundless and I could have given up everything for them, my mind was not free of lust even at that critical moment. This was an unforgivable lack in my service to my father. This is why in spite of my faithfulness to one woman I have viewed myself as someone blinded by sexuality. It took me a long time to free myself of lust and I have had to undergo many ordeals before I could attain this freedom.

Before I close this chapter of my double shame I also want to say that the child born to my wife did not survive for more than a couple of days. What other outcome could there have been?[4]

Sexual passion endangers all the generations, Gandhi seems to say, not only the parents to whom one is morally and filially obliged, but the children conceived in sexual union.

At the age of 18, Mohandas left his wife and family behind (a son had been recently born) as he sailed for England to study law. He faced a good deal of opposition to his plans from his family and his community, which propounded the orthodox view that a man could not remain a good

Hindu if he went abroad. Gandhi could leave for England with his family's consent (the community was not so easily mollified and declared him an outcaste) only after he made a solemn vow to his mother to avoid scrupulously the three inflamers of passion, 'wine, women, and meat'—the anxious Hindu counterpart of the more cheerful 'wine, women, and song'—during his sojourn in that distant island.

Gandhi's account of his three-year stay in England is striking in many ways. V.S. Naipaul has pointed out Gandhi's intense self-absorption, which made him oblivious to all the externals of his surroundings.[5] Gandhi does not mention the climate or the seasons. He does not describe London's buildings and streets, nor touch upon its social, intellectual, and political life.

What he immerses himself in and passionately discovers are fringe groups and causes which the mainstream English society would have unhesitatingly labeled 'eccentric.' An active member of the London Vegetarian Society and the 'Esoteric Christian Union' (many years later in South Africa he would proudly identify himself as the agent for these Societies on his letterhead), he was also a fervent admirer of Annie Besant, the heir of the Russian mystic Madame Blavatsky, and a self-declared 'bride of Christ.'

Knowing that till very recently (and again in the future) the core of Gandhi's self absorption was his concern with his sexuality, the meagre space he devotes to the stirring of sexual desire is even more striking. In the full flush of youth, learning such English graces as dancing, and becoming somewhat of a dandy, this passionate young man—a (however reluctant) sensualist—tells us very little about how he dealt with his desires and their inevitable stimulation in a society where the sexes mingled much more freely that in his native Kathiawar. The only exception to this silence is an incident near the end of his stay, when Gandhi was attending a conference of vegetarians in Portsmouth and stayed with a friend at the house of a woman, 'not a prostitute but of easy, virtue.' At night, while the three of them were playing cards, there was much sexual banter in which Gandhi enthusiastically participated. Gandhi was ready, as he says, 'to descend from speech into action,' when his friend reminded him of his vows.

I was embarrassed, I came to my senses. In my heart I was grateful to the friend. I remembered my vow to my mother. I was trembling when I reached my room. My heart was racing. My condition was that of a wild animal who has just escaped the hunter. I think this was the first occasion I was 'possessed by passion' for a woman not my wife and desired to 'make merry' with her.[6]

This is the only explicit event in which higher duty opposed and conquered sexual temptation that is reported in this part of Gandhi's
autobiography. The earlier sexual preoccupation, I would surmise, went
underground, to reemerge in two different streams which on the surface
seem quite unrelated to genital sexuality. One of these streams is
Gandhi's increasing preoccupation with religious and spiritual matters.
He tells us of his visit to theosophists, conversations with Christian cler-
gymen, the reading of inspirational and religious literature. At times,
Gandhi seems to be quite aware of the connection between his sexual
struggles and his spiritual interests. Thus he notes down the following
verses from the *Bhagavad Gita*:

> If one
> Ponders on objects of the senses there springs
> Attraction; from attraction grows desire,
> Desire flames to fierce passion, passion breeds
> Recklessness; then the memory—all betrayed—
> Lets noble purpose go, and saps the mind,
> Till purpose, mind, and man are all undone.

'These verses,' he says, 'made a deep impression on my mind, and they
still ring in my ears.'[7]

The other stream is his obsession with food, an obsession that was
to remain with him for the rest of his life. Page after page, in dreary
detail, we read about what Gandhi ate and what he did not, why he par-
took of certain foods and why he did not eat others, what one eminent
vegetarian told him about eggs and what another, equally eminent,
denied. The connection between sexuality and food is made quite explicit in Gandhi's later life when his ruminations about his celibacy
would almost invariably be followed by an exhaustive discussion of the
types of food that stimulate desire and others that dampen it. Again, we
must remember that in the Indian consciousness, the symbolism of food
is more closely or manifestly connected to sexuality than it is in the
West. The words for eating and sexual enjoyment, as A.K. Ramanujan
reminds us, have the same root, *bhuj*, in Sanskrit, and sexual intercourse
is often spoken about as the mutual feeding of male and female.[8]

On his return to India, Gandhi was faced with the necessity of
making a living as a lawyer, a task for which he found himself both
professionally and personally ill-equipped. A section of his caste was
still hostile to him, having never forgiven him for his defiance of its
mandate not to go abroad. There were further difficulties in his adjust-

ments to the norms and mores of life in an Indian extended family—and in the family's adjustments to the newly acquired habits and values of its somewhat Anglicized member. Today, with infinitely larger numbers of people moving across cultural boundaries and back again, the urbane Indian might indulgently smile at the tragicomic aspects of this reverse cultural shock. Tea and coffee, oatmeal porridge and cocoa were introduced to the breakfast table of the Gandhi household. Boots, shoes—and smelly socks—were to be worn in the burning heat of Kathiawar. Indeed, as a colonial subject, his identification with the British overlord was so strong that when some years later he was to sail for South Africa, he insisted on his sons being dressed like English public school boys with Etonian collars and ties. Poor Kasturbai was to dress up as a British lady—corset, bustle, high lace collar, laced shoes, and all. Her vehement protests and perhaps the absurdity of it all made him finally relent, though Kasturbai still had to dress up as a Parsi lady, a member of the community most respected by the British.

The marriage was still tempestuous, his driven genital desire the cause of these storms. His stay in England had neither reduced the strength of Gandhi's jealousy nor put an end to the nagging suspicions about his wife's fidelity. At the egging on of his old friend Sheikh Mehtab, Gandhi went so far as to break Kasturbai's bangles—to an Indian girl the dreaded symbol of widowhood—and to send her back to her parents' house. It took him a year before he consented to receive her back and over four years before his suspicion was stilled.[9] Purists can be cruel, especially to those dependent women who threaten to devour their virtue.

Economic, social, and familial conflicts, besides the perennial erotic one, seem to have spurred Gandhi's travels on the spiritual path. In this journey he now acquired a guide, Raichandra, a young jeweller. Raichandra was a man after Gandhi's own heart, more interested in *moksha* (the release from the cycles of birth and death which Hindus believe govern the wandering of the individual soul) than in diamonds. The two men met often to discuss spiritual topics and the depth of Raichandra's sincerity, purpose, and knowledge of Hindu thought and scriptures made a deep impression on Gandhi's mind. Of the three men, he says, who had to greatest influence on his life (the others were Tolstoy and Ruskin), Raichandra was the only one with whom he had a long personal association. Indeed, the young jeweller who talked so eloquently about *moksha* was the nearest Gandhi came to having a guru, and 'In my moments of inner crisis, it was Raichandra with whom I used to seek refuge.'[10]

Unfortunately, in spite of the vast amount written on his life (over 400 biographical items), and the wealth of material contained in the 90 volumes of Gandhi's collected works, we know very little of the subjects of these talks, the letters they exchanged. or the kind of guidance Gandhi sought for his inner turbulence From the available references, scattered in Gandhi's writings, it is evident that a central concern of their earnest exchanges was the relationship of sexuality to 'salvation,' the transformation of sexual potency into psychic and spiritual power— the core issue, in fact, of much of Hindu metaphysics and practice. Gandhi notes that the idea that 'milk gives birth to sexual passions is something which I first learnt from Raichandrabhai,' and he ascribes to the jeweller the predominant role in his decision to become a celibate.[11]

In 1893, at the age of 24; Gandhi left for South Africa where he had been engaged as a lawyer by an Indian businessman. With brief interruptions for home visits, he was to stay there for the next 22 years.

Gandhi's years in South Africa, especially from 1900 to 1910, roughly spanning the fourth decade of his life, were crucial for the formation of Gandhi's historical persona. During these years Gandhi remade himself in that final image which is now evoked by his name. The first great nonviolent political campaigns for the rights of Indians living in South Africa, which introduced and refined the instrument of *Satyagraha* (literally, insistence on truth), took place during this period, at the end of which it would become well-known in many parts of the world. Equally important for our purposes is the fact that it was also during these years that he defined for himself the kind of personal life he would lead, and developed his ideas on the desired relationship between the sexes which would form the foundation for his own marriage with Kasturbai.

Founding and living in communes with disciples and seekers who shared his vision, radically experimenting with food and alternative systems of healing such as nature cure, generally embracing an ascetic lifestyle, the cornerstone of his personal life was *brahmacharya* or celibacy. Indeed *brahmacharya* was one leg of a tripod of which the other two were nonviolence (*ahimsa*) and truth (*satya*), which he adopted as the conscious basis for his adult identity and about which he would later write: 'Nonviolence came to me after a strenuous struggle, *brahmacharya* I am still struggling for, but truth has always come naturally to me.'[12]

The decision for sexual abstinence was taken in 1901, the year in which Raichandra died and in which Gandhi had just become a father for the fourth time (Devdas, the youngest son, was born in 1900). Both these circumstances must have contributed to Gandhi's resolve to renounce sexuality. The birth of the son, as we know from the account of the fateful night of the father's death and the newborn who did not survive because of *his father's* accursed lust, was a reminder of Gandhi's despised genital desires and therefore a stigma. To give them up was an offering made at the altar of Raichandra's (and, we would conjecture, his father's) departed soul. Kasturbai had not been consulted and Gandhi confesses that for the first few years he was only 'more or less successful' in his practice of self restraint.[13] Gandhi had left for India with his family in November 1901 and returned to South Africa the next year after promising his wife that she would soon follow. Yet once he was back in South Africa, Gandhi was reluctant to have Kasturbai join him. Paramount in his decision must have been the fact that his resolve to abstain from sexual intercourse was still fragile. The monetary argument he advances in the letters to his relatives, where he asks their help in persuading his wife to remain behind for two to three years, namely, that the savings he could make in South Africa would enable her and the children to lead an easy life in India,[14] neither jibes with the realities of running a household alone nor with Gandhi's character and temperament. Only a few months earlier, while leaving for India, he had gifted all the gold and diamond jewellery presented to him by a grateful Indian community to a trust, maintaining, 'I feel neither I nor my family can make any personal use of the costly present,' and that what he valued was their affection and not money.[15]

Gandhi finally took the vow to observe complete celibacy in 1906 when he was 37 years old, on the eve of his first nonviolent political campaign in South Africa. The preceding five years of attempted abstinence he felt, had only been a preparation for what would amount to a total and irrevocable renunciation of sexuality. The example of Tolstoy further deepened his resolve. As he writes in 1905, 'He (Tolstoy) used to enjoy all pleasures of the world, kept mistresses, drank and was strongly addicted to smoking. . . . He has given up all his vices, eats very simple food and has it in him no longer to hurt any living creature by thought, word or deed.'[16] Tolstoy's ideas on chastity, not only for the unmarried but also for the married, outlined in the *Kreuzer Sonata* (1889), were combined with the Hindu notions on *brahmacharya* to form Gandhi's own vision of the 'right' relationship between men and women. More than a personal code of conduct, these ideas regulated the life of all those who lived with him in his various communes (*ashrams*) in South Africa and India. Briefly summarized in his own words, this doctrine on the relationship between a couple holds that

The very purpose of marriage is restraint and sublimation of the sexual passion. Marriage for the satisfaction of sexual appetite is *vyabhichara*, concupisence . . . if they come together merely to have a fond embrace they are nearest the devil.

The only rule that can be laid down in such instances (if a child is not conceived) is that coitus may be permitted once at the end of the monthly period till conception is established. If its object is achieved it must be abjured forthwith.

There is not doubt that much of the sensuality of our nature, whether male or female, is due to the superstition, having a religious sanction, that married people are bound to share the same bed and the same room. But every husband and wife can make a fixed resolution from today never to share the same room or same bed at night, and to avoid sexual contact, except for one supreme purpose which it is intended for in both man and beast.[17]

Whatever its other consequences, there is little doubt that Gandhi's vow of celibacy distinctly improved his marriage, perhaps because poor Kasturbai was no longer perceived as a seductive siren responsible for his lapses from a longed-for ideal of purity. Ever since they had been in South Africa, there was much bickering and quarreling between the two. They had fought over her desire to keep her ornaments while Gandhi sought to convince her of the virtues of nonpossession. There was a major explosion, in which Gandhi almost turned her out of the house, over his wish that she clean up after an untouchable Christian visitor, a task abhorrent to a traditional Hindu woman with her deeply ingrained taboos about pollution. There was a running battle between the couple over their eldest son Harilal's wish that he grow up like other boys of his age and be allowed to avail of formal schooling. Gandhi's radical views on education would not allow the son to be sent to school, while Kasturbai was obstinate in the advocacy of her firstborn's cause.

From all accounts, before the vow of *brahmacharya*, Gandhi was an autocrat with his wife, 'completely steel,' as he tried to bend her to his will and get her to embrace what must have appeared to her as eccentric notions that endangered the present and future welfare of the family.

After 1906, their relationship improved steadily and Gandhi could write with some justification that 'I could not steal into my wife's heart until I decided to treat her differently than I used to do, and so I restored to her all her rights by dispossessing myself of any so-called rights as

her husband.'[18] In their later years, though there were occasional dis-
agreements, generally with respect to the children and Kasturbai's
discomfort with the many women in the various *ashrams* who jostled
each other to come closer to Gandhi, the marriage was marked by deep
intimacy and a quiet love which impressed everyone who witnessed the
old couple together.

For Gandhi, celibacy was not only the sine qua non for *moksha*, but
also the mainspring of his political activities. It is from the repudiation,
the ashes of sexual desire, that the weapon of nonviolence which he
used so effectively in his political struggle against the racial oppression
of the South African white rulers and later against the British empire,
was phoenix-like born. As Gandhi puts it :

Ahimsa (nonviolence) means Universal Love. If a man gives his love to one
woman, or a woman to one man, what is there left for the world besides? It
simply means, 'We two first, and the devil take all the rest of them.' As a faithful wife must be prepared to sacrifice her all for the sake of her husband, and a
faithful husband for the sake of his wife, it is clear that such persons cannot rise
to the height of Universal Love, or look upon all mankind as kith and kin. For
they have created a boundary wall round their love. The larger their family, the
farther are they from Universal Love. Hence one who would obey the law of
ahimsa cannot marry, not to speak of gratification outside the marital bond.[19]

As for those who are already married,

If the married couple can think of each other as brother and sister, they are freed
for universal service. The very thought that all women in the world are his
sisters, mothers and daughters will at once enable a man to snap his chains.[20]

The truth of Gandhi's assertion that sexual love limits rather than expands personal concerns and that the narrow role of a husband is
antithetical to the larger identity of one who would husband the world
is not at issue here. Our intention for the moment is to elucidate
Gandhi's conflict in the way he viewed it—in this case, the imperatives
of desire straining against the higher purpose of unfettered service to
community. Yet another of his pansexualist formulations of the conflict
has it that the gratification of sexual passion vies with a man's obligation to enhance personal vitality and psychic power. 'A man who is
unchaste loses stamina, becomes emasculated and cowardly,'[21] is a sentiment often echoed in his writings as is the reiteration that his capacity
to work in the political arena was a result of the psychic power gained
through celibacy. Still another, later formulation is put in religious and
spiritual terms—sexuality compromises his aspiration to become 'God's
eunuch.' Reminiscent of Christ's metaphors of innocent childhood to

describe would-be entrants to the kingdom of heaven and Prophet Mohammed's welcoming of 'those made eunuchs,' not through an operation but through prayer to God, Gandhi too would see sexual renunciation as a precondition for self realization and, Moses-like, for seeing God 'face to face.'

Like his communes, which are a combination of the *ashrama* of the ancient sages described in the Hindu epics and the Trappist monastery in South Africa which so impressed him on a visit, Gandhi's views on the importance and merits of celibacy too seem to be derived from a mixture of Hindu and Christian religious traditions. Where Gandhi proceeded to give these views a special twist, going much beyond the cursory juxtaposition of sexuality and eating made in his culture, was in emphasizing, above all, the relation of food to the observance of celibacy. Experiments with food, to find that elusive right combination which would keep the libido effectively dammed, continued right through to the end of his life. In South Africa, as reported by an admiring yet detached disciple, there were months of cooking without salt or any condiments. Another period witnesses the absence of sugar, dates, and currants being added for sweetening purposes. This was followed by a period of 'unfired' food served with olive oil. Food values were most earnestly discussed, and their effect upon the human body and its moral qualities solemnly examined. For a time a dish of raw chopped onions, as a blood purifier, regularly formed part of the dinner meal. . . Ultimately Mr Gandhi came to the conclusion that onions were bad for the passions, and so onions were cut out. Milk, too, Mr Gandhi said, affected the 'passion' side of human life and thereafter milk was abjured likewise. 'We talk about food quite as much as gourmands do,' I said on one occasion to Mr Gandhi. 'I am sure we talk about food more than most people, we seem to be always thinking of the things we either may or may not eat. Sometimes, I think it would be better if we just ate anything and did not think about it at all.'[22] But for Gandhi food was a deathly serious business.

Control of palate is very closely connected with the observance of *brahmacharya* (celibacy). I have found from experience that the observance of celibacy becomes comparatively easy, if one acquires mastery over the palate. This does not figure among the observances of time-honoured recognition. Could it be because even great sages found it difficult to achieve. Food has to be taken as we take medicine, without thinking whether it is tasty or otherwise, and only in quantities limited to the needs of the body. . . . And one who thus gives up a multitude of eatables will acquire self control in the natural course of things.[23]

The above passage is reminiscent of St Augustine who, too, would take food as physic, strive daily against concupiscence in eating and drinking, and assert that 'the bridle of the throat then is to be held attempted between slackness and stiffness.'[24] St Augustine's attitude toward food, though, is part of his attempt to gain a general freedom from the grip of sensuality, including 'the delights of the ear (that) had more firmly entangled and subdued me'.[25] Augustine treats imbibition as he does all sensory input. Gandhi, on the other hand, makes of food a primary regulator of the genital impulses. 'A man of heightened sexual passion,' he writes, 'is also greedy of the palate. This was also my condition. To gain control over the organs of both generation and taste has been difficult for me.'[26]

A radical cure for his epicurean disease is, of course, fasting, and Gandhi was its enthusiastic proponent. 'As an external aid to *brahmacharya*, fasting is as necessary as selection and restriction of diet. So overpowering are the senses that they can be kept under control only when they are completely hedged in on all sides, from above and from beneath.'[27] Remembering Gandhi's great fasts during his political struggles, we can see how fasting for him would have another, more personal meaning as a protector of his cherished celibacy and thus an assurance against the waning of psychic, and, with it, political power.

Battle, weapons, victory and defeat are a part of Gandhi's image in his account of a life-long conflict with the dark god of desire, the only opponent he did not engage nonviolently nor could ever completely subdue. The metaphors that pervade the descriptions of this passionate conflict are of 'invasions by an insidious enemy' who needs to be implacably 'repulsed'; while the perilous struggle is like 'walking on a sword's edge.' The god himself (though Gandhi would not have given Kama, the god of love, the exalted status accorded him in much of Hindu mythology) is the 'serpent which I know will bite me,' 'the scorpion of passion,' whose destruction, annihilation, conflagration, is a supreme aim of his spiritual strivings. In sharp contrast to all his other opponents, whose humanity he was always scrupulous to respect, the god of desire was the only antagonist with whom Gandhi could not compromise and whose humanity (not to speak of his divinity) he always denied.

For Gandhi, defeats in this war were occasions for bitter self-reproach and a public confession of his humiliation, while the victories were a matter of joy, 'fresh beauty,' and an increase in vigour and self confidence that brought him nearer to the *moksha* he so longed for.

Whatever may be his values to the contrary, a sympathetic reader, conscious of Gandhi's greatness and his prophetic insights into many of the dilemmas of modern existence, cannot fail to be moved by the dimensions of Gandhi's personal struggle—heroic in its proportion, startling in its intensity, interminable in its duration. By the time Gandhi concludes his autobiography with the words:

To conquer the subtle passions seems to me to be far harder than the conquest of the world by the force of arms. Ever since my return to India I have had experiences of the passions hidden within me. They have made me feel ashamed though I have not lost courage. My experiments with truth have given, and continue to give, great joy. But I know that I must traverse a perilous path. I must reduce myself to zero.[28]

no reader can doubt his passionate sincerity and honesty. His is not the reflexive, indeed passionless moralism of the more ordinary religionist.

How did Gandhi himself experience sexual desire, the temptations and the limits of the flesh? To know this, it is important that we listen closely to Gandhi's voice describing his conflicts in the language in which he spoke of them—Gujarati, his mother tongue. Given the tendency toward hagiolatry among the followers of a great man, their translations, especially of the Master's sexual conflicts, are apt to distort the authentic voice of the man behind the saint. The English translation of Gandhi's autobiography by his faithful secretary, Mahadev Desai, in spite of the benefit of Gandhi's own revision, suffers seriously from this defect, and any interpretations based on this translation are in danger of missing Gandhi's own experience. Take, for instance, one famous incident from Gandhi's youth, of the schoolboy Gandhi visiting a prostitute for the first time in the company of his Muslim friend and constant tempter, Sheikh Mehtab. The original Gujarati version describes the incident as follows:

I entered the house but he who is to be saved by God remains pure even if he wants to fall. I became almost blind in that room. I could not speak. Struck dumb by embarrassment, I sat down on the cot with the woman but could not utter a single word. The woman was furious, gave me a couple of choice abuses and showed me to the door [my translation].[29]

The English translation, however, is much less matter-of-fact. It is full of Augustinianisms in which young Gandhi goes into a 'den of vice' and tarries in the 'jaws of sin.' These are absent in the original. By adding adjectives such as 'evil' and 'animal' before 'passions,' the translation seems to be judging them in a Christian theological sense that is missing in Gandhi's own account. St Augustine, for instance—with whose *Confessions* Gandhi's *Experiments* has much in common—was rent asunder because of the 'sin that dwelt in me,' by 'the punishment of a sin more freely committed, in that I was a son of Adam.'[30] Gandhi, in contrast, uses two words, *vishaya* and *vikara*, for lust and passion respectively. The root of *vishaya* is from poison, and that is how he regards sexuality—as poisonous, for instance, when he talks of it in conjunction with serpents and scorpions. The literal meaning of *vikara*, or passion, is 'distortion,' and that is how passions are traditionally seen in the Hindu view, waves of mind that distort the clear waters of the soul. For Gandhi, then, lust is not sinful but poisonous, contaminating the elixir of immortality. It is dangerous in and of itself, 'destructuralizing' in psychoanalytic language, rather than merely immoral, at odds, that is, with certain social or moral injunctions. To be passionate is not to fall from a state of grace, but to suffer a distortion of truth. In contrast to the English version, which turns his very Hindu conflict into a Christian one, Gandhi's struggle with sexuality is not essentially a conflict between sin and morality, but rather one between psychic death and immortality, on which the moral quandary is superimposed.

We can, of course, never be quite certain whether Gandhi was a man with a gigantic erotic temperament or merely the possessor of an overweening conscience that magnified each departure from an unattainable ideal of purity as a momentous lapse. Nor is it possible, for that matter, to evaluate the paradoxical impact of his scruples in intensifying the very desires they opposed. Both fuelled each other, the lid of self-control compressing and heating up the contents of the cauldron of desire, in Freud's famous metaphor, their growing intensity requiring ever greater efforts at confinement.

Gandhi himself, speaking at the birth centenary of Tolstoy in 1928, warns us to refrain from judgments. While talking of the import of such struggles in the lives of great *homo religiosi*, he seems to be asking for empathy rather than facile categorization:

The seeming contradictions in Tolstoy's life are no blot on him or sign of his failure They signify the failure of the observer. . . . Only the man himself knows how much he struggles in the depth of his heart or what victories he wins in the war between Rama and Ravana.* The spectator certainly cannot know that.[31]

*The good and evil protagonists of the Indian epic, *Ramayana.*

In judging a great man, Gandhi goes on to say, and here he seems to be talking as much of himself as Tolstoy,

God is witness to the battles he may have fought in his heart and the victories he may have won. These are the only evidence of his failures and successes. . . If anyone pointed out a weakness in Tolstoy though there could hardly be an occasion for anyone to do so for he was pitiless in his self-examination, he would magnify that weakness to fearful proportions. He would have seen his lapse and atoned for it in the manner he thought most appropriate before anyone had pointed it out to him.[32]

This is a warning we must take seriously but do not really need. Our intention is not to 'analyse' Gandhi's conflict in any reductionist sense but to seek to understand it in all its passion—and obscurity. Gandhi's agony is ours as well, after all, an inevitable by-product of the long human journey from infancy to adulthood. We all wage wars on our wants.

A passionate man who suffered his passions as poisonous of his inner self and a sensualist who felt his sensuality distorted his inner purpose, Gandhi's struggle with what he took to be the god of desire was not unremitting. There were long periods in his adulthood when his sensuality was integrated with the rest of his being. Old movie clips and reminiscences of those who knew him in person attest to some of this acceptable sensuality. It found expression in the vigorous grace of his locomotion; the twinkle in his eye and the brilliance of his smile; the attention he paid to his dress—even if the dress was a freshly laundered, spotless loincloth; the care he directed to the preparation and eating of his simple food; the delight with which he sang and listened to devotional songs; and the pleasure he took in the daily oil massage of his body. The Christian St Augustine would have been altogether shocked. Here, then, the Indian ascetic's path diverges from that trod by the more austere and self-punishing western monk. Here, too, from Gandhi's sensuous gaiety, stems his ability to rivet masses of men not by pronouncement in scripture but by his very presence.

In Gandhi's periods of despair, occasioned by real-life disappointments and setbacks in the sociopolitical campaigns to which he had committed his life, the integration of his sensuality and spirituality would be threatened and again we find him obsessively agonizing over the problem of genital desire. Once more he struggled against the reemergence of an old antagonist whom he sought to defeat by public confessions of *his* defeats.

One such period spans the years between 1925 and 1928, after his release from jail, when he was often depressed, believing that the Indian religious and political divisions were too deep for the country to respond to his leadership and that Indians were not yet ready for his kind of nonviolent civil disobedience. There was a breakdown with a serious condition of hypertension and doctors had advised him long rest. Interestingly, this is also the period in which he wrote his confessional autobiography, where he despondently confides, 'Even when I am past 56 years, I realize how hard a thing it (celibacy) is. Every day I realize more and more that it is like walking on the sword's edge, and I can see every moment the necessity of continued vigilance.'[33] His ideals and goals failing him, Gandhi finds sublime purpose and intent crumbling, exposing desires held in abeyance. These then become prepotent. The psychoanalyst would speak in this instance of the disintegration of 'sublimations'—conversions of base wishes into socially sanctioned aspirations—and the lonely, painful regression which ensues.

In the copious correspondence of the years 1927 and 1928, the two longest and the most personally involved letters are neither addressed to his close political co-workers and leaders of future free India such as Nehru, Patel or Rajagopalachari, nor do they deal with vital political or social issues. The addressees are two unknown young men, and the subject of the letters is the convolutions of Gandhi's instinctual promptings. Responding to Balakrishna Bhave, who had expressed doubts about the propriety of Gandhi placing his hands on the shoulders of young girls while walking, Gandhi conducts a characteristic, obsessive search for any hidden eroticism in his action.[34] The other letter, to Harjivan Kotak, deserves to be quoted at some length since it details Gandhi's poignant struggle, his distress at the threatened breakdown of the psycho-sensual synthesis.

When the mind is disturbed by impure thoughts, instead of trying to drive them out one should occupy it in some work, that is, engage it in reading or in some bodily labour which requires mental attention too. Never let the eyes follow their inclination. If they fall a woman, withdraw them immediately. It is scarcely necessary for anyone to look straight at a man's or woman's face. This is the reason why *brahmacharis*, and others too, are enjoined to walk with their eyes lowered. If we are sitting, we should keep them steady in one direction. This is an external remedy, but a most valuable one. You may undertake a fast if and when you find one necessary. . . . You should not be afraid even if you get involuntary discharges during a fast. *Vaid*s (traditional doctors) say that, even when impure desires are absent, such discharges may occur because of pressure in the bowels. But, instead of believing that, it helps us more to believe that they occur because of impure desires. We are not always conscious of such desires. I had involuntary discharges twice during the last two weeks. I cannot recall any dream. I never practised masturbation. One cause of these discharges is of course my physical weakness but I also know that there are impure desires deep down in me. I am able to keep out such thoughts during waking hours. But what is present in the body like some hidden poison, always makes its way, even forcibly sometimes. I feel unhappy about this, but am not nervously afraid. I am always vigilant. I can suppress the enemy but have not been able to expel him altogether. If I am truthful, I shall succeed in doing that too. The enemy will not be able to endure the power of truth. If you are in the same condition as I am, learn from my experience. In its essence, desire for sex-pleasure is equally impure, whether its object is one's wife or some other woman. Its results differ. At the moment, we are thinking of the enemy in his essential nature. Understand, therefore, that so far as one's wife is concerned you are not likely to find anyone as lustful as I was. That is why I have described my pitiable condition to you and tried to give you courage.'[35]

A 'hidden power,' an 'enemy to be expelled'—in such circumstances the body becomes a strange land inhabited by demons of feeling and impulse divided from the self. With setbacks in unity of intent, there is a further fragmenting of the self. The moral dilemma stirs conflicts of a primeval order, when early 'introjects'—those presences bound to desire out of which we construct our primary self—are awakened, taste blood or better, poison, and threaten our identity—our sense of wholeness, continuity, and sameness.

Another emotionally vulnerable period comprises roughly 18 months from the middle of 1935 onwards, when Gandhi was almost 66 years old. Marked by a 'nervous breakdown,' when his blood pressure went dangerously out of control, Gandhi was advised complete rest for some months by his doctors. He attributed this breakdown to overwork and especially mental exhaustion brought on by the intensity of his involvement and emotional reactions to the personal problems of his co-workers. He considered these as important as those pertaining to the country's independence, regretting only that he had not reached the Hindu ideal, as outlined in the *Gita*, of detachment from emotions. Gandhi used this enforced rest for introspection and decided to give up his practice of walking with his hands on the shoulders of young girls. In 'A Renunciation,' an article he wrote for his newspaper during this time, he traced the history of this particular practice, reiterated the purity of his paternal intentions towards the girls involved, acknowledged that he was not unaware of the dangers of the liberty he was taking, and based his renunciation on the grounds of setting a good example to the younger generation.[36]

What is more significant is that in the very first article he was allowed to write by his doctors, Gandhi, meditating on the causes of his ill-health, comes back to the question of his celibacy. He mentions an encounter with a woman during the period of convalescence in Bombay, which not only disturbed him greatly but made him despise himself. In a letter to Prema Kantak, a disciple and confidante in his Sabarmati *ashram*, he elaborates on this incident further.

I have always had the shedding of semen in dreams. In South Africa the interval between two ejaculations may have been in years. I do not remember it fully. Here the time difference is in months. I have mentioned these ejaculations in a couple of my articles. If my *brahmacharya* had been without this shedding of semen then I would have been able to present many more things to the world. But someone who from the age of 15 to 30 has enjoyed sexuality (*vishya-bhog*)- even if it was only with his wife—whether such a man can conserve his semen after becoming a *brahmachari* seems impossible to me. Someone whose power of storing the semen has been weakened daily for 15 years cannot hope to regain this power all at once. That is why I regard myself as an incomplete *brahmachari*. But where there are no trees, there are thorn bushes. This shortcoming of mine is known to the world.

The experience which tortured me in Bombay was strange and painful. All my ejaculations have taken place in dreams; they did not trouble me. But Bombay's experience was in the waking state. I did not have any inclination to fulfil that desire. My body was under control. But in spite of my trying, the sense organ remained awake. This experience was new and unbecoming. I have narrated its cause.* After removing this cause the wakefulness of the sense organ subsided, that is, it subsided in the waking state.

In spite of my shortcoming, one thing has been easily possible for me, namely that thousands of women have remained safe with me. There were many occasions in my life when certain women, in spite of their sexual desire, were saved or rather I was saved by God. I acknowledge it one hundred percent that this was God's doing. That is why I take no pride in it. I pray daily to God that such a situation should last till the end of my life.

To reach the level of Shukadeva is my goal.** I have not been able to achieve it. Otherwise in spite of the generation of semen I would be impotent and the shedding will become impossible.

The thoughts I have expressed recently about *brahmacharya* are not new. This does not mean that the ideal will be reached by the whole world or even

---

*By remaining inactive and eating well, passions are born in the body.

**Son of Vyasa, Shukadeva is the mythical reciter of the *Bhagavatapurana*. In spite of having married and lived the life of a householder (like Gandhi, he was the father of four sons) in later life he succeeded in conquering his senses to an extent that he rose up to the Heavens and shone there like a second sun.

by thousands of men and women in my lifetime. It may take thousands of years, but *brahmacharya* is true, attainable and must be realized.

Man has still to go a long way. His character is still that of a beast. Only the form is human. It seems that violence is all around us. In spite of this, just as there is no doubt about truth and nonviolence similarly there is no doubt about *brahmacharya*.

Those who keep on burning despite their efforts are not trying hard enough. Nurturing passion in their minds they only want that no shedding of semen take place and avoid women. The second chapter of *Gita* applies to such people.

What I am doing at the moment is purification of thought. Modern thought regards *brahmacharya* as wrong conduct. Using artificial methods of birth control it wants to satisfy sexual passion. My soul rebels against this. Sexual desire will remain in the world, but the world's honour depends on *brahmacharya* and will continue to do so.[37]

Further self-mortification was one of his responses to what he regarded as an unforgivable 'lapse.' Even the ascetic regimen of the *ashram* now seemed luxurious. Leaving Kasturbai to look after its inmates, he went off to live in a one-room hut in a remote and poverty-stricken, untouchable village. Though he wished to be alone—a wish that for a man in his position was impossible of fulfilment—he soon became the focus of a new community.

Another dark period covers the last two years of Gandhi's life. The scene is India on the eve of Independence in 1947. A Muslim Pakistan is soon to be carved out of the country, much against Gandhi's wishes. His dream of Hindus and Muslims living amicably in a single unified state seems to be shattered beyond hope. Gandhi would even postpone Independence if the partition of the country could be averted, but his voice does not resonate quite so powerfully in the councils where the transfer of power is being negotiated. The air hangs heavy with clouds of looming violence. Hindus and Muslims warily eye each other as potential murderers . . . or eventual victims. The killings have already started in the crowded back-alleys of Calcutta and in the verdant expanses of rural Bengal, where the 78-year-old Mahatma is wearily trudging from one village to another, trying to stem the rushing tide of arson, rape, and murder that will soon engulf many other parts of the country. The few close associates who accompany him on this mission of peace are a witness to his despair and helpless listeners to the anguished cries of '*Kya karun, kya karun*? (What should I do? What should I do?)' heard from his room in the middle of the night.[38] 'I find myself in the midst of exaggeration and falsity,' he writes, 'I am unable to discover the truth. There is terrible mutual distrust. Oldest friendships have snapped. Truth and *Ahimsa* (nonviolence) by which I swear and which have to my knowledge sustained me for 60 years, seem to fail to show the attributes I ascribed to them.'[39]

For an explanation of his 'failures' and sense of despair, Gandhi would characteristically probe for shortcomings in his abstinence, seeking to determine whether the god of desire had perhaps triumphed in some obscure recess of his mind, depriving him of his powers. Thus in the midst of human devastation and political uncertainty, Gandhi wrote a series of five articles on celibacy in his weekly newspaper, puzzling his readers who, as his temporary personal secretary, N.K. Bose, puts it, 'did not know why such a series suddenly appeared in the midst of intensely political articles.'[40]

But more striking than this public evidence of his preoccupation were his private experiments wherein the aged Mahatma pathetically sought to reassure himself of the strength of his celibacy. These experiments have shocked many and have come to be known as 'having naked young women sleep with him when he was old,' although their intent and outcome were far removed from the familiar connotations of that suggestive phrase. In the more or less public sleeping arrangements of his entourage while it rested in a village for the night, Gandhi would ask one or another of his few close women associates (his 19-year-old granddaughter among them) to share his bed and then try to ascertain in the morning whether any trace of sexual feeling had been evoked, either in himself or in his companion.[41] In spite of criticism by some of his close co-workers, Gandhi defended these experiments, denying the accusation that they could have ill effects on the women involved. Instead, he viewed them as an integral part of the *Yagna* he was performing—the Hindu sacrifice to the gods—whose only purpose was a restoration of personal psychic potency that would help him to regain control over political events and men, a control which seemed to be so fatally slipping away. Again he exploits his desires (and, admittedly, women) for the sake of his cause—the prideful vice of an uncompromisingly virtuous man.

TWO WOMEN

In his middle and later years, a number of young women, attracted by Gandhi's public image as the Mahatma, his cause, or his fame, sought his proximity and eventually shared his *ashram* life. These women, who in many cases had left their well-appointed middle- and upper-class homes to take upon themselves the rigors of an ascetic lifestyle, were all else but conventional. Some of them were not only 'highstrung' but can fairly be described as suffering from emotional crises of considerable magnitude. Like their counterparts today who seek out well-known gurus, these women too were looking for the therapist in Gandhi as much as the Mahatma or the leader embodying Indian national aspirations. If toning down the intensity of a crippling emotional disturbance and awakening latent productive and creative powers that neither the individual nor the community 'knows' he or she possesses is the mark of a good therapist then, as we shall see later, Gandhi was an exceptional one. From women who were a little more than emotional wrecks, he fashioned energetic leaders directing major institutions engaged in the task of social innovation and actively participating in the country's Independence movement.

Gandhi's relationships with these women are fascinating in many ways. First, one is struck by the trouble he took in maintaining a relationship once he had admitted the woman to a degree of intimacy. Irrespective of his public commitments or the course of political events, he was punctilious in writing (and expecting) regular weekly letters to each one of his chosen women followers when they were separated during his frequent visits to other parts of the country or his lengthy spells of imprisonment. Cumulatively, these letters build up a portrait of the Mahatma which reveals his innermost struggles, particularly during the periods of heightened emotional vulnerability, and the role played therein by Woman, as embodied in the collectivity of his chosen female followers.

At their best, the letters are intensely human, full of wisdom about life and purpose. Even at times of stress, they are invariably caring as Gandhi encourages the women's questions, advises them on their intimate problems, and cheerfully dispenses his favorite dietary prescriptions for every kind of ailment. As he writes to one of them: 'Your diagnosis is a correct one. The pleasure I get out of solving the *ashram* 's problems, and within the *ashram* those of the sisters, is much greater than that of resolving India's dilemmas.'[42]

The second striking characteristic of these letters is what appears to be Gandhi's unwitting effort simultaneously to increase the intimacy with the correspondent and to withdraw if the woman wished for a nearness that crossed the invisible line he had drawn for both of them. The woman's consequent hurt or withdrawal is never allowed to reach a point of breakdown in the relationship. Gandhi employed his consider-

able charm and powers of persuasion to draw her close again, the hapless woman oscillating around a point between intimacy and
estrangement, nearness and distance. The emotions aroused, not only in
the women (who were also in close contact with each other) but to some
degree in Gandhi, simmered in the hothouse *ashram* atmosphere to
produce frequent explosions. In accordance with our narrative intent, let
us look at the stories of two of these women, making of them brief tales
rather than the novel each one of them richly deserves.

Prema Kantak belonged to a middle-class family from a small town
in Maharashtra. She was still a schoolgirl when she heard about Gandhi
and the wonderful work he had done for the cause of Indians in South
Africa. An only daughter among five sons, she was a favourite of her
father and enjoyed more than the usual freedom for a girl of her class
and times.

As Prema grew into youth, she was gripped by the fervour of
nationalist politics and agonized over personal spiritual questions, interests which Gandhi too combined in his person. Had he not maintained
that 'politics without religion is dangerous?'

Her first encounter with the great man took place when Gandhi came
to address students of her college at Poona. After the talk, she remembers going up to the platform where he was sitting so as to touch his
feet in the traditional Indian gesture of respect. Since Gandhi was sitting
cross-legged, his feet were tucked under his body. Prema reports:

Without any mental reservations I touched his knee with my finger and saluted
him. With a start he turned to look at me, reciprocated the greetings and looked
away. If he but knew that by touching him my heart had blossomed forth with
incomparable pride! With the pure touch an electric current ran through my
body and I walked home lost in a world of bliss![42]

Sensitive and emotional, intelligent and idealistic, Prema refused to
follow the traditional life plan of an Indian girl and get married, perhaps
also because of a problematic (most analysts would say 'classically
hysterical') attitude toward sexuality. 'Once, when I was 16, I was reading the *Bhagavata*,' she writes, 'when I came to the conversation
between Kapila and Devahuti,* I learnt how babies come into world. I
remember that my hair stood up on end. I visualized my own conception and was seized with disgust toward my parents and my body! My

---

* Kapila is the legendary expounder of the Samkhya system of Hindu philosophy.
Devahuti is Kapila's mother.

life seemed dirty! This disgust remained with me for many years.'[44] After a bitter quarrel between the daughter and her beloved father, Prema left home to live in a women's hostel. She earned her livelihood by tutoring children while she continued her studies toward a Master's degree.

Prema's fascination for Gandhi and her decision to go and live with him in the *ashram* is quite understandable. In the very nature of the *ashram* life and its ideals, there is a promised protection from disgusting sexuality. In her wishful imagination Gandhi looms up as the ideal parent who will soothe the hurt caused by the disappointment in the real-life one. He is also the admired mentor for Prema's political and spiritual interests, who is capable of comprehending the deeper needs of her soul.

At the age of 23, then, bubbling with innocent enthusiasm, Prema found herself in Ahmedabad in the Mahatma's presence. As was his wont, at first Gandhi discouraged her. He described to her in detail the hard physical work, the chores of cutting vegetables, grinding grain, cooking meals, cleaning utensils and toilets which awaited her if she adopted the *ashram* life. Prema, exultant in her youthful vitality and idealism, dismissed his cautions as trifles. 'I want to do something tremendous!', she exclaimed on one of her very first nights in the *ashram*. With wry humour, Gandhi tried to temper her exuberance without crushing her spirit. 'The only tremendous thing you can do just now is go to sleep,' he said.[45]

At the start of her stay, when Gandhi was out of town for a few days, Prema had the following dream. She is a little girl reclining in Gandhi's lap. From his breast, a stream of sweet, good milk is flowing straight into her mouth. Prema is drinking the milk and the Mahatma is saying, 'Drink, drink, drink more.' Prema is replete but the milk continues to flow and Gandhi keeps insisting that she drink more. Prema's clothes and body are thoroughly soaked in milk but the stream is unending. She wakes up in alarm.[46]

On narrating her dream to Gandhi and asking for an interpretation, Gandhi replied, 'Dreams can have the quality of purity (*sattvik*) or of passion (*rajasik*). Your dream is a pure one. It means that you feel protected with me.'[47] From the orthodox Freudian view, the interpretation cannot be faulted. An instinctive psychoanalyst, Gandhi provides reassurance to the patient and encourages her to give him her trust at this stage of their relationship. Unwittingly following the technical rule of proceeding from the surface to the depths, his interpretation could have been as easily made by an analyst who, for the time being, would have kept his hypotheses on the deeper imports of the dream images— of the symbolic equivalence of milk and semen, Prema's greedy voraciousness, her possible fantasy regarding the persecuting breast and so on—quietly to himself.

In the *ashram*, the competition among women for Gandhi's attention was as fierce as it is in any guru's establishment today. When he went for his evening constitutional, Gandhi would walk with his hands around the shoulders of the *ashram* girls. There was intense jealousy among them as each kept a hawk's eye for any undue favouritism—the number of times a girl was singled out for the mark of this favour, the duration of time a girl had Bapu's hands on her shoulder and so on. At first Prema felt aggrieved when other girls teased her, 'Prema—*ben*, Bapuji does not put his hands on *your* shoulders!' 'Why should he? I am not like you to push myself forward!' Prema would reply spiritedly. 'No, he never will. The *ashram* rule is that he can keep his hands only on the shoulders of girls who are younger than 16.'[48]

Prema felt her deprivation acutely and approached Gandhi who asked her to get the *ashram* superintendent's permission if she wanted him to treat her like the younger girls. Prema's pride was hurt and she responded angrily, 'Why should I hanker after your hand so much that I have to go and get permission?' and stalked off. One night, however, Gandhi had gone to the toilet since he was suffering from diarrhoea because of one of his food experiments. He had fainted from weakness and Prema, who had heard him fall, reached his side. Gandhi walked back leaning his body against her for support and she even lifted him onto the bed. From that night onwards she often accompanied him on his evening walk, with his hand on her shoulder, while she, I imagine, looked around her with the pride of the chosen one, a victor in the secret struggle among the women. In her elation at being closer to him, she tells us, she once kissed his hands saying. 'The hand that has shaken the British throne is resting on my shoulders! What a matter of pride!' Gandhi had laughed, 'Yes, how proud we all are!' and, clowning, he threw out his chest and strutted about in imitation of a stage emperor.[49]

In 1933, when she was 27 years old, Gandhi begged Prema to give him as *bhiksha* (meritorious alms) a life-long vow of celibacy. Prema wrote back that there was no difficulty in her compliance with his wish as celibacy was in any case her ideal. In unreflected arrogance she added, 'I may sleep with any man on the same bed during the whole night and get up in the morning as innocent as a child.' Touched on a sore spot, Gandhi reprimanded her on a pride unbecoming a celibate. From mythology he gave examples of those whose pride in their celibacy had gone before a grievous fall. She was no goddess (*devi*), he said, since she still had her periods. For Gandhi believed that in a really celibate woman menstruation stopped completely, the monthly period being but a stigmata of *vikara*, of the sexual distortions of a woman's soul.[50]

Gradually, Prema was trusted with greater and greater responsibilities in running the *ashram*, though her constant struggle, like those of most other women, was for an intimate closeness with Gandhi. He would try to turn her thoughts toward the *ashram* community, instruct her to regard herself as belonging to the community and vice versa. 'You are dear to me, that is why "your" *ashram* is dear to me. Love wants an anchor, love needs touch. It is human nature that not only the mind needs an anchor but also the body and the sense organs,' she would argue back.[51] He would ask her to sublimate her emotions, affectionately call her hysterical, explaining that by hysterical he meant someone under an excessive sway of emotions. He would berate her for her lapses and then coax and cajole her back if she showed any signs of withdrawal. Prema felt that the 'Old Beloved,' her affectionate name for him, had ensnared her. Gandhi replied,

I do not want to snare anyone in my net. If everyone becomes a puppet of mine then what will happen to me? I regard such efforts as worthless. But even if I try to trap someone you shouldn't lose your self confidence. Your letters prove that you are on guard. Yes, it is true that you have always been fearful of being caught in my net. That is a bad sign. If you have decided (to throw in your lot with me) then why the fear? Or perhaps it is possible that we mean different things by the word 'ensnare'?[52]

Feeling trapped—by the frustration of her own unconscious wishes in relation to Gandhi, the analyst would say—Prema sought to detach herself from him. She fought with him on what in retrospect seem minor issues. Remaining a devoted follower of Gandhi and his ideals, she was aware of a degree of estrangement from the Mahatma. Prema finally went back to Maharashtra in 1939 and set up an *ashram* in a small village. It was devoted to the fulfilment of Gandhi's social agenda—uplift of the poor and the untouchables, education of women, increasing the self sufficiency of the village community, and so on. Like the portentous dream after their initial meeting, the separation too is the occasion for a significant dream. In this dream Prema is alone on a vast plain which meets the sky at the horizon. She is sitting in a chair in the middle of this plain with green grass all around her. Behind the chair, she senses the presence of a man. She cannot see him but has no doubt that the man is her protector and her companion. Suddenly four or five beautiful, well-dressed boys come running up to her with bouquets of flowers in their hands. She begins to talk to the boys. More and more children now appear with bouquets. From the sky, flowers begin to rain down upon her. She wakes up with a start. After waking up, when she thinks of the dream, she is convinced that the man standing behind her is Gandhi and that his blessings will always remain with her.[53]

As I reflect on the dream and its context, I cannot help musing (which is less an interpretation of the dream than my associations to it) that perhaps the dream fulfils some of Prema's contradictory wishes. Once again restored to the centre of her world with Gandhi, from which she has been recently excluded, she is the celibate *devi* of Hindu mythology on whom gods shower flowers from heaven as a sign of their approbation and homage. On the other hand, she has also become the life-companion of the Mahatma, bearing him not only the four sons Kasturbai had borne but many, many more adoring and adorable children.

Since it was the man rather than what he stood for who was the focus of her emotional life, Prema gradually drifted back to her earlier spiritual interests after Gandhi's death. As she consorted with yogis and mystics, the memory of the Mahatma and the years she had spent with him would become locked up in a corner of her mind, to be occasionally opened and savoured privately, a secret solace in times of distress.

In many ways, Madeline Slade was one of the more unusual members of Gandhi's female entourage. Daughter of an admiral in the British Navy who had been a commander of the East Indies Squadron, she was a part of the British ruling establishment, which both despised and feared Gandhi as an implacable foe. Brought up in the freedom of an upper-class English home of the era, Madeline had been dissatisfied and unhappy for years, and tells us that everything had been dark and futile till she discovered Gandhi and left for India when she was in her early 30s.[54] A great admirer of Beethoven—she had thought of devoting her life to the study of his life and music—her plans underwent a drastic change after she read Romain Rolland's book on Gandhi (*Mahatma Gandhi*, 1924). Not wishing to act hastily, she first prepared herself for the ordeal of *ashram* life in India. Madeline went about this task with her usual single-minded determination. She learned spinning and sitting cross-legged on the floor; she became a teetotaller and a vegetarian and learned Urdu. She then wrote to Gandhi expressing her wish and received a cordial reply inviting her to join him.

A tall, strapping woman, handsome rather than pretty, Madeline took avidly to the ascetic part of the *ashram* life. She clung to Gandhi with a ferocity which he found very unsettling, perhaps also because of the feelings which her strong need for his physical proximity in turn aroused in him. During the 24 years of their association, Gandhi would repeatedly send her away to live and work in other *ashram*s in distant parts of the country. She would have nervous breakdowns as a consequence of these separations and 'struggles of the heart' (as she called them) or 'spiritual agony' (as Gandhi put it), impetuously rush back to wherever Gandhi was only to be again banished from his presence. He tried to redirect her from her single-minded concentration on him as a person to the cause they both served.

The parting today was sad, because I saw that I pained you. I want you to be a perfect woman. I want you to shed all angularities. . . .

Do throw off the nervousness. You must not cling to me as in this body. The spirit without the body is ever with you. And that is more than the feeble embodied imprisoned spirit with all the limitations that flesh is heir to. The spirit without the flesh is perfect, and that is all we need. This can be felt only when we practise detachment. This you must now try to achieve.

This is how I should grow if I were you. But you should grow along your own lines. You will, therefore, reject all I have said in this, that does not appeal to your heart or your head. You must retain your individuality at all cost. Resist me when you must. For I may judge you wrongly in spite of all my love for you. I do not want you to impute infallibility to me.[55]

Madeline, now appropriately renamed Mira by Gandhi after the 16th-century Indian woman-saint whose infatuation with Krishna was not much greater than Madeline's own yearning for the Mahatma, was however a battlefield of forces stronger than those amenable to reason. She was like the women described by the psychoanalyst Ralph Greenson, who come to analysis not to seek insight but to enjoy the physical proximity of the analyst.[56] Such patients relate a history of achievement and an adequate social life but an unsatisfactory love life characterized by wishes for incorporation, possession, and fusion. Gandhi's attitude to Mira, like that of the analyst with the patient, combined sympathetic listening with the frustration of wishes for gratification—a certain recipe, the mandrake root, for intensifying and unearthing ever more fresh capacities for love in her.[57] It further enhanced what analysts would call her transference to the Mahatma, a type of intense love felt for people who fulfil a role in our lives equivalent to the one fulfilled by parents in our childhood.

The presumption that their relationship was not quite one-sided and that Mira too evoked complex 'counter-transference' reactions in Gandhi is amply supported by his letters to her. Once, in 1927, when Mira had rushed to Gandhi's side on hearing that he was under severe strain, and had promptly been sent back, Gandhi wrote to her:

I could not restrain myself from sending you a love message on reaching here. I felt very sad after letting you go. I have been very severe with you, but I could not do otherwise. I had to perform an operation and I steadied myself for it. Now let us hope all would go on smoothly, and that all the weakness is gone.[58]

The letter was followed the next day with a post card: 'This is merely to tell you I can't dismiss you from my mind. Every surgeon has a soothing ointment after a severe operation. This is my ointment. . . .'[59] Two days later, yet another letter followed:

I have never been so anxious as this time to hear from you, for I sent you away too quickly after a serious operation. You haunted me in my sleep last night and were reported by friends to whom you had been sent, to be delirious, but without any danger. They said, 'You need not be anxious. We are doing all that is humanly possible.' And with this I woke up troubled in mind and prayed that you may be free from all harm. . . .[60]

From prison, where he was safe from her importunate physicality, Gandhi could express his feelings for her more freely. While translating a book of Indian hymns into English for her, he wrote: 'In translating the hymns for you I am giving myself much joy. Have I not expressed my love, often in storms than in gentle soothing showers of affection? The memory of these storms adds to the pleasure of this exclusive translation for you.'[61] As with his other women, Gandhi could not let Mira get away further than the distance he unconsciously held to be the optimal for his own feelings of well-being.

Like the child on his first explorations of the world who does not venture further from the mother than the length of an invisible string with which he seems attached to her, Gandhi too would become anxious at any break that threatened to become permanent and would seek to draw the woman closer to him.

Chi. Mira,
You are on the brain. I look about me, and miss you. I open the *charkha* (spinning wheel) and miss you. So on and so forth. But what is the use? You have

done the right thing. You have left your home, your people and all that people prize most, not to serve me personally but to serve the cause I stand for. All the time you were squandering your love on me personally, I felt guilty of misappropriation. And I exploded on the slightest pretext. Now that you are not with me, my anger turns itself upon me for having given you all those terrible scoldings. But I was on a bed of hot ashes all the while I was accepting your service. You will truly serve me by joyously serving the cause. Cheer, cheer, no more of idle.

To this, Mira added the commentary, 'The struggle was terrible. I too was on a bed of hot ashes because I could feel the Bapu was. This was one of the occasions when, somehow or other, I managed to tear myself away.'[62]

In 1936, when Gandhi was recovering from his breakdown and had decided to leave Sabarmati to go and live by himself in a remote village, Mira thought she finally had a chance to fulfil her deepest longing, to live with Bapu in the countryside. Gandhi, however, was adamant. He would stay in the village Mira lived in only if she herself shifted to a neighbouring one. 'This nearly broke my heart, but somehow I managed to carry on, and when Bapu finally decided to come and live in Seagaon,' she writes, 'I buried my sorrow in the joy of preparing for him his cottage and cowshed. For myself I built a little cottage a mile away on the ridge of Varoda village, and within a week of Bapu's coming to live in Seagaon I departed for the hut on the hill where I lived alone with my little horse as my companion.'[63] Even this relative nearness was not to last long as political events inexorably pulled Gandhi away on his travels.

In 1948, at the time of Gandhi's death, Mira was living in her own *ashram* near Rishikesh in the foothills of the Himalayas, devoting herself to the care of cattle in the nearby villages. Starting one *ashram* after another, deeper and deeper into the Himalayas, she was to live in India till 1958 after she decided to return to Europe, almost 35 years after she had first left home in search of Gandhi. I visited her with a friend in 1964, in the forests above Baden near Vienna where she now made her home in an isolated farmhouse with a dog and an old Indian servant from Rishikesh. Gracious but reserved, she offered us tea and biscuits and perfunctorily inquired about current events in India. She refused to talk about Gandhi, claiming that he did not interest her any longer. What animated her exclusively and what she enthusiastically talked about was Beethoven whom she saw as the highest manifestation of the human spirit. He had been her first love before she read Romain

Rolland's book on Gandhi that was to change her life. Working on a biography of Beethoven and with his music as her dearest companion she had come back to the composer after a 35-year detour with Gandhi. Somewhat disappointed, we left her to her new love. Walking toward our car parked a few hundred yards away from the farmhouse, we saw the servant come running up to us, desperation writ large on his lined face: 'Sahib, I don't want to live here. I want to go home. Please take me home.' I mumbled our apologies for being unable to help and left him standing on the grassy meadow, peering after us in the mild afternoon sun as we drove away.

To place Gandhi's sexual preoccupations in their cultural context, we should remember that sexuality, whether in the erotic flourishes of Indian art and in the Dionysian rituals of its popular religion, or in the dramatic combat with ascetic longings of yogis who seek to conquer and transform it into spiritual power, has been a perennial preoccupation of Hindu culture. In this resides the reason, puzzling to many non-Indians, why in spite of the surface resemblances between Jungian concepts and Indian thought, it is Freud rather than Jung who fascinates the Indian mind. Many modern Indian mystics feel compelled, in fact, to discuss Freud's assumptions and conclusions about the vagaries and transfigurations of libido while they pass over Jung's work with benign indifference. Indian spirituality is preeminently a theory of 'sublimation.'

Indian 'mysticism' is typically intended to be an intensely practical affair, concerned with an alchemy of the libido that would convert it from a giver of death to a bestower of immortality. It is the sexual fire that stokes the alchemical transformation wherein the cooking pot is the body and the cooking oil is a distillation from sexual fluids. The strength of this traditional aspiration to sublimate sexuality into spirituality, semen into the elixir *Soma*, varies in different regions with different castes. Yet though only small sections of Indian society may act on this aspiration, it is a well-known theory subscribed to by most Hindus, including non-literate villagers. In its most popular form, the Hindu theory of sublimation goes something like this.

Physical strength and mental power have their source in *Virya*, a word that stands for both sexual energy and semen. *Virya*, in fact, is identical with the essence of maleness. *Virya* can either move downward in sexual intercourse, where it is emitted in its gross physical form as semen, or it can move upward through the spinal chord and into the brain, in its subtle form known as *ojas*. Hindus regard the downward movement of sexual energy and its emission as semen as enervating, a debilitating waste of vitality and essential energy. Of all emotions, it is said, lust throws the physical system into the greatest chaos, with every violent passion destroying millions of red blood cells. Indian metaphysical physiology maintains that food is converted into semen in a 30-day period by successive transformations (and refinements) through blood, flesh, fat, bone, and marrow till semen is distilled-40 drops of blood producing one drop of semen. Each ejaculation involves a loss of half an ounce of semen, which is equivalent to the vitality produced by the consumption of 60 pounds of food.

In another similar calculation with pedagogic intent, each act of copulation is equivalent to an energy expenditure of 24 hours of concentrated mental activity or 72 hours of hard physical labour.[64] Gandhi is merely reiterating these popular ideas when he says that

Once the idea, that the only and grand function of the sexual organ is generation, possesses men and women, union for any other purpose they will hold as criminal waste of the vital fluid, and consequent excitement caused to men and women as an equally criminal waste of precious energy. It is now easy to understand why the scientists of old have put such great value upon its strong transmutation into the highest form of energy for the benefit of society.[65]

If, on the other hand, semen is retained, converted into *ojas* and moved upwards by the observance of *brahmacharya*, it becomes a source of spiritual life rather than cause of physical decay. Longevity, creativity, physical and mental vitality are enhanced by the conservation of semen; memory, will power, inspiration—scientific and artistic—all derive from the observation of *brahmacharya*. In fact, if unbroken (*akhanda*) *brahmacharya* in thought, word, and deed can be observed for 12 years, the aspirant will obtain *moksha* spontaneously.

These ideas on semen and celibacy, I have emphasized above, are a legacy of Indian culture and are shared, so to speak, by Hindu saints and sinners alike. Indeed, the very first published case history in Indian psychoanalytic literature sounds like a parody of Gandhi.

The patient is a married young man and is the father of several children. He is of religious bent and his ideal in life is to attain what has been called in Hindu literature *Jivanmukti*, i.e., a state of liberation from worldly bondages and a perfect freedom from all sorts of passions whether bodily or mental. The possibility of the existence of such a state and of its attainment is never doubted by the patient as he says he has implicit faith in the Hindu scriptures which assert that the realization of *brahma* or supreme entity, results in such a liberation. (He believes) . . . that the only thing he has to do is to abstain from sex of all sorts and liberation will come to him as a sort of reward. . . . Since one pleasure leads to another it is desirable to shun all pleasures in life lest they should lead to sex. The patient is against forming any attachment whether it be with his wife or children or friend or any inanimate object. He is terribly upset sometimes when he finds that in spite of his ideal of no-attachment and no-sex, lascivious thoughts of the most vulgar nature and uncontrollable feelings of love and attraction arise in his mind. . . . In spite of his deep reverence for Hindu gods and goddesses filthy sexual ideas of an obsessional nature come into his mind when he bows before these images.[66]

The 'raising of the seed upwards,' then, is a strikingly familiar image in the Indian psycho-philosophical schools of self realization commonly clumped under the misleading label of 'mysticism.' As Wendy O' Flaherty remarks: 'So pervasive is the concept of semen being raised up to the head that popular versions of the philosophy believe that semen originates there.'[67] The concept is even present in the *Kamasutra*, the textbook of eroticism and presumably a subverter of ascetic ideals, where the successful lover is not someone who is overly passionate but one who has controlled, stilled his senses through *brahmacharya* and meditation.[68] Indian mythology, too, is replete with stories in which the gods, threatened by a human being who is progressing toward immortality by accruing immense capacities through celibacy and meditation, send a heavenly nymph to seduce the ascetic (even the trickling down of a single drop of sexual fluid counting as a fatal lapse), and thereby reduce him to the common human, carnal denominator.

Of course, given the horrific imagery of sexuality as cataclysmic depletion, no people can procreate with any sense of joyful abandon unless they develop a good deal of scepticism, if not an open defiance, in relation to the sexual prescription and ideals of the 'cultural superego.' The relief at seeing the ascetic's pretensions humbled by the opulent charms of a heavenly seductress is not only that of the gods but is equally shared by the mortals who listen to the myth or see it enacted in popular dance and folk drama. The ideals of celibacy are then simultaneously subscribed to and scoffed at. Whereas, on the one hand, there are a number of sages in the Indian tradition (Gandhi is only the latest one to join this august assemblage), who are admired for their successful celibacy and the powers it brought them, there are, on the other hand, also innumerable folktales detailing the misadventures of randy ascetics. In the more dignified myths, even the Creator is unable to sustain his chastity and is laid low by carnality.

The heavenly nymph Mohini fell in love with the Lord of Creation, Brahma.

After gaining the assistance of Kama, the god of love, she went to Brahma and danced before him, revealing her body to him in order to entice him, but Brahma remained without passion. Then Kama struck Brahma with an arrow. Brahma wavered and felt desire, but after a moment he gained control. Brahma said to Mohini, go away, Mother, your efforts are wasted here. I know your intention, and I am not suitable for your work. The scripture says, 'Ascetics must avoid all women, especially prostitutes.' I am incapable of doing anything that the Vedas consider despicable. You are a sophisticated woman, look for a sophisticated young man, suitable for your work, and there will be virtue in your union. But I am an old man, an ascetic Brahmin; what pleasure can I find in a prostitute? Mohini laughed and said to him, 'A man who refuses to make love to a woman who is tortured by desire—he is an eunuch. Whether a man be a householder or ascetic or lover, he must not spurn a woman who approaches him, or he will go to Hell. Come now and make love to me in some private place,' and as she said this she pulled at Brahma's garment. Then the sages bowed to Brahma, 'How is it that Mohini, the best of celestial prostitutes, is in your presence?' Brahma said, to conceal his scheme, 'She danced and sang for a long time and then when she was tired she came here like a young girl to her father.' But the sages laughed for they knew the whole secret, and Brahma laughed too.[69]

The piece of gossip that Gandhi 'slept with naked women in his old age' has therefore resounding echoes in the Indian cultural tradition. It arouses complex emotions in both the purveyor or and the listener, namely a malicious relief together with an aching disappointment that he may indeed have done so.

The ultimate if ironic refinement of celibacy is found in the Tantric version, where the aspirant is trained and enjoined to perform the sexual act itself without desire and the 'spilling of the seed,' thus divorcing the sexual impulse from human physiology and any conscious or unconscious mental representation of it. The impulse, it is believed, stirs up the semen in this ritual (and unbelievably passionless) sexual act and evokes energetic forces that can be rechannelled upwards. This and other Tantric techniques were familiar to Gandhi, whose own deeply held religious persuasion, Vaishnavism, was pervaded by many such Tantric notions. On the one hand, as we have seen, Gandhi often sounds like Chaitanya, the 15th-century 'father' of north Indian Vaishnavism, who rejected a disciple for paying attention to a woman, saying: 'I can never again look upon the face of an ascetic who associates with women. The senses are hard to control, and seek to fix themselves on worldly things. Even the wooden image of a woman has the power to steal the mind of a sage. . . .'[70] On the other hand, however, Gandhi in his sexual experiments seems to be following the examples set by other famous Vaishnavas like Ramananda and Viswanatha. Ramananda, Chaitanya's follower and companion, used to take two beautiful young temple prostitutes into a lonely garden where he would oil their bodies, bathe, and dress them while himself remaining 'unaffected.'[71] The philosopher Viswanatha, it is said, went to lie with his young wife at the command of his guru: 'He lay with her on the bed, but Viswanatha was transformed, and he did not touch her, as it had been his custom to do. He lay with his wife according to the instructions of his guru . . . and thus he controlled his senses.'[72]

There are germs of truth in the signal importance Indian cultural tradition attaches to sexuality. The notion, arising from this emphasis, that sexual urges amount to a creative fire—not only for procreation but, equally, in self creation—is indeed compelling. Further, a tradition that does not reduce sexual love to copulation but seeks to elevate it into a celebration, even a ritual that touches the partners with a sense of the sacred, and where orgasm is experienced as 'a symbolic blessing of man by his ancestors and by the nature of things,' is certainly sympathetic.[73] My concern here has to do with the concomitant strong anxiety in India surrounding the ideas of the 'squandering of the sperm' and 'biological self sacrifice.' Such ideas and the fantasies they betray cannot help but heighten an ambivalence toward women that verges on misogyny and phobic avoidance. As for self realization through renunciation of sexual love, I would tend to side with Thomas Mann when he observes:

It is undeniable that human dignity realizes itself in the two sexes, male and female; so that when one is neither one nor the other, one stands outside the human pale and whence then can human dignity come? Efforts to sustain it are worthy of respect, for they deal with the spiritual, and thus, let us admit in honour, with the preeminently human. But truth demands the hard confession that thought and the spirit come badly off, in the long run, against nature. How little can the precepts of civilization avail against the dark, deep, silent knowledge of the flesh! How little it lets itself be taken in by the spirit![74]

How would Freud, who in his mid-life also chose to become celibate, have regarded Gandhi's celibacy and its intended efficacy? In general, Freud was understandably skeptical about the possibility that sexual abstinence could help to build energetic men of action, original thinkers, or bold reformers. Yet he also saw such attempts at the sublimation of 'genital libido' in relative terms:

The relationship between the amount of sublimation possible and the amount of sexual activity necessary naturally varies very much from person to person and even from one calling to another. An abstinent artist is hardly conceivable; but an abstinent young savant is certainly no rarity. The latter can, by his self restraint, liberate forces for his studies; while the former probably finds his artistic achievements powerfully stimulated by his sexual experience.[75]

It is quite conceivable that Freud would have conceded the possibility of successful celibacy to a few extraordinary people of genuine originality with a self-abnegating sense of mission or transcendent purpose. In other words, he would have agreed with the Latin dictum that 'what is allowed to Jove is forbidden to the ox.' The psychoanalytic question is, then, not of sublimation but why Gandhi found phallic desire so offensive that he must, so to speak, tear it out by the very roots.

Some of Gandhi's uneasiness with phallic desire has to do with his feeling that genital love is an accursed and distasteful prerogative of the father. In his autobiography, in spite of expressing many admirable filial sentiments, Gandhi suspects his father of being 'oversexed' since he married for the fourth time when he was over 40 and Putlibai, Gandhi's mother, was only 18. In his fantasy, we would suggest, Gandhi saw his young mother as the innocent victim of a powerful old male's lust to which the child could only be an anguished and helpless spectator, unable to save the beloved caretaker from the violation of her person and the violence done to her body. In later life, Gandhi would embrace the cause wherein the marriage of old men with young girls was adamantly opposed with great zeal. He wrote articles with such titles as 'Marriage of Old and Young or Debauchery?' and exhorted his correspondents who reported such incidents to fight this practice. The older men he respected and took as his models were those who shared his revulsion with genital sexuality. These were the men who (like Tolstoy and Raichandra) had sought to transform sexual passion into a more universal religious quest or (like Ruskin) into a moral and aesthetic fervour.

If phallic desire was the violent and tumultuous 'way of the fathers,' genital abstinence, its surrender, provided the tranquil, peaceful path back to the mother. Here Gandhi was not unlike St Augustine, who, too, inwardly beheld celibacy garbed in soothing, maternal imagery:

. . . there appeared unto me the chaste dignity of Continence, serene, yet not relaxedly gay, honestly alluring me to come and doubt not; and stretching forth to receive and embrace me, her holy hands full of multitudes of good examples; there were so many young men and maidens here, a multitude of youth and every age, grave widows and aged virgins; and Continence herself in all, not barren, but a fruitful mother of children of joys. . .[76]

More specifically, the psychobiographical evidence we have reviewed above is compelling that Gandhi's relationships with women are dominated by the unconscious fantasy of maintaining an idealized relationship with the maternal body. This wished-for oneness with the mother is suffused with nurturance and gratitude, mutual adoration and affirmation, without a trace of desire which divides and bifurcates. Replete with wishes for fusion and elimination of differences and limits, Gandhi 'perceived' sexual desire, *both* of the mother and the child, as the single biggest obstacle to the preservation of this illusion. Many of his attitudes, beliefs, and actions with regard to women can then be understood as defensive manoeuvres against the possibility of this perception rising to surface awareness.

Since the mother is a woman, a first step in the defensive operations is to believe that women are not, or only minimally, sexual beings. 'I do not believe that woman is prey to sexual desire to the same extent as man. It is easier for her than for man to exercise self-restraint,'[77] is an opinion often repeated in his writings. Reflecting on his own experiences with Kasturbai, he asserts that 'There was never want of restraint on the part of my wife. Very often she would show restraint, but she rarely resisted me, although she showed disinclination very often.'[78] Whereas he associates male sexuality with unheeding, lustful violence, female sexuality, where it exists, is a passive, suffering acceptance of the male onslaught. This, we must again remember, is only at the conscious level. Unconsciously, his perception of masculine violence and feminine passivity seem to be reversed, as evident in the imagery of the descriptions of his few erotic encounters with women. In his very first adolescent confrontation, he is struck 'dumb and blind,' while the woman is confident and aggressive; in England, he is trembling like a frightened wild animal who has just escaped the (woman) hunter.

The solution to the root problem between the sexes is then, not a removal of the social and legal inequalities suffered by women—though Gandhi was an enthusiastic champion of women's rights—but a thoroughgoing desexualization of the male–female relationship, in which women must take the lead. 'If they will only learn to say "no" to their husbands when they approach them carnally. . . . If a wife says to her husband: "No, I do not want it," he will make no trouble. But she has not been taught. . . . I want women to learn the primary right of resistance.'[79]

Besides desexing the woman, another step in the denial of her desire is her idealization (especially of the Indian woman) as nearer to a purer divine state and thus an object of worship and adoration. That is why a woman does not need to renounce the world in the last stage of life to contemplate God, as is prescribed for the man in the ideal Hindu life cycle. 'She sees Him always. She has no need of any other school to prepare her for Heaven than marriage to a man and care of her children.'[80] Woman is also

the incarnation of *Ahimsa*. *Ahimsa* means infinite love, which, again means infinite capacity for suffering. Who but woman, the mother of man shows this capacity in the largest measure? Let her transfer that love to the whole of humanity, let her forget she ever was, or can be, the object of man's lust. And she will occupy her proud position by the side of the man as his mother, maker and silent leader.[81]

Primarily seeing the mother in the woman and idealizing motherhood is yet another way of denying feminine eroticism. When Millie Polak, a female associate in the Phoenix *ashram* in South Africa, questioned his idealization of motherhood, saying that being a mother does not make a woman wise, Gandhi extolled mother-love as one of the finest aspects of love in human life. His imagery of motherhood is of infants suckling on breasts with inexhaustible supplies of milk. For example, in a letter explaining why the *Gita*, the sacred book of the Hindus, is called Mother, he rhapsodizes,

It has been likened to the sacred cow, the giver of all desires (sic!). Hence Mother. Well, that immortal Mother gives all the milk we need for spiritual sustenance, if we would but approach her as babies seeking and sucking it from her. She is capable of yielding milk to her millions of babies from her exhaustless udder.

In doing the Harijan (untouchable) work in the midst of calumny, misrepresentations and apparent disappointments, her lap comforts me and keeps me from falling into the Slough of Despond.[82]

Whereas desexualizing, idealizing, and perceiving only the 'milky' mother in the woman is one part of his defensive bulwark which helped in preserving the illusion of unity with the maternal body intact, the other part consists of efforts at renouncing the gift of sexual desire, abjuring his own masculinity. Here we must note that the Hindu Vaishnava culture, in which Gandhi grew up and in which he remained deeply rooted, not only provides a sanction for man's feminine strivings, but raises these strivings to the level of a religious-spiritual quest. In devotional Vaishnavism, Lord Krishna alone is the male and all devotees, irrespective of their sex, are female. Gandhi's statement that he had mentally become a woman or that he envied women and that there is as much reason for a man to wish that he was born a woman, as for women to do otherwise, thus struck many responsive chords in his audience.

If Gandhi had had his way, there would be no art or poetry celebrating woman's beauty.

I am told that our literature is full of even an exaggerated apotheosis of women. Let me say that it is an altogether wrong apotheosis. Let me place one simple fact before you. In what light do you think of them when you proceed to write about them? I suggest that before you put your pens to paper think of woman as your own mother, and I assure you the chastest literature will flow from your pens, even like the beautiful rain from heaven which waters the thirsty earth below,. Remember that a woman was your mother, before a woman became your wife.[83]

Although Gandhi's wished-for feminization was defensive in origin, we cannot deny the development of its adaptive aspects. Others, most notably Erik Erikson, have commented upon Gandhi's more or less conscious explorations of the maternal stance and feminine perspective in his actions.[84] In spite of a welter of public demands on his time, we know of the motherly care he could extend to the personal lives of his followers, and the anxious concern he displayed about their health and well-being, including solicitous inquiries about the state of their daily bowel movements.[85] We also know of the widening of these maternal–feminine ways—teasing, testing, taking suffering upon oneself, and so on—in the formulation of his political style and as elements of his campaigns of militant nonviolence.

We have seen that for Gandhi, the cherished oneness with the maternal-feminine could not always be maintained and was often threatened by the intrusion of phallic desire. His obsession with food at these times, evident in the letters and writings, not only represented a preparation for erecting physiological barriers against desire, but also the strengthening of his psychological defences, and thus a reinforcement of his spiritual armamentarium. In other words, in his preoccupation with food (and elimination), in his persistent investment of edible physical substances with psychological qualities, Gandhi plays out the 'basic oral fantasy,' as described by the psychoanalyst Donald Winnicott—'when hungry I think of food, when I eat I think of taking food in. I think of what I like to keep inside and I think of what I want to be rid of and I think of getting rid of it'—whose underlying theme is of union with the mother. His experiments with various kinds of food and a reduction in its intake—in his later years, he abjured milk completely so as not to eroticize his viscera—appear as part of an involuted and intuitive effort to recover and maintain his merger with his mother.

Gandhi's relationship with women and the passions they aroused are, then, more complex than what he reveals in his own impassioned confession. Nor does a recourse to traditional Hindu explanations and prescriptions for their 'diagnosis and cure' reflect adequately the depths of the inner life in which his desires found their wellsprings. Beset by conflicts couched in moral terms familiar to Christian and classical psychoanalyst alike, he struggled with the yearnings aroused by the goddess of longing besides the passions provoked by the god of desire. Or, to use a well-known Indian metaphor in which a woman is said to have two breasts, one for her child, another for her husband, Gandhi's unconscious effort to shift from the one breast to the other—from man to child—was not always successful. He was a man in spite of himself. We know that the sensuality derived from the deeply felt oneness with a maternal world, a sensuality that challenges death, energized Gandhi's person, impelled his transcendent endeavours, and advanced him on the road to a freedom of spirit from which India, as well as the world, has profited. Yet we have seen that throughout his life, there were profound periods of emotional turmoil when this original and ultimately illusory connection broke down, emptying him of all inner 'goodness' and 'power'.

11

Lovers in the Dark

When I was growing up in the 1940s, going to the cinema, at least in the Punjab and at least among the middle- and upper-classes, was regarded as slightly dissolute, if not outright immoral, and the habit was considered especially dangerous to the growing sensibilities of young children. Of course not all films were equally burdened with disapproval. Like everything else in India—from plants to human beings—there was (and is) a strict hierarchical classification. In the movie caste system, stunt films, the Indian version of Kung Fu movies, were the low-caste Shudras at the lowest rung of the ladder while the Brahmin 'mythological' and the *Kshatriya* 'historical' vied for supremacy at the top. The only time I was admitted to the owner's box of Prabhat Talkies—the cinema owned by a grand-uncle in Lahore—was to see an eminently forgettable mythological called *Kadambari*. In childhood, stunt films were my favourite, although my taste was quite catholic, consisting as it did of indiscriminate adoration. With the complicity of a friendly doorman who doubled as an odd job man in my grand-uncle's adjoining house, I was in the fortunate position of being able to indulge my secret passion for films whenever we visited Lahore. I use the word 'passion' literally and not as a metaphor, since my craving for movies was insatiable and my consumption equally remarkable; I saw *Ratan* 16 times, *Shikari* 14 times, and even *Kadambari* three times after that first viewing from the owner's box.

I remember my movie-going with a nostalgia which cloaks childhood events, at least the good ones, in a unique glow of permanence and ephemerality. In the anonymity of a darkness pierced by the flickering light which gave birth to a magical yet familiar world on the screen, I was no longer a small boy but a part of the envied world of adulthood, although I sensed its rituals and mysteries but dimly. I always joined in the laughter that followed a risqué comment, even if its exact meaning escaped me. I too would hold my breath in the hushed silence that followed a particularly well-enacted love scene, and surreptitiously try to whistle with the O of the thumb and the index finger under the tongue, in imitation of the wolf whistles that greeted the obligatory scene in which the heroine fell into the water or was otherwise drenched. Recently, when in *Satyam Shivam Sundaram* Miss Zeenat Aman's considerable charms were revealed through her wet and clinging saree at the receiving end of a waterfall, I felt grateful to the world of Hindi movies for providing continuity in an unstable and changing world. When I was a child, the movies brought the vistas of a desirable adulthood tantalizingly close; as an adult, I find that they help to keep the road to childhood open.

I have described my engagement with the world of Hindi films at some length, not in order to claim any vast personal experience or specialized knowledge but to stress the fact of an enduring empathic connection with the world of Indian popular, cinema. Today, this cinema, which draws upon images and symbols from the traditional regional cultures and combines them with more modern western themes, is the major shaper of an emerging, pan-Indian popular culture. Though its fixed repertoire of plots, with which the audience is presumably thoroughly familiar, has striking parallels with traditional folk theatre, the popular culture represented by the cinema goes beyond both classical and folk elements even while it incorporates them.

The appeal of the film is directed to an audience so diverse that it transcends social and spatial categories. Watched by almost 15 million people every day, popular cinema's values and language have long since crossed urban boundaries to enter the folk culture of the rural-based population, where they have begun to influence Indian ideas of the good life and the ideology of social, family, and love relationships. The folk dance of a region or a particular musical form such as the devotional *bhajan*, after it has crossed the portals of a Bombay or Madras studio, is transmuted into a film dance or a film *bhajan* by the addition of musical and dance motifs from other regions as perhaps also from the West, and is then relayed back in full technicolor and stereophonic sound to decisively alter the original. Similarly, film situations, dialogue, and decor have begun to colonize folk theatre. Even the traditional iconography of statues and pictures for religious worship is paying homage to film representations of gods and goddesses.[1]

My own approach to popular cinema is to think of film as a collective fantasy, a group daydream. By 'collective' and 'group' I do not mean that Hindi film is an expression of a mythic collective unconscious or of something called a group mind. Instead, I see the cinema as the primary vehicle for shared fantasies of a vast number of people living on the Indian subcontinent who are both culturally and psychologically linked. I do not use 'fantasy' in the ordinary sense of the word, with its popular connotations of whimsy, eccentricity, or triviality, but as another name for that world of imagination which is fuelled by desire and which provides us with an alternative world where we can continue our longstanding quarrel with reality. Desire and fantasy are, of course, inexorably linked. Aristotle's dictum that there can be no desire without fantasy contains even more truth in reverse. Fantasy is the *mise-en-scène* of desire, its dramatization in a visual form.

The origins of fantasy lie in the unavoidable conflict between many of our desires, formulated as demands on the environment (especially on people), and the environment's inability or unwillingness to fulfill our desires, where it does not proscribe them altogether. The power of fantasy, then, comes to our rescue by extending or withdrawing the desires beyond what is possible or reasonable, by remarking the past and inventing a future. Fantasy, the 'stuff that dreams are made of,' is the bridge between desire and reality, spanning the chasm between what is asked for and what is granted. It well deserves psychoanalyst Robert Stoller's paean as 'the vehicle of hope, healer of trauma, protector from reality, concealer of truth, fixer of identity, restorer of tranquillity, enemy of fear and sadness, cleanser of the soul.'[2] Hindi films, perhaps more than the cinema of many other countries, are fantasy in this special sense.

The sheer volume of unrelieved fantasy in one film after another is indeed overwhelming, and it is disquieting to reflect that this exclusive preoccupation with magical explanations and fairy-tale solutions for life's problems could be an expression of a deep-seated need in large sections of Indian society. Some may even consider such a thoroughgoing denial of external reality in Indian cinema to be a sign of morbidity, especially since one cannot make the argument that fantasy in films fulfils the need for escapism of those suffering from grinding poverty. In the first place, it is not the poor who constitute the bulk of the Indian film clientele. In the second, one does not know the cinema of any other country which, even in the worst periods of economic deprivation and political uncertainty, dished out such uniformly fantastic fare. Neither German cinema during the economic crisis of the 1920s nor Japanese cinema in the aftermath of the Second World War elevated fantasy to such an overwhelming principle. And if one considers that neorealism even flourished in Italy during the economic chaos following the Allied victory, then one must acknowledge that economic conditions alone cannot explain the fantasia permeating Indian films.

The reason for the ubiquity of fantasy in the Hindi cinema, I suspect, lies in the realm of cultural psychology rather than in the domain of socio-economic conditions. Now, as in other cultures, we too have our film addicts. These are the unfortunate people who are pressed in childhood to view reality in an adult way and now need the fantasy of the film world to fill up the void left by a premature deprivation of magic in early life. Leaving aside this group, no sane Indian believes that Hindi films depict the world realistically, although I must admit I often feel that our willingness to suspend disbelief is relatively greater than in many other cultures. This is not because the thought processes of Indians are fantasy-ridden. The propensity to state received opinion and belief as observation, to look for confirmation of belief rather than be upon to disturbing new knowledge, to generally think in a loose, associative rather than a rigorous and sequential way, is neither Indian, American, Chinese, Japanese, or German, but common to most human beings. However, I would hypothesize, without passing any value judgment, that, relatively speaking, in India the child's world of magic is not as far removed from adult consciousness as it may be in some other cultures. Because of a specific thrust of the culture and congruent child-rearing practices which I have described in detail elsewhere, the Indian ego is flexible enough to regress temporarily to childhood modes without feeling threatened or engulfed.[3] Hindi films seem to provide this regressive haven for a vast number of our people.

If, as I have indicated above, I regard the Indian cinema audience not only as the reader but also as the real author of the text of Hindi films, what is the role played by their ostensible creators—the producers, directors, scriptwriters, music directors, and so on? In my view, their functions are purely instrumental and akin to that of a publisher who chooses, edits, and publishes a particular text from a number of submitted manuscripts. The quest for the comforting sound of busy cash registers at the box office ensures that the filmmakers select and develop a daydream which is not idiosyncratic. They must intuitively appeal to those concerns of the audience which are shared, if they do not, the film's appeal is bound to be disastrously limited. As with pornography, the filmmakers have to create a work which is singular enough to fascinate and excite, and general enough to excite many. Moreover, in their search for the 'hit,' the ten to 15 films out of the roughly 700 produced every year which evoke the most enthusiastic response, the filmmakers repeat and vary the daydreams as they seek to develop them into more and more nourishing substitutes for reality. Under the general rubric of fantasy, which can range all the way from the most primal images in dreams to the rationalized misinterpretations of reality in everyday life, the Hindi film is perhaps closest to the daydream. Indeed, the visual landscape of these films has a strong daydream quality in that it is not completely situated outside reality but is clearly linked to it. As Arjun Appadurai and Carol Breckenridge point out, while the landscape of the popular film contains places, social types, topological features, and situations which are reminiscent of ordinary experience, these elements are transformed or transposed so as to create a subtly fantastic milieu.[4] Even film speech is reminiscent of real speech. Thus the frequently heard admonition in 'Indinglish,' 'Don't *maro filmi dialogues, yaar*,' (Don't spout dialogues from films at me, friend), is often addressed to someone expressing highly inflated sentiments of friendship, love, or hostility which typify exchanges between the characters of Indian cinema.

Like the adult daydream, Hindi film emphasizes the central features of fantasy—the fulfilment of wishes, the humbling of competitors and the destruction of enemies. The stereotyped twists and turns of the film plot ensure the repetition of the very message that makes, for instance, the fairytale so deeply satisfying to children—namely, that the struggle against difficulties in life is unavoidable, but if one faces life's hardships and its many, often unjust impositions with courage and steadfastness, one will eventually emerge victorious.[5] At the conclusion of both films and fairytales, parents are generally happy and proud, the princess is won, and either the villains are ruefully contrite or their battered bodies satisfactorily litter the landscape. Evil in film, too, follows the same course it does in fairy tales; it may be temporarily in ascendance or usurp the hero's legitimate rights, but its failure and defeat are inevitable. Like the temptations of badness for a child who is constantly forced to be good, evil in Hindi cinema is not quite without its attractions of sensual licence and narcissistic pleasure in the unheeding pursuit of the appetites. It is usually the unregenerate villain who gets to savour the pleasures of drinking wine and the companionship, willing or otherwise, of sexy and attractive women.

Another feature common to both Hindi films and fairy tales is the oversimplification of situations and the elimination of detail, unless the detail is absolutely essential. The characters of the film are always typical, never unique, and without the unnerving complexity of real people. The Hero and the Villain, the Heroine and Her Best Friend, the Loving Father and the Cruel Stepmother, are never ambivalent, never the mixed ticket we all are in real life. But then, unlike in novels, the portrayal of characters in film is neither intended to enhance our understanding of the individual complexities of men and women nor to assist our contemplation of the human condition. Their intention is to appeal to the child within us, to arouse quick sympathies and antipathies, and thus encourage the identifications that help us to savour our fantasies more keenly.

When dogmatic rationalists dismiss Hindi films as unrealistic and complain that their plots strain credibility and their characters stretch the limits of the believable, this condescending judgment is usually based on a restricted vision of reality. To limit and reduce the real to that which can be demonstrated as factual is to exclude the domain of the psychologically real—all that is felt to be, enduringly, the actuality of one's inner life. Or, to adapt Bruno Bettelheim's observation on fairytales, Hindi films may be unreal in a rational sense but they are certainly not untrue. Their depiction of the external world may be flawed and their relevance to the external life of the viewer remote; yet, as we shall see, in their focus on the unconsciously perceived fantasy rather than the consciously perceived story, the Hindi film demonstrates a confident and sure-footed grasp of the topography of desire. The stories they tell may be trite and limited in number, with simple, recognizable meanings which on the surface reinforce rather than challenge cultural convention. yet beneath the surface, the fantasies they purvey, though equally repetitious, are not so trite and add surprising twists to the conscious social understanding of various human relationships in the culture.

Having described the relationship between Indian cinema, culture, and psyche is some detail, let me now turn to the cinema audience's internal theatre of love as they watch the images flicker by on the screen. The composite love story I seek to present here is culled largely from a score of the biggest box-office hits of the last 20 years. Since it would be impossible as well as tedious to narrate the plots of all these films, I will take as my illustrative text only one film. Raj Kapoor's *Ram Teri Ganga Maili* (*Rama, Your Ganga Is Polluted*), the top box-office hit for the year 1986. I shall then use examples from other films to amplify and otherwise complete the prototypical love story of Hindi cinema.

Narendra, the hero of the film, is a student of a Calcutta college and the son of a rich, thoroughly corrupt businessman. His father is a close associate of Bhag Choudhary, a villainous politician, whose only daughter, Radha, is romantically interested in our young hero. Narendra, however, is unaware of Radha's feelings for him. He ignores her not-so-subtle advances and generally treats her in a friendly asexual fashion.

Narendra goes on a college trip to Gangotri, the source of the sacred river Ganges, in the Himalayan hills. He has promised to bring his doting grandmother pure Ganges water from the river's very source, since the water is polluted by the time it reaches the sea at Calcutta. He clambers down a mountainside to reach the stream, but the pitcher he has brought with him slips from his hand and rolls down the slope. As Narendra seeks to retrieve the pitcher, he is saved from falling over a cliff by a shouted warning from the heroine of the movie, Ganga. Ganga is a pretty, young girl of the hills, unspoilt and innocent, and frankly expresses her liking for the city boy. Often enough, she takes the initiative in their budding relationship. She leads him by the hand on their excursions through the mountains, barefooted and impervious to the cold while he both stumbles and shivers. During their courtship they sing duets in meadows full of wild flowers and frolic through streams which, of course, make Ganga's thin white sari wet and cling revealingly to her well-formed breasts. Narendra saves Ganga from being raped by one of his college friends, which deepens the girl's feelings for the boy and increases their mutual attachment.

Although Ganga has been promised in marriage to one of her own people, she decides to break the engagement and marry Narendra. The marriage ceremony is preceded by a rousing (and arousing) folk dance and is succeeded by the wedding night. While inside the room, Narendra undresses Ganga with the gravity and devotion of a priest preparing the idol of the goddess for the morning worship, Ganga's brother and her enraged ex-fiancé are engaged outside in a murderous fight which will end in both their deaths.

Narendra goes back to Calcutta, promising to send for Ganga as soon as he has informed the family of his marriage. There he discovers that his grandmother has betrothed him in his absence to Radha, the politician's daughter, a match welcomed by both the families. After many emotional scenes involving the boy and his parents, in the course of which his grandmother suffers a heart attack and eventually dies. Narendra, defying his parent's wishes, sets out for the hills to fetch Ganga. By virtue of the political influence exercised by Choudhary, he is forcibly taken off the bus by the police before he can reach her village in the hills and is brought back to Calcutta.

In the meanwhile, a letter by Narendra's grandmother to her grandson reaches Ganga, from which she learns of the family's plans for Narendra's betrothal; Ganga believes her husband now to be married to another woman. Their wedding night, however, has had consequences and Ganga gives birth to a child. Since in Hindu tradition children belong to the father, Ganga nobly decides to take the infant son to far off Calcutta and hand him over to Narendra. It is now that the perils of Ganga begin. Alighting from the bus at the foot of the hills and looking for the train station from where she can take the train to Calcutta, Ganga is instead guided to a cheap whorehouse. There she is sold to a customer who would rape her but Ganga manages to escape with the baby clutched to her breast. She then approaches an old priest for directions to the station. He, too, turns out to be lecherous. Ganga is saved from his attentions by the timely arrival of the police. Finally put on the train to Calcutta by a kindly police officer—who for a change does not try to rape her—Ganga is kidnapped on the way by a pimp who brings her to a *kotha* in Benares, a brothel whose customers are first entertained by song and dance in the traditional style of the Indian courtesan. Ganga becomes a well-known dancing girl though all the while retaining her mysterious purity, that 'purity of the Ganges which lies in a woman's heart and which makes a man attracted to her, merge into her.'

Ganga is now sold by the owner of the *kotha* to Choudhary who has come to Benares to find a girl to keep him company in his declining years. Choudhary, her husband's future father-in-law, installs the girl in a house in Calcutta and one day brings Narendra's father along with him to show off the girl's charms. He promises to share Ganga with him once the marriage of their children has been solemnized. On the day of the marriage, Ganga is called upon by Choudhary to entertain the wedding guests. As she sings and dances, Narendra recognizes her and without completing the marriage rites rushes to her side. His father and especially Choudhary and his goons try to stop him but Narendra and Ganga are finally united. Together with their infant son, they go away from the corruption of a degraded older generation toward a hopeful new future.

Superficially, *Ram Teri Ganga Maili* is a syrupy tale of the eternally pure woman whose devotion and innocence triumph over the worst efforts of lustful (mostly older) males to enslave and exploit her. As the third ear is deemed essential for listening in the analytic hour, similarly the analyst may need a third eye to break up the cloying surface of the film into less obvious patterns. Unlike Shiva's third eye which destroys all reality, the Freudian one merely cracks reality's stony surface to release its inner shape of fantasy. Like the dreamer who is not only the author, producer, and director of his dream but often plays all the important leads himself, the creator–audience of the film, too, is not limited to existing within the skin of the hero or the heroine but spreads out to cover other characters. The analyst may then reassign different values to the characters of the story than what has been the dreamer's manifest intent. He will, for instance, be mindful that besides experiencing the overt pity aroused by the hapless Ganga, the audience may well be deriving secret pleasure in the sexual villainy as well as surreptitiously partaking of the masochistic delight of her ordeals. Moreover, the third eye also destroys the very identities of the film's characters, replacing them with those of a child's internal family drama. Thus Ganga's screen image, with the infant clutched perpetually to her breast, becomes the fantasized persona of the mother from a particular stage of childhood. The faces of the various villains, on the other hand, coalesce into the visage of the 'bad' aggressive father, forcing the poor mother to submit to his unspeakable desire. It is then with the third eye that we look at Indian men and women as lovers and at some of the situations and spaces of love they project on the screen.

Bearing a strong resemblance to another girl from the hills, Reshma, played by Nargis in Raj Kapoor's first film *Barsaat* four decades ago, Ganga is the latest reincarnation of the heroine who is totally steadfast in her devotion to a hero who is passive, absent, or both. Independent and carefree before being struck by the love-god Kama's flowery arrows, all that love brings her is suffering and humiliation, particularly of the sexual kind. Indeed, her suffering, like that of such legendary heroines as Laila and Sohni, seems almost a punishment for breaking social convention in daring to love freely. Rape, actual or attempted, is of course the strongest expression, the darkest image of the degradation she must undergo for her transgression.

The question why rape is a staple feature of Indian cinema where otherwise even the kiss is taboo, why the sexual humiliation of the woman plays such a significant role in the fantasy of love, is important. That this rape is invariably a fantasy rape, without the violence and trauma of its real-life counterpart, is evident in the manner of its visual representation. Villains, mustachioed or stubble-chinned, roll their eyes and stalk their female prey around locked rooms. With deep-throated growls of gloating, lasciviously muttering a variant of 'Ha! You cannot escape now,' they make sharp lunges to tear off the heroine's clothes and each time come away with one more piece of her apparel. The heroine, on the other hand, retreats in pretty terror, her arms folded across her breasts to protect her dishevelled modesty, pleading all the while to be spared from the fate worse than death. As in the folk theatre presentations of the scene from the *Mahabharata* where Dushasana is trying to undrape Draupadi, what is being enjoyed by the audience is the sado-masochistic fantasy incorporated in the defencelessness and pain of a fear-stricken woman.

Now masochism is usually defined as the seeking of pain for the sake of sexual pleasure, with the qualification that either the seeking or the pleasure, or both, are unconscious rather than conscious. The specific locus of the rape fantasy for men is the later period of childhood which I have elsewhere called the 'second birth,' when the boy's earlier vision of the mother as an overwhelming feminine presence is replaced by her image, and that of woman generally, as a weak, castrated, suffering, and humiliated being. This is less a consequence of the boy's confrontation with female reality in the Indian family setting and more a projection of what would happen to him if he sexually submitted to the father and other elder males. As the boy grows up into a man, this fantasy needs to be repressed more and more, banished into farther and farther reaches of awareness. In the cavernous darkness of the cinema hall, the fantasy may at last surface gingerly and the associated masochistic pleasure be enjoyed vicariously in the pain and subjugation of the woman with whom one secretly identifies.

The effect of the rape scene on the female part of the audience, even if the movie rape is highly stylized and eschews any pretence to reality, is more complex. On one hand the sexual coercion touches some of her deepest fears as a woman. On the other hand, we must note the less conscious presence of a sexual fantasy due to the fact that the raping 'baddies' of Indian cinema are very often older gurus on whom the woman is dependent in some critical way: employers, *zamindars* (landlords), and so on. The would-be rapists in *Ram Teri Ganga Maili*, apart from the anonymous brothel customer, are the priest and the powerful Choudhary, the future father-in-law of Ganga's husband. In many other movies, the face of the father behind the rapist's mask is more clearly visible. Thus in *Karz*, a box-office hit of 1979, the heroine's step-father stages a mock rape of his step-daughter to test the suitability of the hero as her future spouse. Wendy O'Flaherty has linked the power of this particular scene to the ancient myth in which the father-god (Brahma, Prajapati, or Daksha) attempts to rape his own daughter until she is rescued by the hero, Shiva.[7] She points out that this well-known myth is tolerated and viewed positively in Hindu texts which tell of the birth of all animal life from the incestuous union of father and daughter. I would, on the other hand—a case of cultural psychology complementing mythology—trace the woman's allurement in the fantasy of rape by the villainous father-figure to many an Indian woman's adolescence. This is perhaps the most painful period of a girl's life, in which many renunciations are expected of her and where her training as an imminent daughter-in-law who must bring credit to her natal family is painfully stepped up. Psychoanalysis regularly brings up the powerful wish from this period for an intimacy with the father in which the daughter is simultaneously indulged as a little girl and treated as a young woman whose emerging womanhood is both appreciatively recognized and appropriately reacted to. In part, this is a universal fantasy among women, arising from the fact that a father often tends to withdraw from his daughter at the onset of puberty, feeling that he should not longer exhibit physical closeness, doubtless also because of the sexual feelings the daughter arouses in him. The daughter, however, learning to be at home in a woman's body and as yet insecure in her womanly role, may interpret the father's withdrawal as a proof of her feminine unattractiveness. The wished for father-daughter intimacy becomes a major fantasy in India because of the fact that in the Indian family the father's withdrawal from his daughter is quite precipitate once she attains puberty. The daughter is completely given over to the woman's world which chooses precisely this period of inner turmoil to become increasingly harsh. The rape by the father is then the forbidden, sexual aspect of her more encompassing longing for intimacy. The fearful mask worn by the father is a projection of the daughter's own villainous desire which frees her from the guilt for entertaining it.

Narendra, the hero of the movie, is a passive, childlike character, easily daunted by his elders who put obstacles in the path of the lovers' union. He is a pale shadow of the more ubiquitous romantic hero who suffers the despair of separation or disappointment in love with a suprahuman intensity (by which I mean less that of an inconstant god than of the faithful child lover). Such a hero used to be very popular in

Indian films until about 20 years ago. Since in India nothing ever disappears, whether religious cults, political parties, or mythological motifs, the romantic lover too lives on, though at present he is perhaps in the trough rather than at the crest of the wave. For my generation, however, the images of this lover, as played for example by Dilip Kumar in *Devdas* or Guru Dutt in *Pyasa*, remain unforgettable.

The Majnun–lover, as I would like to label this type after the hero of the well-known Islamic romance, has his cultural origins in a confluence of Islamic and Hindu streams. His home is as much in the Indo-Persian *ghazal* (those elegies of unhappy love where the lover bemoans the loss, the inaccessibility, or the turning away of the beloved) as in the lover's laments of separation in Sanskrit and Tamil *viraha* poetry—of which Kalidasa's *Meghaduta* (*The Cloud Messenger*) is perhaps the best-known example.

Elsewhere, I have discussed the psychological origins of the Majnun-lover as part of the imperious yet vulnerable erotic wishes of infancy.[8] His is the wish for a total merger with the woman; his suffering, the wrenching wail of the infant who finds his budding self disintegrating in the mother's absence. What he seeks to rediscover and reclaim in love is what is retrospectively felt to be paradise lost—the postpartum womb of life before 'psychological birth,' before the separation from the mother's anima took place. These wishes are of course part of every man's erotic being and it is only the phallic illusion of modern western man which has tended to deny them legitimacy and reality.

All soul, an inveterate coiner of poetic phrases on the sorrows and sublimity of love, the romantic lover must split off his corporeality and find it a home or, rather, an orphanage. The *kotha*, the traditional-style brothel, is Hindi cinema's favourite abode for the denied and discarded sexual impulses, a home for vile bodies. Sometimes replaced by the shady night club, a more directly licentious import from the West, the *kotha* provides the alcohol as well as the rhythmic music and dance associated with these degraded impulses. Enjoyed mostly by others, by the villain or the hero's friends, for the romantic lover the sexual pleasures of the *kotha* are generally cloaked in a pall of guilt, to be savoured morosely in an alcoholic haze and to the nagging beat of self-recrimination.

The Krishna-lover is the second important hero of Indian films. Distinct from Majnun, the two may, in a particular film, be sequential rather than separate. The Krishna-lover is physically importunate, what

Indian-English will perhaps call the 'eve-teasing' hero, whose initial contact with women verges on that of sexual harassment. His cultural lineage goes back to the episode of the mischievous Krishna hiding the clothes of the *gopis* (cow-herdesses) while they bathe in the pond and his refusal to give them back in spite of the girls' repeated entreaties. From the 1950s Dev Anand movies to those (and especially) of Shammi Kapoor in the 1960s and of Jeetendra today, the Krishna-lover is all over and all around the heroine who is initially annoyed, recalcitrant, and quite unaware of the impact the hero's phallic intrusiveness has on her. The Krishna-lover has the endearing narcissism of the boy on the eve of the Oedipus stage, when the world is felt to be his 'oyster.' He tries to draw the heroine's attention by all possible means—aggressive innuendoes and double entendres, suggestive song and dance routines, bobbing up in the most unexpected places to startle and tease her as she goes about her daily life (Jeetendra is affectionately known as 'jack in the box'). The more the heroine dislikes the lover's incursions, the greater is his excitement. As the hero of the film *Aradhana* remarks, 'Love is fun only when the woman is angry. '

For the Krishna-lover, it is vital that the woman be a sexual innocent and that in his forcing her to become aware of his desire she get in touch with her own. He is phallus incarnate, which distinct elements of the 'flasher' who needs constant reassurance by the woman of his power, intactness, and especially his magical qualities that can transform a cool Amazon into a hot, lusting female. The fantasy is of the phallus—Shammi Kapoor in his films used his whole body as one—humbling the pride of the unapproachable woman, melting her indifference and unconcern into submission and longing. The fantasy is of the spirited androgynous virgin awakened to her sexuality and thereafter reduced to a grovelling being, full of a moral masochism wherein she revels in her 'stickiness' to the hero. Before she does so, however, she may go through a stage of playfulness where she presents the lover a mocking version of himself. Thus in *Junglee*, it is the girl from the hills—the magical fantasy-land of Indian cinema where the normal order of things is reversed—who throws snowballs at the hero, teases him, and sings to him in a good-natured reversal of the man's phallicism, while it is now the hero's turn to be provoked and play the reluctant beloved.

The last 15 years of Indian cinema have been dominated, indeed overwhelmed, by Amitabh Bachchan who has personified a new kind of hero and lover. His phenomenally successful films have spawned a brand new genre which, though strongly influenced by Hollywood action movies such as those of Clint Eastwood, is neither typically western nor traditionally Indian.

The Bachchan hero is the good–bad hero who lives on the margins of his society. His attachments are few but they are strong and silent. Prone to quick violence and to brooding periods of withdrawal, the good–bad hero is a natural law-breaker, yet will not deviate from a strict private code of his own. He is often a part of the underworld but shares neither its sadistic nor its sensual excesses. If cast in the role of a policeman, he often bypasses cumbersome bureaucratic procedures to take the law in his own hands, dealing with criminals by adopting their own ruthless methods. His badness is not shown as intrinsic or immutable but as a reaction to a development deprivation of early childhood, often a mother's loss, absence, or ambivalence toward the hero.

The cultural parallel of the good–bad hero is the myth of Karna in the *Mahabharata*. Kunti, the future mother of the five Pandava brothers, had summoned the Sun when she was a young princess. Though her calling the Sun was a playful whim—she was just trying out a *mantra*—the god insisted on making something more of the invitation. The offspring of the resulting union was Karna. To hide her shame at Karna's illegitimate birth, Kunti abandoned her infant son and cast him adrift on a raft. Karna was saved by a poor charioteer and grew up into a formidable warrior and the supporter of the evil Duryodhana. On the eve of the great battle, Kunti approached Karna and revealed to him that fighting on Duryodhana's side would cause him to commit the sin of fratricide. Karna answered:

It is not that I do not believe the words you have spoken, *Kshatriya* (warrior caste) lady, or deny that for me the gateway to the Law is to carry out your behest. But the irreparable wrong you have done me by casting me out has destroyed the name and fame I could have had. Born a *Kshatriya*, I have yet not received the respect due to a baron. What enemy could have done me greater harm than you have? When there was time to act you did not show your present compassion. And now you have laid orders on me, the son to whom you denied the sacraments. You have never acted in my interest like a mother, and now, here you are, enlightening me solely in your own interest.[9]

Karna, though, finally promised his mother that on the battlefield he would spare all her sons except Arjuna—the mother's favourite.

The good–bad Bachchan hero is both a product of and a response to the pressures and forces of development and modernization taking place in Indian society today and which have accelerated during the last two decades. He thus reflects the psychological changes in a vast number of people who are located in a halfway house—in the transitional sector—which lies between a minuscule (yet economically and politically powerful) modern and the numerically preponderant traditional sectors of Indian society. Indeed, it is this transitional sector from which the Bachchan movies draw the bulk of their viewers.

The individual features of the good–bad hero which I have sketched above can be directly correlated with the major psychological difficulties experienced by the transitional sector during the course of modernization. Take, for instance, the effects of overcrowding and the high population density in urban conglomerations, especially in slum and shanty towns. Here, the lack of established cultural norms and the need to deal with relative strangers whose behavioural cues cannot be easily assessed compel the individual to be on constant guard and in a state of permanent psychic mobilization. A heightened nervous arousal, making for a reduced control over one's aggression, in order to ward off potential encroachments, is one consequence *and* a characteristic of the good–bad hero.

Then there is bureaucratic complexity with its dehumanization which seems to be an inevitable corollary of economic development. The cumulative effect of the daily blows to feelings of self-worth, received in a succession of cold and impersonal bureaucratic encounters, so far removed from the familiarity and predictability of relationships in the rural society, gives rise to fantasies of either complete withdrawal or of avenging slights and following the dictates of one's personal interests, even if this involves the taking of the law into one's own hands. These, too, form a part of our hero's persona.

Furthermore, the erosion of traditional roles and skills in the transitional sector can destroy the self-respect of those who are now suddenly confronted with a loss of earning power and social status. For the families of the affected, especially the children, there may be a collapse of confidence in the stability of the established world. Doubts surface whether hard work and careful planning can guarantee future rewards of security. The future itself begins to be discounted to the present.[10] The Bachchan hero, neither a settled family man nor belonging to any recognized community of craftsmen, farmers, etc., incorporates the transitional man's collective dream of success without hard work and of life lived primarily, and precariously, in the here-and-now.

The last feature of the portrait is the core sadness of the good–bad hero. On the macro level, this may be traced back to the effects of the population movements that take place during the process of economic development. The separation of families, the loss of familiar village neighbourhoods and ecological niches, can overwhelm many with feelings of bereavement. Sometimes concretized in the theme of separation from the mother, these feelings of loss and mourning are mirrored in the Bachchan hero and are a cause of his characteristic depressive detachment, in which the viewers, too, can recognize a part of themselves.

As a lover, the good–bad hero is predictably neither overly emotional like Majnun nor boyishly phallic like the Krishna lover. A man of controlled passion, somewhat withdrawn, he subscribes to the well-known lines of the Urdu poet Faiz that 'Our world knows other torments than of love and other happinesses than a fond embrace.' The initial meeting of the hero and heroine in *Deewar*, Bachchan's first big hit and widely imitated thereafter, conveys the essential flavour of this hero as a lover. The setting is a restaurant-night club and Bachchan is sitting broodingly at the bar. Anita, played by Parveen Babi, is a dancer—the whore with a golden heart—who comes and sits next to him. She offers him a light for his cigarette and tells him that he is the most handsome man in the bar. Bachchan, who must shortly set out for a fateful meeting with the villain, indifferently accepts her proffered homage as his due while he ignores her sexually provocative approach altogether. Indeed, this narcissistically withdrawn lover's relationships with his family members and even his best friend are more emotionally charged than with any woman who is his potential erotic partner. Little wonder that Shashi Kapoor, who played the hero's brother or best friend in many movies, came to be popularly known as Amitabh Bachchan's favourite heroine!

Afraid of the responsibility and effort involved in active wooing, of passivity and dependency upon a woman—urges from the earliest period of life which love brings to the fore and intensifies—the withdrawn hero would rather be admired than loved. It is enough for him to know that the woman is solely devoted to him while he can enjoy the position of deciding whether to take her or leave her. The fantasy here seems of revenge on the woman for a mother who either preferred someone else—in *Deewar*, it is the brother—or only gave the child conditional love and less than constant admiration.

The new genre of films, coexisting with the older ones, has also given birth to a new kind of heroine, similar in some respects to what Wolfenstein and Leites described as the masculine–feminine girl of the

American movies of the 1940s and 1950s.[11] Lacking the innocent androgyny of Krishna's playmate, she does not have the sari-wrapped femininity (much of the time she is clad in jeans anyway!) of Majnun's beloved either. Like the many interchangeable heroines of Bachchan movies, she is more a junior comrade to the hero than his romantic and erotic counterpart.

Speaking a man's language, not easily shocked, she is the kind of woman with whom the new hero can feel at ease. She is not an alien creature of feminine whims, sensitivities and susceptibilities, with which a man feels uncomfortable and which he feels forced to understand. Casual and knowing, the dull wholesomeness of the sister spiced a little with the provocative coquetry of the vamp, she makes few demands on the hero and can blend into the background whenever he has more important matters to attend to. Yet she is not completely unfeminine, not a mere mask for the homosexual temptation to which many men living in the crowded slums of big cities and away from their women-folk are undoubtedly subject. She exemplifies the low place of heterosexual love in the life of the transitional man, whose fantasies are absorbed more by visions of violence than of love, more with the redressal of narcissistic injury and rage than with the romantic longing for completion—a gift solely in the power of a woman to bestow.

Having viewed some dreams in Indian popular cinema with the enthusiast's happy eye but with the analyst's sober perspective, let me reiterate in conclusion that *oneiros*—dream, fantasy—between the sexes and within the family, does not coincide with the cultural propositions on these relationships. In essence, *oneiros* consists of what seeps out of the crevices in the cultural floor. Given secret shape in narrative, *oneiros* conveys to us a particular culture's versions of what Joyce McDougall calls the Impossible and the Forbidden,[12] the unlit stages of desire where so much of our inner theatre takes place.

IV

Religion and Psyche

12

Ramakrishna and the Mystical Experience

Of the many ways of inner transformation known to man, the mystical path is perhaps one of the most ancient, universal, and highly regarded, even when its practitioners have often lived in an uneasy truce, if not in frank antagonism, with the established religions of their societies.

The mystical path may be one but has many forks. Scholars of religion have distinguished them in various ways. Nathan Söderblom talks of 'mysticism of the infinite,' an elevation of awareness where the unifying experience with the suprahuman eliminates perception of the concrete and abstract elements from the sensate world. He contrasts this to 'mysticism of personal life' where the experience is not rooted in ecstatic rapture, but in a meeting with God in the midst of life's problems and struggles, a meeting experienced at a deep level of faith within normal waking consciousness.[1] Martin Buber and John of the Cross would be two exemplars of Söderblom's mysticism of personal life. Of course, such distinctions are more sign-posts rather than sharp dividers since shades of both 'infinity' and 'personality' will exist in every mystic.

Mysticism of the 'infinite', my own focus of interest, has also been variously categorized—nature mysticism, theistic mysticism, and monistic or soul mysticism—although it is doubtful whether the categories are any different at the level of inner experience. Yet another distinction is the one made by William James between sporadic and cultivated mysticism, which corresponds to Arthur Deikman's separation between untrained–sensate and trained–sensate mystical experiences.[2] Ramakrishna was of course, a 'career' mystic, and though his initial forays into mysticism may have been sporadic and untrained, the latter half of his life was marked by regular and frequent mystical experiences of the cultivated, trained–sensate kind.

A mystical experience may be mild, such as a contact with a 'sense of Beyond' among completely normal people, or it may be extreme with ecstasies and visions. We know from survey studies that more or less mild mystical experiences are widespread, even in countries without an active mystical tradition and where the intellectual climate is not particularly conducive to mystical thought. In the United States, for instance, 35 per cent of the respondents in a large sample study by Andrew Greeley in 1975 reported having mystical experiences, a finding which has been since confirmed by other, comparable studies. It is significant that those who had such experiences were more educated than the national average and in 'a state of psychological well-being' unmarked by any obvious neurotic difficulties.[3]

My focus here, though, is mysticism of the extreme variety and especially ecstatic mysticism. Most dramatically manifested in visions and trances, psychologically it is characterized by an expansion of the inner world, by a consciousness suffusing the whole of the body from inside. The expanding consciousness also fills the external world which appears to be pervaded by a oneness of existence.

The overwhelming feeling is of the object of consciousness, the world, having at last become transparent and more real than its conventional reality. All of this is accompanied by heightened intrapsychic and bodily sensations, culminating in a great feeling of pleasure which eliminates or absorbs all other experience.[4] Variously called cosmic consciousness, peak experience (Maslow), *mahabhava*, ecstatic mystical experience seems to differ from one where consciousness and its object, the world, become one and subject–object differentiations vanish. The *samadhi* of the Hindus, *satori* of Zen masters, and *fana* of the Sufis are some of the terms for this particular mystical experience. Again these distinctions are not either/or categories, the former often leading to the latter, as in the case of Ramakrishna, though not all mystics need to have spanned the whole gamut of mystical experience, each with its specific degree of ineffability and noesis—the conviction of knowing.

We must also remember that Ramakrishna was an heir to the Hindu mystical tradition which in spite of many similarities to the mysticism of other religious faiths, also has its own unique context. First, mysticism is the mainstream of Hindu religiosity, and thus Hindu mystics are generally without the restraints of their counterparts in monotheistic religious traditions such as Judaism, Islam, and to a lesser extent, Christianity, where mystical experiences and insights must generally be interpreted against a given dogmatic theology.[5] A Hindu mystic is thus normally quite uninhibited in expressing his views and does not have to be on his guard lest these views run counter to the officially interpreted orthodoxy. Second, God as conceived in the monotheistic religions does not have the same significance in two major schools of Hindu mysticism. Upanishadic mysticism, for instance, is a quest for spiritual illumination wherein a person's deepest essence is discovered to be identical with the common source of all other animate and inanimate beings. Yogic mysticism strives to realize the immortality of the human soul outside time, space, and matter. Through intensive introspection and practice of disciplines that lead to mastery of senses and mental processes, it seeks to realize the experience of one's 'soul' as an unconditioned, eternal being, distinct from the 'illusory' consciousness of the conditioned being. In both Upanishadic and Yogic mysticism there is no trace of love of or yearning for communion with God, which is considered the highest manifestation of the mystical mood in both Christian and Islamic traditions and without which no *unio mystica* is conceivable. In these two Hindu schools, mystical liberation is achieved entirely through the mystic's own efforts and without the intervention of divine grace. It is only in *bhakti* or devotional mysticism— Ramakrishna's preferred form—where love for the Deity creeps in, where the mystic's soul or 'self' is finally united with God (or Goddess) in an ecstatic surrender, that Hindu mysticism exhibits a strong family resemblance to the mysticism of monotheistic faiths.

Let me state at the outset that given the theoretical uncertainties in contemporary psychoanalysis which threaten its basic paradigm, the earlier equation of the mystical state with a devalued, if not pathological, regression comparable to a psychotic episode is ripe for radical revision. Many analysts interested in the phenomenon would now agree that in spite of superficial resemblances, the mystical retreat is neither as complete nor as compelling and obligatory as psychotic regression. Moreover, in contrast to the psychotic, the mystic's ability to maintain affectionate ties remains unimpaired when it does not actually get enhanced. Given the analyst's commitment to Freud's dictum that the capacity 'to love and work' is perhaps the best outer criterium for mental health, then the mystic's performance on both counts is impressive—that is, if one can succeed in emancipating one's self from a circumscription of the notions of love and work dictated by convention. In short, the full force of the current flowing through the psyche that leads to short circuit in the psychotic may, and indeed does, illuminate the mystic.

Some of the more recent work in psychoanalysis recognizes that mystical states lead to more rather than less integration of the person.[6] The mystics insight into the workings of his or her self is more rather than less acute. Although consciousness during the mystical trance may be characterized by 'de-differentiation' (to use Anton Ehrenzweig's concept),[7] that is, by the suspension of many kinds of boundaries and distinctions in both the inner and outer worlds, its final outcome is often an increase in the mystic's ability to make ever-finer perceptual differentiations. In other words, the point is not the chaotic nature of the mystical experience, if it is indeed chaotic, but the mystic's ability to create supreme *order* out of the apparent chaos. In fact, what I would like to do here is address the question Romain Rolland, in writing of Ramakrishna's initial trances, posed for 'physicians both of the body and of the mind,' namely, 'There is no difficulty in proving the apparent destruction of his whole mental structure, and the disintegration of its elements. But how were they reassembled into a synthetic entity of the highest order?'[8] To put it differently, how does the mystic become master of his madness and of his reason alike whereas the schizophrenic remains their slave?

The timing of my attempt to formulate some kind of answers to these questions is not inopportune. Today, psychoanalysis is in a relatively better position of *adequatio* (adequateness) in relation to mystical phenomena as well as other states of altered consciousness, such as the possession trance. The *adequatio* principle, of course, states that the same phenomenon may hold entirely different sets of meaning for different observers.[9] To a dog, a book belongs to a class of object which can be played with but not eaten. To the illiterate, it may be just a book, ink markings on paper he cannot decipher. To the average educated adult, the book is an impenetrable scientific tome. To the physicist, the volume is a brilliant treatise on relativity which makes him question some of the ways he looks at the universe. In each case the level of meaning is a function of the *adequatio* of the observer. As far as mysticism is concerned, psychoanalysts today are neither dogs nor even illiterates but are, perhaps, just moving beyond the stage of the average educated adult.

The increase in the level of analytical *adequatio* has not come about because of any analyst's personal experience of training in the mystical disciplines (as far as I know). In part, this higher *adequatio* is due to the increased availability of analytically relevant information which is no longer limited to the writings or biographical and autobiographical accounts of a few western mystics such as Teresa of Avila and John of the Cross. In the last 15 years, we have had access to psychodynamically informed interviews with members of mystical cults who have travelled varied distances on the mystical path and have experienced various states of altered consciousness, including the ecstatic trance.[10] In addition, we have at least two detailed case histories of intensive psychoanalytic therapy with patients who had both mystical proclivities and trance experiences.[11]

More than the availability of additional information, the greater *adequatio* of psychoanalysis in relation to mysticism stems from the work of many writers—Erik Erikson, Donald Winnicott, Wilfred Bion, and Jacques Lacan come immediately to my mind—who, in spite of their very different theoretical concerns, pursued a common antireductionistic agenda. The cumulative effect of their writings has been to allow the adoption of what Winnicott, in talking of transitional phenomena, called 'a particular quality in attitude', with which I believe mystical states should also be observed. In other words, my own enhanced feeling of *adequatio* reflects the presence of an unstated project in contemporary psychoanalysis in which the copresence of different orders of experience is tolerated and no attempts are undertaken to explain one in terms of the other without reciprocity. As we shall see later, in their separate efforts to develop a phenomenology of creative experiencing, Winnicott, Lacan, and Bion are directly relevant for a reevaluation and reinterpretation of mystical phenomena.[12] Of the three, whereas Winnicott was more the poet, Lacan and Bion, in their explicit concern with questions of ultimate reality, its evolution and reflection in psychic life, may fairly be described as the mystics of psychoanalysis. (As someone who spent his childhood in India, it is quite appropriate that Bion is radically sincere in his approach to 'O', his symbol for ultimate reality, whereas Lacan, I like to think, as befitting a Frenchman talking of the Real, is more an ironic mystic.)

The psychoanalytic understanding of any phenomenon begins with the narrative, with the echoes and reverberations of individual history. The individual I have selected for my own explorations is the 19th-century Bengali mystic Sri Ramakrishna. Together with Ramana Maharishi, Ramakrishna is widely regarded as the preeminent figure of Hindu mysticism of the last 300 years, whatever preeminence may mean in the mystical context. He is a particularly apt choice for a psychoanalytic study of ecstatic mysticism since Freud's observations on the mystical experience, on what he called the 'oceanic feeling', an omnibus label for all forms of extreme mystical experience, were indirectly occasioned by Ramakrishna's ecstasies.

It was the biography of Ramakrishna which Romain Rolland was working on at the time when he wrote of Freud in 1927, saying the though he found Freud's analysis of religion (in *The Future of an Illusion*) just, he would ideally have liked Freud to 'make an analysis of spontaneous religious feelings, or more exactly, religious sensations which are entirely different from religion proper and much more enduring.'[13] Rolland went to call this sensation oceanic, without perceptible limits, and mentioned two Indians who had such feelings and 'who have manifested a genius for thought and action powerfully regenerative for their country and for the world.'[14] Rolland added that he himself had all his life found the oceanic feeling to be a source of vital revival. Freud's response to Rolland, his analysis of the 'oceanic feeling,' was then spelled out in *Civilization and its Discontents*. It is highly probable that the term 'oceanic feeling' itself is taken from Ramakrishna's imagery to describe the ineffable. For instance, one of Ramakrishna's oft-repeated metaphors is of the salt doll which went to measure the depth of the ocean: 'As it entered the ocean it melted. Then who is there to come back and say how deep is the ocean?'[15]

Of course, ocean as a symbol for boundless oneness and unity in which multiplicities dissolve and opposites fuse not only goes back to the Upanishads in the Hindu tradition, but is one of the preferred metaphors of devotional mystics for the melting of ego boundaries in the Buddhist, Christian and Muslim traditions as well.[16] Christian mystics, for instance, have been greatly fond of the metaphor. 'I live in the ocean of God as a fish in the sea.'

Freud's response to Ramakrishna, as generally to 'Mother India,' was of unease. Although of some professional interest, Ramakrishna's florid ecstasies were as distant, if not distasteful, to his sensibility as the jumbled vision of flesh, the labyrinth flux of the animal, human, and divine in Indian art. In his acknowledgement of Rolland's book about Ramakrishna, Freud writes, 'I shall now try with your guidance to penetrate into the Indian jungle from which until now an uncertain blending of Hellenic love of proportion, Jewish sobriety, and Philistine timidity have kept me away. I really ought to have tackled it earlier, for the plants of this soil shouldn't be alien to me; I have dug to certain depths for their roots. But it isn't easy to pass beyond the limits of one's nature.'[17]

We are, of course, fortunate that the last four years of Ramakrishna's life, from 1882 to 1886, were recorded with minute fidelity by a disciple, Mahendranath Gupta, or M as he called himself with modest self-effacement.[18] In the cases of most mystics throughout history, we have either had to rely on doctrinal writing that is formal and impersonal, or on autobiographical accounts from which intimate detail, considered trifling from transcendental heights, has been excised. M, on the other hand, with the obsessive fidelity of a Bengali Boswell, has left an enormously detailed chronicle of the daily life and conversations of Ramakrishna—his uninhibited breaking out in song and dance, his frequent and repeated ecstasies, his metaphysical discourses full of wisdom and penetrating insight, his parables, jokes, views, anxieties, and pleasures, the times he slept and ate and what he ate—which is rare in hagiographical literature. Let me then begin with the outer scaffolding of the story, a brief narration of events of Ramakrishna's early life. And though we can never know what *really* happened in his or anyone else's infancy and childhood, the former forever beyond the reach of memory, I have no hesitation in extending a qualified belief to Ramakrishna's own version of his life story. Yet, of course, it is not solely his version. As a reteller of his tale, I cannot help but also bring to bear a psychoanalytic sensibility in the choice of events I emphasize and others that I must have underplayed. The biographies by his direct disciples, on the other hand, are shaped by the traditional Hindu religious idiom, while the narration by Romain Rolland is moulded by his more universalistic, spiritual concerns, in the sense of what Adlous Huxley called the 'perennial philosophy.'

Ramakrishna was born in 1836 in a Brahmin family in the village of Kamarpukur in Bengal. The parents were pious and very poor, but what I find exceptional about them in the context of 19th-century village India is their ages at the time of Ramakrishna's birth. At a time when the average longevity was less than 30 years, maternal death during childbirth fairly common, and the sexually reproductive years of the woman over by her early 30s, Ramakrishna's father was 61 and his mother 45 years old when he was born. In the family there was a brother 31 years older, a sister 27 years older, and another brother 11 years older. Yet another sister was born when Gadhadhar, that was his given name, was four years old.

Ramakrishna later remembered his mother Chandra as a simple soul without a trace of worldliness who could not even count money. She said whatever came to her mind, without obfuscation or concealment, and people even called her a 'simpleton.' Devoted to her youngest son, the fruit of old loins, she was nevertheless, as elderly parents often tend to be, inordinately anxious about any harm befalling him when he was not within her ken. A curious and lively child, intent on exploring the world, Ramakrishna did not exactly help in allaying his mother's anxieties. She sought to master these by daily prayers to the family deity wherein she besought the continued welfare of her little boy. Perhaps Ramakrishna's later anxiousness whenever he was physically incapacitated, his almost hypochondriacal concerns at such times, can be directly traced to the elderly mother's anxieties about her youngest son.

The incident given as an example of the boy's wilfulness, which sometimes ignored the conventional rules of conduct, concerns his hiding behind a tree and peeping out at women while they washed clothes and bathed at the village tank. One of the women complained to Chandra who then admonished the boy that all women were the same as his mother. Shaming them was shaming her, insulting their honour was insulting hers. We are told that the mortified boy never again repeated his behaviour. To us post-Freudians, the incident embodies a child's natural sexual curiosity which the mother dampens by associating it with incestuous anxiety. Interestingly, in later life, Ramakrishna would use a mythological version of this personal experience, wherein the incestuous urgings and fears are much more explicit, to explain a part of his attitude toward women. One day, during his childhood, the god Ganesha saw a cat which, as some boys are apt to do, he proceeded to torture in various ways till the cat finally made its escape. When Ganesha came back home he saw to his surprise the bruises and marks of torture on his mother's, the goddess Parvati's body. The mother revealed to her son that all living beings in female form were part of her and whatever he did to any female he did unto his mother. On reaching marriageable age, Ganesha, lest he marry his mother, decided to remain a celibate forever. 'My attitude to women is the same,' was Ramakrishna's final comment.[19]

Khudiram, Ramakrishna's father, was a gentle man who is reported to have never scolded his son. He took a quiet pride in the boy's evident intelligence and phenomenal memory, which were further displayed to advantage when he started attending the village school at the age of five. However, though good at school (but bad at arithmetic), what the boy most enjoyed was painting pictures and spending time with the village potters learning how to make clay images of gods and goddesses. The artistic streak in Ramakrishna was strongly developed, and it seems appropriate that his first ecstasy was evoked by the welling up of aesthetic emotion; an episode of 'nature' mysticism, it was the consequence of an aesthetically transcendent feeling: 'I was following a narrow path between the rice fields. I raised my eyes to the sky as I munched my rice. I saw a great black cloud spreading rapidly until it covered the heavens. Suddenly at the edge of the cloud a flight of snow white cranes passed over my head. The contrast was so beautiful that my spirit wandered far away. I lost consciousness and fell to the ground. The puffed rice was scattered. Somebody picked me up and carried me home in his arms. An excess of joy and emotion overcame me. . . . This was the first time that I was seized with ecstasy.'[20]

Ramakrishna's father, who had been ill for awhile, died when the boy was around eight years of age. The effect of the father's death was to make Ramakrishna withdrawn and fond of solitude. His attendance at school became fitful. He drew closer to his mother and spent much time in helping her with her household duties and her daily prayers to the gods. He became very fond of listening to discourses on spiritual matters and spent hours at a pilgrimage house where wandering ascetics found a bed for a night or two before they resumed their wanderings. The latter activity alarmed his mother who feared that her son might decide to leave home and embrace the renunciant's life.

There were other fainting spells, as on the way to the temple of a goddess or when acting the part of Shiva in a play he lost all external consciousness. He later attributed the states to spiritual stirrings although his family suspected a physical malady and refrained from forcing him to go to school which by now he quite disliked.

The gradually deteriorating condition of the family after Khudiram's death worsened with the marriage of Ramakrishna's second brother. With the advent of the new daughter-in-law, quarrels and bickerings in the household increased markedly, a situation which the family's worsening economic circumstances, driving it to the edge of subsistence, did not help improve. The daily clamour and strife, I imagine, perhaps added its own impetus in pushing the sensitive and artistic boy more and more away from the distasteful discord of everyday reality and toward transcendental, spiritual matters and religious life. The latter too coursed through the village, as it does to great extent even today in rural India, in a powerful stream. There were the many rituals in which everyday life was embedded, frequent recitals from the *Puranas*, and the religious plays and festivals in which Ramakrishna participated by singing and dancing with fervid abandon. And, above all, there were the sudden inward, abstracted states, brought on at the oddest of times by outer stimuli such as listening to a song in praise of a god or to snatches of devotional music.

The young daughter-in-law died in childbirth when Ramakrishna was 13 years old; and the burden of running the household once again fell on the aging shoulders of Ramakrishna's mother. To help alleviate the poverty, his eldest brother left for Calcutta to run a small Sanskrit school. His position as the head of the family now devolved on Ramakr ishna's second brother who was temperamentally disinclined to take over responsibilities for his siblings and was in any case much too busy scrounging around for work.

Thus at the beginning of adolescence, Ramakrishna was left to his own devices, without the paternal guiding voice of his father or eldest brother. School became even more occasional. When he was not an enthusiastic participant in the village's religious life, he was at home with his mother, helping her with household tasks and sharing with her the rhythm of her woman's days. The village women who dropped in on his mother for a visit during the day seem to have adopted him as one of their own. They would ask him to sing- -he had a very sweet singing voice—or to tell stories from the *Puranas*, of which he had an enormous stock. He performed scenes from popular plays for their amusement, playing all the parts himself. He listened to their secrets and woes and would attempt to lift the spirits of a dejected woman by acting out a rustic farce.

He loved putting on women's clothes and ornaments. Dressed thus, with a pitcher under his arm to fetch water from the tank like other village women, he would pass in front of the men and felt proud that no one suspected he was not a woman. Once, disguised as a poor weaver girl, he spent a whole evening in the closely guarded women's quarters of the village shopkeeper's house taking part in their conversation, without being discovered. In his mature years, talking to his disciples, there was a certain wry pride with which he related, and occasionally enacted to their surprised delight, incidents from his youth which showed his ability to mimic women's gestures and movements to perfection.

A fantasy from this period has Ramakrishna imagining that were he to be born again he would become a beautiful child widow with long black hair who would not know anyone else except Lord Krishna as a husband. The girl widow would live in a hut with an elderly woman as a guardian, a spinning wheel, and a cow which she would milk herself. During the day, after finishing household work, she would spin yarn, sing songs about Krishna, and after dusk ardently weep for the god, longing to feed him sweets made from the cow's milk. Krishna would come in secret, be fed by her and go away, his daily visits taking place without the knowledge of others.[21]

In the meantime, Ramakrishna's eldest brother Ramkumar was doing well in Calcutta, running his small school and performing religious services for some rich families. He called the 17-year-old Ramakrishna over to the city to assist him in his priestly duties. Soon after, a new opportunity opened up when a rich woman built and consecrated a temple to the goddess Kali outside Calcutta and employed Ramlcumar as its full-time priest. Ramkumar, who had been ailing for some time, found the task arduous and handed over his duties to Ramakrishna, the younger brother. He died a year later.

Ramkumar's death was to have a profound effect on Ramakrishna. Thirty-one years older, he had looked after Ramakrishna like a father after Khudiram's death. 'Who can say,' Ramakrishna's disciple-biographer asks, 'how far his brother's death contributed to the kindling up of the fire of renunciation in the Master's pure mind, by producing in him a firm conviction about the transitoriness of the world?'[22] In any case his behaviour changed markedly as he became more and more engrossed in the worship of the Mother Goddess. As her priest he had to wake her up early in the morning, bathe and dress her, make garlands of flowers for her adornment. At nine he had to perform her worship, offer her food, and escort her to her silver bed at noon where she rested for the afternoon. Then came the evening worship. For Ramakrishna, these were no longer duties but heartfelt services. He became so absorbed in each one of them that he had to be reminded when it was time to go on to the next ritual.

After the closing of temple at midday and midnight, Ramakrishna shunned all company and disconsolately roamed around in the jungle at the edge of which the temple was located. All he yearned for with all his soul, he was to later tell us, was a vision, the personal *darshan* of the Mother. The spiritual thirst, the clinician would observe, was embedded in all the signs of a full-fledged depression. There was a great restlessness of the body, sleepless nights, loss of appetite in which eating was reduced to the bare minimum, eyes that filled up often and suddenly with tears. The nephew who looked after him became alarmed for his sanity when at night he saw Ramakrishna sitting under a tree naked, having flung off his clothes and even the sacred thread of a Brahmin, or, when he saw him put the leavings from leaf plates from which beggars had eaten to his mouth and to his head.

But now, as we come to a culmination of his 'dark night of the soul,' we need Ramakrishna's own words. 'There was then an intolerable anguish in my heart because I could not have Her vision. Just as a man wrings a towel forcibly to squeeze out all the water from it, I felt as if somebody caught hold of my heart and mind and was wringing them likewise. Greatly afflicted by the thought that I might not have Mother's vision, I was in great agony. I thought that there was no use in living such a life. My eyes suddenly fell upon the sword that was in the Mother's temple. I made up my mind to put an end to my life with it that very moment. Like one mad, I ran and caught hold of it, when suddenly I had the wonderful vision of the Mother, and fell down unconscious. I did not know what happened then in the external world—how that day and the next slipped away. But in my heart of hearts, there was flowing a current of intense bliss, never experienced before. . . . It was as if the house, doors, temples, and all other things vanished altogether; as if there was nothing anywhere! And what I saw was a boundless infinite conscious sea of light! However far and in whatever direction I looked, I found a continuous succession of effulgent waves coming forward, raging and storming from all sides with great speed. Very soon they fell on me and made me sink to the abysmal depths of infirmity.'[23]

Those familiar with mystical literature will recognize many elements in Ramakrishna's vision which are known to us from similar descriptions fiom all over the world, especially the feeling of being flooded by light. In the still controversial studies of near-death experiences, 'seeing the light' and 'entering the light' are said to be the deepest and most positive parts of that particular experience. The incident has not only universal but also cultural aspects. It is a very Hindu story of a man forcing the Goddess to appear by threatening to decapitate himself. This is an old theme, found both in religious and secular literature, for instance in the well-known story which has been so brilliantly retold for western readers by Thomas Mann in his *The Transposed Heads*.

Unlike similar accounts of the first vision in the lives of most mystics, this particular vision, to which we will come back later and to which all his boyhood experiences seem like forerunners, was not suf-

icient to take him out of the 'valley of the shadow of death.' Its after-
taste but whetted an appetite for repeated blissful salvings. Even for the
pious visitors to the temple, accustomed to a wide range in manifestation of religious fervour, Ramakrishna's behaviour appeared bizarre. He
would decorate his own person with the flowers and sandalwood paste
brought for the worship of the goddess. He would feel the statue of the
goddess breathing, try to feed her stony mouth, and carry on playful
conversations as to who, the goddess or her priest, should eat first. Any
diminution in the sense of her presence made him throw himself and
roll violently on the ground, filling the temple with loud wailings at her
absence. At such times his breath would almost stop, and he appeared
to struggle for his very life. When he again received a vision of the goddess, he would beam with joy and become a different person altogether.
The consensus of his employers and others was that he had become in-
sane. Romain Rolland calls this a necessary period of hallucination, and
even Ramakrishna referred to it as a passing phase of *unmada* (insanity), leaving it unambiguous—something he was not wont to do in
respect of the visions in his later life—that the 'madness' was less
divine intoxication than human disintegration, however necessary it
may have been as a prelude to the former. Later in life, he would
wonder at some of his behaviour during this phase—worshipping his
own phallus as that of Shiva, being seized by ecstatic visions while he
defecated, and so on.

The prescribed medical treatment for 'insanity' did not have the
desired effect. Finally, he was taken to his village home where his wor-
ried mother had him ministered to by both an exorcist and an Ayurvedic
doctor. Slowly, he regained his normal state of health. To safeguard the
apparent gains the family arranged his marriage, a step, which I know
from professional experience, is even today considered as the best an-
tidote to threatened or actual psychic breakdown. Of course, as far as
Ramakrishna was concerned, there was never any question of the marriage being consummated. From the very beginning, in relation to his
girl bride, he saw himself either as a woman or, in his ecstatic state, as
a child. In the former case, the husband and wife were both girlfriends
(*sakhis*) of the Mother Goddess while, in the latter, the wife was envisioned as the Goddess herself.

At the age of 24, Ramakrishna, now accompanied by his wife,
returned to Calcutta to resume his priestly duties at the Kali temple.
There was a relapse in his condition, though in an attenuated form.
Whereas his initial visions had been untutored and spontaneous, intiated

by the passionate intensity of his longing for *darshan* of the Goddess, during the next eight years he systematically followed the prescribed practices laid down by the different schools of Hindu mysticism. The disciplines were undertaken under the guidance of different gurus who were amazed at his natural facility and speed in reaching the goal of *samadhi*, a capability they themselves had acquired only after decades of strenuous effort.

First, there were the esoteric meditations of Tantra, fierce and fearful, under the tutelage of a female guru, Brahmani Bhairavi. This was followed by the nondualistic way of Vedanta, of concentration and contemplation techniques which seek to discriminate the Real from the Non-Real, a discipline without the need for any divinity or belief in God, till in the attainment of the *samadhi* all distinctions between I and the Other vanish. Then there were the various ways of Vaishnava mysticism, full of love and devotion for Rama or Krishna, the incarnations of Vishnu, and of Shakta mysticism where the supreme deity is Shakti the primordial energy and the great Mother Goddess. All of these, the Vaishnava and Shakta says, are essentially affective, and to which he felt personally most attuned. Whatever the discipline, his mystical genius was soon recognized by laymen and experts alike. Disciples gathered. Pandits—the theologically learned—came to visit and to partake of his clear insight into the whole gamut of Hindu metaphysics, a product of lived experience rather than scriptural proficiency; in any conventional sense, he was more or less illiterate. Ramakrishna would convey this experience simply yet strikingly through devotional songs, Puranic myths, analogies, metaphors, and parables fashioned out of the concrete details of the daily life of his listeners. Most of all, they were attracted by his riveting presence, even when he absented himself in ecstatic trances many times a day, with a few lasting for several days.

The *samadhi*s did not now come unbidden but when his constantly receptive state crossed a certain threshold either in song or abandoned dance, in contemplation of a natural phenomena or absorption in the image of a divinity. He had become both a great teacher and a great mystic without losing his childlike innocence and spontaneity, which extended well into his final days. At the end of his life, dying of throat cancer, his disciples pleaded with him to ask the Mother Goddess for an easing of his disease so that he could eat some solid food rather than continue to subsist on a little barely water which had been his only nourishment for six months. Ramakrishna reluctantly agreed. On the disciples' inquiry as to the fate of their request, Ramakrishna answered

'I said to the Mother, "I canot eat anything on account of this (showing the sore in his throat). Please do something that I can eat a little." But the Mother said, "Why? You are eating through all these mouths (showing all of you)." I could speak no more for shame.'[24]

In my attempt to understand the meaning of Ramakrishna's inner states, let me begin with Ramakrishna's own version of his experience. Anthropologically speaking, I shall start with the 'native's point of view' on the phenomenology of mystical states.

Although Ramakrishna had successfully practised the 'higher' Vedantic disciplines of monotheistic, soul-mysticism his own personal preference was for devotional, theistic mysticism of the Vaishnava and Shakta varieties. Ultimately, of course, both roads lead to the same destination. The impersonal soul of the Vedantic seer and the God or Mother Goddess—the primordial energy—of the devotee are identical, like fire and its power to burn. At first one may take the *neti, neti* (not this, not this) road of discrimination in which only Brahman is real and all else is unreal. Afterwards, the same person finds that everything in the universe, animate and inanimate, is God himself—he is both the reality and the illusion of the *Maya*. The negation is followed by an affirmation.

Ramakrishna felt that the classical disciplines of yoga were very difficult to follow for most human beings since the identification of the self with the body, which these disciplines seek to undo, was too deeply embedded for any easy sundering. For those who could not get rid of the feeling of 'I,' it was easier to travel on the devotional path where one could instead cherish the idea that 'I am God's servant' (or child, or friend, or mother, or lover, as the case may be). He illustrated this point through the example of the monkey god Hanuman, symbol of *dasa* (servant) devotionalism, who when asked by Rama, by God, how he looked at Him replied, 'O Rama, as long as I have the feeling of "I", I see that you are the whole and I am a part; you are the Master and I am your servant. But when, O Rama, I have the knowledge of truth, then I realize that You are I and I am You.'[25]

Even the passions—lust, anger, greed, inordinate attachment, pride, egoism—which have been traditionally held as obstacles to spiritual progress, do not need to be vanquished in devotional mysticism. The *vairagya*, the renunciation or rather the depassioning, can take place equally well by changing the object of these passions, directing them toward God rather than the objects of the world. 'Lust for intercourse with the soul. Feel angry with those who stand in your way toward God.

Be greedy to get Him. If there is attachment, then to Him; like *my* Rama, *my* Krishna. If you want to be proud, then be like Vibhishana [Ravana's brother in the epic of *Ramayana*] who says, "I have bowed before Rama and shall not bow to anyone else in the world."[26] Devotional mysticism does not demand an elimination of a sense of individual identity, of I-ness, which can instead be used to progress along the spiritual path. Thus in *vatsalya* devotionalism, the attitude of a mother toward God, Ramakrishna gives the example of Krishna's mother as the ideal to be emulated. 'Yashoda used to think, "Who will look after Gopala (Krishna's name as child) if I do not? He will fall ill if I do not look after him." She did not know Krishna as God. Udhava said to Yashoda, 'Mother, your Krishna is God Himself. He is the Lord of the Universe and not a common human being." Yashoda replied, "O who is talking about your Lord of the Universe? I am asking how *my* Gopala is. Not the Lord of the Universe, *my* Gopala. "'[27]

Ramakrishna's preferred mystical style did not need ascetic practices, yogic exercises, or a succession of ever more difficult meditations. What it required of the aspirant was, first , a recovery of a childlike innocence and freshness of vision, a renunciation of most adult categories. 'To my Mother I prayed only for pure devotion. I said "Mother, here is your virtue, here is your vice. Take them both and grant me only pure devotion for you. Here is your knowledge and here is your ignorance. Take them both and grant me only pure love for you. Here is your purity and here is your impurity. Take them both Mother and grant me only pure devotion for you. Here is your *dharma* (virtue) and here is your *adharma*. Take them both, Mother, and grant me only pure devotion for you. "'[28] And at other place, 'Who can ever know God? I don't even try. I only call on him as Mother. . . . My nature is that of a kitten. It only cries "Mew, mew." The rest it leaves to the Mother.'

Being like a child in relation to the Divinity does not mean being fearful, submissive, or meek, but of existing in the bright-eyed confidence of continued parental presence and *demanding* its restoration when it is felt to be lacking or insufficient. 'He is our Creator. What is there to be wondered if He is kind to us? Parents bring up their children. Do you call that an act of kindness? They must act that way. Therefore we should force our demands on God. He is our Father and Mother, isn't He?[29] Being a child, then, meant the joy of total trust, of being in the hands of infinitely powerful and infinitely beneficient forces. The power of this total trust is tremendous; its contribution to reaching the mystical goal vital. One of Ramakrishna's illustrative stories went that Rama who was God Himself had to build a bridge to cross the sea to Lanka. But the devotee Hanuman, trusting only in Rama's name, cleared the sea in one jump and reached the other side. He had no need of a bridge.

But perhaps the most important requirement of devotional mysticism, in all its varieties, was the intensity of the aspirant's yearning to be with God, whether in the dyad of mother–child, or as friend or as servant, or as lover. The longing had to be so intense that it completely took over body and mind, eliminating any need for performing devotions, prayers, or rituals. Ramakrishna illustrated this, his own yearning, through the parable of a guru who took his disciple to a pond to show him the kind of longing that would enable him to have a vision (*darshan*) of God. On coming to the pond, the guru pushed the disciple's head underwater and held it there. After a few seconds he released the disciple and asked, 'How do you feel?' The disciple answered, 'Oh, I felt as if I was dying! I was longing for a breath of air!' 'That's exactly it,' said the guru.[30] Like other kinds of mysticism, affective mysticism too has its developmental stages. Devotion (*bhakti*) matures into (*bhava*), followed by *mahabhava*, *prema*, and then attainment of God in the *unio mystica*. Since the distinctions between *bhava*, *mahabhava* and *prema* seem to me to lie in their degrees of intensity rather than in any fundamental qualitative difference, let me try to understand the nature of only one of the three states, *bhava*, a term which Ramakrishna uses constantly to describe states of consciousness which preceded his visions and ecstatic trances.

Literally translated as 'feeling,' 'mood,' *bhava* in Vaishnava mystical thought means a state of mind (and body) pervaded with a particular emotion. Basing his illustrations on Hindu ideals, Ramakrishna lists the *bhava*s in relation to God as *shanta*, the serenity of a wife's devotion to her husband, *dasya*, the devoted submissiveness of the servant, *sakhya*, the emotion of friendship, *vatsalya*, the feeling of mother towards the child, and *madhurya*, the romantic and passionate feelings of a womam toward her lover. Ramakrishan felt that the last, symbolized in Radha's attitude toward Krishna, included all the other *bhava*s. Indeed, the discourse of passionate love is conducted in many *bhava*s. At times idealizing the lover makes 'me' experience the loved one as an infinitely superior being whom I need outside myself as a *telos* to which or whom 'I' can surrender and obey in *dasya*. At other times, there is the contented oneness of *vatsalya* as the lover becomes as a babe on the breast, not in quiescence, a complacence of the heart, but in voluptuous absorption and repose. At yet other times, there is the serene tranquillity of *shanta*, the peace of the spouses in an ineffable intimacy, a state which the eighth-century Sanskrit poet Bhavabhuti lets Rama, with Sita asleep across his arm, describe as 'this state where there is no twoness in response of joy or sorrow / where the heart finds rest; where feeling does not dry with age / where concealments fall away in time and essential love is ripened.'[31] Besides the compulsions of possessive desire, all these *bhava*s too are at the core of man's erotic being.

Vaishnava mysticism, being a mysticism of love, does not consider awe as a legitimate *bhava* in relation to the Divine. Thus there are no feelings of reverence, of the uncanny, or of mystery. Nor are there the degrees of fear associated with awe where, in extremity, terror and dread can reign. Awe is perhaps the central *bhava* of what Erich Fromm called authoritarian religion. Vaishnava devotionalism, on the other hand, would consider awe as an obstacle in the mystical endeavour. It distances and separates rather than binds and joins.

I am aware that Ramakrishna's immersion in the various *bhava*s at different times in which he even adopted their outward manifestations can make him appear an outrageous figure to unsympathetic and prosaic observers. Practising the *madhurya bhava* of Radha towards Krishna, he dressed, behaved, and lived as a girl for six months. At another time, going through the *dasya bhava* of Hanuman, he attached an artifical tail to his posterior in an effort to resemble the monkey god. When living in the motherly *bhava* of Yashoda toward Krishna, he had one disciple, who felt like a child toward him, lean against his lap as if suckling at his breast while the mystic talked or listened to the concerns of his other disciples.

I have mentioned *mahabhava* and *prema* as the higher, more intense states of *bhava* which most aspirants never manage to reach. *Mahabhava* shakes the body and mind to its very foundations, and Ramakrishna compared it to a huge elephant entering a small hut. *Prema*, on the other hand, which makes visions of the Divine possible, was in his analogy a rope by which one tethered God. Whenever one wanted a *darshan*, one had merely to pull the rope, and He appeared.

Psychologically speaking, I would tend to see *bhava*s as more than psychic looseners that jar the soul out of the narcissistic sheath of normal, everyday, self-limiting routine. They are experiences of extreme emotional states which have a quality of irradiation wherein time and space tend to disappear. We know of these feeling states from our experience of passionate love where, at its height, the loved one's beauty is all beauty, the love cannot be conceived as not being eternal, and where the memories of all past loves dim so precipitately as to almost merge into darkness. We also know *bhava* from our experience of grief which, beginning with a finite loss, irradiates all the world at its height. The world becomes empty, and all that is good is felt to be lost forever. We even know of the quality of *bhava* from states of extreme fear when the smallest sound, the minutest changes of light and shade, the quivering shapes of objects in the dark, all take on an air of extreme menace. The threat becomes eternal, with nary a thought that it might ever end.

Bhava, then, is a way of experiencing which is done 'with all one's heart, all one's soul, and all one's might.' The *bhava* fills the ecstatic mystic, as it did Ramakrishna, to the brim. He is not depleted, and there is no need for that restitution in delusion and hallucination that is the prime work of insanity. In a *bhava*, Ramakrishna rekindled the world with fresh vision, discovering or rather endowing it with newfound beauty and harmony. *Bhava* animated his relation with nature and human beings, deepened his sensate and metaphysical responsiveness.

Bhava, then, is creative experienc:ng, or rather the ground for all creativity—mystical, artistic, or scientific. The capacity for *bhava* is what an ideal analysis strives for, an openness toward experiencing; a capacity for 'experiencing experience' as Bion would call it. All the other gains of analysis—insight into one's conflicts, the capacity to experience pleasure without guilt, ability to tolerate anxiety without being crippled, development of a reliable reality testing, and so on—are secondary to the birth of the analytic *bhava*. Of course, the analytic *bhava*, the total openness to the analytic situation manifested in the capacity to really *free*-associate, is not simply a goal to be reached at the end of analysis, but a state to strive for in every session. In the language of the traditional drive–defence analytic model, if we divide defences into creative and uncreative, the latter by definition pathological, then the capacity for *bhava* is perhaps the most creative of defences and needs a place of honour beside and even beyond sublimation.

From *bhava*, the ground of mystical creativity, let us turn to *darshan*, vision, the mystic's primary creative product, his particular non-material creation or mystical art. Ramakrishna's explanation of visionary experience is simple, heartfelt, and sensuous. 'God cannot be seen with these physical eyes. In the course of spiritual discipline (*sadhana*) one gets a love's body endowed with love eyes, love ears, and so on. One sees God with these love eyes. One hears His voice with these love ears. One even gets a penis and a vagina made of love. With this love body one enjoys intercourse with the soul.'[32]

In my own explorations, I prefer to use the religious term vision rather than its psychiatric counterpart hallucination for the same reason that I have talked of mystical *ecstasy* rather than of euphoria, namely the connotations of psychopathology associated with psychiatric categories. The distinction between the two, though, is not very hard and fast, their boundaries constantly shifting. Both can be produced by severe depression or manic excitement, toxic psychosis due to exhaustion or starvation or sensory deprivation or simply a febrile illness. What is important in distinguishing them is their meaning and content and not their origin.

Visions are like hallucinations in that they too are images, such as flashes of light, which are visually perceived without the external stimulation of the organ of sight. They are, however, not hallucinations in that they occur during the course of intense religious experience rather than during a psychotic episode. They are thus less bizarre and less disorganized. Visions belong more to the realm of perceptions that take place say, during a dream, while falling asleep (hypnagogic) or when awakening (hypnopompic). None of these can be called a consequence of psychic impairment. Visions are, then, special kinds of dreams which find their way into waking life. To have vision is in itself as much a manifestation of mental disorder as is the corresponding process of real events being drawn across the barrier of sleep into the formation of dreams. Freud recognized the special nature of visions when, in an aside on the psychology of the mystic, he remarked, 'It is easy to imagine, too, that certain mystics may succeed in upsettting the normal relations between the different regions of the mind, so that, for instance, perception may be able to grasp happenings in the depths of the ego and in the id which were otherwise inaccessible to it.'[33] Ramakrishna's visions, as perhaps those of other mystics, do not constitute a unitary phenomenon. They span the whole range from what can be fairly described as hallucinations in the psychiatric sense, through more or less conscious visions, to what I would call 'unconscious visions' (or 'visions of the unconscious'?) which cannot be described since the observing ego is absent. Thess are the ineffable 'salt doll' visions which comprise a small, though perhaps the most striking part of the total mystical repertoire.

Before we discuss the various kinds of visions, let us note their central common feature: the intense affect they generate, an affect that endows them with their characteristic sense of noesis. The affect, so strong that it is experienced as *knowing* partakes of some of the quality of the symbiotic state in infancy when the child knew the mother through an interchange of their feelings, when affect and cognition were not differentiated from one another.[34]

The affects are also manifested in the body, and Ramakrishna's visions had certain well-defined physical correlates. At times, he would shudder while tears of joy streamed unchecked down his cheeks. At other times, his eyes would become half closed and unfocussd, a faint smile playing around the mouth while his body became completely rigid and had to be supported by a disciple lest he fall and hurt himself. The accompaniment to certain other trance states was a flushed chest or a strong burning sensation all over the body. Ramakrishna reports that once when in such a state, Brahmani, his tantric guru, tried to lead him to his bath. She could not hold his hand, so hot was his skin, and she had to wrap him in a sheet. The earth that stuck to his body while he was lying on the ground became baked. Then there is the feeling of being famished—one wonders, spiritual receptivity with a bodily analogue (or is it vice versa)? Or there are the bouts of gluttony in which he consumed enormous quantities of food, generally sweets. The craving for a particular dish or a sweet would come upon Ramakrishna unexpectedly, at any time of night or day. At these moments, Ramakrishna would be like a pregnant woman who is dominated by her obsession and cannot rest till the craving is satisfied.

From inside the tradition, all these manifestations are some of the 19 bodily signs of the mystical experience. To the analyst, however, they are a further confirmation of the mystic's access to a period in early life—'oral' in the classical nomenclature—when the boundary between psyche and soma was much more porous than is the case in adulthood. His is the reclamation of a truly dialogical period wherein engendered affects were discharged through the body while physical experience found easy expression in affective states. Ramakrishna's longing for the Mother, accompanied by breathlessness of a kind where he feels he is about to die, for instance, is akin to a certain type of asthmatic bodily manifestation of dammed-up urge for the mother's succour.

Coming back to the various types of visions, the hallucinations, unbidden and unwelcome, belong to his period of insanity (*unmada*): 'I would spit on the ground when I saw them. But they would follow me and obsess me like ghosts. One day after such a vision I would have a severe attack of diarrhoea, and all these ecstasies would pass out through my bowels.'[35]

These hallucinations, or better, nightmarish visions, are not alien but perhaps as much a part of Ramakrishna's personality as are his artistic sensibility or his more elevated, mystical visions. Their essential linkage may be better understood if we take recourse to Ernst Hartmann's work on nightmares.[36]

In his study of nonpsychiatric volunteers who suffered from nightmares since childhood, Hartmann found that these subjects were usually sensitive people with a strong artistic bent and creative potential. More important, they demonstrate what he calls 'thin boundaries of the mind,' a permeability between self and object, waking/sleeping, fantasy/reality, adult/child, human/animal, and other such boundaries, which are relatively fixed for most people. The thin boundary of the mind, Hartmann tries to show, is at the root of both their artistic sensibility and potential for nightmares. It is tempting to speculate that Ramakrishna, and perhaps most other mystics, have a ge*net*ic biological predisposition, reinforced by some early experiences to which we will come later, to thin boundaries, also between nightmarish and ecstatic visions.

The second class of visions are the conscious ones. Welcomed by a prepared mind, they fall on a receptive ground. Conscious visions may be symbolic representations of an ongoing psychic process, the symbols taken from the mystic's religious and cultural tradition. This is true, for instance, of Ramakrishna's vision of his 'enlightenment,' which he 'saw' in the traditional yogic imagery of *Kundalini*, the coiled serpent energy rising through the different centres (*chakra*s) of his body and opening up the 'lotuses' associated with these centres, a specifically Hindu metaphor for mental transformation and the opening up of the psyche to hitherto inaccessible psychic experience. 'I saw a 22, 23-year-old, exactly resembling me, enter the Sushumna nerve and with his tongue 'sport' (*raman*) with the vulva-(*yoni*) shaped lotuses. He began with the centre of the anus, through the centres of the penis, navel, and so on. The respective four-petaled, six-petaled, and ten-petaled lotuses which had been dropping, rose high and blossomed. I distinctly remember that when he came to the heart and sported with it with his tongue, the 12-petaled lotus which had been dropping rose high and opened its petals. Then he came to the 16-petaled lotus in the throat and the two-petaled one in the forehead. And last of all, the 1000-petaled lotus in the head blossomed.'[37] This particular vision, in which self-representation is split into observing and participating aspects, can also be seen through psychiatric glasses as a heutroscopic depersonalization which occurs particularly among individuals with tendeneies toward self-contemplation and introspection. Yet in the absence of any as-sociated painful or anxious affect and the fact that this kind of vision was only one among Ramakrishna's vast repertoire of visions with very different structures and qualities, I would tend to see its ground in a creativity, akin to the heightened fantasy of an artist or a writer, rather than in pathology. Goethe and Maupassant are two instances of creative writers who also experienced the phenomenon of their doubles.[38]

Other conscious visions are visual insights, images full of conviction and sudden clarity, couched either in a universal–mystical or in a par-ticular, cultural–historical idiom. Some examples of the former would be seeing the universe filled with sparks of fire, or glittering like a lake of quicksilver, or all its quarters illuminated with the light of myriad candles. Such visions of light, we mentioned earlier, have been reported by mystics throughout the ages, and, indeed, seeing the divine light has been a central feature of many mystical cults, including 17th-century Quakerism. Another visual insight of the universal variety is seeing everything throbbing with consciousness: 'Sometimes I see the same consciousness playing in small fish that is animating the world. Some-times I see the world soaked with consciousness in the same way as the earth is soaked with water during the rains.'[39]

The full import of the more culturally constituted visions, on the other hand, can only be appreciated if we keep in mind that Ramakrish-na was a Hindu Brahmin living at a time—the 19th century, and place—rural Bengal—in which the ideas of pollution and polluting sub-stances were strong, caste taboos strict, and the threatened loss of caste a horror of the first magnitude. Visions dissolving religious distinctions and caste taboos, such as the ones on touching forbidden substances or taking food from forbidden persons, were thus primarily expressed in a cultural imagery relevant to Ramakrishna's community. For instance, 'Then I was shown a Muslim with a long beard who came to me with rice in an earthen plate. He fed other Muslims and also gave me some grains to eat. Mother showed me there exists only one and not two.'[40] 'Another day I saw excrement, urine, rice, vegetables, and other foods. Suddenly the soul came out of my body and, like a flame, touched everything: excrement, urine, everything was tasted. It was revealed that everything is one, that there is no difference.'[41] Or, when on the repeated egging on by his nephew, he asked the Goddess for occult powers and saw a middle-aged prostitute come up, squat on her haunches with her back to him, and proceed to evacuate. The vision revealed that occult powers were the shit of that whore.

There is another class of visions, or strictly speaking, mystical illusions, since these rest on a transmutation of external stimuli into creations which are nearer to those of the artist. Thus the way an English boy leans against a tree is transformed into a vision of Krishna; a prostitute walking toward him is changed into a vision of the Mother Goddess—both images irradiate his body and mind with beneficence. In Blake's words, these illusions are 'auguries of innocence' enabling the mystic 'to see a world in a grain of sand, and a heaven in a wild flower.'

And finally, there are the indescribable, unconscious visions. 'You see,' Ramakrishna once said to diciples, 'something goes up creeping Gom the feet to the head. Consciousness continues to exist as long as this power does not reach the head; but as soon as it reaches the head, all consciousness is completely lost. There is no seeing or hearing anymore, much less speaking. Who can speak? The very idea of "I" and "You" vanishes. While it (the serpent power) goes up, I feel a desire to tell you everything—how many visions I experience, of their nature, etc. Until it comes to this place (showing the heart) or at most this place (showing the throat) speaking is possible, and I do speak. But the moment it goes up beyond this place (showing the throat) someone forcibly presses the mouth, as it were, and I lose all consciousness. I cannot control it Suppose I try to de.scribe what kind of vision I experience when it goes beyond this place (showing the throat). As soon as I begin to think of them for the purpose of description the mind rushes immediately up, and speaking becomes impossible.'[42]

His feelings during these visions could then only be expressed in metaphors—'I feel like a fish released ffom a pot into the water of the Ganges.' Ramala'ishna, however, does not seem to have been overly enamoured of these states which have been so often held as the apex of the mystical experience. He consciously tried to keep a trace of the observing ego—a little spark of the big fire—so as not to completely disappear, or disappear for a long time, into the *unio mystica* with its non-differentiation of 'I' and the 'Other.' 'In *samadhi*, I lose outer consciousness completely, but God generally keeps a little trace of the ego in me for the enjoyment [here he uses a deliberately sensual metaphor, *vilas*] of intercourse. Enjoyment is only possible when "I" and "You" 'remain.' As he maintained, 'I want to taste sugar, not become sugar.'

Yet in spite of himself he was often the salt doll that went into the ocean.

The unconscious visions, irreducible to language. are different from other visions which are ineffable only in the sense that their description can never be complete. The unconscious visions are a return to the world before the existence of language, visions of 'reality' through the destruction of language that the particular mystical act entails. As Octavio Paz puts it, 'Language sinks its roots into this world but transforms its juices and reactions into signs and symbols. Language is the consequence (or the cause) of our exile from the universe, signifying the distance between things and ourselves. If our exile were to come to an end, languages would come to an end.'[43] The salt doll ends exile, writes a *finis* to language.

The vicissitudes of separation have been, of course, at the heart of psychoanalytic theorizing on mysticism. The yearning to be reunited with a perfect, omnipotent being the longing for the blissful soothing and nursing associated with the mother of earliest infancy (perhaps as much an adult myth as an infantile reality), has been consensually deemed the core of mystical motivation. What has been controversial is the way this longing has been viewed and the value placed on it by different analysts.

The traditional view, initiated by Freud, sees this yearning as reactive, a defence against the hatred directed towards the oedipal father. For writers influenced by Melanie Klein, the longing for the blissful 'good' mother is a defensive denial of her terrifying and hated aspect's.[44] Given the limitation that Ramakrishna did not spend any time on the couch (but, then, neither have other theorists had mystics as patients), I can only say that there is no evidence in the voluminous record of his conversation, reminiscences, and accounts of his visions which is remotely suggestive of any strong hostility toward the Oedipal father. The evidence for the denial of the dreaded aspects of the mother is slightly greater, namely through a plausible interpretation of some elements of his vision in the Kali temple when he had taken up a sword to kill himself. However, seen in the total context of a large number of visions of the Mother Goddess, the ambiguous evidence of one particular vision is not enough to compel an acceptance of the Kleinian notions on mystical motivation.

Paul Horton has advanced a more adaptive view of mystical yearning and mystical states, especially during adolescence.[45] He sees them as a consequence of the pangs of separation in which the felt reality of being utterly and agonizingly alone is *transiently* denied. The mystical experience is then a transitional phenomenon which soothes and reassures much as a baby is soothed by a blanket, a child by a stuffed toy or fairytale, an adult by a particular piece of music—all these various creations, material and nonmaterial, providing opportunities for the controlled illusion that heals.

There is much to be said for the hypothesis that experiences of separation and loss spurred Ramakrishna onto the mystical path. We know that Ramakrishna's first quasi-mystical ecstasy when he became unconscious at the sight of white cranes flying against a background of dark clouds took place in the last year of his father's final illness (according to one place in Ramakrishna's reminiscences, two years after his father's death), that is, at a time of an impending loss. And I have described the marked change that came over Ramakrishna is not unlike some of the Christian mystics in whose lives too, as David Aberbach has demonstrated, one could hypothesize a link between personal loss and their mystical calling.[46] Teresa of Avila's life in the church began with the death of her mother when Teresa was 12 years old. The loss of a parent or parent–surrogate may also be an early one, heightening a later sense of abandonment and the subsequent search for the 'eternal Thou,' as perhaps in the examples of St John of the Cross, whose father died a few months after his birth, or of Martin Buber, whose mother deserted him when he was three.

The mystical path is then also a way of lessening the agony of separation, mitigating the grief at loss, reducing the sadness of bereavement. In my own interviews with members of a mystical cult in India, loss was the single most important factor in their decision to seek its membership. The very embarkation on the mystical path had a therapeutic effect by itself, while any experience of a mystical state had a further marked effect in altering the person's dysphoric state of mind.[47] In contrast to the person's previous feelings of apathy and depression, the turn to mysticism had the consequence of his dealing with grief in a more orderly and more detached, though in a more transcendent, manner. Perhaps T.S. Eliot is correct in observing that 'A man does not join himself with the universe so long as he has anything else to join himself with.'[48]

Of course, Ramakrishna's two actual experiences of loss are not sufficient to explain the totality of his mysticism, the intensity of his yearning throughout life to end the state of separation from the Divine, and the acuteness of his distress at the absence of the Mother. The motivational skein of mysticism, as of any other psychic phenomenon, is composed of many strands. One could speculate that the advanced age of his mother at his birth, his family's poverty and thus his mother's added preoccupations with household tasks, the birth of another sibling when he was four, may have led to the emotional unavailability of the mother at a phase of the child's development when his own needs were driving him closer to her. In other words, the suggestion is that in the crucial 'rapprochement' phase (which occurs later in India than in psychoanalyst Margaret Mahler's timetable), the mother was unavailable at a time when his anxiety about separation, and its convergent depression, were at their apex. This would fix separation and its associated anxiety as the dominant theme of his inner life. Each feared or actual loss would reactivate separation anxiety together with a concomitant effort at combating it by reclaiming in fantasy an adored and adoring intimacy with the maternal matrix. The unity Ramakrishna aimed for is, then, not the mergerlike states of the infant at the breast, though these too prefigured his trances, but the ending of separation striven for by the toddler. It is a state in which both mother and child have boundaries in relation to each other while another boundary encloses their 'double unit' from the rest of the world. Here the enjoyment of the mother's presence is deeply sensuous, almost ecstatic, and informs Ramakrishna's selection of words; images and metaphors that describe his experiences.

Together with the speculated impact of early mother–child interaction in Ramakrishna's psychic life, admittedly a construct derived from analytic theory rather than a reconstruction based on compelling psychobiographical evidence, I would tend to attribute his acute sensitivity to the theme of separation to the mystical gift (or curse) of a specific kind of creative experiencing. This can be understood more clearly, if we take recourse to some ideas of the 'metaphysical' analysts mentioned earlier.

Lacan, for instance, has postulated that man's psychic life constantly seeks to deal with a primordial state of affairs which he calls the Real. The Real itself is unknowable, though we constantly create myths as its markers. Perhaps the principal myth involves the rupture of a basic union; the separation from the mother's body, leaving us with a fundamental feeling of incompletion. The fantasies around this insufficiency are universal, governing the psyche of both patients and analysts alike. In the psyche, this lack is translated as desire, and the human venture is a history of desire as it ceaselessly loses and discovers itself in (what Lacan calls) The Imaginary and, with the advent of language, The Symbolic order. Born of rupture, desire's fate is an endless quest for the lost object; all real objects merely interrupt the search. As the Barandes put it, 'It is the task of the *néoténique* (i.e., immature, even foetalized being] being separated from its original union by its fall into life and into time, to invent detours for itself, deviations of object as well as means and aims. Its condition is inexorably perverse—if perversions must be.'[49] The mystical quest seeks to rescue from primal repression the constantly lived contrast between an original interlocking and a radical rupture. The mystic, unlike most others, does not mistake his hunger for its fulfilment. If we are all fundamentally perverse in the play of our desire, then the mystic is the only one who seeks to go beyond the illusion of The Imaginary and, yes, also the *maya* of The Symbolic register.

One of Ramakrishna's more 'private' visions attempts to paint the issue of separation with crude yet compelling brushstrokes. As Bion would say, here he is like the analyst who knows that emotional truth is ineffable, available only in intimations and approximations. Like the Bionian analyst, the mystic too is compelled to use terms from senuous experience to point to a realm beyond this experience. 'Let me tell you a very secret experience. Sitting in a pine grove, I had the vision of a small, hidden [literally 'thief's door'] entrance to a room. I could not see what was inside the room. I tried to bore a hole with a nail file but did not succeed. As I bored the hole it would fill up again and again. And then suddenly it made a big opening.' He kept quiet and then started speaking again. 'These are all higher matters. I feel someone is closing my mouth. I have seen God residing in the vagina. I saw Him there at the time of sexual intercourse of a dog and a bitch.'[50]

Ramakrishna's vision, followed by an associative sequel, does not need extended analytic gloss. The small secret opening to a room into which he cannot see and which he tries to keep open, the seeing of God in the genitals of a bitch in intercourse, do not encode the mystical preoccupation with opening a way back to the self-other interlocking in any complex symbolic language. This interlocking, the mystical unity, is not unitary. As we saw in Ramakrishna's case, it extends in a continuum fiom the foetalized being's never having known separation from the mother's insides, an expulsion from her womb, through the satiated infant's flowing feelings of merger at the breast, to the toddler being pulled back to the mother as if held at one end of an invisible string.

What I am emphasizing, however, is not the traditional analytic agenda of pathological, defensive, or compensatory uses of these various degrees of dyadic unity in mystical experiencing. As Michael Eigen has elaborated in a series of papers, for Freud, ideal experiencing, that is, states or moments of beatific (or horrific) perfection, in which I would include the mystical states, usually involved something in disguise—mother, father, sex, aggression and so on.[51] Lacan, Winnicott and Bion (and implicitly also Erikson), on the other hand, look at ideal experiencing in its own right, as a spontaneously unfolding capacity for creative experiencing. This capacity can be deployed defensively as has been spelled out in detail in the Freudian literature, but it is not conterminous with defence.

All these authors emphasize the positive, regenerative aspects of this experiencing not as idealists but as empirical analysts who chart out its developmental vicissitudes from early infancy onward. The experiencing itself, they maintain, should not be confused with the introjection of the mother and father images or functions. These only foster or hamper this capacity. 'If one reads these authors carefully, one discovers that the *primary object of creative experiencing is not mother or father but the unknowable ground of creativeness as such*. Winnicott, for example, emphasizes that what is at stake in transitional experiencing is not mainly a self or object (mother) substitute, but the creation of a symbol, of symbolizing experiencing itself. The subject lives through and toward creative immersion (including phases of chaos, unintegration, waiting).'[52] What we should then pay equal attention to is not only the conflicts of the mystic that threaten to deform or disperse his creative experiencing, but the experiencing itself—its content, context, and evolution.

Most of us harbour tantalizing 'forgotten' traces of this kind of experiencing, an apperception where what is happening outside is felt to be the creative act of the original artist (or mystic) within each of us and recognized as such with (in Blake's word) *delight*. For in late infancy and early childhood we did not always see the world as something outside ourselves, to be recognized in detail, adapted, complied with, and fitted into our idiosyncratic inner world, but often as an infmite succession of creative acts.

Mystical experience, then, is one and—in some cultures and at certain historical periods—the preeminent way of uncovering the vein of creativity that runs deep in all of us. For some, it is the throes of romantic love that gives inklings of our original freshness of vision. Others may strive for creative experiencing in art or in natural science. In the West, the similarities between mystics and creative artists and scientists have been pointed out since the beginning of the century. Evelyn Underhill in her path-breaking work on mysticism emphasized the resemblance between artistic geniuses and mystics—though one should hesitate to use the terms as interchangeable—while James Leuba pointed out the similarity at a more mundane level in creative phenomena of the daily kind and at a lower level of intensity.[53] In China, we know that it was the mystical Taoists stressing spontaneity, 'inaction,' 'emptying the mind,' rather than the rational Confucians, who stimulated Chinese scientific discovery. In India, too, in different epochs, the striving for mystical experience through art, especially music, has been a commonly accepted and timehonoured practice. And Albert Einstein writes of his own motivations for the scientific enterprise, 'The most beautiful, the most profound emotion we can experience is the sensation of the mystical. It is the fundamental emotion that stands at the cradle of true art and science.' Einstein goes on to say that there is a need 'to escape from everyday life with its painful crudity and hopeless dreariness, from fetters of one's own shifting desires.' Instead the scientist and the artist creates his own reality, substituting it for the world of experience and thus overcoming it: 'Each makes his own cosmos and its construction the pivot of his emotional life, in order to find in this way peace and security which he cannot find in the narrow whirlpool of personal experience.'[54] Here it seems to me that Einstein is not talking as some who is depressed but with a creative individual's clear-sighted and inevitable response to the world as it is. When Buddha, as the young Siddhartha confronted with illness, old-age, and death proclaims '*Sabbam dukham* (All is suffering)', he too is not depressed but in perfect attunement with the reality principle. To see the world with a creative eye but a sober perspective is perhaps our greatest adaptation to reality—a state where Buddha, Freud and Ramakrishna come together.

SEXUALITY AND THE MYSTICAL EXPERIENCE

Ramakrishna was one with other Vaishnava mystics in his insistence that sexuality, by which he meant male sexuality, phallic desire, constituted the biggest obstacle to mystical experiencing. This is a formulation with which psychoanalysts will not have any quarrel. For both male and female infants, the differentiation between self and object is achieved and ego boundaries constituted by a gradual detachment from the mother. The presence of the father is vital for this process. Whereas the masculinity of the father makes it possible for the boy to overcome his primary femininity, the presence of the paternal phallus also helps to protect the little girl from fusional tendencies with the mother. Male sexuality and male desire may thus be viewed as obstacles in the path of fusion, the phallus as the prime symbol of boundaries the mystic seeks to transcend.

The renunciation of adult masculinity is not only a feature of Hindu devotional mysticism but is also a feature of Christian emotional mysticism of medieval and early modern Europe. Affective prayer or Bernardine mysticism, as it has often been called after the influential sermons of the eleventh-century saint Bernard of Clairvaux, possesses a striking affinity to its Hindu counterpart. Femininity pervades both. In the case of medieval Europe, most of the practising mystics were women. But even the outstanding male mystics—St John of the Cross, Francois de Sales, Fenelon—show strong feminine identifications and produced their most important ideas under the direct influence of women.[55] The psychological stance of Christian ecstatics toward Divinity, paralleling that of the Vaishnava mystics, is either that of the infant toward a loving maternal parent, or of a woman toward a youthful lover. Like the Hindus, the Christian mystics too disavowed or overthrew the paternal phallus as they divested the Judeo-Christian God of much of his original masculinity and sternness, virtually relegating him to the role of a grandfather. The message of the European emotional mystics seems to be the same as that of Ramakrishna: the actual gender of the mystics is not important for his practice. It is, however vital that the mystic accept and cultivate his or her femininity to the point that the female-self part becomes dominant in his or her inner psychic reality.

Of the many mystical disciplines, the one Ramakrishna could never practise was the 'heroic' one of Tantra where, at its culmination, God as a female is sought to be pleased-or perhaps I should say, pleasured-as a man pleases a woman through intercourse. In his own Tantric training, he had escaped the demand for ritual sex by going into an ecstatic state just before he had to actually 'perform'. He repeatedly warned his disciples against *kamini–kanchani* (literally, woman and gold), and his advice to novices on the mystical path was to avoid the female sex altogether, the whirlpool in which even Brahma and Vishnu struggle for their lives. For a renunciant, he felt, to sit with a woman or talk to her for a long time was a kind of sexual intercourse of which there were eight kinds. Some of these were to listen to a woman, to talk to her in secret, to keep and enjoy something belonging to a woman, to touch her, and so on. Given the fact that a vast majority of widely known mystics, at least in medieval Christian and devotional Hindu traditions, have been celibates, one wonders whether clibacy, with its profound influence on hormonal balance, is not an important physiological technique for mystical ecstasy.

The prescribed avoidance of women was only for beginners. Once mystical knowledge was gained, sexual differentiation too vanished: 'Then you don't have much to fear. After reaching the roof you can dance as much as you like, but not on the stairs.' Yet though Ramakrishna constantly reiterated that he looked at the breasts of every woman as those of his mother, that he felt as a child or as another woman with women, his male awareness of women as sexual beings, and of the dangers of a desire that separates and bifurcates, never quite disappeared as his biographers would have us believe. He felt uncomfortable with female devotees sitting in his room and would ask them to go and visit the temple as soon as he could decently get rid of them. Being touched by a woman was not a matter of unconcern but evoked strong physical reactions. 'If a woman touches me, I fall ill. That part of my body aches as if stung by a horned fish. If I touch a woman my hand becomes numb; it aches. If in a friendly spirit I approach a woman and begin to talk to her, I feel as if a curtain has come down between us.'[56] However minimal his sexual conflict, even a great mystic seems to retain at least a vestigial entanglement with the world of desire. In his normal nonecstatic state, Ramakrishna too was never quite free of the sexual *maya* free from the delight, wisdom, beauty, and pain of the 'illusion' which so beguiles the rest of us.

Ramakrishna's attempted renunciation of male sexual desire is the subject of one vision, although as someone who claimed to never having even dreamt of intercourse with a woman, the *conscious* pr ptings of desire could not have been too peremptory. 'During the *sadhana*s, I vividly perceived a heap of rupees, a shawl, a plate of sweets and two women. "Do you want to enjoy any of these things?" I asked my mind. "No," replied the mind. I saw the insides of those women, of what is in them; entrails, piss, shit, phlegm and such things.'[57] We can, of course, try to understand the contents of this vision in biographical terms. Money, shawl, and sweets embody overpowering temptations for a boy who grew up in a poor family whose dire financial straits allowed but the most spartan of fare. Similarly, one posible cause for the hankering after sexual purity in his youth could be a deep feeling of shame he associated with the sexual act. In a country and at a time where women not infrequently became grandmothers in their late 20s, where sexual activity has always been considered a prerogative of the young—sexual desire of older men and women occasioning derisive laughter—Ramakrishna's birth itself (followed by that of the sister) is the sign of a tainted and deeply mortifying sexuality of his old parents. We have already seen how Ramakrishna's enduring wish to be a woman, expressed variously in dressing and moving his limbs like one, his fantasy of being a girl widow who secretly trysts with Krishna every evening, fitted in well with a tenet of Vaishnava mysticism that all mankind is female while God alone is male. Ramakrishna would approvingly cite the opinion that irrespective of biological gender everyone with nipples is a female. Arjuna, the heroic warrior of the *Mahabharata*, and Krishna are the only exceptional males since they do not have nipples. In the *madhurya bhava*, Ramakrishna had even tried to engender in himself female erotic feelings. Moved by an intense love for Krishna, 'such as a woman feels for her lover,' he had stretched out his arms to embrace the Lord's stone idols.

Just as the writings of medieval European female mystics, wherein they wax rhapsodic over their ecstatic union with Jesus, portrayed as an exceedingly handsome and loving bridegroom of the human soul, have been analyzed as expressions of a pathological, hysterical sexuality, it would not be difficult to diagnose Ramakrishna in traditional Freudian terms as a secondary transsexual. He would seamlessly fit in with Robert Stoller's description of the secondary transsexual as being someone who differs om his primary counterpart in that he does not appear feminine from the start of any behaviour that may be classed in gender terms.[58] Under the surface of masculinity, however, there is the persistent impulse toward being feminine, an urge which generally manifests itself in adolescence. The most obvious manifestation of these urges is the wish for the actual wearing of women's clothes. Though these urges may gather in strength and last for longer and longer periods, the masculine aspects of identity are never completely submerged.

Ramakrishna's open espousal and expression of his feminine identifications as a boy, however, also have to do with the greater tolerance of his community and its culture towards such identifications. His urge toward femininity did not meet an unyielding opposition or strenuous attempts at suppression by an enforced participation in masculine play. Any transsexual or homosexual labels may obscure his sense of comfort and easy familiarity with the feminine components of his self. It may hide the fact that the freeing of femininity from repression of disavowal in man and vice versa in a woman may be a great human achievement rather than an illness or a deviation. The deviation may actually lie, as in one view of the etiology of homosexuality, in the *inability* to come to terms with the opposite sexual personality in one's self.[59]

Summarizing, I would say that the male-self part of Ramakrishna's personality was split off in early childhood and tended to grow, if at all, rather slowly. In contrast, the female-self part of his personality dominated his inner psychic reality. Ramakrishna's girl-self was neither repressed nor disassociated but could mature to an extent where psychically he could even possess female sexual equipment and enjoy female sexual experience.

Yet even a celebratory avowal of secondary femininity in a male mystic may not be enough to exhaust the mystery of the link between sexuality and mysticism. For if, together with 'infant-likeness,' secondary femininity and female bodily experience—breastpride, absence of male external genitalia, the presence of vulva and womb—are important for affective mysticism, then women will be seen as having a head start in this particular human enterprise. They naturally are what male aspirants must become. This may be true though it has yet to be demonstrated that gender makes a substantial difference in the making of a mystic. What is perhaps essential in mysticism is not the presence of secondary but of 'primary' femininity—the 'pure female element' (not the female person) in Winnicott's sense of the term. In his theory of the life of male and female elements in a person, the purely male element, in both man and woman, presupposes separateness and tracks in terms of active relating, or being passively related to, and is backed by the whole apparatus of instinctual drives.[60] The female element, on the other hand, relates to the other—the breast, the mother (both with a small and capital 'm'—in the sense of an identity between the two. When this element finds the other, it is the self that has been found. It is the female element that establishes the simplest, the most primary of experiences, the experience of *being*. Winnicott remarks psychoanalysts have perhaps given special attention to this male element or drive aspecf of object relating and yet have neglected the subject–object identity to which I am drawing attention here, which is at the basis of the capacity to be. The male element *does* (active–passive) while the female element *is* (in males and females) and conclude 'After being—doing and being done to. But first *being*.'[61]

Looking at Ramakrishna's sexuality in relation to his mystical experience in terms of oral, anal, and phallic stages of development or of identifications with mother, father and so on, as in classical analytic discourse, is then to forget that this discourse itself may be based on the life of the male element. Our psychology has still little to say of the distilled female element, the primary femininity, at the heart of emotional mysticism. The pure female element, in both men and women, continues to testify to the category of mystery as a basic dimension in which we all, and especially the mystic, live. As analysts, however, we cannot look at mystery as something eternally beyond human comprehension, but as a phenomenon to which we repeatedly return to increase our understanding. As our perspectives change, our earlier views do not get replaced but are subsumed in an ever-widening set of meanings.

13

The Virtuous Virago

To look more closely at the constructed revival of Hindu identity, I have chosen as my text a speech by Sadhvi Ritambhara, one of the star speakers for the *sangh parivar*, the prefix sadhvi being the female counterpart of sadhu, a man who has renounced the world in search of personal salvation and universal welfare within the Hindu religious worldview. It is reported that Ritambhara was a 16-year-old schoolgirl in Khanna, a village in the Punjab, when she had s strong spiritual experience while listening to a discourse by Swami Parmananda, one of the many 'saints' in the forefront of Hindu revivalism.[1] Ritambhara abandoned her studies and home and joined Parmananda's ashram. Soon she began travelling with her guru to religious meetings in the Hindi heartland and after a while addressed a few herself. Her oratorical talents were noticed by the political leadership of the *sangh parivar* and, after being given some training in voice modulation, she was well on her way to become the leading firebrand in the Hindu cause.

The speech I have chosen was given at Hyderabad in April 1991, a few weeks after the general elections for the national Parliament and many state assemblies were announced. The speech is a standard one which Ritambhara has given all over India to the enthusiastic response of hundreds of thousands of people. The political context of the speech is the bid by the BJP, the political arm of the *sangh* family, to capture power in some north Indian states in the coming elections and to emerge as the single largest party in the national Parliament. In the preceding months, the BJP had determined the country's political agenda by its mobilization of Hindus on the issue of constructing a temple to the god Rama at Ayodhya, his reputed birthplace. The construction of this temple had become an explosive and divisive issue since the designated site was already occupied by the Babri Masjid, a mosque built by Babar, the Muslim invader from Central Asia who was the founder of the Mughal dynasty that ruled over large parts of India for over 400 years. There had been much bloodshed five months earlier as many Hindus, the *kar-sevak*s, lost their lives in police firing when they attempted to defy legal orders and begin the temple construction, a step which required demolition or at least relocation of the existing mosque. The killings of unarmed Rama *bhakt*s—devotees of Rama—in Ayodhya led to a spate of riots between Hindus and Muslims in other parts of the country, including Hyderabad, a city with an almost equal proportion of the two communities and where the tension between them over the years had regularly erupted in communal violence.

The political context of the speech, the theme of temple versus mosque, the abundance of imagery and allusions in its text to the narratives of the epics *Ramayana* and the *Mahabharata*, and the person of the speaker herself are all replete with symbolic resonances, evocations, and associations. They virtually reek with a surfeit of meaning that burrows deep into the psychic recesses of the audience, going well beyond the words used as its carriers. Listening to her speak, the earlier question is once again raised: Is she an elite manipulator of Hindu cultural symbols (instrumental theory) or is she an articulator of what many Hindus feel but cannot express (primordialist viewpoint)? The answer is again not in terms of either/or but of the simultaneity of both processes. Ritambhara appeals to a group identity while creating it. She both mirrors her listeners' sentiments and gives them birth. My impression is that the images, metaphors, and mythological allusions of her speech have a resonance for the audience because they also have a resonance for her. This does not imply that the speech is a spontaneous pouring out of her heart. Like an actor she has honed this particular speech through successive deliveries and knows what 'works'. It is not raw feeling but carefully crafted emotion; an epic poem rather than a scream or a shout. Ritambhara's power lies less in her persuasiveness on an intellectual, cognitive plane than on the *poetic* (Greek *poiesis*—a making, shaping) that permeates her speech. It is this poetic which gives a first form to what are for her audience only vaguely or partially ordered feelings and perceptions, makes a shared sense out of already shared circumstances.[2]

As a renouncer of worldly life, a sanyasin, Ritambhara conjures up the image of selflessness. Associatively, she is not a politician stirred by narrow electoral considerations or identified with partisan interest groups but someone who is moved by the plight of the whole country, even concerned with the welfare of all mankind. As an ascetic who has renounced all sexual activity, she evokes the image of the virgin goddess, powerful because virgin, a power which is of another, 'purer' world. There is also a subtle sexual challenge to the men in her audience to prove their virility (*vis-à-vis* the Muslim) in order to deserve her.

The key passages in the text of her speech are delivered as rhyming verses, in the tradition of bardic narration of stories from the Hindu epics. Perhaps people tend to believe verse more than prose, especially in Hindu India where the transmission of sacred knowledge has traditionally been oral and through the medium of rhymed verse. In any event, implicit in her speech is the claim to be less tainted with the corruption of language, a corruption which is widely laid at the door of the politician and which has led people to lose faith in what they hear from public platforms. If Ritambhara is a politician, hers is the politics of magic that summons forces from the deep, engaging through coded ideas and ideals the deeper fears and wishes of her Hindu audiences whom she and the *sangh parivar* are determined to make 'more' Hindu. As I listened to her I was once again reminded of Milan Kundera's statement that 'political movements rest not so much on rational attitudes as on fantasies, images, words and archetypes that come together to make up this or that political kitsch.'

Hail Mother Sita! Hail brave Hanuman! Hail Mother India! Hail the birthplace of Rama! Hail Lord Vishwanath [Shiva] of Kashi [Benares]! Hail Lord Krishna! Hail the eternal religion [*dharma*]! Hail the religion of the vedas! Hail Lord Mahavira! Hail Lord Buddha! Hail Banda Bairagi! Hail Guru Gobind Singh! Hail the great sage Dayananda! Hail the great sage Valmiki! Hail the martyred *kar-sevak*s! Hail Mother India!

In ringing tones Ritambhara invokes the various gods and revered figures from Indian history, ancient and modern. The gods and heroes are not randomly chosen. In their careful selection, they are markers of the boundary of the Hindu community she and the *sangh parivar* would wish to constitute today and believe existed in the past. Such a commemoration is necessarily selective since it must silence contrary interpretations of the past and seek to conserve only certain of its aspects. The gods and heroes are offered up as ego ideals, to be shared by members of the community in order to bring about and maintain group cohesion. Identity implies definition rather than blurring, solidity rather than flux or fluidity, and therefore the question of boundaries of a group become paramount. Ritambhara begins the construction of Hindu identity by demarcating this boundary.

In the context of the preceding year's agitation around the construction of the Rama temple, the god Rama occupies the highest watch-over on the border between Hindu and non-Hindu. Ritambhara starts by raising Rama's wife, the goddess Sita, and his greatest devotee, the monkey god Hanuman, who are then linked to contemporary concerns as she hails Rama's birthplace where the sangh parivar wishes to construct the controversial temple and around which issue it has sought a mobilization of the Hindus.

The 5000-year-old religion, however, with a traditional lack of central authority structures such as a church and with a diffused essence, has over the centuries thrown up a variety of sects with diverse beliefs. It is Ritambhara's purpose to include all the Hinduisms spawned by Hinduism. The presiding deity of the Shaivite sects, Shiva, is hailed, as is Krishna, the most popular god of the Vaishnavas.

The overarching Hindu community is then sought to be further enlarged by including the followers of other religions whose birthplace is India. These are the Jains, the Buddhists, and the Sikhs, and Ritambhara devoutly hails Mahavira, Buddha, and the militant last guru of the Sikhs, Guru Gobind Singh who, together with Banda Bairagi, has the added distinction of a lifetime of armed struggle against the Mughals. Nineteenth-century reformist movements such as the Arya Samaj are welcomed by including its founder Dayananda Saraswati in the Hindu pantheon. The Harijans or 'scheduled castes', the former 'untouchables' of Hindu society, are expressly acknowledged as a part of the Hindu society by hailing Valmiki, the legendary author of the *Ramayana* who has been recently elevated to the position of the patron saint of the Harijans.

From gods and heroes of the past, a link is established to the collective heroism of the *kar-sevak*s, men and women who in their bid to build the temple died in the police firing at Ayodhya. The immortal gods and the mortal heroes from past and present are all the children of Mother India, the subject of the final invocation, making the boundaries of the Hindu community coterminous with that of Indian nationalism.

have come to the Hindus of Bhagyanagar [Hyderabad] with a message. The saints who met in Allahabad directed Hindu society to either bend the government to its will or to remove it. The government has been removed. On fourth April, more than two and a half million Hindus displayed their power at the lawns of Delhi's Boat Club. We went to the Parliament but it lay empty. The saints said, fill the Parliament with the devotees of Rama. This is the next task of Hindu society.

As far as the construction of the Rama temple is concerned, some people say Hindus should not fight over a structure of brick and stone. They should not quarrel over a small piece of land. I want to ask these people, 'If someone burns the national flag will you say "Oh, it doesn't matter. It is only two metres of cloth which is not a great national loss."' The question is not of two metres of cloth but of an insult to the nation. Rama's birthplace is not a quarrel about a small piece of land. It is a question of national integrity. The Hindu is not fighting for a temple of brick and stone. He is fighting for the preservation of a civilization, for his Indianness, for national consciousness, for the recognition of his true nature. We shall build the temple!

It is not the building of the temple but the building of India's national consciousness. You, the wielders of state power, you do not know that the Rama temple is not a mere building. It is not a construction of brick and stone. It is not only the birthplace of Rama. The Rama temple is our honour. It is our self esteem. It is the image of Hindu unity. We shall raise its flag. We shall build the temple!

Hindi is a relatively passionate language. Its brilliant, loud colours are impossible to reproduce in the muted palette of English. As the Rama temple takes shape in Ritambhara's cascading flow of language, as she builds it, phrase by phrase, in the mind of her listeners, it evokes acute feelings of a shared social loss. The Rama temple, then, is a response to the mourning of Hindu society: a mourning for lost honour, lost self esteem, lost civilization, lost Hinduness. It is the material and social counterpart of the individual experience of mourning. In a more encompassing formulation, the Rama birthplace temple is like other monuments which, as Peter Homans perceptively observes:

engage the immediate conscious experience of an aggregate of egos by representing and mediating to them the lost cultural experiences of the past; the experiences of individuals, groups, their ideas and ideals, which coalesce into what can be called a collective memory. In this the monument is a symbol of union because it brings together the particular psychological circumstances of many individuals' life courses and the universals of their otherwise lost historical past within the context of their current or contemporary social processes and structures.[3]

The temple is the body in which Hindu identity is sought to be embodied.

Some people became afraid of Rama's devotees. They brought up Mandal.*

---

*Mandal refers to the reservation policy announced by the government of V.P. Singh at the height of the temple agitation. The policy sought to increase reservations in federal and state employment and admission to educational institutions for the backward castes at the expense of the upper castes.

They thought the Hindu will get divided. He will be fragmented by the reservations issue. His attention will be diverted from the temple. But your thought was wrong. Your thought was despicable. We shall build the temple!

I have come to tell our Hindu youth, do not take the candy of reservations and divide yourself into castes. If Hindus get divided, the sun of Hindu unity will set. How will the sage Valmiki look after Sita? How will Rama eat Shabri's berries [*ber*]?* Those who wish that our bonds with the backward castes and the Harijans are cut will bite dust. We shall build the temple!

Listen, Rama is the representation of mass consciousness. He is the god of the poor and the oppressed. He is the life of fishermen, cobblers, and washermen.** If anyone is not a devotee of such a god, he does not have Hindu blood in his veins. We shall build the temple!

Marking its boundary, making it aware of a collective cultural loss, giving it a body, is not enough to protect and maintain the emerging Hindu identity. For identity is not an achievement but a process constantly threatened with rupture by forces from within and without.

Constant vigil is needed to guard it from that evil inside the group which seeks to divide what has been recently united, to disrupt and fragment what has been freshly integrated. Ritambhara addresses the feeling of threat and singles out the political forces representing this threat which must be defeated at the coming battle of the ballot box.

My Hindu brothers! Stop shouting that slogan, 'Give one more push and break the Babri mosque! The mosque is broken, the mosque is broken!!' What mosque are you talking about? We are going to build our temple there, not break anyone's mosque. Our civilization has never been one of destruction. Intellectuals and scholars of the world, wherever you find ruins, wherever you come upon broken monuments, you will find the signature of Islam. Wherever you find creation, you discover the signature of the Hindu. We have never believed in breaking but in constructing. We have always been ruled by the maxim, 'The world is one family [*Vasudhaiva kutumbakam*]'. We are not pulling down a monument, we are building one.

Scholars, turn the pages of history and tell us whether the Hindu, riding a horse and swinging a bloody sword, has ever trampled on anyone's human dignity? We cannot respect those who have trod upon humanity. Our civilization has given us great insights. We see god in a stone, we see god in trees and plants. We see god in a god and run behind him with a cup of butter. Hindus have you

*The sage Valmiki, reputedly a hunter belonging to a low caste gave asylum to Sita in his forest abode after she was banished by Rama. Shabri was a poor untouchable who fed berries to Rama during his exile.
**All of them belong to the lowest castes.

forgotten that the saint Namdev had only one piece of bread to eat which was snatched by a dog. Namdev ran after the dog with a cup of butter crying, 'Lord, don't eat dry bread. Take some butter too!!' Can the Hindu who sees god even in a dog ever harbour resentment towards a Muslim?

Wherever I go, I say, 'Muslims, live and prosper among us. Live like milk and sugar. If two kilos of sugar are dissolved in a quintal of milk, the milk becomes sweet!' But what can be done if our Muslim brother is not behaving like sugar in the milk? Is it our fault if he seems bent upon being a lemon in the milk? He wants the milk to curdle. He is behaving like a lemon in the milk by following people like Shahabuddin and Abdullah Bukhari.* I say to him, 'Come to your senses. The value of the milk increases after it becomes sour. It becomes cheese. But the world knows the fate of the lemon. It is cut, squeezed dry and then thrown on the garbage heap. Now you have to decide whether you will act like sugar or like a lemon in the milk. Live among us like the son of a human being and we will respectfully call you "uncle". But if you want to behave like the son of Babar then the Hindu youth will deal with you as Rana Pratap and Chatrapati Shivaji** dealt with your forefathers.' Those who say we are against the Muslims lie. We are talking of the birthplace of Rama, not constructing at Mecca or Medina. It is our birthright to build a temple to our Lord at the spot he was born.

We have religious tolerance in our very bones. Together with our 330 million gods, we have worshipped the dead lying in their graves. Along with Rama and Krishna, we have saluted Mohammed and Jesus. With *Vasudhaiva kutumbakam* as our motto, we pray for the salvation of the world and for an increase in fellow feeling in all human beings. We have never said, 'O World! Believe in our *Upanishads*. Believe in our *Gita*. Otherwise you are an infidel and by cutting off the head of an infidel one gains paradise.' Our sentiments are not so low. They are not narrow-minded. They are not dirty. We see the world as our family.

Here, in the construction of the Hindu identity, we see the necessary splitting that enhances group cohesion. The process involves idealizing on the one hand and scapegoating and persecutory processes on the other. What is being idealized is the Hindu tolerance, compassion, depth of insight and width of social concern. These are the contents of a grandiose Hindu group self which makes the individual member feel righteous and pure. It raises each member's sense of worth for belonging to this group.

The increase in self-esteem can be maintained only by projecting the bad, the dirty, and the impure to another group, the Muslim, with which one's own group is then constantly compared. This process is at the roo

*Widely regarded as two of the leaders of Muslim fundamentalism in India.
**Popular embodiments of Hindu resistance to Mughal rule.

of scapegoating and, as Rafael Moses reminds us, this indeed is how the original scapegoat was conceived of in religion: the animal was driven away with all the community's badness inside it so that the community of believers could remain pure and clean (like milk, I am tempted to add).[4] Of course, as a good vegetarian Hindu, Sadhvi Ritambhara conceives the Muslim scapegoat not as an animal but as a lemon. As we shall see below, the Muslim is not only the object of scapegoating but also the subject of persecutory fantasies in the collective Hindu imagination.

Today, the Hindu is being insulted in his own home. The Hindu is not sectarian. How could he if he worships trees and plants! Once [the Mughal emperor] Akbar and [his Hindu minister] Birbal were going somewhere. On the way they saw a plant. Birbal dismounted and prostrated himself before the plant saying, 'Hail mother tulsi!' Akbar said, 'Birbal, you Hindus are out of your minds, making parents out of trees and plants. Let's see how strong your mother is!' He got off his horse, pulled the tulsi plant out by its roots and threw it on the road. Birbal swallowed this humiliation and kept quiet. What could he do? It was the reign of the Mughals. They rode farther and saw another plant. Birbal again prostrated himself saying, 'Hail, father! Hail, honoured father!' Akbar said, 'Birbal I have dealt with your mother. Now, let me deal with your father too.' He again pulled out the plant and threw it away. The plant was a nettle. Akbar's hands started itching and soon the painful itch spread all over his body. He began rolling on the ground like a donkey, with tears in his eyes and his nose watering. All the while he was scratching himself like a dog. When Birbal saw the condition of the king, he said, 'O Protector of the World, pardon my saying that our Hindu mothers may be innocent but our fathers are hard-bitten.' Akbar asked, 'Birbal, how do I get rid of your father?' Birbal said, 'Go and ask forgiveness of my mother tulsi. Then rub the paste made out of her leaves on your body and my father will pardon you.'

I mean to say that the long-suffering Hindu is being called a religious zealot today only because he wants to build the temple. The Muslims got their Pakistan. Even in a mutilated India, they have special rights. They have no use for family planning. They have their own religious schools. What do we have? An India with its arms cut off.* An India where restrictions are placed on our festivals, where our processions are always in danger of attack, where the expression of our opinion is prohibited, where our religious beliefs are cruelly derided. We cannot speak of our pain, express our hurt. I say to the politician, 'Do not go on trampling upon our deepest feelings as you have been doing for so long.'

In Kashmir, the Hindu was a minority and was hounded out of the valley. Slogans

*The reference is to a comparison between the maps of India before and after Partition.

of 'Long live Pakistan' were carved with red-hot iron rods on the thighs of our Hindu daughters. Try to feel the unhappiness and the pain of the Hindu who became a refugee in his own country. The Hindu was dishonoured in Kashmir because he was in a minority. Bu there is a conspiracy to make him a minority in the whole country. The state tells us Hindus to have only two or three children. After a while, they will say do not have even one. But what about those who have six wives, have 35 children and breed like mosquitoes and flies?

Why should there be two sets of laws in this country? Why should we be treated like stepchildren? I submit to you that when the Hindu of Kashmir became a minority he came to Jammu. From Jammu he came to Delhi. But if you Hindus are on the run all over India, where will you go? Drown in the Indian Ocean or jump from the peaks of the Himalayas?

What is this impartiality toward all religions where the mullahs get the moneybags and Hindus the bullets? We also want religious impartiality but not of the kind where only Hindus are oppressed. People say there should be Hindu-Muslim unity. Leave the structure of the Babri mosque undisturbed. I say, 'Then let's have this unity, in the case of the Jama Masjid* too. Break half of it and construct a temple. Hindus and Muslims will then come together.'

You know the doctors who carry out their medical experiments by cutting open frogs, rabbits, cats? All these experiments in Hindu–Muslim unity are being carried out on the Hindu chest as if he is a frog, rabbit or cat. No one has ever heard of a lion's chest being cut open for a medical experiment. They teach the lesson of religious unity and amity only to the Hindus.

In Lucknow there was a Muslim procession which suddenly stopped when passing a temple where a saffron flag was flying. The mullahs said, 'This is the flag of infidels. We cannot pass even under its shadow. Take down the flag!' Some of your liberal Hindu leaders and followers of Gandhi started persuading the Hindus, 'Your ancestors have endured a great deal. You also tolerate a little. You have been born to suffer. take down the flag.' Luckily, I was also there. I said to the leader who was trying to cajole the Hindus into taking down the flag, 'If I took off your cap, gave four blows to your head with my shoe and then replaced the cap, would you protest?' This is not just our flag, it is our honour, our pride. Religious impartiality does not mean that to appease one you insult the other. Hindu children were riddled with bullets in the alleys of Ayodhya to please the Muslims. The Saryu river became red with the blood of slaughtered *kar-sevak*s. We shall not forget.

It is true that for the strengthening of cultural identity, belief of the group members in an existing or anticipated oppression is helpful, if not necessary. yet for the 800 million Hindus who are relatively more advanced on almost every economic and social criteria, to feel oppressed

---

*The best known Indian mosque, located in Delhi.

by Muslims who are one-eighth their number demands an explanation other than one given by the theory of relative deprivation. This theory, as we know, argues that a group feels oppressed if it perceives inequality in the distribution of resources and believes it is entitled to more than the share it receives. There is a considerable denial of reality involved in maintaining that the Hindus are relatively deprived or in danger of oppression by the Muslims. Such a denial of reality is only possible through the activation of the group's persecutory fantasy in which the Muslim changes from a stereotype to an archetype; he becomes the 'arch' tyrant. As in individuals, where persecution anxiety often manifests itself in threats to the integrity of the body, especially during psychotic episodes, Ritambhara's speech becomes rich in the imagery of a mutilated body. Eloquently, she conjures up an India—the motherland—with its arms cut off; Hindu chests cut open like those of frogs, rabbits, and cats, the thighs of young Hindu women burnt with red-hot iron rods; in short, the body amputated, slashed, raped. It is the use of metaphors of the body—one's own and of one's mother (India)—under assault that makes an actual majority feel a besieged minority in imagination, anchors the dubious *logos* of a particular political argument deeply in fantasy through the power of *mythos*.

They said, 'Let's postpone the mid-term elections till the Hindu's anger cools down.' I say, 'Is the Hindu a bottle of mineral water? Keep the bottle open for a while and the water will stop bubbling?' It is 900,000 years since Ravana kidnapped Sita and challenged god Rama. But to this day we have not forgotten. Every year we burn his effigy and yet the fire of our revenge burns bright. We will not forget mullah Mulayam* and his supporter Rajiv Gandhi. I have come to tell the young men and mothers of Bhagyanagar, listen to the wailing of the Saryu river, listen to the story told by Ayodhya, listen to the sacrifice of the *kar-sevak*s. If you are a Hindu, do not turn your face away from the Rama temple, do not spare the traitors of Rama.

After the incident on the ninth of November, many Hindu young men came to me. 'Sister,' they said, 'give us weapons to deal with mullah Mulayam.' I said, 'Why waste a bullet to deal with a eunuch?' Rama had become tired shooting his arrows. Ravana's one head would fall to be immediately replaced by another. Vibhishana [Ravana's brother] said, 'Lord, you will not kill this sinner by cutting off his heads. His life is in his navel.' My brother Hindus, these leaders have their lives in their chairs [of power]. Take away their power and they'll die—by themselves. They are only impotent eunuchs. When Rama was banished from Ayodhya many citizens accompanied him to the forest and stayed

*The chief minister of Uttar Pradesh.

there overnight. In the morning, Rama said, 'Men and women of Ayodhya, go back to your homes.' The men and women went back but a group of hermaphrodites, who are neither men nor women, stayed back and asked, 'Lord, you have not given us any instructions.' Rama is kind. He said, 'In the future Kaliyuga you will rule for a little while.' These, neither-men-nor-women, are your rulers today. They will not be able to protect India's unity and integrity. Make the next government one of Rama's devotees. Hindus, you must unite in the coming elections if you want the temple built. Hindus, if you do not awaken, cows will be slaughtered everywhere. In the retreats of our sages you will hear the chants of 'Allah is Great'. You will be responsible for these catastrophes for history will say Hindus were cowards. Accept the challenge, change the history of our era.

Many say, Ritambhara you are a sanyasin. You should meditate in some retreat. I tell them raising Hindu consciousness is my meditation now and it will go on till the saffron flag flies from the ramparts of the Red Fort.*

The feeling of helplessness which persecution anxiety engenders reverses the process of idealization, reveals the fragility of the group's grandiose self. The positive self image of the Hindu—tolerant, compassionate, with special insight into the relationship between the divine and the natural worlds, between human and divine—exposes another, negative side: the specific Hindu shame and fear of being too cowardly and impotent to change the material or social conditions of life. Indeed, we should always look closely at a group's specific form of self-idealization to find clues to its particular moment of self-doubt and self-hatred. What a group most idealizes about itself is intimately related to its greatest fear. For the Hindu, the positive self image of tolerance has the shadow of weakness cleaving to it. Are we tolerant or are we merely weak? Or tolerant *because* weak?

The crumbling self, with its unbearable state of helplessness, demands restoration through forceful action. Ritambhara channels this need for *agens* into a call for collective and united action in the political arena. She holds out the possibility of some kind of self assertion through the coming electoral process where all the persecutory anti-Hindu forces, from within and without the Hindu fold, can be engaged and defeated. With this prospect, the negative self image begins to fade, the group self becomes more cohesive. The Muslim, too, though remaining alien, becomes less demonic and more human, although still a cussed adversary.

*The symbol of political power in India.

They ask what would happen to the Muslims in a Hindu India? I tell them the Muslims will not be dishonoured in a Hindu state nor will they be rewarded to get their votes. No umbrella will open in Indian streets because it is raining in Pakistan. It there is war in the Gulf then slogans of 'Long Live Saddam Hussein' won't be shouted on Indian streets. And as for unity with our Muslim brothers, we say, 'Brother, we are willing to eat *sevian* [sweet noodles] at your house to celebrate Eid but you do not want to play with colours with us on Holi. We hear your calls to prayer along with our temple bells, but you object to our bells. How can unity ever come about? The Hindu faces this way, the Muslim the other. The Hindu writes from left to right, the Muslim from right to left. The Hindu prays to the rising sun. The Muslim faces the setting sun when praying. If the Hindu eats with the right hand, the Muslim eats with the left. If the Hindu calls India 'Mother', she becomes a witch for the Muslim. The Hindu worships the cow, the Muslim attains paradise by eating beef The Hindu keeps a moustache, the Muslim always shaves the upper lip. Whatever the Hindu does, it is the Muslim's religion to do its opposite. I said, 'If you want to do everything contrary to the Hindu, then the Hindu eats with his mouth; you should do the opposite in this matter too!'

After the laughter subsides, Ritambhara ends by asking the audience to raise their fists and repeat after her, 'Say with pride, we are Hindus! Hindustan (India) is ours!'

The conclusion of Ritambhara's speech complements its beginning. Both the beginning and the end are concerned with the issue of drawing the boundaries of the group of 'us' Hindus. Whereas Ritambhara began with a self definition of the Hindu by including certain kinds of Hinduisms—as personified by heroes, gods and historical figures—she ends with trying to achieve this self definition through contrasts with what a Hindu is decidedly not—the Muslim. At the start, the boundary was drawn from inside out; at the end, its contours are being marked off by reference to the 'them', the Muslims, who lie outside the psychogeographical space inhabited by 'us'. It is, of course, understood that 'their' space is not only separate and different but also devalued. In her enumeration of differences Ritambhara cleverly contrives to end on a note which associates the Muslim with certain denigrated, specifically anal, bodily parts and functions.

I have suggested here that the construction/revival of the new Hindu identity in the text of Ritambhara's speech follows certain well-marked turnings of the plot which are motivated, energized, and animated by fantasy. To recapitulate, these are: marking afresh the boundaries of the religious–cultural community, making the community conscious of a collective cultural loss, countering internal forces which seek to disrupt the unity of the freshly demarcated community, idealizing the community, maintaining its sense of grandiosity by comparing it to a bad 'other' which, at times, becomes a persecutor and, finally, dealing with the persecutory fantasies, which bring to the surface the community's particular sense of inferiority, by resort to some kind of forceful action.

In describing these psychological processes, I am aware that my own feelings toward the subject could have coloured some of my interpretations. This is unavoidable, especially since I am a Hindu myself, exposed to all the crosscurrents of feelings generated by contemporary events. My own brand of Hinduism, liberal–rationalist (with a streak of agnostic mysticism) can be expected to be critical of the new Hindu identity envisaged by the *sangh parivar*. Thus, to be fair (the liberal failing *par excellence*), one should add that the Hindu is no different from any other ethnic community or even nation which feels special and superior to other collectivities, especially their neighbours and rivals. This sense of superiority, the group's narcissism, its self aggrandizement, serves the purpose of increasing group cohesion and thus the enhancement of the self-esteem of its members. Rafael Moses, reflecting on the group selves of the Israelies and the Arabs, asks: 'And is perhaps a little grandiosity the right glue for such a cohesion? Is that perhaps the same measure of grandiosity which is seen in the family and does it serve the same purpose, thereby strengthening the feeling of specialness and of some grandiosity which all of us harbour in ourselves?'[5]

The *sangh parivar* cannot be faulted for fostering a Hindu pride or even trying to claim a sense of superiority *vis-à-vis* the Muslim. These are the normal aims of the group's narcissistic economy. Perhaps we recoil from such aims because narcissism, both in individuals and groups, is regarded with much misgiving. A person who is a victim of passions, sexual and aggressive, may be pitied and even seen by some as tragically heroic. An individual propelled by narcissism, on the other hand, is invariably scorned as mean and contemptible. Whereas the perversions of sex may evoke sympathy, the miscarriages of narcissism, such as a smug superiority or an arrogant self righteousness, provoke distaste among even the most tolerant. The question is not of the *sangh parivar*'s fostering of Hindu narcissism (which, we know, serves individual self possession) but of when this narcissism becomes deviant or abnormal. The answer is not easy for I do not know of any universal, absolute standards which can help us in charting narcissistic deviance or pathology in a group. One would imagine that the promotion of persecutory fantasies in a group to the extent that it resorts to violence against the persecuting Other would be deviant. Yet we all know that a stoking of persecutory fantasies is the stock in trade of all nations on the eve of any war and continues well into the duration of hostilities.

One could say that a group wherein all individual judgement is suspended and reality-testing severely disturbed may legitimately be regarded as pathological. This, however, is an individualistic viewpoint which looks askance at any kind of self transcendence through immersion in a group. In this view, spiritual uplift in a religious assembly, where the person feels an upsurge of love enveloping the community and the world outside, would be regarded with the same grave suspicion as the murkier purposes of a violent mob. It is certainly true that transcending individuality by merging into a group can generate heroic self-sacrifice, but it can also generate unimaginable brutality. To get out of one's skin in a devotional assembly is also at the same time to have less regard for saving that skin when part of a mob. Yet to equate and thus condemn both is to deny the human aspiration toward self-transcendence, a promise held out by our cultural identity and redeemed, if occasionally, by vital participation in the flow of the community's cultural life.

It is, however, evident that it is this group pride and narcissism which have made it possible for the Hindutva forces to offer another alternative vision of India's future as an alternate to those offered by the modernists and the traditionalists. The modernists are, of course, enthusiastic votaries of the modernization project although the Left and Right may argue over which economic form is the most suitable. Both factions, however, are neither interested in nor consider the question of cultural authenticity as important. The traditionalists, on the other hand, including the neo-Gandhians, totally reject modernity solely on the issue of cultural authenticity. The Hindutva forces have tried to offer yet another alternative by reformulating the project of modernity in a way where its instrumentalities are adopted but its norms and values are contested. The pivotal issue for them is not the acceptance of global technoscience or the economic institutions and forms of modernity but their impact on and a salvaging of Hindu culture and identity—as they define it. Cultural nationalism, though, will always have priority whenever it conflicts with economic globalism. It is apparent that such an approach to modernity will have great appeal to the emerging middle classes and sections of the intelligentsia which are committed neither to what I can only call universal modernism nor to a postmodern traditionalism.

The danger of stoking group narcissism, Hindu *garv* (pride) in our example, is that when this group grandiosity (expressed in a belief in its unique history and/ or destiny, its moral, aesthetic, technological, or any other kind of superiority *vis-à-vis* other groups) is brought into serious doubt, when the group feels humiliated, when higher forms of grandiosity such as the group's ambitions are blocked, then there is a regression in the group akin to one in the individual. The negative part of the grandiose self which normally remains hidden, the group's specific feelings of worthlessness and its singular sense of inferiority, now come to the fore. If all possibilities of self assertion are closed, there is a feeling of absolute helplessness, a state which must be changed through assertive action. Such a regression, with its accompanying feeling of vulnerability and helplessness, is most clearly manifested in the sphere of group aggression which takes on, overtly and covertly, the flavour of narcissistic rage. As in the individual who seeks to alter such an unbearable self state through acts as extreme as suicide or homicide, the group's need for undoing the damage to the collective self by whatever means, and a deeply anchored, unrelenting compulsion in the pursuit of this aim give it no rest. Narcissistic rage does not vanish when the offending object disappears. The painful memory can linger on, making of the hot rage a chronic, cold resentment till it explodes in all its violet manifestations whenever historical circumstances sanction such eruptions. I am afraid Ayodhya is not an end but only a beginning since the forces buffeting Hindu (or, for that matter, Muslim) grandiosity do not lie within the country but are global in their scope. They are the forces of modernization itself, of the wonderful attractions and the terrible distortions of the mentality of Enlightenment.

It would also be easy to dismiss Ritambhara's—and the *sangh parivar*'s—evocation of the Hindu past from a postmodern perspective which considers every past a social construction that is shaped by the concerns of the present. In other words, there is no such thing as *the* past since the past is transformable and manipulable according to the needs of the present. Yet as the French sociologist Emile Durkheim pointed out long ago, every society displays and even requires a minimal sense of continuity with its past.[6] Its memories cannot be relevant to its present unless it secures this continuity. In a society in the throes of modernization, the need for continuity with the past, a sense of heritage, essential for maintaining a sense of individual and cultural identity, becomes even more pressing, sharply reducing the subversive attractions of a viewpoint which emphasizes the plasticity and discontinuities of the past. It is this need for a continuity of cultural memory, of a common representation of the past in times of rapid change, even turbulence, which the *sangh parivar* addresses with considerable social resonance and political success.

14

Meeting the Mullahs

The men who have traditionally spearheaded the fundamentalist response of Muslim societies and who are widely regarded as representatives of Islamic conservatism are professional men of religion, the *ulema*, with various degrees of religious learning, who are also known as mullahs in Persia and India. In some ways, my encounter with the mullahs was psychologically the most difficult. The meeting itself was undemanding since besides our animating minds the encounter only involved a disembodied voice on the mullah's part and ears on mine. The mullahs—Qari Hanif Mohammad Multanwale, Syed Mohammad Hashmi, Maulana Salimuddin Shamshi, Riyaz Effendi, and others—came to me through their sermons recorded live at different times during the last decade at various mosques and reproduced in hundreds of thousands of inexpensive audiocasettes which are widely available in the Muslim neighbourhoods of Indian towns and cities.

The encounter with the mullah proved difficult on two counts. First, there was the persistence of my Hindu childhood image of the mullah as the wild-eyed man with a flowing beard who spewed fire and brimstone every Friday afternoon in the mosque with an intent to transform his congregation into a raging mob baying for the blood of the Hindu infidel—mine. Second, the mullah's rhetoric, based on older models from the heyday of Islam in the Middle East, was unpleasantly foreign to me. Openly emotional, using the full register of the voice from a whisper to the full-throated shout, screaming and on occasion weeping as he is overtaken by religious enthusiasm, the mullah's style of public speaking (as of the Hindu zealot) was distasteful to me. My adult sensibility, influenced by psychoanalytic rationalism, recoils at the hectoring tone, the imperative voice, and the moral certainty which recognizes only the black of unbelief (*kufar*) and the white of faith and has neither time nor tolerance for the shades of grey.

Influenced emotionally by fantasies from a Hindu past and cognitively by the concepts of a western-inspired liberalism, my first reaction to the mullah was to label him a 'fanatic', the word itself an 18th-century European coinage meant to denounce rather than describe the religious zealot. The temptation to rip open the mullah's facade of a just man gripped by religious passion to reveal the workings of other, baser motives was overwhelming. Indeed, the speeches of most mullahs, expressing contempt and indifference for everything other than the object of their passion and an unshakeable certitude in the rightness of their beliefs, seem to be verily designed for a psychoanalytically inspired hatchet job. The temptation to pathologize the mullah as an obsessional, if not psychopathic or even paranoid, had to be resisted if I wished to understand Muslim fundamentalism without resort to reductionist psychological cliches.[1] The first step in such an understanding was to listen to the mullah.

Sung in many voices and with varying lyrics, the music of the fundamentalist theme song is easily recognizable from one mullah to another. After a couple of obligatory *ayat*s from the *Qur'an* in Arabic as a prelude, signifying that both the speaker and the listener are now in the realm of the sacred, the fundamentalist generally begins with a lament for the lost glories of Islam as he compares the sorry plight of Muslims today with their earlier exalted status. There may be a sizeable presence of Muslims in all parts of the globe, says one mullah, and the mosque and the *Qur'an* found in every country. Yet nowhere does one hear that Muslims are thriving, successful, or on the ascendant. A hundred and sixty million Muslims are being whipped by two-and-a-half million Jews, says another. Look at the sorry fate of Iraq, a land made sacred by the blood of the Prophet's grandsons. At one time Sultan Salah-al-din Ayubi (Saladin) commanding a force of 13,000 in the battle for Jerusalem fed Richard's army of 700,000 and killed 300,000 Christians on a single day. Once, in the battle for Mecca—and the first battle of Islamic history is every mullah's preferred illustration—the Prophet with a ragtag force of 313 (a number which along with the word 'Karbala' has become the most effective symbol of political mobilization), including women, children, and old men, defeated the 1000 armed warriors of Abu Jahl, many of them on horseback, at the battle of Badr. Today, with all the oil, dollars, and weapons in the world, Muslims are slaves to the dictates of western Christian powers even in the 36 countries of which they are the putative rulers. Once, when the Muslim saint Khwaja Moinuddin Chisti died in Ajmer, nine million *kafirs* (here, the Hindus) began reading the *kalma*, that is, became Muslims. Once, at the sight of Imam Rahimullah's funeral cortege, 20,000 Jews converted to Islam. Today, Muslims have trouble keeping their own faith alive.

The choice of historical illustrations from the early history of Islam, including their legendary elaboration, to bring home the fact of Muslim degeneration and distress in the modern world is a pan-Islamic phenomenon. Few if any civilizations have attached as much importance to history as has Islam in its awareness of itself.[2] 'Recognize your history (*tarikh*)!' is the common fundamentalist exhortation, in contrast to the Hindu revivalist's implied suggestion, 'Live your myth!' From the Prophet's time to the present, it has been Islam which has distinguished between self and other, between brother and stranger, between the faithful and the alien *kafir*, the unbeliever. It is therefore not surprising that in fundamentalist discourse it is the wider, Arab-centred history of Islam rather than the history of Indian Muslims through which a collective Muslim identity is sought to be shaped.

After listing the symptoms of Muslim distress, the mullahs proceed to diagnose the disease. The bad condition of the Muslims, they aver, is not due to any major changes in the outer circumstances of Muslim lives but because of a glaring internal fault: the weakening or loss of religious faith. Muslims have lost everything—political authority, respect, the wealth of both faith. (*din*) and the world (*duniya*)—because they did not keep their pact with Mohammed. At one time Allah gave Muslims the kingdom of the world only in order to test whether they would continue to remain His slaves. Muslims have failed Allah's test. It was their religious zeal which made a small, unarmed group of Muslims succeed on the battlefield against overwhelming odds. (Now the mullah begins to address the listener more directly). Today, you do not respect the *Qur'an*. You do not respect the Prophet who is so pure that not a single fly came near him during his lifetime, a man whose sweat smelt more divine than shiploads of perfume. You may think of yourselves as Muslims but look into the mirror of the *Qur'an* and you will see you are not.

The Arabs lose to the Jews in Palestine because they are fighting for land, even if it is their own land. They are not fighting for Islam, for the Prophet. Sultan Salah-al-din fought for Islam and won Palestine. On the eve of the battle against Richard, he said to his soldiers: 'Paradise is near, Egypt is far.' He did not defend Islam by the sword but by his character as a Muslim. The Christians, as is their wont, used to send beautiful young women to seduce and corrupt Muslim generals, their priests assuring the girls forgiveness for all sins incurred in the service of Christianity. Saladin rejected 13 of the most beautiful Christian girls sent to his palace; in fact, the Christian women, impressed by the Sultan's steadfastness, read the *kalma*. On the other hand the Muslims lost India, not to the British, but because the last Mughal emperors like Mohammad Shah Rangile and Bahadur Shah Zafar were sunk in the quagmire of wine, women, and poetry.

After the diagnosis the physicians proceed to pathogenesis. The disease is caused by the process of modernity which the Muslim body has not resisted. There is no difference today between the home of a Muslim and that of a Hindu, Jew, or Christian. The sickness of television has entered Muslim homes where families fritter away whole evenings in ungodly entertainment rather than in reading from or discussing the *Qur'an*. Some of them say, 'We watch television only for the news.' I ask, 'What news? Of murders and accidents? Is there any news to gladden the heart of the faithful? Where is the news that a Muslim country has conquered an infidel land?' People walk about the streets singing songs from movies, prostitute's songs, rather than with the *kalma* on their lips. They follow educated people who are the thieves of religion, who teach the separation of religion from life and from politics.

Muslims have now taken to these deeply offensive modern fashions. They no longer give a revered name such as Fatima, that of the Prophet's daughter, to their own daughters but prefer instead to name the little girl after some movie actress, a prostitute. Look at the western-style trousers that men wear, with pockets in indecent places. You see man bending forward and taking out money from thc hip pocket, next to the buttocks. In winter you can see them sliding their hands into the side pockets and taking out peanuts or cashews from these disgusting places and putting them in the mouth.

In olden days a ruler would never permit the presence of a woman in official rooms or at public functions. A mullah would not perform the wedding ceremony where women were present. Now some of the rulers cannot even go to the toilet without a woman. Instead of only bowing before Allah, Muslims now bow before graves of various *pirs* (holy men) who are three feet underground. No wonder Islam is bending under the assault of *kufr*, Arabs are bowing before Jews and Christians, you before the Hindus. What is this preoccupation with worldly wealth and success? Allah says, I did not bring you into the world to make two shops out of one, four out of two, two factories out of one, four out of two. Does the *Qur'an* want you to do that? Does the Prophet? No! They want you to dedicate yourself to the faith, give your life for the glory of Islam.

The remedy suggested by the mullahs is a return to the fundamentals of the faith as contained in the *Qur'an*. The *Qur'an* is Allah's book, the light given by God to lift the darkness of mankind. Nothing can be added to or subtracted from the book. No arguments, no discussion, no objections, no asking for proof. It is eternal and unchanging. It is not like the clothes you wear which are different for summer and winter. Follow every rule of the faith, not just the ones which are convenient. It is not what you want or wish but Allah's wish that has to be complied with. It is not your likes but what is liked by the Prophet that must be done. All that is needed to live your life is contained in the examples from the life of the Prophet. All you need is faith—in Allah, the Prophet, the Book, angels, Judgement Day, paradise, and hell—and effort. If you cannot get worldly wealth without putting in an effort, how can you obtain paradise without it? Tell your daughter to offer *namaz* daily in the house; you won't be able to tell them once they are burning in hell.

Psychologically, then, fundamentalism is a theory of suffering and cure, just as modern individualism is another theory of suffering and its cure. The core of psychological individuality is internalization rather than externalization. I use 'internalization' here as a sensing by the person of a psyche in the Greek sense, an animation from within rather than without. Experientially, this internalization is a recognition that one is possessed of a mind in all its complexity. It is the acknowledgement, however vague, unwilling, or conflicted, of a subjectivity that fates one to episodic suffering through some of its ideas and feelings—in psychoanalysis, murderous rage, envy, and possessive desire seeking to destroy those one loves and would keep alive—simultaneously with the knowledge, at some level of awareness, that the mind can help in containing and processing disturbed thoughts. Fundamentalism, on the other hand, identifies the cause of suffering not in the individual mind but in a historical process which, however, is not fatefully deterministic but amenable to human will and eminently reversible. Individual and collective suffering are due to a lapse from an ideal state of religious faith, and the cure lies in an effort to restore faith in one's inner life to its original state of pristine purity.

Another striking aspect of fundamentalist religious discourse is not so much its warlike anger against the enemy—the modernization process, the infidels—held responsible for the contemporary sorry state of the Muslims, but the turning of this rage inward in a collective self-recrimination and masochistic self-hate. The loss of Muslim greatness is not grieved for, a process that would pave the way for an eventual acceptance of its loss and thus enable the community to face the future without a debilitating preoccupation with the past. Instead, the loss is experienced as a persisting humiliation, a narcissistic injury to the group self which keeps on generating inchoate anger rather than the sadness of mourning. The instances from history in the mullahs' sermons are replete with sadomasochistic imagery, betraying an unconscious rage even as they seem to bemoan the lost glories of Islam. Their talk is liberally spattered with blood. Rivers of blood flow in the massacres of Muslims, fountains of the stuff spurt from the chests of children martyred to the faith. The atrocities borne by Muslims, both in modern and medieval periods, are detailed with much relish. It is not the doctors and the officers—the representatives of the modern world—who have sacrificed for the country's independence, says Quri Mohammad Hanif, but the mullahs. Detailing incidents not recorded in history books, 3000 *ulema* were laid on the road to Delhi and the British drove road rollers over their chests. Hundreds were sewn into pigskins and burnt alive. Impaling, burning at the stake, being trampled under elephant feet, and the walling in alive of early martyrs is described with an eye for gory detail. The listeners are asked to visualize the plight of the pious woman who had hundreds of nails driven into her palms and feet saying to her infidel torturer, 'You can drive a hundred nails into my tongue too and I will still take Allah's name.'

In addition to the sadomasochistic imagery, another theme in fundamentalist discourse is the inculcation of guilt. The speeches conjure up images of the ancestors regarding today's generation of Muslims with eyes full of reproach and with a 'Thou hast forsaken us!' refrain on dead lips. Skilfully reactivating the guilt *vis-à-vis* our parents that is our common human legacy from early childhood, fundamentalism stirs anger and guilt in a potent brew.

To trace psychological themes in Muslim fundamentalist discourse is not to reduce this discourse to psychopathology. Illness to the outsider, fundamentalism is a cure for the insider. For many Muslims with an inchoate sense of oppression and the looming shadow of a menacing future, with fractured self-esteem in the wake of historical change that saw an end to their political role and a virtual disappearance of their language, fundamentalism is an attempt, however flawed, to revive the sacred in social and cultural life, to give politics a spiritual dimension, and to recover in their religious verities a bulwark against collective identity fragmentation.

15

Religious Conflict in the Modern World

Our times are witness to a worldwide wave of religious revival. Islam, Hinduism, Buddhism, the new religions in Japan, born-again Christians in the United States, and the Protestant sects in Latin America are undergoing a resurgence which is regarded with deep distrust by all the modem heirs to the Enlightenment. Although a secular humanist might find most manifestations of the current religious zeal personally distasteful, he or she is nonetheless aware that the revitalization of religion at the end of the 20th century constitutes a complex attempt at the resacralization of cultures beset with the many ills of modernity. As Andrew Samuels reminds us, this fragmented and fractured attempt at resacralization to combat the sense of oppression and a future utterly bereft of any vision of transcendent purpose is not only a part of the new religious fundamentalisms but also integral to the so-called left-leaning, progressive political movements.[1] One can discern the search for transcendence even in concerns around ecological issues and environmental protection where at least some of the discourse is comprised of elements of nature mysticism.

However, if we look closely at individual cases around the world, we will find that the much-touted revival is less of religiosity than of cultural identities based on religious affiliation. In other words, there may not be any great ferment taking place in the world of religious ideas, rituals, or any marked increase in the sum of human spirituality. Where the resurgence is most visible is in the organization of collective identities around religion, in the formation and strengthening of communities of believers: What we are witnessing today is less the resurgence of religion than (in the felicitous Indian usage) of com-

munalism where a community of believers not only has religious affiliation but also social, economic, and political interests in common which
may conflict with the corresponding interests of another community of
believers sharing the same geographical space. Indeed, most secular
analysts and progressive commentators have traditionally sought to un-
cover factors other than religion as the root cause of an ostensibly
religious conflict. This has been as true of the anti-Semitic pogroms in
Spain in the 14th century, of 16th-century Catholic–Protestant violence
in France, of anti-Catholic riots in 18th-century London, as of 20th-cen-
tury Hindu–Muslim riots in India.[2] The 'real' cause of conflict between
groups in all these instances has been generally identified as a clash of
economic interests; the explanation embraces some version of a class
struggle between the poor and the rich.

The danger to the material existence of an individual can indeed be
experienced as an identity threat which brings a latent group identity to
the forefront. This heightened sense of identity with the group provides
the basis for a social cohesiveness which is necessary to safeguard the
individual's economic interests. But there are other threats besides the
economic one which too amplify the group aspect of personal identity.
In an earlier chapter, I described the identity–threat which is being
posed by the forces of modernization and globalization to peoples in
many parts of the world. Feelings of loss and helplessness accompany
dislocation and migration from rural areas to the shanty towns of urban
megalopolises, the disappearance of craft skills which underlay traditional work identities, and the humiliation caused by the homogenizing
and hegemonizing impact of the modern world which pronounces ancestral, cultural ideals and values as outmoded and irrelevant. These,
too are conducive to heightening the group aspects of identity as the
affected (and the afflicted) look to cultural–religious groups to combat
their feelings of helplessness and loss and to serve as vehicles for the
redress of injuries to self-esteem.

The identity–threat may also arise due to a perceived discrimination
by the state, that is, a disregard by the political authorities of a group's
interests or disrespect for its cultural symbols. It can also arise as a consequence of changing political constellations such as those which
accompany the end of empires. If Hindu–Muslim relations were in better shape in the past, with much less overt violence, it was perhaps also
because of the kind of polity in which the two peoples lived. This polity
was that of empire, the Mughal empire followed by the British one. An
empire, the political scientist Michael Walzer observes, is characterized

by a mixture of repression for any strivings for independence and tolerance for different cultures, religions and ways of life.[3] The tolerance is not a consequence of any great premodern wisdom but because of the indifference, sometimes bordering on brutal incomprehension, of the imperial bureaucrats to local conflicts of the peoples they rule. Distant from local life, they do not generally interfere with everyday life as long as things remain peaceful, though there may be intermittent cruelty to remind the subject peoples of the basis of the empire—conquest through force of arms. It is only with self-government, when distance disappears, that the political questions—'Who *among* us shall have power here, in these villages, these towns?' 'Will the majority group dominate?' 'What will be the new ranking order?'—lead to a heightened awareness of religious–cultural differences. In countries with multireligious populations, independence coincides with tension and conflict—such as we observe today in the wake of the unravelling of the Soviet empire.[4]

The identity–threats I have outlined above do not create a group identity but merely bring it to the fore. The group aspect of personal identity is not a late creation in individual development but exists from the beginning of the human lifecycle. Although Freud had no hesitation in maintaining that from the very first individual psychology is a social psychology as well, psychoanalysts, with their traditional emphasis on the 'body-in-the-mind', have tended to downplay the existence of the 'community-in-the-mind'.[5] They have continued to regard the social (*polis*) aspects of man's being as an overlay which compromises the wishes and needs of the self or, in the case of the crowd is destructive of individual self and identity. Erikson has been one of the rare psychoanalysts who has called for a revision of this model that differentiates so starkly between an individual-individual and the individual-in-mass who has no individuality at all: 'Yet that a man could ever be psychologically alone; that a man 'alone' is essentially different from the same man in a group; that a man in a temporary solitary condition or when closeted with his analyst has ceased to be a 'political' animal and has disengaged himself from social action (or inaction) on whatever class level—these and similar stereotypes demand careful revision.'[6]

Such revisions would begin with the idea that the inner space occupied by what is commonly called the 'self'—which I have been using synonymously with 'identity'—not only contains mental representations of one's bodily life and of primary relationships within the family but also holds mental representations of one's group and its culture, that is, the group's configuration of beliefs about man, nature, and social relations (including the view of the Other). These cultural propositions, transmitted and internalized through symbols have a strong emotional impact on those who grow up as members of a particular cultural group. The self, then, is a system of reverberating representational worlds, each enriching, constraining, and shaping the others, as they jointly evolve through the lifecycle. A revision of psychoanalytic notions of the self, identity, and subjectivity would also acknowledge that none of these constituent inner worlds is 'primary' or 'deeper', that is, there is no necessity of identity or an 'archaeological' layering of the various inner worlds, although at different times the self may be predominantly experienced in one or other representational mode. It is not only the brain that is bicameral.

At some point of time in early life, like the child's 'I am!' which heralds the birth of individuality, there is also a complementary 'We are!' which announces the birth of a sense of community. 'I am' differentiates me from other individuals. 'We are' makes me aware of the other dominant group (or groups) sharing the physical and cognitive space of my community. The self-assertion of 'We are' with its potential for confrontation with the 'We are' of other groups, is *inherently* a carrier of aggression, together with the consequent fears of persecution, and is thus always attended by a sense of risk and potential for violence. (The psychological processes initiated by an awareness of 'We are', I suggest, also provide an explanation for the experimental findings of cognitive psychologists that the mere perception of two different groups is sufficient to trigger a positive evaluation of one's own group and a negative stereotyping of the other).

The further development of the social-representational world or the group aspect of identity has some specific characteristics which I have discussed in detail at various places in this book in the context of Hindu–Muslim relations. To abstract briefly: this aspect of identity is powerfully formed by the processes of introjection, identification, idealization, and projection during childhood. On the one hand, the growing child assimilates within itself the images of the family and group members. He or she identifies with their emotional investment in the group's symbols and traditions and incorporates their idealizations of the group which have served them so well—as they will serve the child—in the enhancement of self-esteem for belonging to such an exalted and blessed entity. On the other hand, because of early difficulties in integrating contradictory representations of the self and the parents—the 'good' loving child and the 'bad' raging one; the good, caretaking parent and the hateful, frustrating one—the child tries to disown the bad representations through projection. First projected to inanimate objects and animals and later to people and other groups—the latter often available to the child as a preselection by the group—the disavowed bad, representations *need* such 'reservoirs', as Vamik Volkan calls them. These reservoirs—Muslims for Hindus, Arabs for Jews, Tibetans for the Chinese, and vice versa—are also convenient repositories for subsequent rages and hateful feelings for which no clear-cut addressee is available. Since most of the 'bad' representations arise from a social disapproval of the child's 'animality', as expressed in its aggressivity, dirtiness, and unruly sexuality, it is preeminently this animality which a civilized, moral self must disavow and place in the reservoir group. We saw this happening in the Hindu image of the dirty, aggressive, and sexually licentious Muslim, and we encounter it again and again in both modern and historical accounts of other group conflicts. Thus in 16th-century France, Catholics 'knew' that the Protestants were not only dirty and diabolic but that their Holy Supper was disordered and drunken, a bacchanalia, and that they snuffed out the candles and had indiscriminate sexual intercourse after voluptuous psalm singing. Protestants, on their part, 'knew' that Catholic clergy had an organization of hundreds of women at the disposal of priests and canons who, for the most part, were sodomites as well.[7]

The psychological processes involved in the development of 'We are' not only take recourse to the group's cultural traditions—its myths, history, rituals, and symbols—to make the community a firm part of personal identity but also employ bodily fantasies as well as family metaphors to anchor this aspect of identity in the deepest layers of individual imagination. The 'pure' us versus a 'dirty' them, the association of a rival group with denigrated, often anal, bodily parts and functions, representations of one's group in metaphors of a body under attack or as a 'good' son of the mother(land) while the rival group is a 'bad' son, are some of the examples from Hindu and Muslim discourse which I have discussed in earlier chapters.

We must, however, also note that there are always some individuals whose personal identity is not overwhelmed by their religious or cultural group identity even in the worst phase of violent conflict. These are persons capable of acts of compassion and self-sacrifice, such as saving members of the 'enemy' group from the fury of a rampaging mob even at considerable danger to their own physical safety. There are yet others—the fanatics—whose behaviour even in times of peace and in the absence of any identity-threat seems to be exclusively dictated by the 'We are' group aspect of their identity. What the social and psychological conditions are that make one person wear his or her group identity lightly whereas for another it is an armour which is rarely taken off is a question to which the answers are not only of theoretical interest but also of profound practical importance and moral significance.

RELIGIOUS IDENTITIES AND VIOLENCE

The development of religious identity follows the same lines through which the more global aspects of individual and group identities are also constructed. The individual track, which may be called religious selfhood, is an incommunicable realm of religious feeling which quietly suffuses what D.W. Winnicott termed 'the isolated core of the true self' requiring isolation and privacy, a core which 'never communicates with the world of perceived objects [and] must never be communicated with.'[8] In an integrated state, religious selfhood is a quiet self-experience, marked by a calmness of spirit that comes from being alone in the presence of the numinous. With its access to preverbal experience which can link different sensory modalities of image, sound, rhythm, and so on, religious selfhood deepens religious feeling and consolidates religious identity. In a state of fragmentation or threatened disintegration, religious selfhood is prey to a variety of dysphoric moods. For a few, the saints, whose religious identity constitutes the core of their being, the dysphoria can extend to the state of utter despair, the 'dark night of the soul.'

Together with religious selfhood, the 'I-ness' of religious identity, we have a second track of 'We-ness' which is the experience of being part of a community of believers. Religious community is the interactive aspect of religious identity. In contrast to the quietness of religious selfhood, the individual's experience of religious community takes place in an alert state. Optimally, this facet of religious identity expands the self and creates feelings of attunement and resonance with other believers. A threat to the community aspect of religious identity, however, gives birth to communalism, intolerance, and the potential for social violence. In the communal phase, the feeling of intimacy and connectedness characterizing the religious community are polluted by an ambience of aggression and persecution. Whereas both the selfhood and community facets of religious identity are only partially conscious, the change from community to communalism is accompanied and, indeed, initiated by a heightened awareness of 'We-ness', making the community aspect of religious identity hyperconscious. This awareness can be put in the form of declarations similar to the ones Oscar Patterson suggests take place in the inner discourse of an individual who, as a consequence of a shared threat, is in the process of self-consciously identifying with his or her ethnic group.[9] First, I declare to all who share the crisis with me that I am one with them—a Hindu, a Muslim. Second, from my multiple identities I choose the identity of belonging to my religious community though (paradoxically) I have no other choice but to belong. Third, this is my most basic and profound commitment and the one which I am least likely to abandon.

Communalism as a state of mind, then, is the individual's *assertion* of being part of a religious community, preceded by a full *awareness* of belonging to such a community. The 'We-ness' of the community is here replaced by the 'We are' of communalism. This 'We are' must inevitably lead to intolerance of all those outside the boundaries of the group. The intolerance, though, is not yet religious conflict since it can remain a province of the mind rather than become manifest in the outer, public realm; its inherent violence can range from a mild contempt to obsessive fantasies around the extermination of the enemy–Other rather than find explosive release in arson, rioting, and murder. The psychological ground for violence, however, has now been prepared. In mapping the sequence of religious violence from the inner to the outer terrain, I do not mean to give group psychology primacy but only precedence. Riots *do* start in the minds of men, minds conditioned by our earliest inner experience of self affirmation and assertion.

For the outbreak of violence, the communal identity has to swamp personal identity in a large number of people, reviving the feelings of love connected with early identifications with one's own group members and the hate toward the outgroup whose members are homogenized, depersonalized, and increasingly dehumanized. For social violence to occur, the threat to communal identity has to cross a certain threshold where the persecutory potential becomes fully activated and persecutory anxiety courses unimpeded through and between members of a religious group. Amplified by rumours, stoked by religious demagogues, the persecutory anxiety signals the annihilation of group identity and must be combated by its forceful assertion.

Acting demonstratively in terms of this identity as a Hindu or Muslim, though, threatens members of the rival community who too mobilize their religious identity as a defence. The spiral of threats and reactive counterthreats further fuels persecutory anxiety, and only the slightest of sparks in needed for a violent explosion.

The involvement of religious rather than other social identities does not dampen but, on the contrary, increases the violence of the conflict. Religion brings to conflict between groups a greater emotional intensity and a deeper motivational thrust than language, region, or other markers of ethnic identity. This is at least true of countries where the salience of religion in collective life is very high. Religious identity, for instance, is so crucial in the Islamic world that no Muslim revolutionary has been able or willing to repudiate his religious heritage.[10] To live in India is to become aware that the psychological space occupied by religion, the context and inspiration it provides for individual lives, and its role in fostering the cultural identity and survival of different groups—Hindus, Muslims, Sikhs, Christians, Parsis—is very different from the situation, say, in the United States. An Indian atheist cannot go along with an American counterpart's casual dismissal of religion as 'important, if true' but must amend it to 'important, even if not true.'

With its historical allusions from sacred rather than profane history, its metaphors and analogies having their source in sacred legends, the religious justification of a conflict involves fundamental values and releases some of our most violent passions. Why this is so is not only because religion is central to the vital, 'meaning-making' function of human life, causing deep disturbance if the survival of all that has been made meaningful by our religious beliefs is perceived to be under attack. Religion excites strong emotions also because it incorporates some of our noblest sentiments and aspirations—our most wishful thinking, the sceptic would say—and any threat to a belief in our 'higher' nature is an unacceptable denuding of self-esteem. Our wishful construction of human nature—that 'man is naturally good or at least good-natured; i he occasionally shows himself brutal, violent or cruel, these are only passing disturbances of his emotional life, for the most part provoked or perhaps only consequences of the inexpedient social regulations h has hitherto imposed on himself,'[11]—is matched by our equally wishfu constructions around religion. Religion, we like to believe, is abou love—love of God, love of nature, and love of.fellow man. Religio we feel, is essentially about compassion and strives for peace and ju tice for the oppressed. Indeed, freedom from violence, an enduring wish of mankind, is reflected in various religious visions of heaven.

This construction is confronted with the reality that violence is present in all religions as a positive and even necessary force for the realization of religious goals. Religious violence has many forms which have found expression in the practice of animal or human sacrifice, in righteous and often excruciatingly cruel punishment envisaged for sinners, in the exorcism of spirits and demons, killing of witches or apostates and in ascetic violence against the self.[12] The point is, as John Bowker has vividly demonstrated, that every religion has a vision of divinely legitimized violence—under certain circumstances.[13] In the Semitic religions, we have the Holy War of the Christians, the Just War of the Jews, and the Jehad of the Muslims where the believers are enjoined to battle and destroy evildoers. In other religions such as Hinduism and Buddhism, with their greater reputation for tolerance and nonviolence, violence is elevated to the realm of the sacred as part of the created order. In Hinduism, for instance, there is a cycle of violence and peacefulness as the Kali Age is followed by the Golden Age. Buddhist myths talk of Seven Days of the Sword where men will look on and kill each other as beasts, after which peace will return and no life is taken. Although Islam (especially in its current phase) and medieval Christianity have had most violent reputations, the question as to which religions have unleashed the greatest amount of violence is ultimately an empirical one.[14] In any event, fundamentalists can unleash any violence contained in a religion even if the religion is rarely perceived to have a violent potential, as amply demonstrated by our experience of Buddhist violence in Sri Lanka and Hindu violence in India. Moreover, as Natalie Davis has observed of Catholic–Protestant violence in 16th-century France and as we saw in the case of the Hyderabad riots, so long as rioters maintain a given religious commitment they rarely display guilt or shame for their acts of violence.[15]

Rhythms of religious ritual, whether in common prayer, processions or other congregational activities, are particularly conducive to breaking down boundaries between members of a group and thus, in times of tension and threat, forging violent mobs. I have called these instruments of the community's violence 'physical' groups since the individual's experience of group identity here is through unconscious bodily communication and fantasies rather than through the more consciously shared cultural traditions. Physical groups seem to come into existence more effortlessly in religious than in other kinds of conflict.

HISTORIES AND FUTURES

In this book, I have attempted to contribute a depth-psychological dimension to the understanding of religious conflict, especially the tension between Hindus and Muslims. I am aware that this may be regarded by some as 'psychologizing' an issue which demands social and political activism and which could well do without the introduction of psychological complexities, that 'pale cast of thought', which can only sow doubt and sap the will for unself-conscious action. In retrospect, I realize I have gone about this task in consonance with my professional identity as a clinician, though not as a psychoanalyst with an individual patient but more akin to the psychotherapist with a family practice who is called upon for assistance in a disintegrating marriage. I looked at the history of the Hindu–Muslim relationship, made a diagnostic assessment of what has gone wrong, and considered the positive forces in the relationship which were still intact. At the end, it is time to weigh the possible courses of action.

The awareness of belonging to either one community or the other—being a Hindu or Muslim—has increased manifold in recent years. Every time religious violence occurs in India or in some other part of the subcontinent, the reach and spread of modem communications ensure that a vast number of people are soon aware of the incident. Each riot and its aftermath raise afresh the issue of the individual's religious–cultural identity and bring it up to the surface of consciousness. This awareness may be fleeting for some, last over a period of time for others, but the process is almost always accompanied by a preconscious self interrogation on the significance of the religious–cultural community for the sense of one's identity and the intensity of emotion with which this community is invested. For varying periods of time, individuals consciously experience and express their identity through their religious group rather than through traditional kinship groups such as those of family and caste. The duration of this period, or even whether there will be a permanent change in the mode of identity experience for some, depends on many factors, not the least on the success of revivalist and fundamentalist political and social groupings in encouraging such a switch. They do this, we saw in our analysis of the speeches by Ritambhara and Azmi, by stoking the already existing persecution anxiety—its combination of aggression and fear weakening the individual sense of identity. The needed support to a weakened persona identity is then provided by strengthening its social, group aspec through an invitation to the person to identify with a grandiose representation of his or her community. The shared 'contemplation' and growing conviction of the great superiority of Hindu or Muslim culture and ways is then the required tonic for narcissistic enhancement and identity consolidation around the religious–cultural community as a pivot.

As for the future, there is more than one scenario for the likely evolution of Hindu–Muslim relations. The Hindu nationalist, who views the conflict as a product of Hindu and Muslim cultural and institutional traditions, believes the only way of avoiding future large-scale violence is a change in the Muslim view of the community's role, traditions, and institutions so that the Muslim can 'adapt'—the word meaning anything from adjustment to assimilation—to the Hindu majority's 'national' culture. To ask the Muslims to recognize themselves in the Hindu nationalist history of India, to expect them to feel their culture confirmed in Hindu symbols, rituals, and celebrations is asking them to renounce their cultural identity and to erase their collective memory so that they become indistinguishable from their Hindu neighbours. To be swamped by the surrounding Hindu culture has been historically the greatest fear of the Indian Muslim, articulated even by some medieval Sufis who are commonly regarded as having been closest to the Hindu ethos. Such an assimilation is feared precisely because it is so tempting, holding the promise of a freedom from fear of violence and an active and full participation in the majority culture and life, especially now when the majority is also politically dominant. The Hindu nationalist's dilemma is that the Muslims continue to decline an offer the nationalist believes they cannot refuse. The nationalist finds that the Muslim was willing to undertake the exercise in assimilation voluntarily, a highly improbable scenario, the task would involve the immensely difficult understanding of how religious–cultural traditions are transmitted and internalized and how those processes can be effectively interfered with and halted.

The secularist, who views the conflict as rooted in social–structural considerations, especially economic, is more sanguine on the future of Hindu–Muslim relations. In the long run, the secularist believes, the inevitable economic development of the country will alter social–structural conditions and thus assign the conflict, as the cliché would have it, 'to the dust heap of history' as religious identities fade and play less and less of a role in private and public life. A sceptical note on the belief in the primacy of political and economic structures in the shaping of consciousness, however, needs to be sounded. Cultural traditions—including the ideology of the Other—transmitted through the family can and do have a line of development separate from the political and economic systems of a society. This is strikingly apparent if one takes the case of Germany where recent studies indicate that, after living for 40 years under a radically different political and economic system, the political orientation and values of the young in relation to the family in eastern Germany are no different from those of their counterparts in the western part of the country; cultural socialization patterns within the family have survived the change in political systems relatively untouched and are stronger than the logic of the political superstructure.[16]

The optimistic realist, a breed with which I identify, believes that we are moving towards an era of recognition of Hindu–Muslim differences rather than pursuing their chimerical commonalities. We are moving toward a multiculturalism, with majority and minority cultures, rather than the emergence of a 'composite culture'. Such a multiculturalism is neither harmful nor dangerous but necessary, since it enables different religious groups to deal with the modernizing process in an active way rather than making them withdraw in lamentation at the inequities of modernization or endure it as passive victims. The problem is to ensure that one identity, Hindutva, does not dominate or assimilate other religious-cultural identities which are also embarked on the same quest as the Hindus. I can understand the validity of the nationalist call to the Hindus to find new meaning in customs, practices, and symbols of Hindu culture. But by the same logic why should this be denied to the Muslims who, too, are engaged in the same struggle to find meaning in the modern world? The realist would say that the solution is to build a state which protects the equal rights of Hindus and Muslims to be different. He believes that we must work toward building a polity which respects the beliefs of both Hindus and Muslims however odd or perverse they may seem to each other and however scornful they may be of the other community in private. Being a sceptic, he is also aware that the creation of such a public realm may be a long drawn-out affair accompanied by much tension and open conflict between the communities which will strain the social and political fabric of the country.

This realist agrees with the Hindu nationalist that clouds of violence loom over the immediate future of Hindu–Muslim relations. He is convinced, though, that achieving the desired goal of a truly multicultural polity will ultimately generate much less tension than the permanen discord which is the probable consequence of the nationalist vision. I can only hope that the violence is short-lived and that it will hasten the creation of a common, tolerant public realm. Our experience of needless suffering and cruelty can sometimes have the effect of jolting us out of accustomed ways of interpreting the world and making us more receptive to fresh ideals and new social–political arrangements. When stress and anxiety are at their greatest there is perhaps enough survival need in humans to suddenly make them reasonable. I hope the poet Theodore Roethke is right that 'In a dark time, the eye begins to see.'[17] This realist is not a cynic since unlike the latter, he still has hope. And even if the hope turns out to be illusory, he knows that, in the words of the *Mahabharata*, 'Hope is the sheet anchor of every man, When hope is destroyed, great grief follows, which is almost equal to death itself' This applies not only to individuals but also to communities and nations.

Notes and References

1. MOTHERS AND INFANTS

1. I am adopting Simmel's term 'dyad' for the mother–infant relationship since no other word conveys so well the feeling of complementarity and interdependence of two independent entities.
2. Sigmund Freud, *An Outline of Psychoanalysis* (1940), Standard Edition, vol. 23, p. 188. For a comprehensive historical account of Freud's writings on the mother–infant relationship, see John Bowlby, 'The Nature of the Child's Tie to His Mother', *International Journal of Psychoanalysis*, **39**, 1958, pp. 350–73.
3. The literature on the earliest human relationship has grown rapidly during the last few years; a complete bibliography of sources would cover many pages. The most important psycho-analytic writings upon which this summary is based are René A. Spitz, *The First Year of Life*, New York: International Universities Press, 1965; D.W. Winnicott, *The Family and Individual Development*, London: Tavistock Publications, 1952; Erik H. Erikson, *Childhood and Society*, New York: W.W. Norton, 1950; Edith Jacobson, *The Self and the Object World*, New York: International Universities Press, 1964, especially Part 1; Margaret S. Mahler, *On Human Symbiosis and the Vicissitudes of Individuation*, New York: International Universities Press 1969; L.B. Murphy, 'Some Aspects of the First Relationship', *International Journal of Psychoanalysis*, **45**, 1964, pp. 31–43; and J. Bowlby, *Attachment*, New York: Basic Books, 1969. And of course no psychoanalytic study of motherhood (however liable to cultural specialization) can be complete without reference to Helene Deutsch, *The Psychology of Women*, vol. 2 (*Motherhood*), New York: Grune and Stratton, 1945.
4. Spitz, op. cit., p. 96.
5. For an elaboration of this view, see Bowlby, *Attachment*, pp. 265–96.
6. Spitz, op. cit. p. 95.
7. For a psycho-analytic consideration of some of these issues see for exam-

ple, Grete L. Bibring *et al.*, 'A Study of the Psychological Processes in Pregnancy and of the Earliest Mother–Child Relationship', *The Psychoanalytic Study of the Child*, vol. 16, New York: International Universities Press, 1961, pp. 9–72, and H.A. Moss, 'Sex, Age and State as Determinants of Mother–Infant Interaction', *Merrill Palmer Quarterly*, 13, 1967, pp. 19–36.

8. Although the patrilineal and patrilocal family type is dominant all over India, there are some castes and communities, especially in Southern India, which are matrilineal and in which women enjoy relatively greater freedom. For the similarities and contrasts in kinship organization of different regions in India, see Irawati Karve, *Kinship Organization in India*, 3rd edn., Bombay: Asia Publishing House, 1968.

My remarks are intended to apply only to the dominant patriarchal culture where by unconscious necessity it is the *mater* who is of primary symbolic significance, or, as the Jungians would put it, the mother is the primary constituent of a man's *anima*. The problem of feminine figures in the myths of a patriarchal society is compounded by the fact that these *animas* are not solely male projections but also represent some aspects of feminine psychology in these cultures. The reason for this intertwining of *anima* images and feminine psychology is that very early in childhood, girls learn to accurately perceive and conform to the patriarchal images of femininity entertained by the men around them in the household. In this connection see Marie-Louise von Franz, *The Feminine in Fairy Tales*, Zurich: Spring Publications, 1972.

9. The anthropological accounts which have a bearing on this section are T.N. Madan, *Family and Kinship: A Study of the Pandits of Rural Kashmir*, Bombay: Asia Publishing House, 1965; Leigh Minturn and John T. Hitchcock, 'The Rajputs of Khalapur, India' in *Six Cultures: Studies of Child-rearing*, ed. B.B. Whiting, New York: John Wiley and Sons, 1963, pp. 301–61; L. Minturn and W.W. Lambert, *Mothers of Six Cultures*, New York: John Wiley, 1964; Oscar Lewis, *Village Life in Northern India*, New York: Vintage Books, 1958; S.C. Dube, *Indian Village*, New York: Harper and Row, 1967; M.N. Srinivas, *Marriage and Family in Mysore*, Bombay: New Book Co., 1942; Edward B. Harper, 'Spirit Possession and Social Structure', in *Anthropology on the March*, ed. B. Ratnam, Madras: The Book Centre, pp. 165–97; and Aileen D. Ross, *The Hindu Family in its Urban Setting*, Toronto: University of Toronto Press, 1961. Two other useful studies, essentially descriptive, based on intensive interviewing with women who represent the progressive, well-educated parts of Indian society are Margaret Cormack, *The Hindu Woman*, Bombay: Asia Publishing House, 1961, and Promilla Kapur, *Love, Marriage and Sex*, Delhi: Vikas Publishing House, 1973. For older, impressionistic yet sensitive studies of Indian women, see Mary F. Billington, *Woman in India* (18—

?), New Delhi: Amarko Book Agency, 1973, and Frieda M. Das, *Purdah, the Status of Indian Women*, New York: The Vanguard Press, 1932.

10. The infant mortality rate in 1969 for females was 148.1 as compared to 132.3 for males; the life expectancy between 1961–71 was 45.6 for females, 47.1 for males, while the number of girls enrolled in the educational system in 1970–1 was 18.4 per cent as compared to 39.3 per cent for boys. See the relevant statistical tables in Indian Council of Social Science Research, *Status of Women in India: A Synopsis of the Report of the National Committee on the Status of Women* (1971–4), New Delhi: Allied Publishers, 1975, pp. 140–75.

11. *Atharvaveda*, VI. 2. 3, quoted in R.M. Das, *Women in Manu and His Seven Commentators*, Varanasi: Kanchana Publications, 1962, p. 43. See also *Atharvaveda*, VIII. 6. 25, VI. 9. 10, III. 23. 3, for prayers in a similar vein.

12. A.A. MacDonell, *Vedic Religion*, p. 165, quoted in R.M. Das, op. cit., p. 43.

13. See, for example, Minturn and Hitchcock, op. cit., pp. 307–8; Madan, op cit., p. 77; Dube, op. cit., pp. 148–9; Cormack, op. cit., p. 11. See also, William J. Goode, World Revolution and Family Patterns, New York: The Free Press, 1963, pp. 235–6; and D.G. Mandelbaum, *Society in India*, vol. 1, Berkeley: University of California Press, 1970, p. 120. Cases of *post-partum* depression, for example, are much more commonly reported among mothers who give birth to a daughter than among those who have a son. See M.R. Gaitonde, 'Cross-Cultural Study of the Psychiatric Syndromes in Out-Patient Clinics in Bombay, India, and Topeka, Kansas', *International Journal of Social Psychiatry*, **4**, 1958, p. 103.

14. Lewis, op. cit., p. 195.

15. Karve, op. cit., p. 206.

16. See Das, op. cit., p. 44. A contemporary Bengali proverb expresses this thought more bluntly, 'Even the piss of a son brings money; let the daughter go to hell.'

17. Sudhir Kakar, 'Aggression in Indian Society: An Analysis of Folk Tales', *Indian Journal of Psychology*, **49 (2)**, 1974, p. 124.

18. Ibid., pp. 125–6.

19. Cormack, op. cit., pp. 75–8.

20. Karve, op. cit., p. 210.

21. See Ross, op. cit., pp. 150–1; Dube, op. cit., pp. 148–9; Srinivas, op. cit., p. 173; Whiting, op. cit., p. 303; Harper, op. cit., pp. 171–2; Madan, op. cit., p. 77; and Cormack, op. cit., p. 9. Folk songs from all over India also bear witness to this close mother–daughter tie. See, for example, songs no. 4, 5, 6, 7, 8, and 9 in Karve, op. cit., p. 205.

22. Karve, op. cit., p. 205.

23. As Helene Deutsch expresses it, 'In her relation to her own child, woman

repeats her own mother–child history.' See *The Psychology of Women*, vol. 1, op. cit., p. 205. See also Nancy Chodorow, 'Family Structure and Feminine Personality', in *Woman, Culture and Society*, ed. M. Rosaldo and L. Lamphere, Stanford : Stanford University Press, 1975, pp. 52–3.

24. Thus in many ballads whereas the women are depicted as tolerant, self-sacrificing and faithful, the men are weak, timid and faithless. See Sankar Sen Gupta, *A Study of Women of Bengal*, Calcutta: Indian Publications, 1970, p. 107.
25. Srinivas, op. cit., p. 195.
26. For example, in the *Dasa Puttal Brata* of Bengali girls it is wished that 'I shall have a husband like Rama, I shall be *sati* like Sita, I shall have a *devara* (younger brother-in-law) like Lakshman; I shall have a father-in-law like Dasharatha; I shall have a mother-in-law like Kousalya; I shall have sons as Kunti had; I shall be a cook like Draupadi; I shall acquire power like Durga; I shall bear the burden like earth; I shall be like Sasthi whose offspring know no death.' See Akshay Kumar Kayal, 'Women in Folk Sayings of West Bengal', in Sen Gupta, op. cit., p. xxii.
27. Das, op. cit., p. 49.
28. Ibid., p. 72.
29. Jerome S. Bruner, 'Myths and Identity', *Daedalus*, Spring 1959, p. 357. In a study carried out in the north Indian province of Uttar Pradesh 500 boys and 360 girls between the ages of 9 and 22 years were asked to select the ideal woman from a list of 24 names of gods, goddesses and heroes and heroines of history. Sita was seen as the ideal woman by an overwhelming number of respondents: there were no age or sex differences. See P. Pratap, 'The Development of Ego Ideal in Indian Children', unpublished Ph.D. Thesis, Banaras Hindu University, 1960.
30. *Ramayana of Valmiki*, trans. H.P. Shastri, vol. 1 (Ayodhyakanda), London: Shantisadan, 1962, p. 233.
31. Philip Slater, *The Glory of Hera*, Boston: Beacon Press, 1966, p. xi.
32. In this connection see also J.A. Arlow, 'Ego Psychology and the Study of Mythology', *Journal of American Psychoanalytic Association*, **9**, 1961, p. 375.
33. *Mahabharata*, trans. P.C. Roy, Calcutta: Oriental Publishing Co., n.d., vol. 3 (Vanaparva), p. 634.
34. Ibid., p. 633. The Savitri myth is also a striking demonstration of Ernest Jones's thesis that the conscious fantasy of dying together possesses the unconscious significance of the wish to have children. See E. Jones, 'On "Dying Together" with Special Reference to Heinrich von Kleist's Suicide' and 'An Unusual Case of Dying Together', *Essays on Applied Psychoanalysis*, London: Hogarth Press, 1951, pp. 9–21.
35. Ibid., p. 488.
36. Ibid., pp. 506–7.

37. *Siva Purana*, 2. 2. 5. pp. 1–68, 6. pp. 1–62. The translation is from W. O'Flaherty, *Asceticism and Eroticism in the Mythology of Siva*, London: Oxford University Press, 1973, p. 64–5. A perusal of Hindu law texts reveals that our ancient law-givers—Manu, Kautilya, Kullika, Medhatithi—were obsessed with the chastity of young, unmarried girls. The punishments for all conceivable kinds of chastity-violation, depending on the castes of the actors, their sex (whether the violator is a man or a woman), the degree of consent and so on, are elaborately detailed. Thus, for example, if a man forcibly 'pollutes' a maiden with his fingers, the fingers shall be amputated and he shall pay a fine of 500 *panas*. If the man is of equal caste, the fine is reduced. If the fingers have been inserted with the consent of the maiden, the fingers are not amputated and the fine is reduced to 200 *panas*. If the initiative is taken by the girl, the punishment is lighter or non-existent; instead, her guardians are to be punished in so much as they presumably did not keep a proper watch on her. There are similar fines in the case of an older woman seducing a young girl, depending on their castes and the 'violation'. See Das, op. cit., pp. 63–70.

38. *Rangila Bhasur go tumi keno deyor haila na.*
    Tumi jodi haita re deyor khaita batar pan
    (aar) ranga rasa kaitam katha juraito paran.
    Sen Gupta, op. cit., p. 94.

39. The mean age according to the 1961 census was 15.8 years. For a discussion of the subject, see K.P. Singh, Women's Age at Marriage', *Sociological Bulletin*, **23 (2)**, 1974, pp. 236–44. See also William J. Goode, op. cit., pp. 232–6.

40. See Ross, op. cit., p. 151.

41. Lewis, op cit., p. 161; see also Karve, op. cit., p. 137 for evidence on the widespread existence of this custom.

42. Here is an example from Bengal (freely translated):
    O, Kaffu [a bird], you are from my mother's side.
    Speak, O speak in the courtyard of my parents.
    My mother will hear you;
    She will send my brother to fetch me.
    O what sorrowful days have come!
    I wish to get out of this,
    I wish to reach my father's house.
    Sen Gupta, op. cit., p. 149.

43. Folk-lore especially singles out the *sas* (mother-in-law) and the *nanad* (sister-in-law) as the natural enemies of the young bride. See Karve, op. cit., p. 130. Here are lines from some of the songs in Bengal depicting the bride's plight (and her anger) in these two relationships. 'My husband's sister is nothing but a poisonous thorn, her poisonous stings give me much pain'; 'My mother-in-law expired in the morning, if I find time in

the afternoon after eating lunch, I will weep for her.' In north India the bride sings:

O my friend! My in-laws' house is a wretched place.
My mother-in-law is a very hard woman
She always struts about full of anger,

and so forth. There are also many songs which complain of the husband's indifference. For example, see songs no. 39, 40, 41, in Karve, op cit., pp. 209–10. The presence of hidden hostility towards the new husband can also be inferred from the results of a Thematic Apperception Test administered to forty school girls in the South who were shown a picture of a death scene, with a covered unidentifiable body in the centre of the room and a doctor nearby consoling a young woman. In the stories written by the girls, by far the largest number (45 per cent) 'saw' the covered figure as the body of a dead husband. See D. Narain, 'Growing up in India', *Family Process*, **3**, 1964, pp. 132–3.

44. *The Laws of Manu*, trans. G. Buhler, in M. Müller (ed.), *Sacred Books of the East*, vol. 25, Oxford: Clarendon Press, 1886, p. 196.

45. Ibid., p. 197.

46. Madhav S. Gore, 'The Husband–Wife and Mother–Son Relationship', *Sociological Bulletin*, **11**, 1961, pp. 91–102. See also Ross, op. cit., p. 147, for evidence of a similar relationship existing in urbanized families.

47. *The Laws of Manu*, op. cit., p. 85. Similar sentiments are expressed in the *Mahabharata*.

48. See, for example, Mandelbaum, op. cit., p. 88, and Lewis, op. cit., p. 195.

49. Geeta Majumdar, *Folk Tales of Bengal*, New Delhi: Sterling Publishers, 1911, p. 17.

50. The Laws of Manu, op. cit., p. 344.

51. Ibid., p. 56.

52. *Mahabharata*, trans. P.C. Roy, vol. 1 (Adi-parva), pp. 177–8.

53. *Brahmavaivarta*, 3. 2. pp. 19–24, in O'Flaherty, op. cit., p. 225.

54. *The Laws of Manu*, op cit., p. 354. Although it is primarily the son who is responsible for the performance of these rites, in case a couple has no son the rites may be performed by the daughter's son.

55. The Hindu attitude is similar to Malinowski's characterization of the Melanesians: 'The woman shows invariably a passionate craving for her child and the surrounding society seconds her feelings, fosters her inclinations, and idealizes them by custom and usage.' See B. Malinowski, *Sex and Repression in Savage Society*, New York: Harcourt, 1927, p. 21.

56. Helene Deutsch, *The Psychology of Women*, vol. 2, Ch. II.

57. Unless specifically mentioned, the following sections deal with the male infant only, the pattern being somewhat different in the case of daughters.

58. For anthropological accounts which confirm the widespread existence of this pattern of attachment all over India, see G.M. Carstairs, *The Twice*

Born, London: Hogarth Press, 1957, pp. 63–4; S.C. Dube, *Indian Village*, pp. 148–9; Dhirendra N. Narain 'Growing up in India', *Family Process*, **3**, 1964, pp. 134–7; John W. Elder, 'Industrialization in Hindu Society; A Case Study in Social Change', unpublished Ph.D. Thesis, Harvard University, 1959, p. 242.

59. Gardner Murphy, *In the Minds of Men*, New York: Basic Books, 1953, p. 56.
60. See Adrian C. Mayer, *Caste and Kinship in Central India*, London: Routledge and Kegan Paul, 1970; Ross, op. cit.; Gore, op. cit.; and D. Narain, 'Interpersonal Relationships in the Hindu Family', in R. Hill and R. Konig (eds), *Families in East and West*, Paris: Mouton, pp. 454–80.
61. Jawaharlal Nehru, *Toward Freedom*, Boston: Beacon Press, 1961, p. 22.
62. Paramhansa Yogananda, *Autobiography of a Yogi*, Los Angeles: Self Realization Fellowship, 1972, p. 4.
63. Sigmund Freud, *Introductory Lectures on Psychoanalysis* (1916), Standard Edition, vol. 16, p. 407.
64. W.J. Wilkins, Hindu Mythology (1882), Delhi: Delhi Book Store, 1972, pp. 107–12 and 238–47.
65. E.H. Erikson, 'Ontogeny of Ritualization', in R.M. Loewenstein *et al.* (eds.), *Psychoanalysis—A General Psychology: Essays in Honor of Heinz Hartmann*, New York: International Universities Press, 1966, p. 604.
66. *Vaivarta Purana*, quoted in Wilkins, op. cit., p. 244.
67. J. Bowlby, *Separation: Anxiety and Anger*, London: Hogarth Press, 1973.
68. Ibid., p. 314.
79. *Satapatha Brahmana*, quoted in Wilkins, op. cit., p. 286.
70. J. Hitchcock, 'Pregnancy and Childbirth', quoted in D. Narain, 'Growing up in India', op. cit., p. 139.
71. William S. Taylor, 'Basic Personality in Orthodox Hindu Culture Patterns', *Journal of Abnormal Psychology*, **43**, 1948, p. 11. See also P. Spratt, *Hindu Culture and Personality*, Bombay: Manaktalas, 1966, pp. 181–6.
72. See Bowlby, *Separation*, p. 359, and D.W. Winnicott, 'The Capacity to be Alone', *International Journal of Psychoanalysis*, **39**, 1958, pp. 416–20. A similar position has also been adopted by the intellectual spokesmen of what has come to be known as the 'counter-culture' in the United States. Thus Philip Slater suggests that the present American social order deeply frustrates three fundamental human needs: 'The desire for *community*—the wish to live in trust and fraternal cooperation with one's fellows The desire for *engagement*—the wish to come directly to grips with social and interpersonal problems. The desire for *dependence*—the wish to share the responsibility for the control of one's impulses and the direction of one's life.' See *The Pursuit of Loneliness:*

American Culture at the Breaking Point, Boston: Beacon Press, 1970, p. 5.

73. Sigmund Freud, *Introductory Lectures on Psychoanalysis* (1916), Standard Edition, vol. 16, p. 408 and *Inhibitions, Symptoms, and Anxiety* (1926), Standard Edition, vol. 20, p. 167.
74. See Bowlby, *Attachment*.
75. Erich Neutmann, *The Great Mother: An Analysis of the Archetype* (2nd edn.), Princeton: Princeton University Press, 1963, pp. 147–203.
76. Slater, *The Glory of Hera*, p. 68. Slater's brilliant discussion of the mother–son constellation in ancient Greece shows some parallels, though not a complete identity, with the corresponding situation in modern India and has been a rich source of comparative material.
77. *Kalika Purana*, 47. pp. 114–119, paraphrased from O'Flaherty, op. cit., p. 190.
78. *Matsya Purana*, 155. pp. 1–34.
79. William N. Stephens, in a cross-cultural study of the family, has demonstrated these taboos to be positively correlated with indicators of sexual arousal. See *The Family in Cross-Cultural Perspective*, New York: Holt, 1963, pp. 80 ff.
80. *The Laws of Manu*, op. cit., p. 135.
81. *Aitareya Brahmana*, 1. 6. pp. 1–6; see O'Flaherty, op. cit., p. 275.
82. Dube, op. cit., pp. 190–7.
83. Karen Horney, 'The Dread of Woman', *International Journal of Psychoanalysis*, **13**, 1932, pp. 349–53.
84. Brahma Purana, 81. pp. 1–5; paraphrased from O'Flaherty, op. cit., p. 204.
85. *Thirty Minor Upanishads*, trans. K.N. Aiyar, quoted in Spratt, op. cit., p. 118.
86. *Mahabharata*, vol. 2 (Vanaparva), pp. 102–5.
87. *Padma Purana*, 5. 26. pp. 91–125; O'Flaherty, op. cit., p. 280.
88. *Ramayana of Valmiki*, vol. 1 (Aranyakanda), 18: pp. 15–16. In psychoanalytic literature, it was Wilhelm Stekel who pointed to the relationship between the nose and feminine genitalia, basing some of his conclusions on the earlier work of Wilhelm Fliess, *Die Beziehungen zwischen Nase und weiblichen Geschlechtsorganen in ihrer biologisches Bedeutungen* (Vienna, 1897); see Stekel, *Conditions of Nervous Anxiety and their Treatment*, London: Paul Trench and Trubner, 1923, p. 49.
89. Spratt, op. cit., p. 254.
90. Ibid., pp. 252–7.
91. I suspect this will be corroborated convincingly by clinical evidence, once this evidence becomes available in sufficient quantity and depth. Meanwhile, we cannot dismiss the common game of 'playing the wife' among boys of a certain age. The case history of a young boy who used to tie a piece of string around his prepuce and draw his penis so tightly

into the scrotum that it was covered by the folds of the scrotum, thereby giving the genitalia a remarkable female resemblance is one aberrant manifestation of this identification. See G. Bose, 'The Genesis and Adjustment of the Oedipal Wish', *Samiksa*, **3**, 1949, p. 231. This behaviour is reminiscent of the commonly accepted (and admired) ability of Hatha-Yogis to draw the penis and the testes back into the pubic arch so that the whole body takes on the appearance of a woman.

92. The second version of the Ganesha myth, in which Sani first avoids and then looks at the infant Ganesha (thus depriving him of his head) is reminiscent of cases of scotophilic women whose compulsive avoidance of, and looking at, men's genitals is a distorted expression of their castration wish.

93. *Mahabharata*, vol. 10 (Anusasnaparva), pp. 35–8.

94. Spratt, op. cit., p. 193, and p. 237.

95. Warner Muensterberger, 'Psyche and Environment', *Psychoanalytic Quarterly*, **38**, 1969, p. 204.

96. For Freud's distinction between the primary and the secondary processes, see *Formulations on the Two Principles of Mental Functioning* (1911), Standard Edition, vol. 12.

97. This is of course an impressionistic generalization based on personal and professional experience in Indian and western societies. Empirical studies comparing Indian and western children are rare. For an older study lending support to the impression that primary thought processes persist well beyond infancy in Indian childhood, see J.C. Hoyland, *An Investigation Regarding the Psychology of Indian Adolescence*, Jubbulpore: Christian Mission Press, 1921. In a study based on student responses to Rorschach cards, Asthana concludes that fantasy and imagination characterize the entire sample with some subjects given to intense and vivid imagery. See Hari S. Asthana, 'Some Aspects of Personality Structuring in Indian (Hindu) Social Organization', *Journal of Social Psychology*, **44**, 1956, pp. 155–63.

98. Pinchas Noy, 'A Revision of the Psychoanalytic Theory of the Primary Process', *International Journal of Psychoanalysis*, **50**, 1969, pp. 155–78.

99. Ibid., pp. 176–7.

100. See E.H. Erikson, *Identity: Youth and Crisis*, p. 174, for a discussion of the concept of negative identity.

101. Henry Whitehead, *The Village Gods of South India*, Calcutta: Association Press, 1921, p. 18.

102. *Mahabharata*, vol. 4 (Virataparva), p. 12.

103. Milton Singer, 'The Radha–Krishna Bhajans of Madras City', in M. Singer (ed.), *Krishna: Myths, Rites, and Attitudes*, Honolulu: East–West Center Press, 1966, p. 130.

104. Swami Saradananda, *Sri Ramakrishna, The Great Master*, Madras: Ramakrishna Math, n.d., p. 238.

2. THE CHILD IN INDIAN TRADITION

1. I shall be greatly surprised if *jatakarma*, the Hindu birth ritual, has ever taken place exactly in the same way as I have described it above. I have constructed the birth and the ritual from the texts of Ayurvedic medicine and the elaborately detailed instructions given in the *Grihyasutras*, the ancient texts which contain directions for the various *samskaras*—the mandatory nexus of ceremonies, sacraments and rites which accompany a Hindu from the moment of his conception in the womb till the hour of death, and even further through the funeral ceremonies beyond death. In actual practice, of course, depending upon the region, the caste and the historical period, many of the prescribed samskaras, including the one at birth, have been shortened and condensed, blended with others or omitted altogether.

2. Excepting the folk songs, this material essentially belongs to the literate traditions of the upper castes. Yet, as Kosambi has pointed out in another context, such traditions are basically much the same in many lower groups; their continuous and continuing survival in large sections of society being one of the most distinctive features of Indian culture. See D.D. Kosambi, *The Culture and Civilization of Ancient India in Historical Outline*, New Delhi: Vikas, 1970, p. 16.

3. See George Buhler (tr.), *The Laws of Manu in Sacred Books of the East* (F. Max Müller, ed.), vol. XXV, Oxford: Clarendon Press, 1886; III, p. 114; VIII, pp. 66–71; IX, p. 283.

4. Ibid., V, pp. 67–71.

5. Ibid., III, p. 114.

6. Ibid., IV, p. 179.

7. Ibid., IV, pp. 282–3.

8. Ibid., VIII, pp. 299–300; IX, p. 230.

9. See Jerome Carcopino, *Daily Life in Ancient Rome*, New Haven: Yale University Press, 1940, Chapter IV on 'Marriage, Woman and the Family'.

10. Richard B. Lyman Jr., 'Barbarism and Religion: Late Roman and Early Medieval Childhood', in L. De Mause (ed.), *The History of Childhood*, New York: Harper Torchbooks, 1975, p. 84.

11. *Caraka Samhita*, with Hindi translation by Jaideva Vidyalankar, Delhi: Motilal Banarsidass, 1975, Sarira 2. pp. 33–6.

12. *Caraka*, Sarira 4. pp. 15–9.

13. See Debiprasad Chattopadhya, *Science and Society in Ancient India*, Calcutta: R.I. Publishers, 1977, who has emphasized this fact.

14. The Ayurvedic view is identical to that of modern psychoanalysis which holds that in early life the infant must be thought of, not as an individual but only as a part of a nurturing unit, from which he gradually differentiates, as an individual, with the mothering partner serving as a catalyst and a living buffer'; Margaret Mahler, *On Human Symbiosis and the Vicissitudes of Individuation*, New York: International Universities Press, 1968, p. 229.

15. *Caraka*, Sarira 8. p. 96.

16. *Susruta*, Sarira 10. p. 38.

17. See for instance *Mahabharata* (M.N. Dutta, tr.), 12 vols., Calcutta: Oriental Publishing Co., n.d., vol. 1, pp. 107–80; vol. 2, p. 217; vol. 11, pp. 4, 55, 87.

18. Ibid., vol. 1 (Adiparva), pp. 107–8.

19. Ibid., vol. 2 (Sabhaparva), p. 217.

20. Ibid., vol. 1 (Adiparva), p. 510.

21. Ibid., pp. 177–8.

22. Ibid., vol. IV (Udyogparva), p. 210.

23. Ibid., pp. 374–5.

24. Ibid., vol. IX (Santiparva), p. 105.

25. Ibid., p. 136.

26. Ibid., p. 349.

27. See, for instance, vol. 1 (Adiparva), p. 177; vol. IX (Santiparva), pp. 267, 269.

28. Ibid., vol. X (Anusasanaparva), p. 155.

29. Bhavabhuti, *Uttara Rama-Charita*, 6. p. 13 and 6. p. 22; Banabhatt, *Harshacarita*, 5. p. 99.

30. Kalidasa, *Raghuvamsha*, 3. pp. 45–6.

31. Srinivas Sharma, *Adhunik Hindi Kavya Vatsalya Rasa*, quoted in Chandrabhan Rawat, *Sur Sahitya*, Mathura: Jawahar Pustakalaya, 1967, p 230.

32. Rawat, *Sur Sahitya*, p. 229 (my translation).

33. Jadunath Sinha (ed.), *Ramaprosad's Devotional Songs*, Calcutta: Sinha 1966, p. 7.

34. David R. Kinsley, *The Sword and the Flute: Kali and Krishna, Dark Versions of the Terrible and the Sublime in Hindu Mythology*, Berkeley University of California Press, 1975, pp. 12–19.

35. Surdas, *Sursagarsar* (D. Verma, ed.), Allahabad: Sahitya Bhawan, 197. p. 59 (my translation).

36. Goswami Tulsidas, *Kavitavali* (R.P. Tripathi, ed.), Allahabad: Bhara Niketan, n.d., p. 3 (my translation).

37. This is Huizinga's phrase to describe human play; quoted in Erik H. Erikson, *Toys and Reasons*, New York: W.W. Norton, 1977, p. 43.

38. Surdas, p. 57.

39. Tulsidas, *Gitavali* (translated in Hindi by V.N. Prasad), Gorakhpur: Gita Press, n.d., pp. 30–40 (my translation).

40. For a comparison of *ashramadharma* with a modern scheme of psychosocial development see my 'The Human Life Cycle: Traditional Hindu View and the Psychology of Erik Erikson', *Philosophy East and West*, **18** (3), 1968

41. V.B. Athavale, *Balaveda*, Bombay: Pediatric Clinics of India, 1977, p. 1.

42. For a discussion of the psychology of rituals and ritualization see Erik H. Erikson, 'Ontogeny of Ritualization in Man' in *Psychoanalysis—A General Psychology* (R M. Loewenstein *et al.*, eds), New York: International Universities Press, 1966, pp. 601–6.

43. The contents of the *samskaras* have been extensively described in Raj B. Pandey, *Hindu Samskaras*, Delhi: Motilal Banarsidass, 1969.

44. See R. Sankrantyan and D.K. Upadhyaya (eds), *Hindi Sahitya ka Vrihat Itihas*, Kashi: Nagaripracharni Sabha, vol. 16 (part 3), 19, p. 111.

45. P.V. Kane, *History of Dharmasastra*, Poona: Bhandarkar Oriental Research Institute, vol. 2 (part 1), 1933, p. 180.

46. In a study of growing up in 700 families in the urban complex of Poona, Champa Aphale tells us that *namakarana* was generally celebrated except in some families in the case of girls; *nishkramana* was confined to the children of upper and intermediate castes, *annaprasana* was omitted in the case of lower castes and *chudakarana* (*caula munda* in the local language) was universally performed except for girls of the upper castes. Girls were also excluded from the rite of *upanayana* which is not performed for boys belonging to the lower castes either. See Champa Aphale, *Growing Up in an Urban Complex*, New Delhi: National, 1976, pp. 53–6.

47. *Hindi Sahitya ka Vrihat Itihas*, p. 16.

48. In the literature on the *samskaras*, the age at which a particular *samskara* should be performed is not laid down with great rigidity but is flexible within certain, albeit wide, limits. Chronological flexibility, however, is characteristic of all schemes of 'stages of development'—Freud's stages of psychosexual development, Erikson's stages of psychosocial development, Piaget's stages of cognitive development and so on. As with these schemes, the Hindu ritual literature too gives us the earliest possible age for a given transition, the latest possible one and sometimes the optimal one.

49. In this connection, see the various contributions in *The History of Childhood*, and especially de Mause's review essay, 'The Evolution of Childhood', pp. 1–73.

364 / *Notes and References*

50. de Mause identifies the following childrearing models: 1. Infanticidal (Antiquity to 4th century AD); 2. Abandonment (4th–13th centuries) 3. Ambivalent (13th–17th century) 4. Intrusive (18th century); 5. Socialization (19th–mid-20th century) 6. Helping (Begins mid-20th century). See de Mause, 'The Evolution of Childhood', pp. 51–4.

51. For example, as William Langer has shown, infanticide (contrary to the popular assumption that it was solely an Eastern practice) of both legitimate and illegitimate children was a regular practice in western antiquity: See William L. Langer 'Infanticide: A Historical Survey', *History of Childhood Quarterly*, **1** (3), pp. 353–65. In fact, it has been established that the killing of legitimate children in Europe was only slowly reduced during the Middle Ages and that illegitimate children continued to be regularly killed right into the 19th century: See de Mause, 'Evolution of Childhood', p. 25.

52. John Demos, 'The American Family in Past Time', *American Scholar*, **43** (3), 1974, p. 427.

3. THE REVOLUTIONARY YOGI: CHILDHOOD OF SWAMI VIVEKANANDA

1. Sister Nivedita, *The Master as I Saw Him*, Calcutta: Udbodhan Office, 1910, pp. 125–6.
2. See in this connection Pamela Daniels, 'Militant Nationalism in Bengal: A Study in the Shaping of Nations', unpublished Master's Thesis, Harvard University, 1963.
3. Swami Vivekananda, *The Yogas and Other Works*, (S. Nikhilananda, ed.), New York: Ramakrishna–Vivekananda Center, 1953, p. 118.
4. Ibid., p. 119.
5. Swami Vivekananda, *The Complete Works of Swami Vivekananda*, vol. 4, Almora: Advaita Ashrama, 1923, p. 337.
6. Letter to Mary Hale in Vivekananda, *The Yogas and other Works*, p. 92.
7. Ibid., pp. 157–8.
8. Erik H. Erikson, *Young Man Luther*, New York: W.W. Norton, 1958, p. 34.
9. Bhupendra Nath Datta, *Swami Vivekananda: Patriot–Prophet*, Calcutta: Nababharat Publishers, 1954, p. 147. For details of Vivekananda's childhood and youth, I have checked the facts against two authoritative accounts: Sailendra Nath Dhar, *A Comprehensive Biography of Swami Vivekananda*, vol. 1, Madras: Vivekananda Prakashan Kendra, 1975; and the official biography, *The Life of Vivekananda*, 8th edn., by His Eastern and Western Disciples, Almora: Advaita Ashrama, 1974.
10. Ibid. See also Dhar, op. cit.

11. Vivekananda, *The Yogas and other Works*, p. 1.
12. Datta, op. cit., p. 114.
13. Ibid., p. 115.
14. Ernest Jones, *The Life and Work of Sigmund Freud*, vol. l, New York: Basic Books, 1953, p. 5.
15. Letter to Mary Hale, in Vivekananda, *The Yogas and other Works*, p. 165.
16. Nivedita, op. cit., p. 249.
17. Vivekananda, *The Yogas and other Works*, p. 2. In addition, since Indian mothers take care of infants much longer than the age given by Vivekananda for his childhood memory (even if portions of later childhood are incorporated in this memory), it is developmentally probable and reasonable in the Indian context to assume that by 'family' Vivekananda indeed means his mother.
18. Letter to Mrs Ole Bull, in Vivekananda, *The Yogas and other Works*, p. 945. See also Nivedita, op. cit., pp. 206–7.
19. Letter to Mary Hale in Vivekananda, *The Yogas and other Works*, p. 916.
20. Swami Vivekananda, *Lectures from Colombo to Almora*, Almora: Advaita Ashrama, 1933, p. 223.
21. Nivedita, op. cit., pp. 162–8.
22. Ibid., p. 170.
23. Datta, op. cit., pp. 97, 102 and 105.
24. Vivekananda, *The Yogas and other Works*, p. 128 (ital. in original).
25. Ibid., p. 151.
26. Ibid., p. 102.
27. Vivekananda, *Complete Works*, vol. 3, p. 224.
28. Ibid., vol. 4, p. 143.
29. Nivedita, op. cit., p. 297.
30. Letter to Nivedita, in Vivekananda, *The Yogas and other Works*, p. 951.
31. Letter to Mary Hale in Vivekananda, *The Yogas and other Works*, p. 950.
32. Letter to Miss Macleod, in Vivekananda, *The Yogas and other Works*, p. 951.
33. See H. Kohut, *The Analysis of the Self*, New York: International Universities Press, 1971, pp. 108–9.
34. Vivekananda, *The Yogas and other Works*, p. 5.
35. Daniels, op. cit., p. 27.

4. LORD OF THE SPIRIT WORLD

1. For a detailed description of various kinds of Indian spirits, see J. Hastings (ed.), *Encyclopaedia of Religion and Ethics*, 13 vols., Edinburgh, 1908–16, vol. 4, pp. 602 ff.
2. For the local legend of the temple and its deities see Anon., *Shri-Balajidham-mahatmya*, Vrindavan: Matrapith, n.d..

366 / *Notes and References*

3. Ibid., p. 48.
4. The classic work on the Asclepius cult is C.A. Meier, *Ancient Incubation and Modern Psychotherapy*, Evanston, Ill.: Northwestern University Press, 1967.
5. See, for instance, John A. Sanford, *Healing and Wholeness*, New York: Paulist Press, 1977, pp. 49–51.
6. For psychiatric and sociological views on spirit possession in India see Stanley S. Freed and Ruth S. Freed, 'Spirit Possession as Illness in a North Indian Village', *Ethnology*, 3, 1964, pp. 152–71; Edward B. Harper, 'Spirit Possession and Social Structure', in *Anthropology on the March* (B. Ratnam, ed.), Madras: The Book Centre, 1963, pp. 165–97; J.S. Teja, B.S. Khanna and T.B. Subhramanyam, 'Possession States in Indian Patients', *Indian Journal of Psychiatry*, 12, 1970, pp. 71–87. For a cultural view of spirit possession see Peter Claus, 'Spirit Possession and Spirit Mediumship from the Perspective of Tulu Oral Traditions', *Culture, Medicine and Psychiatry*, 3 (1), 1979, pp. 29–52.

   Of the twenty-eight patients interviewed at Balaji, ten were male and eighteen female. They ranged in age from sixteen to sixty-five years, with a median age of twenty-seven years. They hailed from large metropolises, small towns, and villages in almost equal number. All of them belonged to the upper castes and were predominantly of middle and lower-middle class status. Almost all had a few years of schooling and seven had even some college education.
7. On the concept of negative identity, see Erik H. Erikson, *Identity: Youth and Crisis*, New York: W.W. Norton, 1968, pp. 172–6.
8. See Colleen Ward, 'Spirit Possession and Mental Health: A Psychoanthropological Perspective', *Human Relations*, 33 (1), pp. 149–63.
9. Sigmund Freud, 'Studies on Hysteria' (1895), in *The Standard Edition of the Complete Psychological Works of Sigmund Freud* (J. Strachey, ed.), vol. 2, London: Hogarth Press, 1958, ch. 2.
10. Alan Krohn, *Hysteria: The Elusive Neurosis*, New York: International University Press, 1978.
11. Ibid., p. 188.
12. Erikson, *Childhood and Society*, New York: W.W. Norton, 1954, p. 36.
13. The link between spirit possession among women and their social powerlessness has been also emphasized by Harper, op. cit., and Teja, *et al.*, op. cit.
14. Thomas S. Szasz, *The Myth of Mental Illness*, New York: Harper and Row, 1974, p. 230.
15. Hastings, op. cit., p. 604.
16. Gananath Obeyesekere, 'Psychocultural Exegesis of a Case of Spirit Possession in Sri Lanka', in V. Crapanzano (ed.), *Case Studies in Spirit Possession*, New York: John Wiley, 1976, p. 289.

17. For whatever it's worth, eleven of the twenty-eight patients (and their relatives) reported 'considerable improvement' in their condition at the end of their stay at Balaji. The breakdown of those reporting improvement was hysteria, eight; manic depressive, one; obsessive–compulsive, one; and undiagnosed (complaining symptom, white patches on skin), one.
18. Quoted in Virginia Adams, 'Freud's Work Thrives as Theory, Not Therapy', in *The New York Times*, August 14, 1979.

5. THE GURU AS HEALER

1. Pupul Jayakar, *J. Krishnamurti: A Biography,* Delhi: Penguin, 1987, p. 9. Here I must add the caution contained in Brent's observation that 'In a country where there were perhaps ten million holy men, many with their own devotees, acolytes and disciples, some of them gurus with hundreds of thousands of followers, all of them inheritors of a tradition thousands of years old, nothing that one can say about them in general will not somewhere be contradicted in particular.' See P. Brent, *Godmen of India*, Harmondsworth: Penguin, 1973), p. 22.
2. For a comprehensive historical discussion of the evolution of the guru institution, on which this introductory section is based, see R.M. Steinmann, *Guru–Sisya Sambandha: Das Meister–Schuler Verhältnis im Traditionellen und Modernen Hinduismus,* Wiesbaden: Franz Steiner, 1986. See further W. Cenker, *A Tradition of Teachers: Sankara and the Jagadgurus Today,* Delhi: Motilal Banarsidas, 1983.
3. Cenker, *Tradition of Teachers,* p. 41.
4. Cited in D. Gold, *The Lord as Guru,* Delhi: Oxford University Press, 1987, p. 104.
5. Cited in Steinmann, *Guru–Sisya Sambandha,* p. 87.
6. Ibid., p. 103.
7. L. Babb, *Redemptive Encounters,* Delhi: Oxford University Press, 1987, p. 218.
8. *Kulanirvana Tantra,* cited in Steinmann, p. 103.
9. S. Abhayananda, *Jnaneshvar,* Neples, FL: Atma Books, 1989, p. 122–3.
10. See, for instance, Badrinath Chaturvedi, 'Sense and Nonsense about the "Guru" Concept', *Times of India,* 13 February 1990.
11. Steinmann, *Guru–Sisya Sambandha,* pp. 188–9.
12. Swami Saradananda, *Sri Ramakrishna, The Great Master,* 2 vols., Mylapore: Sri Ramakrishna Math, 1983, vol. 1, p. 521.
13. Jayakar, *Krishnamurti,* p. 4.
14. Ibid., p. 5.
15. Ibid., p. 211.

368 / Notes and References

16. See S. Kakar, *Shamans, Mystics and Doctors*, New York: Knopf, 1982, ch. 5.

17. S. Kakar, *The Inner World: A Psychoanalytic Study of Childhood and Society in India*, Delhi: Oxford University Press, 1978, ch. 4.

18. See H. Kohut, *The Analysis of the Self*, New York: International Universities Press, 1971, and *The Restoration of the Self*, New York: International Universities Press, 1977.

19. Ernest Wolf, *Treatment of the Self*, New York: Guilford, 1989, p. 52.

20. See A. Deutsch, 'Tenacity of Attachment to a Cult Leader: A Psychiatric Perspective', *American Journal of Psychiatry*, **137**, 1982, pp. 1569–73. See also S. Lorand, 'Psychoanalytic Therapy of Religious Devotees', *International Journal of Psychoanalysis*, **43**, 1962, pp. 50–5.

21. Wolf, *Treatment of the Self*, p. 100.

22. S. Nacht, 'Curative Factors in Psychoanalysis', *International Journal of Psychoanalysis*, **43**, 1962, p. 208. See also S.M. Abend, 'Unconscious Fantasy and Theories of Cure', *Journal of the American Psychoanalytic Association*, **27**, 1979, pp. .579–96.

23. Cited in Steinmann, *Guru–Sisya Sambandha*, p. 36.

24. Swami Satyanand Saraswati, *Light on the Guru and Disciple Relationship*, Munger: Bihar School of Yoga, 1983, p. 92.

25. Ibid., p. 77.

26. William James, *The Varieties of Religious Experience*, New York: Longmans, Green, 1902, pp. 107, 195.

27. Cited in D. Nurbaksh, 'Sufism and Psychoanalysis', *International Journal of Social Psychiatry*, **24**, 1978, p. 208.

28. Swami Muktananda, *The Perfect Relationship*, Ganesh–Puri: Gurudev Siddha Vidyapeeth, 1983, p. ix.

29. Saradananda, *Sri Ramakrishna*, p. 454.

30. Muktananda, *Perfect Relationship*, p. 35.

31. Ibid., p. viii.

32. Christopher Bollas, 'The Transformational Object', *International Journal of Psychoanalysis*, **60** (1978), pp. 97–107.

33. Muktananda, *Perfect Relationship*, p. 4.

34. Steinmann, *Guru–Sisya Sambandha*, p. 290.

35. Muktananda, *Perfect Relationship*, p. 85.

36. Babb, *Redemptive Encounters*, p. 173.

37. Jayakar, *Krishnamurti*, p. 3.

38. Cited in Steinmann, *Guru–Sisya Sambandha*, p. 235.

39. Ibid., p. 234.

40. M.L. Moeller, 'Self and Object in Countertransference', *International Journal of Psychoanalysis*, **58**, 1977, pp. 356–76.

41. S. Kakar, 'Psychoanalysis and Religious Healing: Siblings or Strangers?' *Journal of the American Academy of Religion*, **53 (3)**, 1985.

42. Muktananda, *Perfect Relationship*, p. 37.
43. Ibid., p. 109.
44. Jayakar, *Krishnamurti*, p. 8.
45. S.L. Bady, 'The Voice as a Curative Factor in Psychotherapy', *Psychoanalytic Review*, **72**, 1989, pp. 677–90.
46. S. Kakar, *Shamans, Mystics and Doctors*, pp. 129–30.
47. Muktananda, *Perfect Relationship*, p. 4.
48. Moeller, 'Self and Object', p. 373.

6. THE BODY IMAGE

1. For a psychoanalytic discussion of the body image see Paul Schilder, *The Image and Appearance of the Human Body*, New York: International Universities Press, 1950; see further Phyllis Greenacre, *Emotional Growth*, vol. 1, New York: International Universities Press, 1971, pp. 22–5, and pp. 113–27; W. Hoffer, 'The Development of the Body Ego', *The Psychoanalytic Study of the Child*, **5**, 1950, pp. 18–24; G.J. Rose, 'Body Ego and Reality', *International Journal of Psychoanalysis*, **47**, pp. 502–9.
2. Phyllis Greenacre, *Emotional Growth*, vol. 1, New York: International Universities Press, 1971, p. 118.
3. Krsna-dhan Cattopadyaya, *The Doctrine of the Body* (1878) (Adati Nath Sarkar, tr.; Ralph Nicholas, ed.), Department of Anthropology, University of Chicago, unpublished ms., p. 31.
4. Francis Zimmermann, 'Remarks on the Conception of the Body in Ayurvedic Medicine', paper presented at the ACLS-SSRC Seminar on the Person and Interpersonal Relations in South Asia, University of Chicago, 1979, p. 7
5. Wendy O'Flaherty, *Women, Androgynes and Other Mythical Beasts*, op. cit., chap. 2.
6. *Caraka Samhita*, 1. 5. pp. 15–19.
7. Ibid., 1. 5. pp. 57–62.
8. Ibid., 1. 5. pp. 78.
9. Ibid., 1. 5. pp. 68–89.
10. Ibid., 1. 5. pp. 96–7.
11. Ibid., 1. 6. pp. 17 and 32.
12. Lawrence Kubie, 'The Fantasy of Dirt', *Psychoanalytic Quarterly*, **6**, 1937, p. 391.

7. CLINICAL WORK AND CULTURAL IMAGINATION

. Berg, *Crow with No Mouth: Ikkyu—15th Century Zen Master*, Port Townsend: Copper Canyon Press, 1989.

C. Bollas, *Being a Character: Psychoanalysis and Self-experience*, New York: Hill and Wang, 1992.

S. Kakar, *The Inner World: A Psychoanalytic Study of Childhood and Society in India*, Delhi: Oxford Univ. Press, 1978.

———, *Shamans, Mystics and Doctors*, New York: Alfred Knopf, 1982.

———, 'The Maternal–feminine in Indian Psychoanalysis', *Int. Rev. of Psychoanalysis*, **16** (3), 1989.

———, *Intimate Relations: Exploring Indian Sexuality*, Chicago: Univ. of Chicago Press, 1990.

H. Kohut, 'The Two Analyses of Mr. Z', *Int. Journal of Psychoanalysis*, **60**, 1979.

S. Kurtz, *All the Mothers are One: Hindu India and the Cultural Reshaping of Psychoanalysis*, New York: Columbia Univ. Press, 1992.

S. Muktananda, *The Perfect Relationship*, Ganeshpuri: Guru Siddha Vidyapeeth, 1983.

A. Roland, *In Search of Self in India and Japan*, Princeton: Princeton Univ. Press. 1990.

8.   THE MATERNAL–FEMININE IN INDIAN PSYCHOANALYSIS

K. Abraham, *Dreams and Myths: A Study in Race Psychology*, New York: Journal of Nervous and Mental Health Publishing Company, 1913.

G. Bose, 'A New Theory of Mental Life', *Samiksa*, **2**, 1948, pp. 108–205.

———, 'The Genesis and Adjustment of the Oedipus Wish', *Samiksa*, **3**, 1949, pp. 222–40.

———, 'The Genesis of Homosexuality', *Samiksa*, **4**, 1950, pp. 66–85.

J. Chasseguet-Smirgel, 'Feminine Guilt and the Oedipus Complex', in *Female Sexuality* (J. Chasseguet-Smirgel, ed.), Ann Arbor: University of Michigan Press, 1964.

P. Courtright, *Ganesa*, New York: Oxford University Press, 1986.

M. Egnor, *The Ideology of Love in a Tamil Family*, Hobart & Smith College, 1984, unpublished mss.

E. Erikson, *Childhood and Society*, New York: Norton, 1950.

S. Freud, 'Creative Writers and Daydreaming', *S.E.*, 1908, p. 9.

———, 'New Introductory Lectures on Psychoanalysis', *S.E.*, 1922, p. 22.

S. Kakar, *The Inner World: A Psychoanalytic Study of Childhood and Society in India*, Delhi and New York: Oxford University Press, 1978.

———, 'Psychoanalysis and Anthropology: A Renewed Alliance', *Contributions to Indian Sociology*, **21**, 1987, pp. 85–8.

S. Kakar and J.M. Ross, *Tales of Love, Sex and Danger*, London: Unwin Hyman, 1987.

H. Kohut, *Self Psychology and the Humanities*, New York: Norton, 1985.

J. Long, 'Culture, Self-object and the Cohesive Self', unpublished paper presented at American Psychological Associacion Meeting, 1986.

G. Obeyesekere, *Medusa's Hair*, Chicago: University of Chicago Press, 1981.

———, *The Cult of Pattini*, Chicago: University of Chicago Press, 1984.

T.C. Sinha, 'Psychoanalysis in India', in *Lumbini Park Silver Jubilee Souvenir*, Calcutta: Lumbini Park, 1966.

D.P. Spence, 'Narrative Smoothing and Clinical Wisdom', in *Narrative Psychology* (T. Sarbin, ed.), New York: Praeger, 1986.

9. THE CLOISTERED PASSION OF RADHA AND KRISHNA

1. The verses from the *Gitagovinda* quoted here are taken from the scholarly yet intensely lyrical translation by Barbara Stoler Miller. See her *Love Song of the Dark Lord: Jayadeva's Gitagovinda* (New York: Columbia University Press, 1977).

2. Maurice Valency, *In Praise of Love* (New York: Macmillan, 1958), p. 18.

3. Lee Siegel, *Sacred and Profane Dimensions of Love in Indian Tradition*, Delhi: Oxford Universiry Press, 1978, pp. 26–7.

4. For a discussion of erotic love in ancient India see Sushil K. De, *Ancient Indian Erotics and Erotic Literature*, Calcutta: Firma K.L. Mukhopadhyaya, 1959; J.J. Meyer, *Sexual Life in Ancient India*, New York: E.P. Dutton, 1930.

5. Miller, p. 15.

6. W.H. Auden, *Forewords and Afterwords*, London: Faber, 1973, p. 67

7. W. Shakespeare, Sonnet 130.

8. On this see A.K. Ramanujan, *Hymns for the Drowning*, Princeton: Princeton Universiry Press, 1981, pp. 127–33.

9. For a further discussion, see Siegel, pp. 178–84, and Ramanujan, *Hymns for the Drowning*, pp. 152–7.

10. Translated by Edward C. Dimock and D. Levertov, *In Praise of Krishna: Songs from Bengali*, New York: Anchor Books, 1967, p. 18.

11. Frédérique Marglin, 'Types of Sexual Union and Their Implicit Meanings', in *The Divine Consort* (J.S. Hawley and D.M. Wulff, eds), Berkeley: Religious Studies Series, 1982, pp. 305–7.

12. Ibid., pp. 306–7.

13 Auden, *Collected Poems*, p. 536.

14. Miller, p. 89. See also the poems in Dimock, p. 7 and p. 11.

15. D. Bhattacharya, *Love Songs of Vidyapati*, London: George Allen and Unwin, 1963, p. 41.

16. Denis de Rougemont, *The Myths of Love*, London: Faber, 1963, p. 21.

17. Robert Stoller, *Sexual Excitement*. New York: Pantheon, 1979, p. 21.
18. The third-century Tamil epic of *Shilappadikaram* (The Ankle Bracelet) is perhaps the earliest illustration of the 'separate but equal' attraction of the adulterous and the conjugal for the Indian man. See Ilango Adigal, *Shilappadikaram* (The Ankle Bracelet) (A. Danielou, trans.), New York: New Directions, 1965.
19. *Mahabharata*, XIII, 104. p. 20 ff. Cited in Meyer, pp. 246–7. See also *The Laws of Manu*, XII, 165. p. 63 ff.
20. Daniel H.H. Ingalls, *An Anthology of Sanskrit Court Poetry*, Cambridge, Mass: Harvard University Press, 1965, p. 256.
21. W.S. Merwin and J. Moussaief Masson, *Sanskrit Love Poetry*, New York: Columbia University Press, 1977, p. 169.
22. Dimock, p. 28.
23. Andreas Capellanus, *The Art of Courtly Love*, John J. Parry, trans.), New York: Columbia University Press, 1941, book I, ch. VI, Seventh Dialogue.
24. Walter M. Spink, *Krishnamandala*, Ann Arbor, Michigan: Center for South and South East Asian Studies, 1971, p. 88.
25. Dimock, *In Praise of Krishna*, p. 56.
26. Miller, p. 113.
27. Quoted by Barbara Miller, 'The Divine Duality of Radha and Krishna', in *The Divine Consort*, p. 25.
28. A.J. Alston, *The Devotional Poems of Mirabai*, Delhi: Motilal Banarasidass, 1980, pp. 24–25.
29. Ramanujan, *Hymns for the Drowning*, p. 154.
30. Ibid.
31. Sigmund Freud, 'Psychoanalytic Notes Upon an Autobiographical Account of a Case of Paranoia', *Standard Edition*, vol. 12, 1911, pp. 3–82.
32. Miller, *Love Song of the Dark Lord*, p. 92.
33. M.S. Randhawa and S.D. Bambri, 'Basholi Paintings of Bhanudatta's Rasamanjari', *Roop Lekha*, **36**, n.d., p. 99.
34. Miller, *Love Song of the Dark Lord*, p.122.
35. Quoted by D.M. Wulff, 'A Sanskrit Portrait: Radha in the Plays of Rupa Gosvami', in *The Divine Consort*, p. 39.
36. Dimock, *In Praise of Krishna*, p. 21.

10. GANDHI AND WOMEN

1. For psychoanalytic perspectives on autobiography, see Robert Steele, 'Deconstructing Histories: Toward a Systematic Criticism of Psychological Narratives', in *Narrative Psychology* (T.R. Sarbin, ed.), New York: Praeger, 1986. See also Erik H. Erikson, 'In Search of Gandhi: On the Nature of Psychohistorical Evidence', *Daedalus*, Summer 1968.

2. For a discussion of Nobokov's *Speak, Memory*, see Sudhir Kakar and John Ross, *Tales of Love, Sex, and Danger*, London: Unwin Hyman, 1987, ch. 8.
3. M.K. Gandhi, *Satya no Prayoga athva Atma-Katha* (translated by Mahadev Desai as *The Story of My Experiments with Truth*), Ahmedabad: Navjivan Prakashan Mandir, 1927, p. 10; henceforth referred to as *Autobiography*.
4. Ibid., p. 31.
5. V.S. Naipaul, *India: A Wounded Civilization*, New York: Knopf, 1976, pp. 102–6.
6. Gandhi, *Autobiography*, p. 75.
7. Ibid., p. 69.
8. A.K. Ramanujan, 'Hanchi: A Kannada Cinderella', in *Cinderella: A Folklore Casebook*(A. Dundes, ed.), New York: Garland Publishing, 1982, p. 272.
9. M.K. Gandhi, *Bibi Amtussalam ke nam patra* [*Letters to Bibi Amtussalam*], Ahmedabad: Navjivan, 1960, p. 70.
10. Gandhi, *Autobiography*, p. 91.
11. Ibid, p. 205.
12. Pyarelal, *Mahatma Gandhi: The First Phase*, Bombay: Sevak Prakashan, p. 213.
13. Ibid, p. 207.
14. M.K. Gandhi, *The Collected Works of Mahatma Gandhi*, Delhi: Publication Division, Government of India, 1958, vol. 3, letters of 30 June 1906 to Chaganlal Gandhi and H.V. Vohra, pp. 352–4; henceforth referred to as *Collected Works*.
15. Ibid, pp. 208–9.
16. Gandhi, *Collected Works*, vol. 5, p. 56.
17. M.K Gandhi, *To the Women*, Karachi: Hingorani, 1943, pp. 49–50, 52.
18. Gandhi, *To the Women*, p. 194.
19. M.K. Gandhi, 'Yervada Mandir', in *Selected Works*, vol. 4, Ahmedabad: Navjivan, 1968, p. 220.
20. Ibid.
21. MK. Gandhi, 'Hind Swaraj,' in *Collected Works*.
22. Millie G. Polak, *Mr. Gandhi: The Man*, Bombay: Vora & Co., 1949, pp. 63–4.
23. Gandhi, 'Yervada Mandir', p. 223.
24. St Augustine, *The Confessions* (E.R. Pusey, trans.), New York: Modern Library, 1949, p. 227.
25. Ibid, p. 228.
26. Gandhi, *Autobiography*, p. 324.
27. Ibid, p. 210.
28. Ibdi., p. 501.

29. Ibid., p. 24.
30. St Augustine, *Confessions*, p. 162.
31. Gandhi, *Collected Works*, vol. 37, 1928, 'Speech on the Birth Centenary of Tolstoy', 10 September 1928, p. 258.
32. Ibid, p. 265.
33. Gandhi, *Autobiography*, p. 209.
34. Gandhi, *Collected Works*, vol. 37, 1928, p. 258.
35. Gandhi, *Collected Works*, vol. 36, 1927–8, letter to Harjivan Kotak, p. 378.
36. Gandhi, 'Ek Tyag', in *Harijanbandhu*, 22.9.35.
37. M.K. Gandhi, *Kumari Premaben Kantak ke nam patra* [*Letters to Premaben Kantak*], Ahmedabad: Navjivan, 1960, pp. 260–2 (my translation).
38. The best eyewitness account of Gandhi's Bengal period is by N.K. Bose, Gandhi's temporary secretary, who was both a respectful follower and a dispassionate observer: see his *My Days with Gandhi*, Calcutta: Nishana, 1953.
39. Ibid., p. 52.
40. Ibid., p. 189.
41. In his *Key to Health*, rewritten in 1942 in the middle of another depressive phase following the widespread violence of the 'Quit India' movement and the death of his wife in prison, Gandhi had hinted at this kind of self-testing: 'Some of my experiments have not reached a stage when they might be placed before the public with advantage. I hope to do so some day if they succeed to my satisfaction. Success might make the attainment of *brahmacharya* comparatively easier.' See *Selected Works*, vol. 4, p. 432. For a compassionate and insightful discussion of these experiments, see also Erik H. Erikson, *Gandhi's Truth*, New York: Norton, 1969), p. 404.
42. Gandhi, *Kumari Premaben Kantak ke nam patra*, p. 16.
43. Ibid., p. 19.
44. Ibid., p. 188.
45. Ibid.
46. Ibid., p. 39.
47. Ibid.
48. Ibid.
49. Ibid.
50. Ibid., p. 190.
51. Ibid., p. 151.
52. Ibid., p. 173.
53. Ibid., p. 369.
54. See Mira Behn, ed., *Bapu's Letters to Mira* (1924–48), Ahmedabad: Navjivan, 1949 and *The Spirit's Pilgrimage*, London: Longman, 1960.
55. Behn, ed., *Bapu's Letters to Mira*, pp. 27–8.

56. R. Greenson, *The Technique and Practice of Psychoanalysis*, New York: International University Press, 1967, pp. 338–41.
57. See Martin S. Bergman, 'Transference Love and Love in Real Life', in *International Journal of Psychoanalytic Psychotherapy* (J.M. Ross, ed.), **11**, 1985–6, pp. 27–45.
58. Behn, ed, *Bapu's Letters to Mira*, p. 42.
59. Ibid.
60. Ibid., p. 43.
61. Ibid., p. 71.
62. Ibid., p. 88.
63. Ibid., p. 166.
64. For an elaborate description of some of these popular psychological ideas in English, see Swami Sivananda, *Mind: Its Mysteries and Control*, Sivanandanagar: Divine Life Society, 1974, ch. 28, and Swami Narayanananda, *The Mysteries of Man, Mind, and Mind-Functions*, Rishikesh: Universal Yoga Trust, 1965), ch. 19.
65. Gandhi, *To the Women*, p. 71.
66. G. Bose, 'All or None Attitude in Sex', *Samiksa*, **1**, 1947, p. 14.
67. Wendy O'Flaherty, *Women, Androgynes, and Other Mythical Beasts*, Chicago: University of Chicago Press, 1980, p. 45.
68. See Wendy O'Flaherty, *Asceticism and Eroticism in the Mythology of Siva*, London: Oxford University Press, 1973, p. 55.
69. *Brahmavaivarta Purana*, 4.31, 4.32, 1.20, 4.33, 1.76; English translation abridged from O'Flaherty, *Asceticism and Eroticism in the Mythology of Siva*, p. 51.
70. Cited in Edward C. Dimock, Jr., *The Place of the Hidden Moon*, Chicago: University of Chicago Press, 1966, p. 154.
71. Ibid, p. 54.
72. Ibid, p. 156.
73. See Ramchandra Gandhi, *Brahmachacya*, Department of Philosophy, Univexsity of Hyderabad, 1981, unpublished, p. 26.
74. Thomas Mann, *Joseph and His Brothers*, London: Secker and Warburg, 1959, p. 719.
75. Sigmund Freud, 'Civilized Sexual Morality and Modern Nervousness', *Standard Edition*, vol. 9, 1908, p. 197.
76. St. Augustine, *Confessions*, p. 165.
77. Gandhi, *To the Women*, p. 81.
78. Ibid., p. 60.
79. Ibid., p. 57.
80. Polak, *Mr. Gandhi*, p. 34.
81. Gandhi, *To the Women*, pp. 28–9.
82. Behn, ed., *Bapu's Letters to Mira*, p. 141.
83. Gandhi, *To the Women*, p. 102.

84. Erikson, *Gandhi's Truth*.
85. Ved Mehta, *Mahatma Gandhi and His Apostles*, New Delhi: Indian Book Co., 1977, p. 13.
86. D.W. Winnicott, 'Appetite and Emotional Disorder', in *Collected Papers*, London: Tavistock Publications, 1958, p. 34.

11. LOVERS IN THE DARK

1. On the influence of film values on Indian culture, see Satish Bahadur, *The Context of Indian Film Culture*, Poona: National Film Archives of India, n.d.. See also the various contributions in *Indian Popular Cinema: Myth, Meaning, and Metaphor*, special issue of the *India International Quarterly*, **8 (1)**, 1980.
2. Robert J. Stoller, *Perversion*, New York: Pantheon Books, 1975, p.55.
3. Sudhir Kakar, *The Inner World: A Psychoanalytic Study of Childhood and Society in India*, Delhi: Oxford University Press, 1978, ch. 3.
4. Arjun Appadurai and Carol Breckenridge, 'Public Culture in Late Twentieth Century India', Department of Anthropology, Pittsburgh: University of Pennsylvania, July 1986, unpublished.
5. See Bruno Bettleheim, *The Uses of Enchantment*, New York: Knopf, 1976.
6. Some of these films are *Junglee, Bees Saal Baad, Sangam, Dosti, Upkaar, Pakeeza, Bobby, Aradhana, Johnny Mera Nam, Roti Kapda aur Makan, Deewar, Zanjeer, Sholay, Karz, Muqaddar ka Sikandar*, and *Ram Teri Ganga Maili*.
7. Wendy O'Flaherty, 'The Mythological in Disguise: An Analysis of *Karz*', in *Indian Popular Cinema*, note 1 above, pp. 23–30.
8. Sudhir Kakar and John M. Ross, *Tales of Love, Sex, and Danger*, London: Unwin Hyman, 1987, ch. 3.
9. *Mahabharata*, 5. 144. pp. 5–10. The English translation is taken from *The Mahabharata* (J.A.B. von Buitenen, ed. and trans.), Chicago: University of Chicago Press, 1978, p. 453.
10. The psychological effects of modernization have been discussed in *The Child in His Family: Children and Their Parents in a Changing World* (E. James Anthony and C. Chiland, eds), New York: John Wiley, 1978.
11. Martha Wolfenstein and Nathan Leites, *Movies: A Psychological Study*, Glencoe, Ill.: Free Press, 1950.
12. Joyce McDougall, *Theatres of the Mind*, New York: Basic Books, 1986.

12. RAMAKRISHNA AND THE MYSTICAL EXPERIENCE

1. N. Söderblom, *Till mystikens belysning* (Lund, 1985), cited in H. Aker-

berg, 'The Unio Mystica of Teresa of Avila,' in *Religious Ecstasy* (N.G. Holm, ed.), Stockholm: Almqvist and Wiksell, 1981, pp. 275–9.

2. William James, *The Varieties of Religious Experience*, New York: Longmans, Green, 1902.

3. Andrew M. Greeley, *The Sociology of the Paranormal: A Reconnaissance*, Beverly Hills: Sage Publications, 1975, p. 62.

4. For a psychological description of the structure of mystical experience see Committee on Psychiatry and Religion, *Mysticism: Spiritual Quest or Psychic Disorder*, New York: Group for Advancement of Psychiatry, 1976. See also H. Hof, 'Ecstasy and Mysticism', in Holm, *Religious Ecstasy*, pp. 243–9.

5. R.C. Zaehner, *Hindu and Muslim Mysticism*, London: Athalone Press, 1960. The authoritative work on Hindu mysticism remains S.N. Dasgupta (1927), *Hindu Mysticism*, Delhi: Motilal Banarsidas, 1987.

6. See Committee on Psychiatry and Religion, *Mysticism*, especially pp. 782–6. For specific psychoanalytic contributions stressing the ego-adaptive aspects of the mystic experience see Paul C. Horton, 'The Mystical Experience: Substance of an Illusion', *Journal of the American Psychoanalytic Association*, **22**, 1974, pp. 364–80; David Aberbach, 'Grief and Mysticism', *International Review of Psychoanalysis*, **14**, 1987, pp. 509–26.

7. Anton Ehrenzweig, *The Hidden Order of Art*, London: Weidenfeld and Nicolson, 1967.

8. Romain Rolland, *The Life of Ramakrishna*, Calcutta: Advaita Ashram, 1986, p. 38.

9. For the arguments against a psychoanalytic, 'scientific' study of mysticism, see Roger N. Walsh *et al.*, 'Paradigms in Collision', in *Beyond Ego: Transpersonal Dimensions in Psychology* (R.N. Walsh and F. Vaughan, eds.), Los Angeles: Tarcher, 1980, pp. 36–52.

10. See Peter Buckley and Marc Galanter, 'Mystical Experience, Spiritual Knowledge, and a Contemporary Ecstatic Experience', *British Journal of Medical Pyschology*, **52**, 1979, pp. 281–9.

11. For the case histories see P.C. Horton, 'Mystical Experience', and Committee on Psychiatry and Religion, *Mysticism*, pp. 799–807.

12. For a comprehensive comparison of the three see Manfred Eigen, 'The Area of Faith in Winnicott, Lacan and Bion', *International Journal of Psychoanalysis*, **62**, 1981, pp. 413–34.

13. Cited in Irving B. Harrison, 'On Freud's View of the Infant–Mother Relationship and of the Oceanic Feeling—Some Subjective Influences', *Journal of the American Psychoanalytic Association*, **27** (1979), p. 409.

14. Ibid.

15. J.M. Masson suggests a different passage from the writings of Ramakrishna as the source for the term 'oceanic feeling'; see his *The Oceanic*

378 / Notes and References

Feeling: The Origins of Religious Sentiment in Ancient India, Dordrecht: Reidel, 1980, p. 36.

16. Dushan Pajin, 'The Oceanic Feeling: A Reevaluation', Belgrade, 1989, manuscript.

17. Letter to R. Rolland, 19 January 1930, in The Letters of Sigmund Freud (E. Freud, ed.), New York: Basic Books, 1960, p. 392.

18. Mahendranath Gupta, Sri Ramakrishna Vachanamrita (trans. into Hindi by Suryakant Tripathi 'Nirala'), 3 vols., Nagpur: Ramakrishna Math, 1988.

19. Swami Saradananda, Sri Ramakrishna, The Great Master, 2 vols., Mylapore: Sri Ramakrishna Math, 1983, vol. 1, pp. 276–7.

20. Rolland, Life of Ramakrishna, pp. 22–3.

21. Saradananda, Sri Ramakrishna, vol. 1, pp. 276–7.

22. Ibid, p. 156.

23. Ibid, pp. 162–3.

24. Saradananda, Sri Ramakrishna, vol. 1, p. 424.

25. Gupta, Vachanamrita, vol. 1, p. 71.

26. Ibid., p. 301.

27. Ibid., p. 320.

28. Ibid., pp. 135–6.

29. Ibid., p. 41.

30. Ibid., vol. 2, p. 241.

31. Bhavabhuti, Uttara Rama Charita, in Six Sanskrit Plays, Bombay: Asia, 1964, p. 368.

32. Gupta, Vachanamrita, vol. 1, p. 90.

33. S. Freud, New Introductory Lectures (1933), Standard Edition, vol. 22, pp. 79–80.

34. Nathaniel Ross, 'Affect as Cognition: With Observation on the Meaning of Mystical States', International Review of Psychoanalysis, 2, 1975, pp. 79–93.

35. Gupta, Vachanamrita, vol. 3, pp. 238–89.

36. Ernst Hartmann, The Nightmare: The Psychology and Biology of Terrifying Dreams, New York: Basic, 1984.

37. Gupta, Vachanamrita, vol. 3, p. 289.

38. J.M.R. Damas Mora et al., 'On Heutroscopy or the Phenomenon of the Double', British Journal of Medical Psychology, 53, 1980. pp. 75–83.

39. Gupta, Vachanamrita. vol. 1, p. 388.

40. Ibid, vol. 3, p. 109.

41. Ibid., vol. 1, p. 431.

42. Saradananda, Sri Ramakrishna, vol. 1, p. 417.

43. Octavio Paz, The Money Grammarian (Helen Lane, trans.), New York Seaver Books, 1981, p. 133.

44. For representative statements of the classical Freudian view see

Salzman, 'The Psychology of Religious and Ideological Conversion', *Psychiatry*, **16**, 1953, pp. 177–87. For the Kleinian view see Irving B. Harrison, 'On the Maternal Origins of Awe', *The Psychoanalytic Study of the Child*, **30**, 1975, pp. 181–95.
45. P.C. Horton, 'Mystical Experience'.
46. For a detailed discussion of the link and parallels between the process of mourning and mysticism see Aberbach, 'Grief and Mysticism', pp. 509–26.
47. S. Kakar, *Shamans, Mystics and Doctors*, New York: Knopf, 1982, chap. 5. See also Buckley and Galanter, 'Mystical Experience', p. 285; P.C. Harton, 'The Mystical Experience as a Suicide Preventive', *American Journal of Psychiatry*, **130**, 1973, pp. 294–6.
48. Cited in Aberbach, 'Grief and Mysticism', p. 509.
49. I. Barande and R. Barande, 'Antinomies du concept de perversion et epigenese del' appetit de excitation', cited in S.A. Leavy, 'Male Homosexuality Reconsidered', *International Journal of Psychoanalytic Psychotherapy*, **11**, 1985–6, p. 163.
50. Gupta, *Vachanamrita*, vol. 1, p. 388.
51. Eigen, 'Area of Faith', 'Ideal Images, Creativity and the Freudian Drama', *Psychocultural Review*, 3, 1979, pp. 278–98; 'Creativity, Instinctual Fantasy and Ideal Images', *Psychoanalytic Review*, **68**, 1981.
52. Eigen, 'Area of Faith', p. 431.
53. E. Underhill, *Mysticism* (1911), New York: E.P. Dutton, 1961; J.H. Leuba, *The Psychology of Religious Mysticism*, New York: Harcourt, Brace, 1925.
54. A. Einstein, *Ideas and Opinions*, New York: Crown Publishers, 1954, p. 75.
55. Herbert Moller, 'Affective Mysticism in Western Civilization', *Psychoanalytic Review*, **52**, 1965, pp. 259–67. See also E.W. McDonnel, *The Beguines and Beghards in Medieval Culture*, New Brunswick: Rutgers University Press, 1954, pp. 320–32.
56. Gupta, *Vachanamrita*, vol. 3, pp. 535–6.
57. Ibid, p. 107.
58. Robert Stoller, 'The Gender Disorders', in *Sexual Deviation*, (I. Rosen, ed.), Oxford University Press, 1979, pp. 109–38.
59. J.O. Wisdom, 'Male and Female', *International Journal of Psychoanalysis*, **64**, 1983, pp. 159–68.
60. D.W. Winnicott, 'Creativity and its Origins', in *Playing and Reality*, London: Tavistock, 1971, pp. 72–85.
61. Ibid, p. 85.

13. THE VIRTUOUS VIRAGO

1. For Ritambhara's biographical details, see 'Virtuous Virago', *The Times of India*, 19 July 1991 and 'Hindutva by the Blood of Her Words', *The Daily*, 9 June 1991.
2. On the poetic function of rhetoric, see John Shotter, 'The Social Construction of Remembering and Forgetting', in *Collective Remembering* (D. Middleton and D. Edwards, eds), London: Sage, 1990, p. 124.
3. Homans, p. 277.
4. Rafael Moses, 'The Group Self and the Arab–Israeli Conflict', *International Review of Psychoanalysis*, **9**, 1982, p. 56.
5. Moses, 'The Group Self', p. 63.
6. Emile Durkheim, *The Elementary Forms of Religious Life* (1912), New York: Free Press, 1965.

14. MEETING THE MULLAHS

1. For a psychopathological treatment of fanaticism, see *Fanaticism: A Historical and Psychoanalytical Study* (A. Haynal, ed.), NewYork: Schocken Booms, 1983.
2. Lewis, *The Political Language of Islam*, p. 7.

15. RELIGIOUS CONFLICT IN THE MODERN WORLD

1. Andrew Samuels, *The Political Psyche*, London: Routledge, Kegan and Paul, 1993, pp. 11–12.
2. See Phillipe Wolff, 'The 1391 Pogrom in Spain: Social Crisis or Not? *Past and Present*, **50**, 1971, pp. 4–18; George Rude, *The Crowd in History: A Study of Popular Disturbances in France and England, 1848* New York: 1964; Janine Estebe, *Tocsin pour un massacre*, Paris, 1968 For the 'clash of economic interests' theory of religious–ethnic conflict in South Asia see *Mirrors of Violence* (Veena Das, ed.), Delhi: Oxfor University Press, 1990.
3. Michael Walzer, 'Nations and Minorities', in *Minorities: Community an Identity* (C. Freud, ed.), Berlin: Springer-Verlag, 1982, pp. 219–27.
4. The leading proponent of the theory that the international environmen especially the ending of colonial rule, is responsible for ethnic conflict D. Horowitz; see his *Ethnic Groups in Conflict*, Berkeley and Los Angele University of California Press, 1985.
5. Sigmund Freud, 'Group Psychology and the Analysis of the Ego' (1921 *Standard Edition*, vol. 18.

6. Erikson, *Identity: Youth and Crisis*, p. 46. See also Janine Puget, 'The Social Context: Searching for a Hypothesis', *Free Associations*, **2 (1)**, 1991.

7. Davis, pp. 156–60.

8. D.W. Winnicott, 'Communicating and Not Communicating Leading to a Study of Certain Opposites', in his *The Maturational Process and the Facilitating Environment*, New York: International Universities Press, 1963, p. 187. For a succinct discussion of contemporary psychoanalytic thinking on self and relatedness, see Alice R. Soref, 'The Self, in and out of Relatedness', *The Annual of Psychoanalysis*, **20**, 1992, pp. 25–48.

9. Oscar Patterson, 'The Nature, Causes and Implications of Ethnic Identification', in Fried, pp. 25–50.

10. David Rapoport, 'Comparing Militant Fundamentalist Movements', in Marty and Appleby, *Fundamentalism Observed*, op. cit., p. 443.

11. Sigmund Freud, 'New Introductory Lectures' (1993), *Standard Edition*, vol. 22, p. 104.

12. See Heinrich von Stietencorn, 'Angst und Gewalt: Ihre Funktionen und ihre Bewältigung in den Religionen', in Stietencorn Ihrg, *Angst und Gewalt: Ihre Präsenz und Ihre Bewaltigung in den Religionen*, Düsseldorf: Patmos Verlag, 1979, pp. 311–37.

13. John W. Bowker, 'The Burning Fuse: The Unacceptable Face of Religion', *Zygon*, 21 (4), 1986, pp. 415–38; see also Elise Boulding, 'Two Cultures of Religion as Obstacles to Peace', *Zygon*, **21 (4)**, 1986, pp. 501–18.

14. Rapoport, op. cit.

15. Davis, p. 165.

16. Hans Bertram, 'Germany—One Country with Two Youth Generations?', paper presented at the Seminar on Childhood and Adolescence, Goethe Institut, Colombo, Sri Lanka, February 1994, pp. 17–21.

7. Cited in Kanan Makiya, 'From Cruelty to Toleration', unpublished paper read at the conference on *Religion and Politics Today*, organized by the Rajiv Gandhi Foundation, New Delhi, January 30–February 2, 1994.

Bibliography

BOOKS

Non-Fiction

1. *Frederick Taylor: A Study in Personality and Innovation*, Cambridge, MA: MIT Press, 1970.
2. (with K. Chowdhry) *Conflict and Choice: Indian Youth in a Changing Society*, Bombay: Somayia, 1971.
3. *The Inner World: A Psychoanalytic Study of Childhood and Society in India*, Delhi: Oxford University Press, 1978, 9th Printing, 1997; Spanish translation, Mexico: Fonda de Cultura, 1987; French translation, Paris: Les Belles Lettres, 1985; German translation, Frankfurt: Nexus Verlag, 1988.
4. Editor and contributor, with an introduction, *Identity and Adulthood*, Delhi: Oxford University Press, 1980. Paperback, 1992, 1998.
5. *Shamans, Mystics and Doctors: A Psychological Inquiry into India and its Healing Traditions*, New York: A. Knopf, 1982; Indian edition, Delhi: Oxford University Press, 1982; British edition, London: Allen and Unwin 1984; Paperback, Boston: Beacon Press, 1983, and Chicago: University of Chicago Press, 1991; German translation, Munich: Biederstein Verlag 1984; Hindi translation, Delhi: Rajkamal (in press); Spanish translation Mexico: Fondo de Cultura, 1990; French translation, Paris: Seuil, 1997 Marathi translation, Bombay: Majestic, 1993; Italian translation, Parma Pratiche Editrice, 1993 and 1998.
6. (with J. Ross) *Tales of Love, Sex and Danger*, Delhi: Oxford University Press, 1986); British edition, London: Unwin Hyman, 1987; U.S. edition New York: Blackwell, 1988; German translation, Munich: Beck Verlag 1986; French translation, Paris: PUF, 1987; Japanese translation, Osaka Sogensha (in press); Italian translation, Como: Lyra Libri, 1982.
7. *Intimate Relations: Exploring Indian Sexuality*, Chicago: University of Chicago Press, 1990; Indian edition, Delhi: Viking, 1989; Paperback Penguin Books, 1991; Marathi translation, Pune: Raghuvanshi Prakasha 1992; French translation, Paris: Des Femmes, 1990; German translation Munich: Verlag Waldsgut, 1994; Italian translation, Parma: Pratic Editrice, 1995; Hindi translation, Delhi: Vani Prakashan (in Press).

8. *The Analyst and the Mystic*, Chicago: University of Chicago Press, 1992; Indian edition, Delhi: Penguin-Viking, 1991.
9. (with C. Clement) *La Folle et le Saint*, Paris: Seuil, 1993; German translation, Munich: Beck Verlag, 1993; Portuguese translation, Rio de Janeiro: Relume Dumara, 1997; Italian translation, Rome: Corbaccio, 1997.
10. *The Colors of Violence: Religious–Cultural Identities and Conflict*, Chicago: University of Chicago Press, 1996; Indian edition, Delhi: Penguin-Viking, 1995; German translation, Munich: Beck Verlag, 1997; Hindi translation, Delhi: Rajkamal (in press).
11. *Culture and Psyche*, Delhi: Oxford University Press, 1997; U.S. edition, New York: Psyche Press, 1997.
12. (with Wendy Doniger) *The Kamasutra or Book of Love, A New Translation*, London: Oxford University Press (in press).

Fiction

1. *The Ascetic of Desire: A Novel*, Delhi: Penguin, 1998; U.S. edition, New York: Overlook Press, 2000; German translation, Munich: Beck Verlag, 1999; Hindi translation, Delhi: Rajkamal, 1999; Italian translation, Rome: Neri Pozza, 2000; French translation, Paris: Seuil (in press); Portuguese translation, Rio de Janiero: Companhia das Letras, 2000; Spanish translation, Barcelona: Plaza y Janes (in press).
2. (ed.) *Indian Love Stories*, Delhi: Roli Books, 1999.
3. *Ecstasy: A Novel*, Delhi: Penguin (in Press), German translation, Munich: Beck Verlag (in press); Hindi translation, Delhi: Rajkamal (in press).

CHAPTERS IN BOOKS

On Domestic Violence, in F. Mayor (ed.), *Taking Action for Human Rights in the Twenty-first Century*, Paris: UNESCO, 1998.
The Search for Middle Age in India, in R. Shweder (ed.), *Welcome to Middle Age (And Other Cultural Fictions)*, Chicago: University of Chicago Press, 1998.
Religious Conflict in the Modern World, in R. Ivekovic and N. Pagon (eds), *Otherhood and Nation*, Ljubljana: Institutum Studiorum Humanitatis, 1998.
The Construction of a New Hindu Identity, in K. Basu and S. Subramanyan (eds), *Unravelling the Nation*, Delhi: Penguin, 1996.
Klinische Arbeit und Kulturelle Imagination, in P. Mohring and R. Apsel (eds), *Interkulturelle Psychoanalytische Therapie*, Frankfurt: Brandes and Apsel, 1995.

Gandhi et le fantasme de l'érotisme, in L. Lapierre (ed.), *Imaginaire et leadership*, Montréal: Presses HEC, 1992.

Some Unconscious Aspects of Ethnic Violence in India, in V. Das (ed.), *Mirrors of Violence*, Delhi: Oxford University Press, 1990.

Psychoanalysis in India: Text and Context, in J. Stigler and R. Shweder *et al.* (eds), *Cultural Psychology*, New York: Cambridge University Press, 1989.

Health and Medicine in the Living Traditions of Hinduism, in L. Sullivan (ed.), *Health in World Religious Traditions*, New York: Macmillan, 1989.

Das Hindustische Weltbild & Der Mensch in Ayurveda, in D. Reimenschneider (ed.), *Shiva tanzt: Das Indien Lesebuch*, Zurich: Union Verlag, 1986.

Psychotherapy and Culture: Healing in the Indian Tradition, in S. Pollack and M. White (eds), *The Cultural Transition*, New York: Basic Books, 1986.

The Child in India, in *Aditi* Catalogue, Washington: Smithsonian Press, 1985. Also in A. Cohn and L. Leach (eds), *Generations*, New York: Pantheon, 1987.

Fathers and Sons: The Indian Experience, in S. Cath, A. Gurwit and J. Ross (eds), *Father and Child: Developmental and Clinical Perspectives*, Boston: Atlantic Little Brown, 1982.

Six Chapters on The Healthy Personality, in *Encyclopedia of Health*, Vol. 3, Lausanne: Editions Grammont, 1982.

(In Spanish) *La Personalidad Sana*, Barcelona: Salvat Editores, 1982.

(with Ashish Nandy) Culture and Personality in India in U. Pareek (ed.), *Review of Research in Psychology*, New Delhi: Indian Council of Social Science Research.

Images of the Life Cycle and Adulthood in Hindu India, in E. James Anthony and C. Chiland (eds), *The Child in His Family: Children and their Parents in a Changing World*, New York: John Wiley, 1978.

SELECTED PAPERS IN PROFESSIONAL JOURNALS

2000   The Time of Kali: Violence between Religious Group in India, *Social Research*, 67(3).

1998   La Double Quête: La Vie des Femmes dans l'Inde Moderne, *Bulletin d'Information des Cadres*, 37.

Gesundheit und Kultur, Heilung in östlicher und westlicher Perspektive, *Jahrbuch für Komplexität in den Natur-, Sozial- und Geisteswissenschaften*, Bd. 7

1995   Clinical Work and Cultural Imagination, *Psychoanalytic Quarterly*, 64 (2).

1994   Encounters of the Psychological Kind: Freud, Jung and India, *The Psychoanalytical Study of Society*, 19.

1992   Ramakrishna and the Mystical Experience, *Annual of Psychoanalysis*, **20.**

1989   The Maternal–Feminine in Indian Psychoanalysis, *International Review of Psychoanalysis*, **16 (3).**

Notes on the History and Development of Indian Psychoanalysis, *Revue Internationale d'histoire de la Psychanalyse*, **2.**
Also in P. Kutter (ed.), *Psychoanalysis International*, vol. 2, Stuttgart: Frommann, 1995.

Doctors and Patients in the Hindu Tradition, *Indian Horizons*, **37.**

1988   Psychoanalytic Reflections on Religion and Mysticism, *Zen Buddhism Today*, **6.**

1987   Psychoanalysis and Anthropology: A Renewed Alliance, *Contributions to Indian Sociology*, **21 (1).**

1986   Male and Female in India: Identity Formation and its Effects on Cultural Adaptation, *Studies in Third World Societies*, **38.**

1985   Psychoanalysis and Non-Western Cultures, *International Review of Psychoanalysis*, **12 (4).**

Psychothérapie et Culture: La guérison dans la tradition, *Confrontations*, **13.**

Les mères et leurs fils en Inde, *Frayages*.

Erotic Fantasy: The Secret Passion of Radha and Krishna, *Contributions to Indian Sociology*, **19 (1).**

Psychoanalysis and Religious Healing: Siblings or Strangers? *Journal of American Academy of Religion*, **53 (3).**
Also in R. Hart (ed.), *Trajectories in the Study of Religion*, Atlanta: Scholars Press, 1988.

1982   Reflections on Psychoanalysis, Indian Culture and Mysticism: A Review Essay, *Journal of Indian Philosophy*, **10.**

1981   The Person in Tantra and Psychoanalysis, *Samiksa*, **35 (4).**
Also published in *International Journal of Asian Studies*.

1980   Observations on the 'Oedipal Alliance' in a Patient with a Narcissistic Personality Disorder, *Samiksa*, **32 (4).**

1979   A Case of Depression, *Samiksa*, **33 (3).**

Childhood in India: Traditional Ideals and Contemporary Reality, *International Social Science Journal*, **31 (3)**; German translation: 'Kindheit in Indien', *Kindheit*, **1.**

1977   Relative Realities: Images of Adulthood in Psychoanalysis and the Yogas, *Samiksa (Journal of Indian Psychoanalytic Society)*, **31 (2).**

Authority in Work Organizations, *Vikalpa*, **2 (4)**.

Leaders, Power and Personality, *Vikalpa*, **2 (2)**.

1976   Curiosity in Children and Adults: A Review Essay, *Indian Journal of Psychology*, 51 (2).

Leadership Training in Industry and Administration: A Critical Review, *Management in Government*.

1975   Neurosis in India: An Overview and Some Observations, *Indian Journal of Psychology*, **50 (2)**.

1974   Indische Kultur und Psychoanalyse (Indian Culture and Psychoanalysis), *Psyche*, **28 (7)**.

Aggression in Indian Society: An Analysis of Folk Tales, *Indian Journal of Psychology*, **49 (2)** (a shorter version in *Journal of Social Psychology*, **87**).

1972   Authority Relations in Indian Organization, *Management International Review*, **1**.

1971   Rationality and Irrationality in Business Leadership, *Journal of Business Policy*, **2 (2)**.

Authority Patterns and Subordinate Behavior in Indian Organizations, *Administrative Science Quarterly*, **16 (5)**.

The Theme of Authority in Social Relations in India, *Journal of Social Psychology*, **84**.

1970   The Logic of Psychohistory, *Journal of Interdisciplinary History*, **1 (1)**.

1968   (Co-author) Time and Content of Significant Life Experience, *Perceptual and Motor Skills*, **27**.

The Human Life Cycle: The Traditional Hindu View and the Psychology of Erik Erikson, *Philosophy East and West*, **18 (5)**.

Index

ERRATUM
The last line on page xvi is:
became passionless. (The anthropologically-minded
Stanley Kurtz — with an altogether